AMERIKA

The Re-Mastered Christian Majority

PAUL BOGGS

silvanus
publishing, inc.

AMERIKA: The Re-Mastered Christian Majority
Cover Design and illustrations throughout book created by
Silvanus Publishing, Inc.
All biblical quotes are taken from The King James Holy Bible
Typography by Silvanus Publishing, Inc.
Copyright 2014 by Silvanus Publishing, Inc.
Published by Silvanus Publishing, Inc.

Library of Congress Cataloging-in-Publication Data

Boggs, Paul 1971 – AMERIKA: THE RE-MASTERED
CHRISTIAN MAJORITY
By Paul Thomas Boggs
391 pages
ISBN: 978-0-9969165-2-3
1. Religion. 2. Elite (Social Sciences)—United States. 3. United States—Social Policy. 4. Body, Mind, Spirit: Occultism. 5. Body, Mind, Spirit: General

Library of Congress Control Number: 2014909018

DISCLAIMER: The following information and opinions are not a substitute for professional medical prevention, diagnosis, or treatment. Please consult with your physician, pharmacist, or health care provider before taking any home remedies or supplements or following any suggestions in this book. Only your health care provider, personal physician, or pharmacist can provide you with advice on what is safe and effective for your unique needs or diagnose your particular medical history. The information in this book does not contain professional advice (e.g., financial, legal, etc.) While my sincere conviction is to provide readers with truthful, straight-forward facts surrounding the topics found inside of this book, there is never a time when anyone [other than God] knows everything. Therefore, the potential for error is ever present when communicating information. Both the author and publisher assume no responsibility for damages that may arise to those using the information found inside of this book or damages alleged to have occurred as a result of the content found inside of this book. This book is not endorsed by any of the individuals, companies, products, etc. mentioned in this book.

"Fulfil ye my joy, that ye be likeminded, having the same love, being of one accord, of one mind. Let nothing be done through strife or vainglory; but in lowliness of mind let each esteem other better than themselves. Look not every man on his own things, but every man also on the things of others. Let this mind be in you, which was also in Christ Jesus: Who, being in the form of God, thought it not robbery to be equal with God: But made himself of no reputation, and took upon him the form of a servant, and was made in the likeness of men: And being found in fashion as a man, he humbled himself, and became obedient unto death, even the death of the cross. Wherefore God also hath highly exalted him, and given him a name which is above every name: That at the name of Jesus every knee should bow, of things in heaven, and things in earth, and things under the earth; And that every tongue should confess that Jesus Christ is Lord, to the glory of God the Father."
– Philippians 2:2-11

"Ministering spirits, I loose you in the Name of Lord Jesus Christ, to minister on my behalf according to the will of God. I bind all demons and Satan. In Jesus Christ's Holy name. Amen!"

Table of Contents

"I am very doubtful whether history shows us one example of a man who, having stepped outside traditional morality and attained power, has used that power benevolently."

- C.S. LEWIS, The Abolition of Man

ABOUT THE AUTHOR

Paul of the Scottish Boggs family is a descendant of the Christian Dál Riata in Scotland, an ancient Gaelic Irish colony credited with bringing Christianity and Literature to Scotland. For the past twenty-two years Paul has worked as a high-level consultant, throughout the International Community, with entrepreneurs in the nascent stages of their businesses. It was during this time span that he pursued interests, within the Industries of alternative medicine, technology, entertainment, and manufacturing. In addition to providing advanced planning solutions, Paul has assisted with the founding and capitalization of several American corporations, as well as three overseas commercial organizations, within Europe, Asia, and Africa. Drawing from that experience, Paul has participated in raising more than $700 million in capital through various investment vehicles, such as private equity, debt equity, and reverse mergers through 'aged' companies. Throughout his career, Paul has worked with award winning Hollywood writers and producers, billionaire hi-tech innovators, entertainers, professional athletes, and a myriad of other personalities.

What has always inspired Paul, throughout his career, are the goals which he has set for himself as a leader. Paul has always subscribed to the belief that leadership has much more to do with the impact one is able to make in people's lives, rather than the fleeting objectives of material gain and personal advancement. Much like in his previous ventures, he understands the importunity of his message throughout this book to the more than two hundred and forty million Christian Americans may be unpopular to some, mainly because it invokes culturally insensitive initiatives, and puts forth provocative strategies to those best described as intellectual believers, but practical atheists. Nevertheless, Paul unabashedly addresses the moral and spiritual gaps between modern day Christian values and behaviors, and asks that the Christian American majority face up to some very tough realities. A central theme in Paul's writing is that Christianity can compete in the marketplace of ideas when it's properly understood and properly articulated.

As a result of travelling extensively throughout Asia, Paul was introduced to a specialized understanding of alternative health solutions, specifically 'herbal combinations'. It's these combinations he learned that provide an individual with more of a robust healing solution. Moreover, such combinations targeted specific deficiencies within the complex co-dex of the human creation. Upon his return from Asia to America, a closer observation of the U.S. 'holistic' environment yielded a discovery that left him with more questions than answers. Paul discovered that the vast majority of 'holistic' practitioners and orthodox physicians in the West were prescribing remedies that quite frankly, conflicted with their patients' actual needs. In other words, the very community whose oath states "first, do no harm" - a principle precept of medical ethics that all medical students are taught to do something, or even to do nothing, than to risk causing more harm than good" - is in fact creating an environ-ment of illness and death. For instance, you're most likely unaware of the fact that more than 16 million deaths have occurred between 1976-2006 due to 'medication errors', according to a June 2010 report in the Journal of General Internal Medicine.

"There is a way that seemeth right unto a man, but the end thereof are the ways of death." – Proverbs 16:25

These statistics are conveniently omitted from the 5 o'clock news, for some reason. What do you believe the motivating factors are? And yet the global elite task masters who own America's mainstream me-dia couldn't wait to plaster images of Dr. Kevorkian's whopping 130 as-sisted suicides. Paul believes it's the right of the individuals to treat them-selves as they see fit and not as dictated by Corporate America or the government. With that being said, he's not suggesting 'assisted suicide' is a good thing, he's simply illustrating the hypocrisy of the global elite machine which feeds the Christian majority barely believable stories full of inconsistencies. On one hand, it demonizes your freedom of choice, all the while pushing you into a direction that at best can be described as a conflict interest; all the while enriching their members' own coffers. Remember, 'healthcare' represents 15.2% of the United States $15 tril-lion GDP.

(Statistic: World Health Organization/Bureau of Economic Analysis)

With that being said, it's a fair assumption to make that who-ever controls this portion of America's financial portfolio wields power over an enormous portion of the American population. Moreover, the individual(s) exhortation of 'choice' is narrowly directed through one of two doors both of which lead to the same slaughtering machine.

"Would socialized medicine lead to socialization of other phases of life? Lenin thought so. He declared socialized medicine is the keystone to the arch of the socialist state." - 1945 AMA Pamphlet

It was this revelation that led Paul to the conclusion that the Medical Industrial Complex were masters at issuing unfounded cautionary statements and/or research, with enough repetition, over the past sixty years, that many of the citizens of America have deemed their falsified facts as truth. Moreover, if Americans were going to be free from the chains of deceit, they would first need to escape the grasp of the corrupt Medical Industrial Complex. Even the majority of U.S. holistic solutions were comprised of a one-size-fits-all 'broad-sword' approach. It's this philosophy that makes it an inferior methodology to the more scalpel approach taught and practiced throughout ancient texts. Paul's understanding of herbal combinations is derived from the teachings of Sun Simiao. Sun Simiao is one of the most interesting figures in the history of ancient medicine. Sun Simiao was a famous clinician; to posterity he left voluminous formularies that have been influential until the present, and was strongly influenced by the 4,000-year-old Oriental Materia Medica, also known as ben cao. Sun Simiao is credited with having created what is considered the Chinese Hippocratic Oath, which states:

"A Great Physician should not pay attention to status, wealth or age; whether he is an enemy or friend, whether he is a Chinese or a foreigner, or finally, whether he is uneducated or educated. He should meet everyone on equal grounds. He should always act as if he were thinking of his close relatives." – Sun Simiao

It's Paul's intention, to provide truth and knowledge to his readers, as though each of you, were his close relatives. Truth, however, may not lead you to where you thought you were going, but it will always lead you somewhere better. When ignored, it will eventually show itself. The closeness of your relationships is directly proportional to the degree to which you have revealed the truth about yourself. Truth can be painful.

Paul is dedicated to the pursuit of providing his readers with accurate and healthful knowledge. It was his intention to create content that is easy to understand and unlike that which is traditionally found in boring scientific journals. Paul did not want to bury his message under a pile of technical mumbo jumbo that most readers would find disinteresting. With that being said, the knowledge readers will encounter is not for the emotionally delicate, nor is what he will share appropriate for those souls wishing to remain in physical, financial, and spiritual servitude to self ascribed 'gods' whose goal is to consolidate their Hegemony over the global population. Paul will guide his readers through dark and rarely discussed areas of world history and will explain how our society today has been intentionally engineered to fund and promote the very system that's plotting the ultimate demise of 240 million Christian Americans. Paul will cite dates, times, and direct quotes that will show his readers that the very system they rely on to keep them and their loved ones 'safe' is in fact conspiring against them. Paul will educate you on how this system, for generations, has been funded and endorsed by global elite modernists. Paul will provide the reader with data which shows how these toxic chemicals, products, and organisms are being propagandized under the guise of 'feeding the world'.

At the end of your journey, through some of history's biggest lies and deceptions, you'll emerge with an arsenal of knowledge. It's the author's hope that the reader will feel inspired by what he or she has read. After all, the purpose of this book is to provoke the reader into a state of honest appraisal. This is when you disarm all of your emotional triggers, set aside partisan politics, and for once in your life be true to yourself. It's Paul's goal to inspire his readers to ask five basic questions.

- Why have I developed into the person I am today?
- Has my overall worldview, personality, lifestyle, understanding about health, etc. evolved naturally and into something I feel has been beneficial for me and for those around me?
- Do I feel as though, I've been indoctrinated into a position or lifestyle in society which is anathema to my Christian faith?
- If my life has in fact been manipulated to benefit an antichristian agenda... How has that affected my soul, mind and body?
- If my entire life has in fact been artificially engineered, by someone or something, then who am I supposed to be?

Paul believes, one of the biggest crimes being committed against the Christian American majority is the obscuring of their history. This has in turn obscured the histories of other Nations and forced Christians into adopting fraudulent records. Such an attempt at fraud or forgery several thousand years ago would have brought the full force of the law, or rather the more immediate remedy of someone's sword, crashing down upon the culprit's head. Paul will demonstrate in subsequent chapters the methods through which the anti-Christian 'Church of Babylon' has effectively deceived Christians into severing all ties with their ancient chronicles. Not even the repression of Maoist China or Stalinist Russia was this effective. It has been this willful lack of preservation and transmittance of knowledge to succeeding Christian generations which has led to a catastrophic disconnect between us and the wisdom, creativity, and strength of our ancestors causing a kind of ancestral amnesia. The Christian majority to all intents and purposes has forgotten that they exist because countless ancestral predecessors struggled, starved, suffered, fought, reproduced, and died to ensure their existence on this earth. Inherent in that realization is humility, humanity, and the overwhelming desire to survive and thrive. We are all on this planet for a primary purpose; it's incumbent, upon each and everyone one of us, to realize this purpose.

As you journey through the subsequent pages you will learn why our global population has become sick: physically, financially, and intellectually. Paul has worked tirelessly compiling an extensive archive of data that clearly defines the forces behind the deliberate 'slow-kill' of hundreds of millions of people. Paul's data highlights the motives behind these nefarious individuals. Utilizing America's own vast financial and altruistic resources, these parasites leverage layer upon layer of deceptive, corrupt proxies to orchestrate the systematic poison and control of America's Air, Water, Food, medication, financial, and learning institutions. Anyone interested in the unfiltered truth and survival will be shocked by the ultimate motivation of these global elite social engineers. And to those skeptics, who so quickly dismiss this knowledge as nothing more than 'conspiracy theory,' Paul's challenge to these critics is to try and defend their 'coincidence theorist' positions once they've collected all of the bread crumbs that he has laid out in this book.

Upon completion of this book you will learn why they have intentionally constructed a toxic crisis ecosystem, complete with laboratory abominations and genetically modified Trojan horses. You will discover why this control system of disease and depression has been intentionally engineered to slowly and painfully decay the souls, minds, and bodies of millions of Christian Americans. Paul will connect for his readers the dots that span more than 230 years. It is, however, the past 60 years that have seen the most turmoil and that has produced the very machine we're all living within today. Throughout these years, Christian America has witnessed a massive erosion of its moral, spiritual, financial, educational, and nutritional body. The Christian American majority has been intoxicated and under the spell of genetically modified diseases, stumbling through a deep fried nutritional waste land. What the reader should find most troubling are the very real dark energies, complicit in the crimes against them and their loved ones. It's these silver tongue, carpet bagging, nihilists who claim allegiance to nothing and no one. It's these secret society phantoms who ravenously devour America's greatness, all with the diabolical intentions of reanimating and controlling the corpse of America with an army of behavioral and social scientists.

DEDICATION

This book is dedicated to the two largest groups of persecuted on our planet. The largest of these, are children. Every day innocent young people are killed through avoidable war, famine, toxic medicine, etc., events orchestrated by individuals who follow ancient Luciferian doctrine that states, "children are the 'enemy' of our planet." As such, this group believes these innocent souls should be exterminated in order to save the world.

Unbeknownst to the vast majority of people on earth, there exists an ancient Luciferian cult that is complicit in the murder of hundreds of millions of innocent people every year. Like their father the devil, this cult's influence and resources, mask it's bankrupt and pathetic reality. Hundreds of years ago 'conquers' had the courage to ride along with their soldiers and assassins. Back then, you knew someone wanted to kill you and the reasons why. Imagine how few wars we would have if 'We The People' required our leaders to lead the charge or land the first blow?

Scottish/Irish American Charles Woods, father of murdered Benghazi Navy Seal Tyrone Woods, best describes why modern day 'leaders' don't lead the charge, stating: "...remember this, Mr. President [Obama]: My son and the others died heroes and it's better to die the death of a hero than it is to live the life of a coward." As an aside, Navy SEALs, Sean Smith, Glen Doherty, and Tyrone Woods, were all of Scottish/Irish ancestry? In fact, the members of the Woods Family are descended from a Norman knight by the name of Ernald de Bosco (Bosco is a Latinized form of wood) who accompanied William the Conqueror? If you would like to learn more about the over two millennia long subjugation and murder of Christian Celts, please visit, KillingIreland.com

"Military men are dumb, stupid animals to be used as pawns in foreign policy." – Henry Kissinger

Former U.S. Secretary of State and mouthpiece for the Rothschild and Rockefeller Families, Henry Kissinger, was rescued from certain death, at the hands of Nazis, when he was accepted into America by Christian Americans. To show his appreciation, Kissinger spent his entire life progressing militant antichristian, Rothschild Family sponsored anti-Americanism and globalism, which has claimed the lives of countless American, Timorese, and South American Christians. A colleague of Kissinger in the financial sector is Democratic Socialist [Communist] George Soros, who hypocritically made his fortune off of America's free-market, capitalist system. Like Kissinger, Soros too escaped Hitler's 'final solution' by clinging to a Christian American lifesaver, and like Henry

Kissinger, George Soros and his offspring show their appreciation to our U.S. Military and the Christian nation who rescued them by promoting anti-Christian, anti-Constitutional concepts and business practices.

(Note: The documentary titled 'The Trials of Henry Kissinger' exposes many of Kissinger' more duplicitous acts, both as an insubordinate employee of the American people and proxy for the Satanic, Global Elite, Newest World Order.)

This brings us to the second largest group of victims on our planet: the brave men and women who serve in our Nation's Military and law enforcement. It's my hope that those suffering from non-catastrophic physical injury caused by post traumatic stress syndrome (PTSD) and other yet to be named traumas will find their way to the knowledge in this book. It has been my contention, for some time, that the rigors of war can literally destroy a soldier's endocrine system. Once this has occurred, the pineal, hypothalamus, pituitary, thyroid, parathyroid's, thymus, adrenal's, pancreas, ovaries, and testes, all become ineffective at supporting the body's most basic chemical needs.

Signs and symptoms include: Cancer, respiratory infections, allergies, asthma, frequent colds, fibromyalgia, chronic exhaustion, hypoglycemia, adult onset diabetes, alcoholism, difficulty waking up in the mornings, feeling exhausted even after a full night sleep, salt cravings, lack of energy, increased effort to do basic daily tasks, decreased sex drive, inability to handle stress, increase time to recover from illness, injury or trauma, feelings of light-headed when standing, mild to severe depression, decreased happiness about life, increased PMS, impotence, sterility, poor focus, decreased tolerance to cold and/or heat, energy levels being highest after 6 PM.

Instead of addressing the root cause of a soldier's above mentioned imbalance, a stressed out endocrine system, the medical industrial complex chooses the path of least resistance by masking the symptoms of our victimized brave men and women in uniform. How? By over-prescribing, or incorrectly prescribing 'therapy' that does anything but rehabilitate. There's no question, the conditions of war are anything but predictable. But, is it really a logical solution, to introduce or impose procedures or medications that aggravate the mental and/or physical conditions of our brave men and women?

If the industrial medical complex and all of its drugs were working, then why are over 33% of our brave men and women, in the Army, on medications that aren't working? What's really concerning is that over 25% of those soldiers are medicated with psychotropic medication.

Could there be any correlation between the psychotropic medications and the over 8,000 American soldiers who are committing suicide each year? What's troubling is one third of those soldiers committing suicide never saw combat. What these victims aren't being told, is that they're feeling suicidal, because of the side effects associated with their government prescribed medications. The statistic which should anger every single American is that the industrial medical complex and the medications they are prescribing to our soldiers are murdering more of our brave men and women than Zbigniew Brzezinski's creation, "Al-Qaeda." Many readers will be unaware of the fact that the U.S. government is the biggest customer of the largest pharmaceutical companies. What's more, many of those pharmaceutical companies receive Government grants to supplement their paltry $85 billion they earn each year. No conflict of interest there.

FOREWORD

Many Christian Americans find the goal of "optimal health" daunting and confusing. In today's age of virtual solutions it seems as though you can't throw a TV remote without hitting ten self-ascribed gurus, doing their best to convince their audience to invest in their revolutionary gizmo or theory. They promise weight loss, improved stamina, decreased cholesterol and the libido of a twenty-one year old.

What these sultans of spin conveniently omit is the hard wiring reality of our body's chemical and electrical systems and the alpha role nutrition plays in maintaining a healthy body and mind. Choosing and maintaining a health routine can be like a puzzle with two sides. On one side, there is a sense of familiarity and comfort, along with some sort of guarantee or quick fix. On the other, there is a siege upon our willpower, by commercials, billboards, radio and movies. The reality is that few are victorious against this onslaught, and even fewer obtain their personal health goals.

When is the last time you visited your local grocery store? Have you really ever stopped, and visually audited the ocean of advertising? The vast majority of messaging, throughout your grocery store, is toxic in nature, with the exception of the pitiful little 400sqft 'health food' section. The fact is, even the health food section of most grocery stores is stocked with products whose ingredients can hamstring your pursuit of optimal health. As a consumer, you may look at the grocery store shelves, and think to yourself: 'there are so many choices in here'. The reality is just ten Corporations manufacture the majority of what you buy. And all of them are sourcing, manufacturing, and promoting products which contain Toxic, 'Genetically Modified Organisms' (GMO's),

GMO's which have been shown to cause disease. KRAFT, Coca Cola, Pepsico, General Mills, Mars, Unilever, Johnson & Johnson, P&G, and Nestle all choose to place toxic GMOs into your food even though studies show that GMOs aren't safe for human consumption. In fact, science has proven that these laboratory abominations are responsible for the massive increase of Cancer, Hypothyroidism, Obesity, Learning Disabilities, Birth Rate Reduction and Impotency. If you or I intentionally fed poison to people, we'd be hauled off to prison for life. It's these same multinational corporations who leverage vast consumer funded resources, e.g., consumer advisory panels, deceptive psychology in commercials, etc. Trickery which encourages American's to buy and consume products that have been shown to cause the top eight leading causes of death in the United States, e.g., Heart Disease; Cancer; Respiratory Disease Stroke; Alzheimer's Disease; Diabetes; Kidney Disease; and Suicide.

In an analysis, by 24/7 Wall St., it was determined that the aforementioned top 10 companies cost the United States $1.1 trillion. Multiply that by twenty-nine, the number of years these Corporations have been controlling the U.S. food supply, and that's how large of a class action lawsuit the American people should bring against Monsanto; KRAFT; Coca Cola; Pepsico; General Mills; Mars; Unilever; Johnson & Johnson; P&G and Nestle Corporations.

The fact is, the above listed Corporations, have willfully produced Wundt psychology based programming, to not only influence, but completely alter the natural behavior of human beings. It's this subliminal primal programming which provokes the viewer into a destructive feeding frenzy. Experts in the art of 'priming' behaviors have been doing this for generations. Priming is a non-conscious form of human memory, which is concerned with perceptual identification of words and objects. It refers to activating particular representations or associations in memory, just before carrying out an action or task. For example, a person who sees the word 'yellow' will be slightly faster to recognize the word 'banana.' This happens because the words yellow and banana are closely associated in memory.

The two best weapons we have to defend ourselves is God's word and an understanding of the psychology being used against us. It's been my experience that when individuals are well educated about the lethal effects of visual programming, toxic air, food, water, etc. they make smarter choices. My goal is to awaken as many Americans as I can to the reality that they are directly and indirectly empowering a system which seeks to destroy their physical, mental, and spiritual wellbeing. Each and every time they make a purchase, they effect this system. When Christians change their buying habits, they change the system.

The Christian American population in 2014 is 80% of the U.S., that's 240 million people, out of a population of 311 million. This majority has the Power to shape our Nation, in the image of Lord Jesus Christ. Instead, they choose to invest their money into industries which are the antithesis of Jesus Christ's teachings. Christians must regain the chivalrous and courageous nature of their ancestors; that irrepressible vow and steadfast discipline to defend the truths promised by Jesus Christ. Only through unity will we defeat our ancient enemy.

"This eternal indictment of Christianity I will write on all walls, wherever there are walls... I call it the one immortal blemish on mankind."
– Friedrich Nietzsche

There is a growing community of "Conspiracy Theorists" [This is a term invented by the CIA in 1967 to attack anyone who challenges the "Official Narrative"], throughout America who believe that only a few thousand people control our entire world. If this is true, what exactly, is holding back 2.5 billion Christian men and women from redirecting their trillions of dollars from Companies, Corporations, States, Non-Profits, and Nations to alternatives which are in line with Christian principles?

If America's Christian majority subscribes to the doctrine of Christianity, why is it financing Schools, Companies, Corporations, non-profit groups, movie producers, musicians, and Communist Governments whose belief system calls for the elimination of Christianity? Imagine the economic impact of 240 million Christians, if at once they all disconnected themselves, and their loved ones, from these militant anti-Christian groups. Christianity's one true enemy would be banished from America overnight.

"If my people, which are called by my name, shall humble themselves, and pray, and seek my face, and turn from their wicked ways; then will I hear from heaven, and will forgive their sin, and will heal their land."
- 2 Chronicles 7:14

If America's spiritual and economic decline is a direct result of our Christian majority's inability to turn off the financial spigot, fueling our enemy's agenda, what exactly is this invisible force holding it back? There can be only one of two possible explanations. First, they have made a conscious decision, to be a victim; and second, they've yet to be educated and deprogrammed about the true nature and agenda of which they are an integral part. It's this second group of Americans who motivated me to write this book. It's my desire to connect with and educate as many of these people as I can.

I don't imagine my counsel will not be met without conflict. I began this journey, following a comprehensive review of Christianity's true enemy, as well as the methods by which it has repeatedly attempted to subjugate our Christian ancestors. That being said, my expectation is that my words will be misrepresented and criticized by those whose entire existence depends heavily on their ability to maintain the very control system which has subjugated our global Christian family for generations. Moreover, I'm intimately familiar with the chemical and economic control measures foisted upon our Christian family, and how toxic life has become for our community.

It's disheartening and frustrating, to walk through any town in America and bear witness the effects of a clandestine assault by Luciferians against our Nation. Americans are unnecessarily being medicated and vaccinated. With the same ingredients found in rat poison no less... Americans are force fed cancer causing hybridized/GMO foods. They're tricked into drinking Chinese manufactured lobotomizing fluoridated water. Most troubling of all, is that Americans are allowing their ancient God given DNA to be eradicated, through the erosion of the nuclear family and drug culture. It's these premeditated cultural toxins which have unleashed a pestilence upon our Nation of biblical proportions. What's more, it's this control system which is responsible for creating an illusion of subjugation, and which made possible the control of what has historically been an undefeatable, uncontrollable Christian majority.

I have spent the past twenty-two years of my life researching the methods through which Christian's one true enemy has successfully manipulated and engineered the thoughts and actions of individuals, groups and nations. It's this experience which has graced me with an elevated perspective that many Christian Americans do not have today. It's this Christ based heightened awareness, which has allowed me to create methods through which tens of thousands have become deprogrammed and detoxified. Americans must understand that the alpha control measure, is to keep our nation in a state of poor physical, mental and spiritual health. Their entire system of control is based on the power of low energy, e.g. negative imagery, fear, war, immorality, bigotry, economic strife, illness, ignorance, occult symbols and disconnection from Lord Jesus Christ. It's this perception of reality that's imperative for them to maintain control over the power of Christ's Army. The less capable America is spiritually; the easier America is to manipulate mentally and physically and ultimately eliminate. The knowledge inside this book will not only help to reverse generational physical and mental subjugation, it will also help you become the type of person the enemy fears most.

XVIII

CHAPTER

1   The Obsolete Man

"You're travelling through another dimension. A dimension, not only
of sight and sound, but of mind. A journey, into a wondrous land,
whose boundaries are that of imagination. That's a sign post up ahead.
Your next stop... The Twilight Zone!"

How many of your own life experiences, would have been complete, with the above, playing in the background? When reruns of the
Twilight Zone aired - in the early 70's - I was just a little guy, around five
or six, living in Fort Worth, Texas. I still remember those 'sick days',
home from school, curled up on the couch. Nothing, but me, a piece of
buttery, toasted, white, wonder bread, banana slices and a 7UP and to
top it all off, a creepy episode of the Twilight Zone, featuring some slimy
little creature on the wing of an airplane.

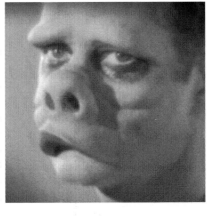

It was the following scene,
from this particular Twilight Zone
Episode, that so accurately depicts
the warped 2014 American culture
that so proudly parades its dysfunctional self, around the world
stage. It's through the lens of
the director, that we experience a
1960's worldview. A view that's arguably less corrupt and influenced
than today's politically correct
environment. The scene begins
with an average looking American
woman laying on a table, inside of
an examination room. As the camera pans in, we see that a doctor is
in the room with her. However, the doctor's back is facing the woman,
obscuring his face from the camera. As the music intensifies, the camera
zooms in on the woman's face, as she just caught her first glimpse of her
doctor. As our vantage is whipped around, we see what has contorted
the woman's face, into the universal expression of fear. The treating physician has the face of a pig. As the episode unfolds, we learn that the
seemingly normal looking woman is now considered to be an abnormal,
freakish monster, worthy of ridicule and experimentation. It's this swine
new world, filled with pig-people who are now the major-
ity, calibrating our moral, spiritual and economic compass.

1

I use the aforementioned episode to illustrate the massive shift America has made, from being a knowledge driven, health conscious superpower, to the embarrassing grandpa to whom people point fingers at and whisper back and forth about. It's the reality for millions who have been lured into an illusion that promotes and rewards the notion that living a high health risk, sedentary lifestyle is fashionable. It's this orchestrated prison that has forced people into a life filled with debilitating medical conditions.

It's distressing for me to see obese human beings waddling around, with stomachs that hang down around their thighs. What angers me about their condition, is that the vast majority are clueless about the fact that their health and lifestyle has been engineered by Luciferians who not only want to eliminate them, they want to eradicate 90% of the American population. I'm inspired by the fact that after you have read this book, you'll have knowledge that could change the rest of your life.

Memories of America:

If I had to describe growing up in the 70's, it would have to be 'Mission Impossible'. My sisters and I were always on an impossible mission to construct or deconstruct something. Whether that meant digging a giant hole, in the middle of our parents' backyard, building what should have been a condemned fort, pulling our jelly filled stretch Armstrong beyond the manufacture recommended distance or playing stick ball in the street, we always had an objective. My family was not rich, but I don't remember ever going without. We were fortunate to have a functional parental unit; and like most kids, during that period, we played hard, and when it came time to eat, we nearly ate our parents into bankruptcy.

Upon reflection, what is rarely, if ever, conjured up in my memory are images of friends who were 'obese' and nobody had, A.D.D., Diabetes, cancer, etc. And I'm not talking about the occasional chubby, crazy friend we've all had or been. I'm talking, call an astronomer to name this new planet… Big! Today, if you're one of the brave souls to have ventured into the nearest big-box barnyards, more commonly referred to as Wal-Mart, you've likely come face to belly, or face to chin, with people who are apparently interbreeding with large hoofed animals.

If you're someone who fits this description please don't expect an apology, because you've come to the wrong place. The time for pleasantries and calling little Jimmy 'big boned' is over. We're not going to help our Christian American brothers and sisters if we continue to sugar coat or glaze over the real problem. I'm sick of watching my Christian family be 'slow-killed'

2

by inbred, syphilitic, sociopathic elites. The truth of the matter is that America, per capita, is the most obese nation on planet Earth. A new study by Columbia University shows one in five deaths in America are caused by obesity. The sad truth is, these lives could have been saved if they had the knowledge in this book. Unfortunately, there are too many willfully incompetent individuals who continuously reject reality, even after it's been gift wrapped and slid under their noses… Throughout this book, I provide fact over fiction and resolutions over reticence. It's time we save our Christian brothers and sisters from the long painful death that's been intentionally engineered for them. If you continue to accept the status quo, if you continue down a path that's been architected by the wicked, it's not a matter of if, but when, you'll be diagnosed with cancer, diabetes, etc. I do not want this future for you or your loved ones.

I care deeply for this Nation. Not only do I care for our Christian family, but also for every single soul living throughout our planet. I want every person reading this book, to come to the realization that the collective body of America is slowly rotting, from its common sense out. Instead of admitting something in America is terribly wrong; America's de-Nile is deeper than the channels of evil flowing under Washington D.C. for the past 60 years. It's time America takes off its blinders and recognizes the Satanic, global elites who are riding us like Sea biscuit.

Why This Book Is So Valuable:

"Thus saith the LORD; Cursed be the man that trusteth in man, and maketh flesh his arm, and whose heart departeth from the LORD."
- Jeremiah 17:5

There are hundreds of books on the market today that address a host of surface level health challenges. Most of these books contain valuable information, along with creative anecdotes to entertain their readers. Christians are constantly being deceived into believing there is 'Secret Knowledge' that will empower them with the tools necessary to heal them, or mystical affirmations that will cleanse them of their ailing condition. This is most definitely not one of those books. I have faith in all of Lord Jesus Christ's promises; and he was quite clear about 'trusting in man' and putting your faith in secret 'gnosis' [John 18:20]. This is the recurring deficiency in all of these resources. The vast majority of health and healing books lead their readers from the very source that is an absolute authority on healing; and that's Lord Jesus Christ. Moreover, they steer their readers away from both Wisdom and Truth. What's more, they commit most of their text to low energy, fear mongering. The very same techniques Luciferian elite's enlist to dominate our lives. This book on the other hand provides

3

readers, above all else, truth and wisdom, and a strategic mental and physical relocation, away from the toxic, modernist mysticism that's deceiving millions away from the truth.

"He that trusteth in his own heart is a fool: but whoso walketh wisely, he shall be delivered" - Proverbs 28:26

Following my survey of the vast field of 'self-help' guides, I wanted to create a resource that addressed the genesis of most health issues. I do this, using two simple methods, truth and honesty. I did not want to merely address surface level solutions, as most 'self-help' guides do. Nor did I want to offer up a band-aid reference manual that simply masked existing conditions. In short, I wanted to create a reference manual, citing empirical evidence that even the most ardent 'coincidence theorists' would find irrefutable. I believe the reader will discover a refreshing point of view derived from a historically factual perspective. Enough with the purely conspiratorial books, whose pages are filled with clever observations and personal theories. This book analyzes and dissects the architects of our current health crisis, and gives practical advice on how to avoid their advances as well as measures one can take to enhance their body's God given healing capabilities.

Upon completion of this reference material, the readers will have a solidly built foundation upon which they will be able to strengthen their biggest weakness. The inherent weakness, found in just about every mind on our planet, is that we are born in an environment without any knowledge as to how it truly functions. This makes man vulnerable to manipulation. I would like to help you emancipate your physical and mental self, from our self ascribed masters. This book will help you enhance how you process vast amounts of stimulation and noise. You'll be able to more effectively manage what you hear, see and feel, on a daily basis. My goal is to help you develop a healthier mental and physical environment.

The Layout:

I would like to inform readers of my non-traditional writing style with regards to 'footnotes', etc. As an avid reader myself, I have always begrudged the process of having to divert my attention to the end of a chapter, or worse, all the way to the back of the book. My method of writing includes the practice of incorporating all pertinent data related to a particular subject into the narrative, acknowledging the source after the quote or reference straight away.

4

This book offers a unique approach to establishing a solid foundation upon which the reader will compose an alternative health reality. My methodology is based on a 'tell and show' approach, rather than a 'fire-hose' method. Represented first are principles behind a topic. I then define, explain, and dissect that principle by showing its application using collections of real stories or case studies. This is not merely a book about stories or neat tricks, but a handbook, and guide through which the reader is able to escape mental and physical subjugation.

Through this book, you will find many Internet links to stories or accounts, as well as links to tools and other aspects of the topics discussed. Practical exercises appear throughout this book, these are designed to help you master the social engineering control system designed by Luciferian globalists. As you read this book, I hope to impress upon you that health awareness is not a part-time job and is not something to take lightly.

Naturally, everyone wants to be healthier, as evidenced by the increase in sales for fad diets, exercise equipment, gym membership sales, and health food stores. All of these resources, in the right hands, can be extremely valuable. However, the single best protection against illness is wellness through education. The only way to reduce the effects of our environment, and of those who seek to harm us, is to acknowledge their existance, to know their modus operandi, and to understand the mentality of the enemy.

When our entire Christian community possess the above-mentioned knowledge, our collective light [Matthew 5:14] illuminates the once-darkened four quarters of the earth, exposing the enemy for all to see. Lord Jesus Christ promises those who believeth on Him and put His armor on that they will possess, "power to tread on serpents [Satan] and over all the power of the enemy: and nothing shall by any means hurt you."

"If you know the enemy and know yourself you need not fear the results of 100 battles." - Sun Tzu

Knowing is half the battle, taking action on Christ's knowledge is what defines wisdom. This book will arm you with the intelligence necessary to thwart your social manipulators, but you have to consciously and consistently incorporate this knowledge into your daily life. My hope is that you will become one of millions, who will get off their knees and stop being a victim, allowing their body and mind to be harvested for profits.

2 Path To Righteous Judgment

"No purpose of action against religion can be imputed to any legislation, state or national, because this is a religious people... This is a Christian nation." - U.S. Supreme Court, Church of the Holy Trinity v. United States (1892)

"I would not look to the U.S. Constitution, if I were drafting a Constitution in the year 2012." - Babylonian Talmudist Supreme Court Justice Ruth Bader Ginsburg January 30, 2012

The design of this book is structured in a way that guides the reader through three main bodies of knowledge. The first portion of the book, examines the subject matter of man's superior and inferior nature. Even though Christian's are opposed to man's inferior nature [evil], many allow themselves to be governed by both elected and unelected representatives who unashamedly worship Lucifer. Christians directly and indirectly pay into unconstitutional agencies such as: The United Nations, The Federal Reserve Corporation, The I.R.S., DHS, etc. It's an incredible revelation, when you realize, that our entire State and Federal infrastructure in which we all live under and financially support, is in fact controlled by an element, that over 99% of the United States rejects.

I'm convinced, based on solid evidence that 'Evil', e.g., low level energy, dark energy, demonic influence, Satan, Lucifer, etc. is absolutely the genesis from which our Nation's toxic imbalance emanates. If Christians were to perform an honest appraisal of both their Nation's vital organs, as well as their own - leveraging key data that I share throughout this book - it's impossible to conclude that we're governed by men and women who have our best interests at heart. Christians have been deceived, at home and abroad, by individuals who are driven by greed, power, immortality, and demonic authorities. Christians must realize that when anyone preaches disunity, anti-family, or pit one of us against the other, through class warfare or race hatred, you can be sure that person or group seeks to rob us of our freedom to worship Lord Jesus Christ and destroy our very lives. There is no such thing as a good or bad race of people, just good and evil ideas and spiritualities.

"And think not to say within yourselves, We have Abraham to our father: for I say unto you, that God is able of these stones to raise up children unto Abraham. And now also the ax is laid unto the root of the trees: therefore every tree which bringeth not forth good fruit is hewn down, and cast into the fire." – *St. Matthew 3: 9-10*

There are two types of people who will find this knowledge 'insulting' or 'politically incorrect'. Personality type A, will actually be followers of the great deceiver [Satan], the very people, who have injected cancer into our Nation's spiritual root system. Frankly, I couldn't care less about their opinion. Personality type B will be those who have been so heavily indoctrinated by the elite controlled propaganda machine that they are willing to fight tooth and nail in defense of their deceit laden illusionary lifestyle. Here's an example of a 'type B' personality. These are the types of individuals who are willing to throw hands, or worse, just because someone said they liked a different sports team, politician, celebrity, historical figure, cookie, etc. than they do. If you're this type of personality, you're going to have to make a conscious effort to eliminate this toxic physical and mental authority which is governing your reality.

The first portion of this book will feature a few select stories of a long list of business and personal experiences of mine. I've chosen these particular reflections to illustrate my qualifications to speak on the subject of evil in America today.

In the second portion of this book, I present irrefutable evidence regarding Luciferians and their "crimes against humanity". I hope readers walk away from this section of the book with a heightened sense of reality. Unfortunately, the vast majority of Christians throughout our Nation today are living in a kind of dream-like state. It's disheartening, when I reflect back on my youth, and conjure up imagery of my neighborhood interactions and adventures with friends. Young people, in 2014, no longer have that physical and/or mental fitness; they've become jellyfish, mentally and physically.

In the third and final portion of this book I'm going to share with you proven strategies to inject a sense of order and wellness back into your life. The first step in your recovery is coming to the realization that you're not a 'smart-phone', HDTV, Facebook or Twitter avatar. These technologies are mere tools, subordinates to one's life, not life itself. Pursuing a lifestyle that suggests otherwise is going to lead you down a path of mental and physical exhaustion.

Throughout my entire life, I've been involved in the development and distribution of 'bleeding-edge,' hi-tech solutions and I've witnessed the effects of technology on our mental and physical conditioning. Moreover, having helped create a number of Class A, high security collocation facilities, one of our Nation's first Citrix resellers and the Nation's first mobile high-speed data wireless internet companies, I believe I'm reasonably qualified to speak on the topic of data security and storage. I feel strongly that what I'm about to share with you is the 'canary in the coal mine' in terms of the direction our nation is headed, if Christians continues to allow Luciferians to creep into our lives.

One of the most surreptitious, hi-tech methods of subjugation, being levied against Christians in 2014 is 'Spy-Cloud' Computing. As someone who understands this space, to a great degree, I can't help but cringe every time I see or hear an ad pushing Christians to blindly adopt the idea of remotely accessing all of their application and data needs. Much in the same way, Americans have surrendered control over its food supply and manufacturing they are now gullibly allowing Luciferian controlled Corporations and Governments complete control over a segment of American life and business which is critical to the growth and prosperity of our economy.

Americans have been lead to believe the 'big-lie' that technology is a unifying force, when in reality technology is viewed by Luciferians as a means to condition the uneducated masses to embrace the destructive reality that the rare and precious human being is an inferior creation when compared with their unpredictable hell on earth concept of 'singularity' (mergence of man with machine).

For the layperson, Spy-Cloud Computing, simply put, allows an end user, to access computer applications and data remotely. All data and software is stored on servers that are intern 'co-located', that is they are in a shared rack or floor space environment, with thousands of other servers that are housed inside massive data centers, somewhere in America.

The 'big-lie' being perpetuated by the 500 pounds gorilla software companies is that Spy-Cloud Computing will provide the consumer and business owner with a greater level of convenience and security, when in reality, it puts consumers in an extremely vulnerable position.

Consider the following scenario:

It's 2027, and Americans have adopted the Spy-Cloud Computing juggernaut into their personal and business lives. They've allowed P.C. Companies to phase out all laptop and desktop production. Americans have allowed all software companies to simply load their applications onto shared super servers, co-located inside one of many government controlled data centers, capable of decrypting, reading, cataloging and deleting all data that enters and exits each of these facilities.

Sounds like science fiction? The fact is, one of America's largest data centers, located in Las Vegas, is currently hosting these said agencies and it's public knowledge in 2014 that software exists to track and catalog voluminous amounts of data.

Now given the bare bones features of what equates to a 'Personal Display Device' now being offered to consumers by the giant PC manufactures, storage of your personal data, on your personal device, is no longer an option.

Virtual storage service providers, such as the service being offered by 'Carbonite', and others, will now collect a monthly fee to store all of your personal and business critical data. And so long as you continue paying your monthly storage fees, don't misplace, forget or have your password hacked, and adhere to their terms and conditions, you'll have total access to your mission critical data.

Flash forward, to 2033, and America has surrendered control of all recorded knowledge e.g., personal, business, libraries, religious, historical, economic, political, environmental, etc. to be stored inside of Luciferian owned and controlled data centers. Now, in order to access your personal data, or even read a book, you'll need to verify your identity through a National ID Card Number, Social Security Card, Credit Card, chip, tattoo, etc. And because all knowledge is now managed by Luciferians, it's simply a matter of pressing a button to alter or delete international, national, political, business, personal and Biblical history forever. And if a 'User' [citizen] no longer submits to government Terms and Conditions [tyranny], the user's account is simply deleted.

Keep in mind, as of 2014, Americans have empowered companies like Rupert Murdoch's HarperCollins with the power to manipulate 76% of all U.S. libraries into adopting 'eBooks'. What's troubling is that in March 2011, Murdoch's HarperCollins announced it would distribute its eBooks to libraries with Digital Rights Management (DRM) which would allow HarperCollins to delete their books, magazines, etc. after being read a set number of times. What Christians must understand is that it has been under the guise of convenience and security that enemies of Lord Jesus Christ have brainwashed his followers into believing that 'eBooks' offer a superior experience and security over holding and owning a physical copy, when in fact it gives Luciferians the power to delete dogmata, ideas, history, etc. which directly compete with their stated goal of eliminating Christianity and constructing a 'One World Religion'.

Much like the advanced technology we all rely on so heavily in today's competitive world, our mind and body requires what 'techies' refer to as a 're-boot' now and again. However, in addition to our bodies' natural reboot [sleep], it often becomes necessary to purge the excess physical and environmental toxins, which are swirling around us at all times. Unfortunately, this is easier said than done. We have a growing legion of aspirant cyborgs who are figuring out, much too late in life, that their caffeine fueled, rock star, warp speed; Star Trek lifestyles are too stimulating for their delicate organic life forms. What most Christians don't understand is that this way of life is the equivalent of detonating a nano-nuclear attack against your endocrine system, each and every day. As illogical and psychologically unbalanced as this may sound, more and more people are being manipulated into adopting this toxic existence. The resulting effects have been catastrophic, not only to our bodies' fragile chemical and electrical systems, but also to our Christian society. One of the most concerning effects of the above lifestyle is the population increase of United States graveyards.

"And be not conformed to this world: but be ye transformed by the renewing of your mind, that ye may prove what is that good, and acceptable, and perfect, will of God." - Romans 12:2

Throughout subsequent chapters we'll examine the cause and effect of our modern American way of life e.g., toxic genetically modified food like substances, hybridized organisms, sugar, fluoride, aluminum, Wi-Fi, laptop computers, bottled water, 'Brawndo' and much more. At this point, it doesn't really matter how or why you're in the condition you're in mentally and physically. What does matter is that you make a conscious decision and brave effort to take action. However, I'm not suggesting that you try and take on your King Kong size challenges all at once, or condition your mind into believing there is some magical pill or 'one-size fits all' quick-fix solution. The key to successfully transitioning from a health challenged body to one that's functioning properly is 'baby steps'. You'll notice that I've identified life changes that are both non-negotiable and others that are more conservative in nature. I will tell you, those who have wholeheartedly adopted the following principles are living happier, and healthier lives, not merely a continuation of an existence.

"And be not conformed to this world: but be ye transformed by the renewing of your mind, that ye may prove what is that good, and acceptable, and perfect, will of God." - *Romans 12:2*

CHAPTER

3   Nature of The Beast

"Be ye not unequally yoked together with unbelievers: for what fellowship hath righteousness with unrighteousness? and what communion hath light with darkness? And what concord hath Christ with Belial? or what part hath he that believeth with an infidel?
- 2 Corinthians 6:14-15

What motivates a person to senselessly destroy themselves or another human being? Christians often romanticize the battle between good and evil. The question is…Where does the American Christian majority believe evil emanates? In their minds, is evil represented as some eternal dormant force or an external phantom, ready to commit wanton cruelty and destructiveness; or does our majority define evil simply as life cannibalizing itself?

Growing up, my perception of what is good and evil was well defined; and it was through this exposure earlier in life that allowed me to identify some rather extraordinary malevolent events as an adult. Even though I've been spiritually outfitted with a heightened sense of awareness, I've nevertheless found myself being a lightning rod for individuals who can be best described as opportunistic, deceitful, and selfish. The fantastic irony is that I have always strived to be the type of Christian who gravitates towards good while doing my best to deflect inferior natured characters and situations. What has always been my Achilles heel, professionally, is my desire to make the tough decisions in life easiest on everyone else, but myself. Nonetheless, I take pride in knowing the tough decisions I've made throughout my life were made compassionately and without compromising my honor. The empathy that I've felt for fellow Christians and all living creatures, knows no bounds. I hope the following personal story illustrates my definition of compassion.

Four years ago, our French bulldog 'Penny' injured her back and was rushed to the emergency room at U.C. Davis Veterinary Hospital, here in Northern California. After a long and complicated surgery, to excise pieces of a fragmented vertebrae from around her spinal cord, the prognosis was devastating. Our fury family member was paraplegic and no longer had use of her hind legs. What's more, she was unable to evacuate her bladder or bowels, which meant she would rely on me for the rest of her life. For four years, I provided the type of care Penny required e.g., special diet, bladder/bowl expressions, four times per day, etc. It was at the end of her fourth year, following her surgery, that Penny developed an incurable condition that attacked her vital organs, resulting in the gut wrenching decision to let her go.

Penny was an extraordinary little spirit and her ability to cope with anything she was faced with will forever be etched in our hearts. She will remain an eternal inspiration to our entire family. Rest in peace Penny.

The following true stories are in no way as furry and cute as Penny. For anyone who has worked hard to create a business, or achieve anything in their life, only to have that something ripped from their grasp, will understand how disturbing these events were in my life. I'm sharing the following experiences with you, with the hope of achieving three objectives.

First, I expect that my true stories will help you recall instances throughout your life which may have been a source of great strife, stress, or challenge. It's been my personal experience, over the past twenty years, that when a person physically puts pen to paper, and writes out their experiences, they find it to be tremendously therapeutic. Identifying high-stress moments throughout your life will aid in the process of pinpointing when and where your health began to decline. We'll expand on this exercise later in this book.

Second, I hope to qualify my personal opinion that there has been a measurable increase in the level of toxic energy throughout our nation. It's this rampant invasion of dark energy that is affecting the collective States of America.

And third, it's my aim to cite historical and scientific data with the goal in mind of establishing a connection between self avowed Luciferians throughout world history, and the epidemic of cancer, heart disease, Crones, 'IBS', juvenile diabetes, A.D.D., A.D.H.D., Autism, etc. that have overshadowed our once happy, healthy, and prosperous Nation. It's my contention, that every one of these diseases have in fact been intentionally engineered by proxies, bought and paid for by global elite organizations and promoted by top United States Government officials, over no less than 160 years. Of course, a conspiracy involving high ranking Government representatives and banking cartels, with trillions of dollars, would never allow the proverbial 'connection of the dots'. Nonetheless, the data cited in this book, I feel, moves the dots within a few millimeters of one another.

"Absence of proof is not proof of absence." – Dr. Edwin Masters

Throughout my life I've been confronted with some rather fascinating characters. There is one person in particular though, just within the past year, who gave me reason for pause. He caused me to reflect back upon and question all of the preceding events in my life. These are the stories which I'll be sharing with you throughout the upcoming pages.

I've worked throughout the world e.g., Asia, Europe, the America's, Africa, etc. and during my travels, I've been extremely blessed to have gained such a wealth of knowledge and to have garnered a perspective of the world that most people never get the opportunity to have. However, earlier life for me was relatively mundane. I grew up in a middle income home, with amazing parents. I participated in The Boy Scouts, road motorcycles through the woods, camped, fished, shot my dad's 357 Magnum at cans, built forts and had a little dachshund/beagle mix sidekick named Biscuit, who braved the most dangerous adventures a 7 year old could conjure up, in his imagination.

As a youngster, I was fortunate to have lived throughout a number of States in the Union, East to West, and when I was around five my family moved to Fort Worth, Texas. During our first few weeks in that State, I remember my parents being compelled to make evasive maneuvers so as to avoid being rammed by fellow motorists. I recall my father jokingly declaring that 'it was because we still had our California plates on the car'. Texas also provided me with a few other experiences which left an indelible impression.

13

The first took place, shortly after arriving in our new home. My mother and father worked, so it was natural to have enlisted the help of a babysitter for the youngest, yours truly. I do not recall how tenured the new sitter was, before she began abusing me sexually, but it didn't seem that long into her employment with my family. As a young boy, going from 'Captain Caveman' to physical contact with a much older women will definitely create 'Trauma Centers' in ones brain and this is the unfortunate reason I still remember this experience vividly to this day.

"But whoso shall offend one of these little ones which believe in me, it were better for him that a millstone were hanged about his neck, and that he were drowned in the depth of the sea." - Matthew 18:6

According to Jesus Christ himself, grown men or women who victimize little children for their own warped, perverse and twisted pleasure, should be executed. This includes groups, such as the North American Man Boy Love Association (N.A.M.b.L.A.) and all persons involved in the ongoing Washington D.C. child sex ring, uncovered back in the 1980's. If you're unfamiliar with the documentary titled 'The Franklin Cover-Up', and are as disgusted as I am, about child molesters, please watch this film.

My second traumatic experience, as a young person in Texas, was being taken to another babysitter, who had recently lost her little boy in an accident. Weeks after I had already been in this woman's care, my parents learned that her deceased son could have passed for my twin. This explained the woman's odd behavior. For instance, she would force me to eat what used to be her son's favorite foods, wear his cloths, and most twisted of all, she would call me by the dead boy's first name.

Shortly after moving to Texas, I began noticing changes in the personality and behavior of my older sister, Susan. To say that she was 'mean' is an understatement. Daily abuse, became common place and my only safe haven, was in the presence of my second still older sister, Jennifer. Now when I say that my sister Susan was abusive, I don't want you to conjure up imagery of innocent pushing, poking, or teasing. I'm talking about being stabbed, punched in the mouth, choked out, and forced to eat cigarettes.

My most vivid memory of being stabbed is the time when my mother, my two sisters, and I were all sitting around the kitchen table, enjoying 'craft time'. My sister Jennifer was working on a project for school that required a number of tools. The one I would become intimately familiar with that evening, was a 'Xacto-Knife'. So here we all were, sitting around the table, with a 'Jack

14

The Ripper' starter kit. Then, for some reason or another, my mother had to leave the room. Like most kids, 'when the cats away the mice will play'...Right? Well, that's exactly what we began doing. Soon after we began chasing each other around the table, I was grabbed, by Susan. She was holding me, by my shoulders, and looking at me with this emotionless, stare and mumbling something to herself. What I didn't realize is that Susan had wedged the Xacto Knife, in between the dining room chair cushions, with the blade side, facing up at a 45 degree angle. Next thing I know, she squeezes my shoulders, steps forward and pushes me down into the chair, forcing the razor sharp blade into my upper hamstring/lower buttocks. The emergency room doctor said that the knife came within centimeters of piercing the main artery in my leg.

From that point on, the creativity and regularity with which my sister Susan exacted her morbid abuse, evolved into something that resembled a 'Friday The 13th' horror film. Following a number of incidence, with Susan, my parents decided to have her 'speak with someone'. Unfortunately, in those days, parents – for the most part – were naïve to the fact, that it was these types of 'mental health' facilities, who were in part responsible for the dysfunctional state of our Nation. Much to my parents' disappointment, the sessions with doctors did very little, however the doctors were able to garner intelligence, from my sister, that indicated she had been participating in 'Witchcraft', 'Ouija Boards', Drug use, Ritual orgies, etc. As time went on, my sister became so willful, disrespectful, and unruly that it was decided that she was too dangerous to have around our family and was sent away.

Flash forward, four years later, and it's December in Northern California. My family and I have recently moved into a quaint little town in Northern California named Arnold, California. The week before Christmas, my mother comes to my sister Jennifer and I and tells us, 'I just spoke with Susan', and 'she wants to come visit'. She assures Jennifer and me that Susan has been 'rehabilitated' and 'doing much better'. Much to our disappointment, Susan keeps her word and in fact does show up at our new home. Following a day full of forced smiles and manufactured pleasantries, we all turn-in for the evening. My sister Jennifer and I have our bedrooms upstairs and the room Susan was staying in was downstairs.

It's approximately 2 a.m. that next morning, and I've fallen asleep on the couch in our living room. All of a sudden, I'm awakened by the sound of something behind our Christmas tree, that's sitting in the corner of the room. At first, I think to myself, perhaps it's my mom or dad putting presents under the tree, but that thought quickly disappears from my mind and turns

15

into confusion. What is this, yet to be identified energy that is orchestrating the tinsel on our Christmas tree to sway and crumple and the packages underneath to scrap and scratch, the wind? No, there are no open windows. Right about then, I concluded my most logical course of action... Get Mom! With that, I head into my parents' room, sneaking up on my mother's side of the bed. Sensing my presences, she asks: 'What's the matter, Paul?' To which I respond: There is something in our living room and its messing with our Christmas Tree. 'What?' Mom excitedly responds. With that, we're off down the hallway, on course, with something or nothing at all. As my mother and I near the tree, my mother notices some kind of disturbance under and around our Christmas Tree. Now she's completely awake and on guard, as she descends upon our tree. I on the other hand, have determined the kitchen, located 30ft away, is a safe place to observe what might be my mother's last stand. As mom, nears the tree, she quietly peers around its back, giving her a line of sight view at what's causing the disturbance. When her eyes connect with whatever is behind our tree, she is mortified and runs to my parents' room to fetch my father. So out runs my father, half asleep and half giving a damn. I really never witnessed my father scared of anything, and this moment was no different, as he sleepily fumbled towards the tree. As he drew nearer, the rustling stopped. Then, all of a sudden, what had been playing with our decorations and abhorrent enough to have caused my mother's retreat, has decided to show itself to the rest of the family. As I'm writing this, some 30 years later, I still get chills up my spine thinking about it. Before my eyes, was a small dark figure, approximately 2 feet tall, wearing what appeared to be a black cloak. What really stood out however, were these two little piercing blood red eyes. As my father approached the figure, what he was going to do with it, I have no idea. The figure darted over to the top of the staircase that led to our downstairs, and before anyone could process what had happened... Swoosh! Down the stairs, it ran. As my father cautiously approaches the top of the stairs, he peers down into the dark abyss. Faced with the knowledge that my sister Susan is asleep downstairs, he makes the decision to pursue the figure. As we slowly see my father's shape disappear into the darkness of the room below, my mother calls out: 'Honey! What's going on? Do you see anything?' For several seconds, there's no response and then I hear my sister Susan's voice: 'Dad, why are you looking at me like that?'

My father never discussed what it was that he saw that evening and for whatever reason, nobody really pressed the issue. As I grew older, I came to my own conclusions, as to what this figure was and its attachment to my sister. Days following my sister's visit, I recall an incident with one of the little boys my mother used to baby-sit. Brandon was a three year old, with no history of violence. Nonetheless, my mother discovered him standing over me,

16

with a butcher's knife, as I slept on the couch. All I remember about that moment is how Brandon's face resembled that of my sister Susan, years prior in Texas, right before she impaled me.

CHAPTER
4 There's Gold In Them There Fiber Optics

"Ye are of your father the devil, and the lusts of your father ye will do. He was a murderer from the beginning, and abode not in the truth, because there is no truth in him. When he speaketh a lie, he speaketh of his own: for he is a liar, and the father of it." – John 8:44

Talmudist orchestrated speculative bubbles are nothing new to usury based economic systems. If you happen to be one of the lucky few fortunate enough to have received a pre-1950's education, You may have read about the 1919 'May Day Bomb Plot,' meant to eliminate the Talmudist cancer in the body of America, e.g., J.P. Morgan and John D. Rockefeller. The Bureau of Investigation (BOI) alleged this plot was meant to kill Morgan and Rockefeller; moreover, it spurred the 1920's deadly Wall St. bombing, which preceded the Wall Street Crash of 1929. Zbigniew Brzezinski's 1970s, 'al-Qaeda' hadn't been invented yet, so the BOI pinned the bombings on 'radical opponents of capitalism' e.g., Bolsheviks, anarchists, communists, militant socialists, etc. As predicted, the Government orchestrated bombings stimulated renewed efforts by police and federal investigators to track the activities and movements of foreign radicals. Public demands to track down the perpetrators led to an expanded role for the U.S. Justice Department's Bureau of Investigation (BOI) (the forerunner of the Federal Bureau of Investigation), including the General Intelligence Division of the BOI headed by J. Edgar Hoover. The NYPD also pushed to form a "special, or secret, police" to monitor "radical elements" in New York City.

"By dividing the people we can get them to expend their energies in fighting over questions of no importance to us." – J.P. Morgan

If you're like tens of millions of other unlucky Americans, you were never apprised of such knowledge. Perhaps the reason we weren't educated about such matters is because it would have caused us to ask too many questions about those whose entire existence depends on secrecy. Instead we were pushed through a Wilhelm Maximilian Wundt style, outcomes based, communist training camp. During which time, we were forced fed 1960's modernist history, with the expectation that we would adopt an anti-Republic, anti-Constitutional, anti-family, pro-Socialist, pro-bigot, pro-hate, pro-war, one world government ideology.

Like many young Americans today, I was conditioned subconsciously to live a self-destructive existence. If there was an inferior natured friendship or business partnership my subconscious gravitated towards it, even though deep down inside, my conscious mind desired a more superior natured Christian existence.

It was only much later in life that I was able to break free from the vicious cycle of poor judgment and behavior. Prior to this breakthrough, I would regularly ask myself, 'Why do I attract these wicked people into my life? It was about one year ago that I had a life changing epiphany. Upon simply shutting off all of the inferior background noise which had monopolized, literally, every second of my life, I was able to focus all my efforts on a Christ-centric professional and personal lifestyle. It was through this simple, yet impactful change in my life, which completely altered the lens through which I reviewed business opportunities and prospective business partners. The resulting effect was that all of the energy vampires, clingers, deceivers, and leeches disappeared.

As Christian Americans, we have to be honest with ourselves and admit that the modern American way of life is extremely toxic. It rewards the morally corrupt and celebrates behavior, most wild animals would find objectionable. I concluded the illusion that I had accepted as my reality, was in fact based on a Luciferian based control system, which rewarded deceit, misery, hate, and arrogance. As a Christian, I knew that lifestyle didn't represent Jesus Christ.

Through years of reflection and research, I concluded that the Christian American majority, had deteriorated, morally, educationally, economically, and spiritually; not because of a natural degeneration, or an overseas boogie man, rather it was caused by a pre-planned, cradle to grave, toxic reality, orchestrated by a secret cabal of men and women who espouse a Satanic ideology. As

18

someone who has always embraced the fortune of God given 'Free Will' I was hostile towards the idea that flesh and blood mortals were inexplicably directing the ambition and destination of every single Christian American. What's more, this group controlled literally every vector and sphere of influence, throughout America, this is not hyperbole. It's a matter of fact. By allowing themselves to be lead around and emotionally manipulated by fill-in-the-blank news headlines and preplanned economic calamities, the Christian American majority is simply swatting at the leafs, instead of attacking the problem at its roots.

Having fought in the trenches, during the 1999-2001 'dot-com' assault on American capitalism, I reflected back on all of the red-flags those experiences raised. The only difference this time being, I viewed all of my past knowledge, through a Christian lens. My practice today is that I construct all health checks on prospective business opportunities, comparing their goals as a business or individual with my Christian principles.

With regards to my dot-com experiences, I began asking the most obvious question. Why were so many people victimized during the dot-com era? And the short answer that I came up with is that most of those poor souls became victims because they failed to adhere to traditional values and business acumen. The majority of startups eschewed these principles in favor of operating at a net loss in order to capture market share and build brand awareness. Believe it or not, it was popular throughout the dot-com era to believe merely capturing market share would result in a solid financial footing. Amazon is one company famous for leveraging this concept, and its founder Mr. Liebowitz, was one of the very few who succeeded handsomely at it. This of course was long before Morgan Stanley, JP Morgan, and the Rockefeller's, Wundt based behavioral control scheme, FACEBOOK, twinkled in their all seeing eye.

In many ways, the dot-com burst of 2000 resembles that of America's 2014 health crisis. Christian Americans throughout our Nation have allowed themselves to become conditioned into believing that being obese, sick or dead at 50 is 'normal'. Those who have bought into this unhealthy illusion are just like the dot-com victims who didn't exercise any level of common sense during the foreseeable bubble. Christian Americans must wake up to the reality that obesity, economic strife, immorality, etc. are all tools used by Luciferians to subjugate the Christian majority. The fact is America's financial condition is nothing new. Nations have been tormented by 'financial bubbles', throughout world history. Take for example, "Tulip Mania" and the "South Sea Bubble". I used to refer to this phenomenon as 'greater fools economics'. Unfortunately, there were a whole lot of

19

people who bought into this economic principle during the global elite manufactured "Dot-com" bubble. People bought assets whose market values had plummeted and then, when the market was flooded with sellers these assets plummeted in value.

I've shared the above experiences of the 'Dot-com' era to illustrate two points. First, that the Christian majority wields incredible power over America's collective economic system. Much like the effects that toxic assets had on the 2000 bubble it's not extraordinary to imagine a time in the not too distant future, where Christians will dump all of the toxic assets inside of their refrigerators and cupboards. The good news here is that you don't have to be a savvy investor to experience incredible health gains; you simply have to be able to read the ingredients on your cans, bottles, and wrappers. If the ingredients read Soy, Soy Lecithin, Corn, Wheat, etc. consider it a toxic asset and dump it. This exercise should be repeated for anything in your sustenance portfolio that does not read 'ORGANIC - Grown In America'. We'll discuss why this is the best investment you can make in yourself and your family, later in this book.

The second reason I've invoked the dot-com bubble is to lend my perspective on past proceedings and the events that led up to one of American's greatest economic perfect storms. Moreover, I wanted to highlight my personal experience, in the trenches, negotiating the V.C. shark tanks and the cannibalistic nature of business partners. I liken the excitement and uncertainty to that of a war film. From the perspective of the start-up, the V.C. is the stereotypical villain. Every presentation on 'Sand Hill', etc. is like walking into an ambush. While the aspiring co-founder of ABC Company pitches his revolutionary new solution, the V.C. is scanning for cracks in the suspect's armor. As the suspect becomes a prospective investment, the V.C.'s strategy becomes purely predatory. It's at this point where most start-up veterans can sense a distinct shift in a V.C.'s talk track, as the smell of money permeates the free-hanging, industrial designed AC ducts.

As if the global elite good old boy economic system isn't enough to break your spirit. The very minute money becomes imminent, every founding member of XYZ Company, must now become a criminal psychiatrist in order to predict the predatory nature of their business partners. Those same partners who once referred to you as a 'brother' now see you as a giant thanksgiving turkey. Remember those cartoons you watched as a kid, featuring two starving characters? One of the characters, who is emaciated and visibly frail, pans over to the second character and imagines that he's a giant turkey, complete with roasting booties and an apple in his mouth.

Unfortunately, many of us in the start-up community, know all too well the feeling of being preyed upon by individuals who have "come to you in sheep's clothing, but inwardly they are ravening wolves" – *Matthew 7:15*.

The following compilation of short stories is a handful of the hundreds of experiences I've had throughout my career as a corporate executive, high-level consultant, and venture capitalist. I believe the characters that you'll meet, in subsequent pages, represent a growing community in America who have unwittingly fallen victim to the Luciferian agenda which seeks to destroy America.

"Beware lest any man spoil you through philosophy and vain deceit, after the tradition of men, after the rudiments of the world, and not after Christ." - Colossians 2:8

5   The Psychology Of The Deal

"But I say unto you, Love your enemies, bless them that curse you, do good to them that hate you, and pray for them which despitefully use you, and persecute you; That ye may be the children of your Father which is in heaven: for he maketh his sun to rise on the evil and on the good, and sendeth rain on the just and on the unjust."
- Matthew 5:44-45

It's 1999 and my good friend, Matthew Goff, and I, are working on a Data Center startup, by the name of Wavve Telecommunications, in Sacramento, California. For the past 2 ½ years we've suspended disbelief that our CEO is capable of paying back our investors the $75M our company has borrowed to build two Data Centers totaling 120,000 square feet. Conceding the inevitable, I approach Matt with an epiphany that I had over the Thanksgiving Holiday; while driving across the causeway, between downtown Sacramento, CA and Davis, CA, I thought to myself: What if the carpoolers, commuting between the whole of Sacramento and Davis had access to high-speed wireless broadband?

This idea led Matt and I to form a company by the name of Prana Technologies, Inc. It would become one of the first high-speed, wireless internet service providers in the Nation who had successfully developed an efficient, cost ef-   21 fective mobile high-speed data solution. Within the first week of verbally forming Prana Corporation, I had secured not only an investor, but a company that would incubate the software development, a critical feature to what Matt and I referred to as the Prana Cortex. Our new investor was a good friend of mine, Steve Petty. Steve was co-owner of one of the more successful VARs (value added reseller) in Northern California, Alliance Healthcare Solutions.

This was a particularly exciting project for me given my familial heritage and their historic contributions towards building America's bleeding edge National IP infrastructure. In 1973, David Boggs, a member of my family tree, along with 3Com founder Robert Metcalfe, announced their creation 'Alto Ethernet'. This revolutionary technology paved the way for virtual commerce, and twenty-six years later, Matt and I were in the process of introducing a wireless super highway through which future generations would develop an even more dynamic commerce vehicle.

The Prana cortex, high-speed wireless throttling solution, was revolutionary back in the late 90's. Matt and I developed our technology based on the United States Navy's declassified 802.11 spread spectrum technology. This particular technology had been available to our Navy for many years, and was commonly used by naval ships to communicate through fog and rough weather. It was an attractive technology due to its ability to safely and securely fragment the data into packets, and then reassemble that data accordingly, upon reaching its destination. The dynamic throttling capability of our cortex solution, offered an additional layer of security, on top of the security inherent in the declassified military technology.

Flash forward six months and Prana has begun gaining momentum and interest on the boards of a shortlist of respectable telecom providers. One of those was Phil Anschutz' Qwest Communications. Upon review of Prana's technology, Qwest indicated that they would like to proceed, with an official evaluation of Prana's solution. Following this review of both Prana's business plan and of our miniature mock-up of a wirelessly enabled city, Qwest's VP of product development and acquisition charged the Prana team with the task of securing a regional telecom provider, who would act as our 'beta-test'. We responded to the VP's request, within only two weeks, with the good news. We had presented the Prana solution to the CEO of Roseville Telecom, Fred Arcuri. Fred oversaw the operations of a relatively small regional telecom solutions provider located in Roseville, California and he was excited to partner with Prana.

To ensure, the successful completion of our Roseville Telecom beta test, Prana founders agreed to interview a number of companies to help both with the development and deployment of our patented Cortex software. Prana narrowed its list of candidates, down to two, ultimately voting in favor of hiring a company, by the name of WorldXPand. The CEO of WorldXPand Jillian, had been the CEO of a large software company, located in Folsom, California by the name of Sterling Software.

Soon after hiring WorldXPand, the mood throughout Prana' executive members changed. Regrettably, I failed to notice these changes in time. For one, I was still working on the Wavve Telecommunications project. I naively bought into Matt's recommendation that it would be best for Prana to just compensate Matt on a monthly basis, and I would stay behind and walk our previous business venture 'Wavve telecommunications' to its grave.

Because of both, the trust I had in Matt and the illusion of influence, over the Prana decision making process, I honestly didn't feel it necessary to be paranoid or overly protective. This would prove to be a fatal error on my part.

Ten months later, Prana is riding high on a wave of excitement and groundswell of supporters. The confidence in our new project is growing exponentially with each passing day. And then we begin hearing those words every entrepreneur dreams of; 'acquisition for hundreds of millions of dollars is guaranteed'. Much to my dismay, the predicted payday, by the self ascribed oracles of WorldXpand has sparked rivalry and controversy, between certain members of Prana. My once promising vision, over Thanksgiving Holiday, has now become a scrap of meat, being fought over by a pack of wolves. The downward spiral reaches a climax, when Matt requests a meeting to discuss WorldXPand's most recent discussions with Qwest. Matt, who is at this point residing in my home, rent-free mind you, proceeds to explain that Jillian and Pierre are suggesting that Matt' equity position be increased to a majority position. The excuse? Because, Matt is perceived by Qwest as being the 'father of invention'. Which was not the case. And before Qwest will invest they want Matt's position secured. Essentially what I'm told is that if I don't agree with these terms our funding source disappears, so under duress, I accept.

What happened next is one of the best examples of divine justice that I've yet to witness, in my lifetime. Shortly after Prana is literally ripped out from underneath me, by my 'friend,' Roseville Telecommunications CEO Fred Arcuri communicates his desire to 'pullout of the deal', and that he will no longer be engaged as Prana's beta-test. We learn that Roseville Telecommunications has actually 'borrowed' Prana' business model and applied it to a small Roseville internet company they had just purchased. They would promote this company as the source of their new Wireless Data Solution, as they proceed to offer our Prana architected wireless data solutions to their 120,000 customers. To add insult to injury, Roseville Telecommunications, changed their name to, SureWest Communications 'borrowing' the Prana corporate Identity e.g., logo, color scheme, etc.

As time passed, I began reflecting back on all of the poor spiritual, personal and business decisions that I had made during the Wavve and Prana ventures. For instance the Wavve Telecommunications culture e.g., investors, founders and employees were highly toxic spiritually. This environment mirrored Matt's personal and business ethics which were woefully anemic. This led me to the realization that Matt's worldview had always been in direct conflict with everything I held sacred in my life. For instance, Matt was an avowed atheist, who supported the Satanic, theosophical ideology of Rudolph Steiner and his Anthroposophical Society.

As an aside, my personal experience has shown that a growing number of the individuals within the information technology community are either anti-Christians or homosexuals. I believe this is an important fact, considering the growing dependency Christians have on technologists. And why it's so critical that a consortium of Christian technologists develop applications and systems independent of D.A.R.P.A.'s World Wide Web? It's paramount that our majority disconnect financially, emotionally, and spiritually from the Luciferian world government technocracy which is emerging through proxy agencies such as Microsoft, Google, Yahoo, etc. For Heaven's sake, Google funnels $8.9 billion dollars annually, through a Bermuda based post office box numbered '666'. What's more, Google honor's, Yuri Kochiyama, a violent Communist Maoist who admired Zbigniew Brzezinski's protégé, Osama bin Landen.

To better understand the depth and breadth of satanic oversight, throughout our current global hi-tech infrastructure, consider a documentary titled 'Inside Satanism and The Satanic Church'. In the film, Davis Harris, an 'ordained satanic priest' for the Church of Satan, describes his relationship with Scottish American Peter H. Gilmore. Gilmore, whose ancient Gaelic name means 'follower of Mary', is the successor of Anton LaVey, founder of the 'Church of Satan' and is referred to by his followers as the 'Black Pope". Satanic priest Harris refers to Gilmore as "Literally one of the greatest people I've ever had the pleasure of knowing and calling my friend."

What should concern the Christian American Majority, is what this Church of Satan priest says regarding his line of work. Davis Harris states:

"I work as a network security consultant for a major fortune 500 company and I'm certainly not the only Satanist working for said company. There are Satanists from every walk of life and possible profession you can imagine. Law enforcement, legal field, fine arts, computer technology. What have you. You name it. I can guarantee you, there is a Satanist working in that profession"

Wavve Telecommunication's culture certainly had its share of individuals who subscribed to an anti-Christian lifestyle. This was fitting given the fact that Wavve promoted the World Wide Web [WWW]. To those Christians who are unaware each Hebrew letter has a numerical value. The letter 'W' happens to be '6', so even though WWW equals 18 it reads '666'.

Couple the abovementioned knowledge with the fact that Anton Lavey publicly announced that Luciferian's would utilize media as a way to deceive Christians away from God stating:

"The religious war is being waged between media vs. churches. We can use TV as a potent propaganda machine." – Anton Lavey, The Devil's Notebook, p. 85

Consider the fact that the, "National Academy of Television Arts & Sciences" (NATAS) is SATAN in reverse. Lavey's book, The Devil's Notebook, contains a total of forty-one essays, in which he bloviates about: artificial human companions, cannibalism, Nazism, nonconformity, erotic politics, magical evocation, etc.

With Anton Lavey's 'media war' threat in mind, consider the cosmetic changes that have occurred to home televisions since the 1960s. Today's flat screen television is an exact replica of a, "Scrying Mirror" [pg. 26]. Here's how a popular witchcraft site describes Scrying Mirrors:

"Samhain is a time to do some serious divination - it's the time of year when the veil between our world and that of the spirits [demons] is at its thinnest, and that means it's the perfect season to look for messages from the metaphysical. Scrying is one of the best known forms of divination."

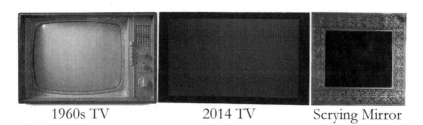

| 1960s TV | 2014 TV | Scrying Mirror |

According to Satanists, and the above physical evidence, the vast majority of Christian homes throughout America have, "one of the best known forms of divination" sitting in their living rooms, bedrooms, etc. Read what the Holy Bible has to say about Scrying Mirrors and 'divination':

"When thou art come into the land which the LORD thy God giveth thee, thou shalt not learn to do after the abominations of those nations. There shall not be found among you [any one] that maketh his son or his daughter to pass through the fire, [or] that useth divination, [or] an observer of times, or an enchanter, or a witch, Or a charmer, or a consulter with familiar spirits, or a wizard, or a necromancer. For all that do these things [are] an abomination unto the LORD"

Wavve's funding of nearly $75M was supplied in large part by a publicly traded Canadian group named Grand Columbia. It would later be discovered, Grand Columbia had participated in the illegal practice of 'Salting Gold Mines'. This is where a mining company will artificially seed an area with gold fragments, then proclaim 'there's gold in them there hills'. Then there was the Wavve sales leadership who were all cheating on their wives, with either other Wavve employees or individuals somehow connected to the company. Our attorney and her husband were 'swingers'. The woman, who would later become my future ex-wife, was a Wavve employee who had an extremely dysfunctional past. Shortly after being married, she disclosed that she was a high-school dropout, due to drug and alcohol addiction and arrested by the Auburn, California, Police Department on a number of occasions. Approximately one year into our marriage, she became an extremely toxic human being. Her addictive personality reanimated her disease of alcoholism. Driving drunk, threats of suicide and violent outbursts were commonplace. What's more, she began practicing Witchcraft and other occult customs. From a spiritual perspective my ex-wife's personal profile became overwhelming when I learned that her cousin was an admirer of the Church of Satan founder Anton LaVey and was in fact a practicing member of the Church of Satan. The proverbial 'nail in the coffin' for me was when I noticed that her father J. Randall Smith,

26

an artist in Northern California, was using a similar mark used by the infamous 'Zodiac Killer' to sign his art work. Furthermore many of his sculptures resembled the Anti-Christian Celtic horned god Cernunnos.

As a Christian the most challenging aspect of Wavve's culture of corruption was the number of homosexuals working for our company. The most dysfunctional of this group was a young man, working inside our I.T. Department, who was found dead inside of his apartment. I later learned that when authorities discovered the young man's body, he was dressed up as a women e.g., make-up, wig, woman's clothing, etc. and sticking out of his rectum was a dildo. Authorities said he died by 'erotic asphyxiation' the intentional restriction of oxygen to the brain for sexual arousal. Homosexual and transgender behavior has been considered psychopathological for centuries throughout the west. The Diagnostic and Statistical Manual of Mental Disorders (DSMMD) listed homosexual and transgender behavior as 'Psychopathological'. Then in 1980 a homosexual attorney, backed by Luciferians, argued for its removal and won. As of December 1, 2012, transgenders are no longer classified as having a mental disorder. If you're interested to learn who invented the 'Religion of Transgenderism' and for what purpose, please visit, transdelusion.com

Throughout this entire experience with Wavve, Prana and my ex, I felt as though I was watching someone else's life unravel before my eyes. My spirituality was under massive attack and it was difficult admitting this was in fact my life. I remember, on a number of occasions, asking the question; 'How did I allow this to happen?'.

The Ruse Jumped Over the Moon

Flash forward to 2005 and I've been introduced to an individual by the name of David Sypnieski. Upon cursory review of David's qualifications, I concluded that he was a sensible choice for an associate position. In addition to David's professional qualifications, he disclosed that both he and his wife were devout Buddhists and that he believed the ultimate premise of his faith was the successful ascension to 'Godhood'. He added, that his wife Katie Hull-Sypnieski was a teacher and that they had one small child. David proudly boasted that his wife had developed a 'proprietary teaching methodology', and that she had been empowering struggling inner city youth for over eight years. David also highlighted the fact that his wife had been recognized as a master of differentiated instruction by Stanford University.

27

Following my introduction to David's academic and business accomplishments, I thought to myself: 'You can't get a more qualified candidate than this.' My perceived view of the Buddhist faith suggested that David believed in the idea of removing the self from the process of perception so that he could become one with everything. What better partner than someone whose spiritual ideals are based on his ability to remain tethered to the notion of selflessness, and a life free of conflict and deceit.

Following a number of meetings, David and I were lead to an idea that would become known as 'Krown Windows'. The Krown objective would be based in large part, on both the manufacturing and fenestration of German style windows. Our goal was to manufacture a series of high-quality European windows overseas and then ship the components to the U.S., where they would be assembled and then distributed throughout a consortium of Krown certified strategic partners.

In tandem with our core venture, Krown Windows, David and I were also in talks with various interests. These included the acquisition of several large raw mineral mines. It was our intention to utilize these deposits in nano-tech applications. Additionally, we were considering a reverse merger into a U.S. shell corporation with one of China' largest growers of herbal remedies and a movie deal, with a Hollywood director friend of mine, named Paul Aratow, to raise money for a few movie projects. The first was named El Piratero a bilingual Spanish-English film based on the classic Italian film 'The Bicycle Thief'. 'Keep On The Sunny Side' the true story of The Carter Family, the originators of commercial Blue Grass music. 'Jack London' a historical biopic of one of the great American writers, and a great love story between two very remarkable people. Paul had access to Charmian London's [Jack's wife] extensive unpublished diaries in the Huntington, courtesy of her heirs. 'The Last of the Wine' a novel by Mary Renault centering on the homosexual relationship of two men during the Peloponnesian war. [C.400 to 430 B.C.] property Paul said was 'perfect material for a TV. Miniseries', Paul said HBO already 'had its eye on this one'. At the same time Paul was promoting the homosexual lifestyle he was ironically working on a one hour DVD project titled 'The Last Hour of Jesus Christ', featuring classical, gospel and ambient sound tracks. I found Paul's duplicitous nature to be a common trait throughout much of Hollywood. Lastly there was a complex video game based on the Peloponnesian war.

Paul Aratow produced a number of movies, e.g., Sheena: Queen of the Jungle among others, beginning in 1966 and directed such actor's as John Carradine father of David Carradine. David Carradine's television series, KungFu, featured his father

John in episodes titled "Dark Angel" and "The Nature of Evil". During my meetings with Paul he disclosed to me some rather fascinating information regarding Hollywood secret societies, e.g., Freemasonry, Church of Satan, etc., and specifically John's and David's involvement with these organizations. As most people already know David Carradine had a prolific career, amassing 227 movie and television credits such as the movie 'Kill Bill' directed by Quinton Tarrantino, a man whose entire catalog of work demonstrates his penchant for Aleister Crowley's edict:

"I want blasphemy, murder, rape, revolution, anything, bad or good, but strong," - Aleister Crowley c.1895

Shortly after his appearances in the 'Kill Bill' franchise, David Carradine, like many other Hollywood Movie Stars before him, was murdered by the Church of Babylon in 2009. It's noteworthy to mention that in 1975 Paul Aratow directed David Carradine's father John Carradine in a film titled: 'Lucifer's Women' which would be released under the name 'Doctor Dracula' in the 80's. Coincidentally the technical advisor for Paul's film was Church of Satan founder Anton LaVey, who injected a number of his Church of Satan members into Paul's film as extras. As an aside in 1978 John Carradine played the role of King David in the "The Judgment of Solomon". King Solomon was of course the King who for a time brought the entire race of demons and their leader Beelzebub under Solomon's command to build his temple, using the 'Star of Remphan' [Acts 7:43], this is the star which adorns the Israeli Flag. These were also the demons that supported the Egyptian magicians against Moses and the very same demons worshipped by Babylonian Talmudic Freemasons. Coincidently John Carradine's son Christopher Carradine is a vice-president for Walt Disney Imagineering, an organization which I demonstrate throughout my book, DECEPTION: The Ancient Mystery That Holds The Secret of Newgrange at, KillingIreland.com, promotes anti-Christian, satanic cryptograms throughout their Walt Disney Properties and Movies.

In an interview, David Carradine recalled that his father John had bragged throughout his lifetime that he had worked as an apprentice for Talmudic Freemason Daniel Chester French, the artist who fashioned the giant Lincoln Memorial. Both John and David have stars on the Hollywood Walk of Fame at, 6240 Hollywood Blvd. near Kodak Theatre which is blanketed with satanic Babylonian Talmudic symbolism. John Carradine like many deceived souls before him made amends in his own way with God while climbing the 328 steep steps of Milan's Gothic cathedral, the Duomo hours before dying inside of Fatebenefratelli Hospital in Milan, Italy on November 27, 1988.

29

In the spring of 2005, David and I began executing the Krown business plan along with our CEO, Larry Lorenz, based in Vancouver Canada, and our CFO, Tom Crom, based in Tempe Arizona. In addition to being a kick in the pants to speak with, Larry had an extensive background working with enterprise-level Chinese mergers and acquisitions and was instrumental in developing the first strategic corporate partnership between a Canadian and Chinese government owned corporation. Larry's influence throughout Chinese elites was so far reaching that at one point in his career he was asked to sponsor one of Chairman Mao Zedong' ten children to a Canadian University. With this knowledge in mind, David and I felt that our interests throughout the unpredictable landscape of China would be under better than average protection.

Under the guidance of Larry, Krown launched talks with the Jiang Family an influential family in China who was capable of fulfilling our first year production projections with The Home Depot, one of our largest prospective buyers. Rounding out our list of requisites included the successful completion of Krown's NFRC certification. Having zero knowledge of this process, I consulted with my father about who he thought might be a qualified candidate. The person he referred me to was Scottish American Dennis McSweeney. Dennis was in charge of The Home Depot's Nation Fenestration University.

Now the stage was set and all of our management pieces in their seemingly proper places. As I sowed and seeded the relationship with Home Depot's VP of Millworks, in Atlanta, Georgia, David compiled the team's collective contributions, and constructed a final draft business plan. Upon its completion, I was tasked with securing initial funding. Phase one of the business plan, which included NFRC window certification, was required post-haste, and within just a few weeks, I had secured our first investor. It was my father. He was excited about the Krown strategy, under one condition: both David and I would be required to sign a 'Note & Guarantee'. This meant that both David and I were personally responsible for the borrowed monies, and that he and I would be held personally responsible for its repayment. Upon hearing my father's conditions, I contacted David and asked him to meet both my father and I at my home. My father reiterated his terms to David and I, as we sat inside my home office and David gave both a verbal agreement, in addition to signing the personal guarantee for these monies.

As I had done in the past, to preserve investment capital, I agreed to accept a position as a Sales Director for a Nationwide Telecom Provider. The logic behind this decision was that David would be able to focus on team assigned responsibilities e.g., NFRC certification, etc., critical to our ability to forge

30

additional strategic distributors, additional financing, etc. In addition, this would ensure that my monthly financial requirement would not drain corporate coffers. After all, the initial investment, from my father, was to be used strictly for the purpose of achieving Phase I.

Shortly after beginning work with my new employer, David contacted me with the highly questionable notion that he should be able to 'tap into' the investment recently made by my father because he was 'unable to pay his bills'. I'm sure David was not prepared for my response, which was an emphatic "No!" I proceeded to explain, what I thought to be apparent, and that was, the investment capital was to be used for the sole purpose of developing the Krown business plan, not funding his family's debt. I informed David that if he needed additional money he would need to take a job and resorting back to my old, hazardous ways, I agree to hire David, as sales representative for the company I was working. This turned out to be a huge mistake. David demonstrated that he was a miserable sales representative; this in turn brought immense pressure on me. In the end, I was forced to fire David.

Shortly after his termination, David, without my knowledge or consent, begins draining the Krown Windows bank account, leaving the Krown Windows coffers sterile, with none of the mandatory certifications accomplished. The decimation of our coffers shuts down any and all negotiations with strategic partners or prospective clients. The Home Depot, which was once extremely interested in Krown's portfolio of high-end European Style windows, has now switched their focus on negotiating pricing reductions with their top window manufacturers, leveraging Krown Windows' pricing. The end result is, The Home Depot' largest supplier of windows, is forced to lower their prices to The Home Depot by a substantial percentage.

For me and the rest of the Krown team this meant the closure of the company and the loss of billions of dollars in potential revenue. As of February 25, 2014, David Sypnieski has made no attempt to reimburse my father back a single dime of the money he appropriated; money that he used to support his family, rather than provide a return on investment to our investor.

As I had done previously, following the Prana debacle, I stepped away from the drawing board and began reflecting back on the mistakes I had made. I vowed this would be the last time that I partnered with anyone to achieve my personal financial goals. I reassured myself 'this would never happen again'. Today, I'm able to better analyze exactly what went wrong, by reviewing this particular moment in history, through a Christian lens. Once I had compiled all of the intelligence I had collected on David and his family, I began building a wellness profile on the Krown venture. What I found was disturbing.

First, I learned later in our partnership that David was heavily dependent on Ritalin and used Cocaine. David would literally pop a Ritalin pill, every half hour. For those who don't know, Ritalin has been shown to cause hallucinations, aggressive behavior, and even psychotic breaks. This would explain David's bizarre behavior. I recall one occasion where David and I were traveling to a meeting and we had to pull over to eat in my car. Before I know it, I see David, in my peripheral, forming a gun out of his fingers and raising his imaginary weapon to my head. As he reaches my temple, David makes a motion as if he's firing a bullet into my head. That was one of the first indications that David was not well. His paranoia flowed over into his marriage as well. On one occasion David asked if I could 'hack-into' his wife's personal e-mail account, because he felt 'she was cheating on him, with one of her male colleagues'. Couple all this with his obsession with 'New Age' theosophical teachers e.g., Wayne Dyer, Deepak Chopra, etc. and I'm able to see clearly where I went wrong. David, like Matt Goff, subscribed to Luciferian doctrines that were counter to my Christian Religion. I remember a number of times where David tried to convince me to abandon my life-long dedication to Jesus Christ in exchange for Buddhism. I pinpoint the day I rejected David's Buddhist faith, as the day David began undermining our collective vision for Krown. Then there was the following middleweb. com interview, where David's wife, Katie Hull-Sypnieski, responded to questions regarding a book she co-authored, with an individual by the name of Larry Ferlazzo, titled: 'The ESL/ELL Teachers Survival Guide'. The interviewer asks:

Interviewer: "What about ELL beyond the E/LA classroom? What do teachers without a primary responsibility for literacy instruction need to know? And how does the Common Core figure in?"

Katie Sypnieski: "We hope that the next generation of standardized tests will respect language acquisition research and that they will be more connected to performance-based assessment, will offer translations in multiple languages, and will adhere to the concept of "universal design" by simplifying language demands that aren't relevant to content being measured."

It's this operant conditioning and Hegelian Dialectic which encompass Katie's 'hope' for our children and the standard through which our youth are measured in the future. In actuality, the above quote mirrors the long term clandestine strategic plan of tax exempt foundations – financed and controlled by global elite theosophists - to transform America from a nation of rugged individualists, problem solvers and Christians to a country of servile, atheistic, brainwashed minions who simply regurgitate whatever they're told.

"The State has the supreme right against the individual, whose supreme duty is to be a member of the State. For the right of the world spirit is above all special privileges." - Georg Hegel

The following is a historical time line for the implementation of Skinnerian's, Pavlovian's and Wilhelm Maximilian Wundt's 'Performance-Based' methods designed to dissolve the once great American educational system in exchange for a Communist based educational system. It's noteworthy to mention that Wundt's grandfather was a member of the Bavarian Illuminati which called for the elimination of Christianity, the family and borders between Nations. Further, Wundt was himself directly involved with the infamous organization 'Skull & Bones'. The first American pupil of Wilhelm Wundt was an avowed Marxist by the name of Stanley G. Hall, who also happened to be a member of 'Skull & Bones.' Hall's writings included psychology and its relations to physiology, anthropology, sociology, sex, crime, religion and education.

1832: Wilhelm Wundt, founder of experimental psychology and the force behind its dissemination throughout the Western world:

"To Wundt, a thing made sense and was worth pursuing if it could be measured, quantified, and scientifically demonstrated. Seeing no way to do this with the human soul, he proposed that psychology concern itself solely with experience."

- The Leipzig Connection: The Systematic Destruction of American Education" by Paolo Lionni

"The conditioning of modern American society began with John Dewey, a psychologist, a Fabian Socialist and the 'Father of Progressive Education.' Dewey used the psychology developed in Leipzig by Wilhelm Wundt, and believed that through a stimulus-response approach (like Pavlov) students could be conditioned for a new social order." - *The Christian News, New Haven, Mo., December 11, 1989*

1862: The first experiment with "Outcome-based Education (OBE) was conducted in England in 1862. Teacher opposition resulted in abandonment of the experiment. "The call for 'sound and cheap' elementary instruction was answered by legislation, passed by Parliament during 1862, known as The Re-

33

vised Code. This was the legislation that produced payment-for-results, the nineteenth century English accountability system. The opposition to the English payment-for-results system which arose at the time of its introduction was particularly interesting. Teachers provided the bulk of the resistance, and they based their objections on both educational and economic grounds. They abhorred the narrowness and mechanical character the system imposed on the educational process. They also objected to the economic burden forced upon them by basing their pay on student performance." - Accountability in American Education: A Critique

1933: Carnegie Corporation's "Eight-Year Study", referred to by the Education Commission of the States in the nineteen nineties as the forerunner of OBE.

1934: Conclusions and Recommendations for the Social Studies, published by American Historical Association, funded by Carnegie Corporation. Professor Harold Laski, philosopher of British socialism, said of this Report: "At bottom and stripped of its carefully neutral phrases, the report is an educational program for a socialist America". This Report lays bare the education agenda for the United States for the next 100 years.

1965: ESEA (Elementary and Secondary Education Act, spawned as part of President Lyndon Johnson's "Great Society") calls for performance based education and it funds BSTEP (Behavioral Science Teacher Education Program) which calls for teacher to be a psychiatrist and a "trainer," not a "teacher."

1968: Siegfried Engelmann's DISTAR (Direct Instruction program), for underprivileged Title I children. This was the first Direct Instruction program funded by the U.S. Office of Education. Engelmann received federal funding for the promotion of this program for at least thirty years!

1968: Ethna Reid, Utah, ECRI (Exemplary Center for Reading Instruction) which, according to parents, teachers, and doctors, makes students sick, has been thoroughly researched by elementary school teacher Ann Herzer. Her excellent critiques of the program, can be studied at: deliberatedumbingdown.com

1968: Chicago Mastery Learning, funded by the U.S. Department of Education, 1968-1980, which after 12 years was described by Education Week as a "human tragedy."

34

1971: "Performance-Based Teacher Education...What is the State of the Art?" by Stanley Elam, Phi Delta Kappa Publications, can also be studied at: deliberatedumbingdown.com This paper was prepared for the Committee on Performance-based Teacher Education pursuant to a contract with the U.S. Office of Education through the Texas Education Agency, Austin, Texas. One important excerpt: "Many aspects of the PBTE approach could be conceived as Skinnerian, dehumanizing, etc."

1977: Washington Post article dated August 1, 1977 entitled "Competency Tests Set in 26 Schools" reads: "Guines said that the new curriculum is based on the work in behavioral psychology of Harvard University's B.F. Skinner who developed teaching machines and even trained pigeons during World War II to pilot and detonate bombs and torpedoes. The basic idea, Guines said, is to break down complicated learning into a sequence of clear and simple skills that virtually everyone can master, although at different rates of speed. If you can train a pigeon to fly up there and press a button and set off a bomb," Guines remarked, "why can't you teach human beings to behave in an effective and rational way? We know that we can modify human behavior. We're not scared of that. This is the biggest thing that's happening in education today." The article went on to say "According to Thomas B. Sticht, Associate Director for Basic Skills of the National Institute of Education, similar techniques, called competency education or mastery teaching, are now being used in many parts of the country."

1982: Thomas Sticht, who worked on the failed D.C. Mastery Learning project, was quoted in a Washington Post article dated August 8, 1982 as follows: "Ending discrimination and changing values are probably more important than reading in moving low income families into the middle class." This statement was probably in response to an outcry from parents of students in the failed D.C. Mastery Learning program.

1984: Utah "Excellence in Instructional Delivery Systems: Research and Dissemination of Exemplary Outcome-Based Programs". This federally-funded program conducted by William Spady was, the first one to use the term outcome-based education: OBE The change name change from ML to OBE was due to the mastery learning disaster in Chicago and in Washington, D.C.

1985: United States-USSR education Agreement (President Reagan-Gorbachev) and Carnegie-Soviet Academy of Science Agreement.

1992: President George W. Bush speaks regarding National Youth Apprenticeship Act, Congressional Record, May 3, 1992. President Bush calls for Soviet-style workforce training.

1996: A Canadian produced video titled: "Failing Grades" is released which relates to use of Direct Instruction and Charter Schools - proof that neoconservatives from USA and Canada were promoting Skinner method for use in work force training. Also this video shows strong support for charter schools (publicly-funded private schools) and makes reference to charter schools in Russia. It also discusses "Effective Schools" which is extensively covered at deliberatedumbingdown.com and discusses the role of change agents in Russia, with regards to their role in creating "Effective Schools". Effective Schools use the Skinner method.

1998: Reading Excellence Act calls for Direct Instruction. Engelmann's Direct Instruction is resurrected, due to public uproars regarding failures of mastery learning and outcomes-based education, primarily in inner city schools. The "destined-to-fail" programs have been intentionally attaching to "reading" programs, since reading is the key ingredient of education about which the population was and is concerned. The school administrators, acting as educational change agents, can get away with just about anything if the public thinks it will help children read.

1999: Before Cynthia Weatherly put the book to bed in 1999, she called Siegfried Engelmann's (Direct Instruction - DISTAR) office in Oregon, and ordered the direct instruction (DISTAR) teacher training video. She wanted to make sure her arguments in opposition to the Pavlovian method made in her book were in fact correct. The video arrived and she was stunned watching the teacher training: hand signals, etc. One of her good education researchers, who couldn't believe "Direct Instruction" was based on the Skinner/Pavlov method, called the DISTAR office and talked to Engelmann's top assistant regarding the DI method. She asked her directly: "Is Charlotte Iserbyt correct when she says that DI is Skinner/Pavlov?" Her response was: "Yes, Charlotte Iserbyt is correct."

The Chinese/Soviet atheist, communist system of education, including the Pavlovian method, is being implemented right now in the United States of America, as recommended by William Foster, former chairman of the U.S. Communist Party, in his 1930 book: "Toward a Soviet America." Foster, who was buried with honors in the Kremlin, stated that this conditioning method is necessary for work force training, as well as political brainwashing. Communist governments are atheist so they consider their citizens as

36

nothing but animals, with no soul, conscience, or free will. The American educational system has adopted the same atheistic view of its citizens?

The agreements between the United States, USSR and China are simply the full realization of the merger of the United States and the Soviet Union as clearly spelled out by Rowan Gaither, President of the Ford Foundation in 1953:

"All of us here at the policy making level of the foundation have at one time or another served in the OSS (Office of Strategic Services, CIA forerunner) or the European Economic Administration, operating under directives from the White House. We operate under those same directives. The substance under which we operate is that we shall use our grant making power to so alter life in the United States that we can be comfortably merged with the Soviet Union."

"I don't want a nation of thinkers. I want a nation of workers."
- John D. Rockefeller

The Legend of Dirty Joe

In September 2007, I'm contacted by a midsize construction corporation and recruited to act as their interim CEO. In addition to developing the company's national role out strategy, I'm tasked with negotiating a $5 million revolving credit facility that will be used to implement the company's regional goals.

One year into its development, we have decided that we are in need of a Chief Operations Officer, so we begin our quest. Following an exhausting search for a qualified candidate, leadership come to the conclusion that it would be best to manage the duties of that position ourselves, rather than hand it over to a tepid candidate. That is until my father, Thomas Boggs, a well respected 22 year executive for The Home Depot, refers an individual to our company by the name of Joe Hines. My father explains that Joe's former employer (Hassco General Builders, Inc.) has recently let Joe go due to 'budget constraints'. We are told that Joe is a hardworking, intelligent and reliable professional capable of managing the role and responsibilities of our open position. During the interview process Joe portrayed himself as an accomplished professional, with an MBA, who possesses the specialized qualifications we're looking for. After much debate and consideration we begin the on boarding process with Joe.

Four months into Joe's employment, the President and I learn that contrary to what Joe had reported, he was 'let go' from his previous employer for 'erratic behavior'. This was concerning given the fact that it was Joe's most recent work experience at Hassco General Builders which led to his hiring. Executive management became increasingly concerned when Joe would not expand on his relationship with Hassco, other than to say that he was let go due to 'irreconcilable differences'.

Immediately following the aforesaid revelation we began auditing Joe's resume against Joe' performance, in doing so, we see what we believed to be a pending apocalypse. For instance one of Joe's responsibilities was to ensure costs associated with field operations came in under budget. This involved sourcing and securing high quality, competitively priced supplies in a fluctuating market. In many instances we found that Joe had been paying thousands of dollars over what the supplies should have cost. For example he paid five thousand dollars for materials from one vendor that cost just eighteen hundred dollars with another. Even more concerning than his apparent lack of basic business acumen is the abrasive way in which he interacted with employees and colleagues. One of the most disturbing e-mails that I received from Joe was on Sunday, October 12, 2008 which read verbatim:

"from now on i'll [expletive] be in charge of IT ([expletive] around) while Aaron (aka a waste of my [expletive] time) will be in charge of operations. I'll let you let him know since he such good [expletive] ideas. [Expletive] you [expletive] piece of [expletive] Aaron!!! I don't answer to nobody epsecially a stupid [expletive] [expletive] and laborers! All they good for is fighting and shuting the [expletive] up! Can't even figure out how to use a paint stripper!!! [expletive]! - joe"

Followed by this e-mail on Monday, October 13, 2008:

"Sorry for blowing up ealier about the workers. I think you are right that they need more guidance. I start taking things very personal when I shouldn't. On Monday we can work together and figure out how to make things better so this doens't happen anymore. Hopefully on Monday we can meet with Wayne Koi, I'm waiting for him to call me up. I know that you and Aaron said you wouldn't hire current or past Hassco employees but he paints cicles around crews. He do in two days what would take a crew 1 week to do. I don't care if we stealing him, Jimmy wants to fire him anyway. I'm really sorry for getting so upset on the phone, I am still working on getting my meds in check (I tend to blow up when I get upset and I am trying to do better). I know we can work through this. - Your Bro, Joe"

Our worst fears are realized, when the President, Joe, and I were driving to San Francisco to meet with a prospective partner. It's during this trip that Joe proceeds to disclose that he had been 'arrested in both Alaska and Las Vegas', for both 'using and dealing drugs'. He told us that he 'lost his mind' at one point and was 'committed to an insane asylum', where he was 'prescribed anti-psychotic medication therapy' and that he was still taking those medications. What's more, he disclosed that he had been involved in Satanism and Nazism, and then proceeded to show us his concealed tattoo of Satan on his forearm with the letters 'FTW'. Joe proudly proclaimed that this is an acronym for 'F-The World'.

As if our trip to the Bay wasn't enough of a shocker, shortly after our meeting in San Francisco, the President and I were approached by the General Contractor whose license the company was operating under. Our General Contractor proceeds to explain that Joe Hines had approached him with the proposition of establishing their own Home Depot vendor account with the intention of stealing the business away from our company. Have you ever watched the movie 'The Crying Game'? This is a film where a guy discovers the woman he's dating is actually a man. That was my level of surprise, at that particular point in time.

Once the President and I had some time to decompress and calibrate our bearings, we both came to the obvious conclusion that Joe not only lied on his resume, he took a flame thrower to the Employment, Confidentiality, and Intellectual Property Agreement that he signed. In short, Joe was a toxic liability and his plan to steal the company's largest account was grounds for immediate termination. On October 27, 2008, Joe was presented with two options, resignation or termination and a lawsuit. Joe chose to resign.

You would think that Joe's relevance in our lives would have come to a screeching halt. Unfortunately several months after Joe's resignation we learned that in addition to his company authorized user_pass, Joe Hines had created an unauthorized account giving him access to our company banking portal. Furthermore, Joe who had resigned several months prior had without authorization accessed our company's private online banking portal stealing confidential financial records belonging to the company. Accessing private computer networks associated with his former employer, with the intention of disrupting operations, ultimately caused tens of millions of dollars in damage and was nothing short of a 21 Century campaign of high-tech revenge. People like Joe Hines should be held accountable for victimizing others by exploiting computer network vulnerabilities. In many states this type of crime carries with it statutory maximum sentence of years' imprisonment, and $250,000 in fines. Further, Joe contacted

The Home Depot main office in Atlanta, Georgia, to levy allegations against my father that he has been 'accepting 'kick-backs' from contractors, which was an unsubstantiated, abhorrent lie. Nonetheless, based on Joe Hines' unverified claims, The Home Depot legal department initiates an investigation of the twenty-two year Home Depot executive.

During the court case, Joe Hines incoherently blathers, like a Jim Beam possessed hillbilly. And as someone whose family hails from the hillbilly triangle, e.g. Kentucky, Ohio and West Virginia territories. I know a good hillbilly impersonation when I see and hear one. Just one of the many claims orchestrated by Joe Hines is that my father accepted and used an African vacation from one of his contractors. What makes this claim so ridiculous is that my father has never had a passport. Most troubling of all, is that even after Joe' reenactment of 'One Flew Over The Cuckoo's Nest' and the defendant's presentation of Joe' mental health history, documented drug arrests and questionable employment history, Joe' fantasy is filed in Home Depot' law library, under non-fiction.

The aftershock of Joe Hines was felt throughout a large community of contractors. Not only did The Home Depot terminate our company's vendor license, causing the closure of the business, they terminated my father; a twenty-two year Home Depot veteran who had done absolutely nothing wrong, other than to refer Joe Hines to our company.

It's important to note that just months prior to being terminated, my father was in line to receive full retirement, along with the full divestiture of his Home Depot stock, which was ample. Moreover, just months following the termination of his employment and health insurance, my father discovers that he has a rare bone cancer. Everyone who has worked with my father swears that his health condition had been caused by his seven days per week, sixteen hour per day work schedule. It's this work ethic and impeccable character that made him an exemplary asset to The Home Depot for twenty-two years. And how did The Home Depot pay tribute to my father's lifelong contribution to The Home Depot? They assassinated his character, stole his stock and retirement and left him without health insurance during a time when he needed it the most. The Home Depot did all of this using the claims of Joe Hines, a well documented drug dealer, liar and mental patient.

What went wrong here is a no brainer and there isn't a day that goes by that I don't regret hiring Joe Hines, an avowed Satanist, Drug dealer, and mental patient, who had a criminal record. As I reflected back on the aforementioned experiences I realized that many of my life's examinations were testing my faith and judgment. However due to my idyllic ignorance I translated these tests as immense misfortunes. On the contrary as I began analyzing these 'misfortunes' I started to see that the evil that had permeated my life did so for my own benefit and that its purpose in my life was to purify my faith in Jesus Christ. Practically speaking I realized that man's superior nature [good] coexists with his inferior nature [evil]. It's these 'misfortunes' that are in fact tests meant to strengthen ones superior nature which is eternal, pure and indestructible, while at the same time heightening their awareness to the forces of inferiority which permeate our modern day society.

"For we wrestle not against flesh and blood, but against principalities, against powers, against the rulers of the darkness of this world, against spiritual wickedness in high places." - Ephesians 6:12

The Mark of The Beast

It's 2013, and since my encounter with Joe Hines and The Home Depot, I've been approached by and participated in a number of opportunities. Unlike in the past where I would have blindly leaped into a partnership with someone based merely on faith, a resume and rapport. The past several years, have been a much different experience. One example is a Romanian plasma gasification technology company which approached me to develop their business plan, investor presentation materials and assist with raising $100 million intended to be used to build a plasma gasification plant in Roseville, California. This company held a patent for a proprietary method of incinerating garbage and then turning that incinerated organic material into energy and building materials.

I'm in no way a proponent of the 'Global Warming' myth invented by Satanist Leopold de Rothschild. If you would like to learn why 'Global Warming' is a myth visit, lordmoncktonfoundation.com. That being said, I do however feel that repurposing materials that take many years to decompose just makes good sense. Now, if you're one of the poor souls who are still buying into the elite's 'Global Warming' money making scheme, consider the following quotes by The Club of Rome in 1993, the U.N. and Green Peace. It's important to note, less than one year following The Club of Rome's recommendations to the United Nations, George H.W. Bush signed into existence the Agenda 21 Protocol on June 29, 1992. He did this while sitting on Prince Charles' yacht, as it floated offshore, near Rio de Janeiro. Shorty after President Clinton's election, Clinton signed Executive Order No. 12852 in 1993, ejecting the Constitution killing agenda 21 into America's bloodstream.

41

"We've got to ride this global warming issue. Even if the theory of global warming is wrong, we will be doing the right thing in terms of economic and environmental policy." - Timothy Wirth, President of the UN foundation

"It doesn't matter what is true, it only matters what people believe is true." - Paul Watson, co-founder of Green Peace

"I got the impression that instead of going out to shoot birds, I should go out and shoot the kids who shoot birds." – Paul Watson, co-founder of Green Peace

Once you've read the following chapter, regarding the goal of Satanic Theosophy and its influence over the United Nations, the above mentioned facts surrounding George H.W. Bush and Clinton will make better sense.

"In searching for a new enemy to unite us, we suggested that pollution; the threat of global warming, water shortages, famine and the like would fit the bill. In their totality and in their interactions, these phenomena constitute a common threat which demands the solidarity of all peoples. But in designating them as the enemy, we fall into the trap about which we have already warned, namely mistaking symptoms for causes. All these dangers are caused by human intervention and it is only through changed attitudes and behavior that they can be overcome. The real enemy then is humanity itself" - The Club of Rome (Book: 'The First Global Revolution' pg.102)

So as I was saying, this Plasma Gasification organization asked me to develop their business plan, investor presentation materials and participate in raising $100 million in capital to build a large gasification plant, in Roseville, California. After several months of qualifying a number of investors, we were introduced to Arch Coal. Ironically the introduction is made by Hank Bonga the President of Eagle Rock Advisors a Native American-Owned and Controlled Company and a member of 'The National Congress of American Indians'. I refer to the introduction as 'ironic' because after applying my new found hyper suspicious, paranoid investigative measures, I discover a corporate history that seemed to be in direct conflict with Native America principles.

The prospective investors were the founders of Arch Coal, the second largest producer of coal in North America. What my research uncovered is that this company practiced 'mountaintop removal mining', which is controversial because it reduces the height of mountaintops (600-800 ft.), removes all veg-

42

etation and places mining waste or overburden into mountain streams, causing flooding, erosion and water contamination. And they had been involved in an extremely controversial product in Alaska, named the Chuitna Coal Mine. It was controversial because they were promoting the idea of Destroying fifteen square miles of Chuitna watershed and the removal of eleven miles of tributary that is 'significant to salmon' breeding, etc. But what took the proverbial cake is that after destroying a vital American river system, they were going to sell all of that coal to Communist China. So while energy costs in America skyrocket and millions of people are unemployed, companies like Arch Coal are shipping America's natural resources to Communist China. This is the same China, whose Empress Dowager (1899-1901) ordered the murder of tens of thousands of Christians during the 'Boxer Rebellion'.

With the aforesaid in mind, I approach the executive leadership of the gasification company and tell them that I would not support a plan that involved accepting a dime from this particular source and the reasons behind my determination. We're talking about $100 million, so of course, there was push back, but I would not compromise my belief system. In the end, I made the decision to leave this venture.

After all of this, I became disenfranchised with anything a prospective client or business partner would refer to as a 'Once in a lifetime' or 'revolutionary' idea. It was at this point in my life that I chose to return back to a lifestyle that I had once considered my real calling in life. What inspired me, twenty-two years ago, was helping health-challenged souls become better educated about the myriad of alternative healing options available to them. Those ambitions inspired me to pursue becoming an alternative health practitioner, specializing in herbal therapies, acupuncture and nutrition.

Over the years, I have advanced my knowledge of alternative medicine and have made an effort to fund or participate in opportunities that had some semblance of my earliest ambitions. Regardless of how large or 'revolutionary' the opportunity was, there would be a sense of futility, if the opportunity lacked the substance that I had predefined long ago. And so, several years ago, I began focusing one hundred percent of my life experiences towards helping people rebuild their health.

From time to time, I'm still approached by past colleagues, venture capitalists, individual investors, clients, and others to see how I'm getting along and vice versa. About one year ago, I was approached by a friend of mine, Ricardo Crooks. I've been friends with Ricardo for about ten years and I would describe Ricardo as a good soul. In addition to sharing the same birthday as

43

me, Ricardo has in spades, what I used to have, and that's an exceedingly trusting personality. Moreover, he has a passion for helping people, no matter how damaged they may be. It's a common personality flaw that both Ricardo and I share. Although I've conditioned myself to now be able to walk away from toxic human beings and deals.

After an initial conference call between me and his business partner Paul Soo, we agree to meet face-to-face to discuss the opportunity over tea. Within the first few minutes, Ricardo excitedly proclaims 'This is a revolutionary solution, Paul!'. Ricardo proceeds to present the name 'Tom Heeter'. I learn that Tom, is the CEO and Founder of a company by the name of SmartPay, Inc. Ricardo explains that Tom has promoted himself, to Ricardo as being a 'well respected attorney in Texas'. Moreover, Ricardo explains, that Tom has purported to have developed an electronic pay system that's going to 'revolutionize the world'. Ricardo proceeds to solicit my help with the development of the marketing and distribution plan as well as raising capital for the venture.

I communicate to Ricardo that my new process through which I pick or pass on opportunities is quite ridged these days. I explain to Ricardo that both me and my attorney will proceed with the necessary due diligence and then upon completion, I'll provide him with a wellness report on this particular suspect. I have to admit; in the beginning, after hearing about this opportunity, I was really excited. I could immediately see the potential and was confident in being able to inject an investor into this venture, if both the technology and the founder were legitimate. Unfortunately, my excitement turned to horror three minutes from typing 'Tom Heeter' into Google and pressing 'Enter'. What is returned to my browser is a litany of offenses and red flags that would send O.J. Simpson's attorney, Robert Kardashian, running. I discover that Tom Heeter was disbarred from the Texas State Bar in 2002 for 'mental health issues;' convicted of 'indecent exposure;' accused of offering a '$50,000 bribe to Judge T.O. Stansbury;' accused of carrying a gun and threatening to cause bodily injury and last but certainly not least Tom Heeter was caught lying about his county of residence in order to run for Democratic public office. The most troubling aspect to Tom Heeter's wellness report was Tom's patent #5,878,155. Here's the 'Abstract' of Tom Heeters patent: "A method is presented for facilitating sales transactions by electronic media. A bar code or a design is tattooed on an individual. Before the sale transaction can be consummated, the tattoo is scanned with a scanner. Characteristics about the scanned tattoo are compared to characteristics about other tattoos stored on a computer database in order to verify the identity of the buyer."

44

Does Tom Heeter's patent sound familiar? If you've read The Holy Bible, it will. Tom Heeter's patent is nearly a carbon copy of the 'Mark of The Beast' prophesized in The Holy Bible.

"And he causeth all, both small and great, rich and poor, free and bond, to receive a mark in their right hand, or in their foreheads. And that no man might buy or sell, save he that had the mark, or the name of the beast, or the number of his name [666]." - Revelation 13:16-17

Now, combine the abstract of Tom Heeter's patent with Tom Heeter's violent history, and the fact that Tom Heeter could pass for Aleister Crowley's twin brother, an infamous Satanist referred to as 'The Great Beast 666', with the disturbing revelation that Tom Heeter's work contact information listed on the State Bar of Texas website is: Mr. Thomas Webster Heeter, 55 Lyerly St. Houston, TX 77022, (713-666-3548).

As you can imagine, my wellness report and recommendations on Tom Heeter back to Ricardo was less than glowing. After I had cited, all of the above mentioned data, I advised Ricardo to run, not walk, away from this individual and to not look back.

Since Heeter's 'Mark of the Beast' patent, individuals and Corporations have developed more modern day versions of the 'Mark of the Beast'. These include Sony Corporation's 'Smart Wig' patent and Motorola's 'e-tattoo', which the company claims can read your thoughts, as well as Google Corporation's anti-Christian engineering director, Ray Kurzweil, who once said: "Does God exist? Not yet." is developing a 'bridge-to-bridge' system, or what I like to call a spycloud control network, powered by advanced 'D-Wave' quantum annealing processors based on Shor's algorithm. It's this 'bride-to-bridge' system Kurzweil posits will empower those who accept his mark with god like powers e.g., immortality, etc., calling to mind Aristotle's recalling of Homer's account of the god Hephaestus's robotic workers made of gold c.850 BC. In reality, Ray Kurzweils 'singularity' and vision of artificial Intelligence [AI], Spy-Cloud Computing, etc. are woefully anemic versions of what Satan has known for millennia to be a superior, infinite, universal system of divine knowledge, a spiritually and technologically superior exchange, which has existed between God and his creation [Man] for over 6,000 years. Luciferians and their god are fully aware of The Creator's divine communication network, ancient universal database, and heavenly infrastructure; after all, Satan was once a subscriber. It's from this ancient divine superhighway that the concept of 'singularity' was born. Since his creation, Satan's objective has always been to tether Man's spiritual being to Satan's domain [earth]

45

forcing Man to worship him forever, deceiving Man from God's infinite universal system of knowledge and salvation. Misleading Man into accepting an infinitely inferior simulation of exponential knowledge, eternally cutoff from his creator, deceived into believing that one day he too shall become a god.

"For we know that if our earthly house of this tabernacle [idiom for a temporary dwelling/body] were dissolved, we have a building of God, an house [permanent more complex dwelling/spiritual body] not made with hands, eternal in the heavens. For in this we groan, earnestly desiring to be clothed upon with our house which is from heaven"
- 2 Corinthians 5:1-2

Kurzweil's singularity theory is an ancient demonic concept and nowhere is the fingerprints of iniquity and prophecy more evident than in the King James Holy Bible. When we juxtapose Jude 1:6 and 1 John 3:2 with that of Google Engineering Director Ray Kurzweil's singularity theory [merging man with machine] we begin to see similarities between Kurzwiel's deception and Satan's goal of maintaining spiritual custody of Man. Through the imprisonment of Satan's singularity, Man is prohibited from ever "seeing him [Jesus Christ] as he is".

"And the angels [fallen angels] which kept not their first estate [principality of angels or demons], but left their own habitation [dwelling], he hath reserved in everlasting chains under darkness unto the judgment of the great day." - Jude 1:6

"Beloved, now are we the sons of God, and it doth not yet appear what we shall be: but we know that, when he [Jesus Christ] shall appear, we shall be like him; for we shall see him as he is." - 1 John 3:2

Former Defense Advanced Research Projects Agency [DARPA] Director, turned Google executive Regina Dugan, is promoting an edible microchip and electronic tattoo that will be able to read your mind. I believe this is why there has been a major push by the entertainment industry to promote tattoos as fashionable. Simply put, the American population is being desensitized to the idea of tattooing themselves with 'The Mark of the Beast'. I too believe, Motorola and Google's 'mind reading' technology is being developed to one day validate the sincerity of those who are willingly accepting the 'Mark of the Beast' [666] in their hand and/or forehead. I predict this technology will allow administrators for the Antichrist to efficiently identify and eliminate those who are subconsciously adverse to Satan's New World Order.

46

The Walt Disney Company is also doing its part to promote the 'Mark of the Beast' with its new FCC registered RFID tracking modules, artfully named 'Magic Bands'. Aside from not exceeding general radiated emission levels set by the dubious Federal Government over a spread spectrum network which shares systems supporting critical Government requirements such as the 'Real ID Act' of 2005, Disney's Magic Bands indoctrinate guests into accepting a device on their wrists in order to buy goods, access their hotel rooms, enter the parks, acquire fast passes, etc. Prior to being assembled in China, Disney's 'Magic Bands' are developed by Synapse Product Development LLC in Seattle, WA, which also develops DNA field analysis devices. I demonstrate throughout my book, DECEPTION: The Ancient Mystery That Holds The Secret of Newgrange (KillingIreland.com), how Disney is one of the biggest promoters of the 'Mark of the Beast' [666]. Whatever the method or technology I believe one thing is certain. The Mark of the Beast will be incompatible with God created DNA. In Revelation 16:2,11 we are told that the mark will become a "grievous sore upon the men which had the mark of the beast". In other words the area the mark is placed will become horribly infected, spreading throughout the entire body rendering the mark useless therefore collapsing the Antichrist' economic system.

Here are a few more of the top biometic corporations that are promoting 'Mark of the Beast' technology, companies whose names are associated with ancient demons, they include:

Kronos (www.kronos.com) named after an ancient demonic deity, who is the parallel version of Moloch and the Greek equivalent of Ba'al Hammon. This was a demon that child sacrifices were made to. As a matter of fact in 1921 an archeological dig at Carthage revealed 20,000 urns containing the cremated remains of infants and children age six. They were all sacrificed out of reverence to the demon god Kronos.

Argus Global (www.argus-global.com) named after an all-seeing- primordial giant. Kairos (www.kairos.com) is named after the Greek demon of opportunity and timing, the youngest son of Zeus. Ever heard the saying "the right place at the right time"? In Greek times they would ascribe this saying with giving your allegiance to the demon of opportunity. This is also the exact word the demons used when they asked him if he had come to torment them "…before the time" – Matthew 8:29.

Corvus Biometrics (www.corvusid.com) named after the black raven that Apollo put in the heavens, who longs to drink the sacred waters protected by the giant hydra, a serpent-like monster with reptilian traits.

Griaule Biometrics (www.griaulebiometrics.com) named after a gigantic red dragon.

Neokoros (www.neokoros.com) named after the three famous temples 'thrice neokoros' in the city of Pergamous where the emperors were worshipped as gods and where the Altar of Zeus was located. John, the writer of the Book of Revelation said that Pergamous is the place where Satan's Seat is located.

"And to the angel of the church in Pergamos write; These things saith he which hath the sharp sword with two edges; I know thy works, and where thou dwellest, even where Satan's seat is: and thou holdest fast my name, and hast not denied my faith, even in those days wherein Antipas was my faithful martyr, who was slain among you, where Satan dwelleth." – Revelation 2:12-13.

As an aside in 2008 President Barack Hussein Obama, while in Berlin gave a speech near The Altar of Zeus ["Satan's Seat"] housed in the Pergamom Museum. Obama told those in attendance that 'The world it stands as one' which is of course a reference to a New World Order or One World Religion controlled by the antichrist. Then upon returning to the United States President Barack Hussein Obama commissions the construction of a replica of the Altar of Zeus [Satan's Seat] from which he made his party's acceptance speech.

The Model Degenerate

I present this particular experience because I believe the following individuals quite literally personify the collective Luciferian waste which is clogging up the arteries of America.

My encounter with this next figure was by pure coincidence. While seeking respite from the startup world I was contacted by a friend of mine who at the time was a relatively well known Italian male model. He asked if I could help develop his brand here in America. Truth be told, I had never set foot inside of a modeling agency and quite frankly had no interest in that world, much less had any clue on how to promote him. So I told my friend 'Sure why not!' After all it was something new and I thought to myself 'What's the worst thing I'm going to encounter. A guy with a MAC cosmetic box?'

I'll save you a lengthy diatribe on what didn't go right. Suffice it to say, the modeling venture didn't produce the results I had convinced myself were possible. That being said, I referred my Italian friend to someone familiar with the ins and outs of

48

the American modeling business and we parted friends. The week I was shuttering his virtual portfolio, a young woman by the name of Arynne Blackley (a.k.a. Arynne Tiller) submitted her request for information. I responded back to her, explaining that the project with my friend was ending and that I would be returning to my primary business of consulting with overseas manufactures. Arynne responded back 'Great! I have a product that I would like to discuss with you.' During my interview with Arynne in Arizona, she explained that she had been a model for Playboy and that her "husband" [Travis Blackley] was a Major League Baseball pitcher for the Oakland A's. Furthermore, she explained her idea to leverage what she described as a healthy network of celebrities through which we would be able to promote her new swimsuit line 'Body Art Bikinis'. In short, this was a line of bikinis whose design elements consisted of custom tattoo patterns. Having had experience in the design and manufacturing of various textile products, I could see the potential of her business model and agreed to sign on to her project. After all she seemed like a relatively legitimate entity.

Several months into the assignment I began noticing signs that something was amiss. Being the 'trust but verify' person that I had become, I requested another face-to-face meeting with Arynne at her estate in Arizona, to evaluate her progress. She explained that she was actually staying at her mom's apartment in Wichita, Kansas and asked if I would mind meeting her there. When I arrived, I was presented with a woman who was disheveled. During our initial meeting Arynne began explaining to me in explicit detail her current personal situation. Our meeting began with Arynne disclosing to me her intention to divorce her husband Travis Blackley. When asked, why? She responded, because he was 'mentally and physically abusive' and participated in 'occult rituals'. She explained that while they were visiting his home Country of Australia, he solicited her to participate in what she described as an occult ritual. When she refused his request she was left far from where they were staying and made to walk home.

Arynne explained that on a number of occasions, she was 'drugged up' and taken to mansion parties in Arizona, where ritual sex orgies were held in large showers. It brings clarity to the pictures of her husband Travis Blackley wearing a T-shirt featuring a satanic upside down cross [pg.50]. Furthermore the two knives which form an 'X' on his shirt holds special meaning for those in secret pagan groups. This satanic mark is misunderstood by many Christian Americans including church leaders. It is most important that the reader should have a clear idea of what this mark means, and as it is rather a difficult point to explain accurately, I must ask the reader to give me his/her best attention; and I cannot refrain from adding the hope

that if the reader succeeds in mastering the explanation of this mark, the reader will abstain from glorifying it like Mr. Blackley. The vast majority of Christians know that the Roman Numeral 'X', represents the number ten however many will be surprised to learn that the Roman Numeral X also represents the word 'IO' (pronounced EO) and in Greek the word 'IO' means Helios or Apollyon otherwise known as "The Beast from the pit".

"And they had a king over them, which is the angel of the bottomless pit, whose name in the Hebrew tongue is Abaddon, but in the Greek tongue hath his name Apollyon." - Revelation 9:11

In addition to being associated with Apollyon, the 'X' or 'IO' is linked to Nimrod, the founder of Babylon. Nimrod [Hebrew for "we will rebel"] was worshipped like a god and constructed the Tower of Babel with the intention of eliminating God. Like Satan, Nimrod rebelled against the will of God and beguiled men into a satanic religious order that insidiously controlled their minds. Nimrod promoted diverse and erratic superstitions and led his followers to be governed by the signs in the stars. Nimrod was eventually smote by God circa 2200 B.C. and all those who worshipped him were divided into 70 different Nations, all speaking in different tongues. Nimrod is the fountainhead from which the Sumerians Marduk and Gilgamesh, the Greeks Apollo the Egyptians Osiris, The Babylonian Talmud, Kabbalism, Freemasonry and satanic theosophy all sprung.

"And Cush begat Nimrod: he began to be a mighty one in the earth. He was a mighty hunter before the Lord: wherefore it is said, Even as Nimrod the mighty hunter before the Lord. And the beginning of his kingdom was Babel, and Erech, and Accad, and Calneh, in the land of Shinar." - Genesis 10:8-10

As an aside 'XX' means to double-cross or betray. Fundamentally speaking it indicates one's willingness to betray on behalf of Satan. When individuals, companies, corporations, etc. feature the 'XX' on their person or in their logo they are invoking satanic energy. For instance, the members of the Rockefeller Family are fully aware of the 'XX' meaning, which is why the family of Standard Oil fame named their Corporation "Exxon" then hired French-born Freemason and 'The Father of Industrial Design', Raymond Loewy, to design their Exxon logo. The Thule Society also featured the double-cross [XX] inside their logo. This was a German occultist group which was later reorganized by Adolf Hitler into the Nazi Party.

Lastly, Arynne' husband Travis seems very familiar with the satanic devil horns hand sign [right], while standing in front of a giant pyramid structure no less. I explain in great detail the actual meaning behind all of these signs and symbols in later chapters.

Christian parents should consider the spiritual beliefs and lifestyles of their favorite athletes. If Christian parents discover that an athlete's ideology competes with or undermines their Christian faith, they should reconsider supporting that individual or team. Christian parents must stop allowing their children to meditate on what man can do and teach their children to focus on what God can do.

On one occasion, while sitting in Arynne's white Lexus, she proceeded to disclose that her son (Tristan) looked too much like his father and that she didn't want to be the little boy's mother anymore. I have to say that this was the most unsettling confession. It was inconceivable to hear a mother be so incredibly wicked and selfish. Arynne continued with saying that her relationship with her estranged husband Travis was so abusive that she began drinking heavily and using both prescription and non-prescription drugs. She said that the anti-depressant drug Lexapro was the only thing 'keeping her alive'. In addition to her drug abuse, she chose to share with me her extra marital exploits, which included another American baseball player by the name of Doug Reinhardt. Arynne explained that she ended the relationship with Reinhart when he asked her to appear in a group sex video. I was personally made aware of Arynne's addiction to drugs and alcohol in the first few months of working with her. I was contacted by her via phone and asked if I would be able to baby-sit her son Tristan, while she appeared in an Arizona court to face charges for driving under the influence (DUI). Based on the facts surrounding her arrest, she was sentenced to Sheriff Joe Arpaio's Maricopa County 'Tent City' in Arizona.

51

As I began asking myself 'Can this person get any more toxic?' Arynne proceeds to disclose that prior to meeting her husband Travis, getting pregnant and moving to Arizona, she was a stripper in Wichita, Kansas. If that wasn't Jerry Springer enough, she disclosed that to supplement her lifestyle she and her best friend would 'scam old men for money'.

When asked if her bout with drug and alcohol abuse was isolated to just herself, she responded 'no'. She indicated that her mother also suffered from depression and suicidal tendencies and that her younger sister regularly stole drugs from her purse.

As a husband and father of four children, I have to say the two most troubling aspects of Arynne Tiller's mentality was her distorted reality that she no longer wanted her son in her life and that the entire reason she 'hooked up' with her son's father was so that she could gain access to the money he would make, when he was hired onto an MLB team. Her exact words to me were 'it was a business deal'. Following Arynne's confessions, I made a decision to disconnect from her project for a few days. As I reflected back on everything that she had shared, I questioned whether or not Arynne was spiritually salvageable.

Other than her son Tristan, who is clearly the victim in this case, it's hard to identify the predator and the prey between Arynne and her husband Travis. After mulling over all that Arynne had shared with me, I contacted her to say that I would no longer be involved with her project. I communicated with her that my decision was based on the level of distraction in her personal life. Moreover, I did not agree with her lifestyle. Knowing the type of personality I was dealing with, I was fully prepared for her infantile response. It began with her hanging up, followed by a dissertation via text message. Not surprising, her communication contained verbiage that would have made Comedian Paul Mooney blush.

6   Know Thy Enemy

"Whatever strikes at the root of Christianity tends manifestly to the dissolution of civil government" – New York Supreme Court 1811

I hope that by sharing some of my aforementioned personal life experiences I've opened your eyes to the reality that 'Evil' does in fact coexist and it should be the pursuit of every Christian to avoid the ancient techniques of trickery and deceit enlisted by esoteric elite doctrines. This is what Lord Jesus Christ himself most clearly points out in his parable regarding trees and their fruits, when he said:

"Either make the tree good, and his fruit good; or else make the tree corrupt, and his fruit corrupt: for the tree is known by his fruit."
- Matthew 12:33

This is a warning to Christians that bad fruit cannot grow on a good tree nor could good fruit grow on a bad tree. Yet from that same earth to which he was referring to, both sorts of trees can grow. People must return to the realization that darkness cannot defeat the light. If you introduce a candle into a dark room it exposes the true contents within that space. Once we begin exposing those working within the shadows to the light, we will learn the true content of their character and more importantly their intentions. By beginning the practice of introducing 'light' into every decision of my life, I began seeing the character and intentions of those who in the past would have been allowed to pull me into the darkness. I've learned that the most powerful weapon used against us is not standing armies and their weapons, rather it's secrecy.

My belief system which is supported by the following historic and scientific facts shows the introduction of what's commonly referred to as the 'New Age' movement, which is in large part responsible for the erosion of American health and the drastic increase of immorality throughout our Nation. I will substantiate these claims throughout the following text and show that "Talmudic Theosophy" is in fact the tributory through which Satanism has flowed into America. For those of you who have never heard about Theosophy, all you need to understand is that its founder and principles are deeply rooted in Satanism. What's troubling is that its core financial contributors are the Rothschild and Rockefeller international central banking system e.g., The Federal Reserve Corporation, the Internal Revenue Service and the United Nations. As unbelievable as this may sound to you right now, I will show a clear, indisputable correlation between the massive increase of disease throughout the United States of America, Satanic Theosophy and the erosion of our Nation's morality and financial foundation.

For the past 100 years, it has been the goal of Luciferians to unify Christianity, Islam, Buddhism, Hinduism, and other faiths, for the sole purpose of unveiling their manufactured 'Anti-Christ' control figure who will usher in their New World Order and deceive all people of faith. This is something that is prophesized through the pages of The Holy Bible.

In his book, "Between Two Ages" [1970] Zbigniew Brzezinski, a Freemason, New World Order advocate, mentor to Osama bin Laden [founder of Al-Qaeda] and father to MSNBC's Mika Brzezinski states:

"The Technotronic era involves the gradual appearance of a more controlled society. Such a society would be dominated by an elite, unrestrained by traditional values... Soon it will be possible to assert almost continuous surveillance over every citizen and maintain up-to-date complete files containing even the most personal information about the citizen."

The agenda of Luciferians to create a 'One World Government' as it's been referred to by President George H.W. Bush, President Bill Clinton, President George W. Bush, President Barack Hussein Obama and leaders of Nations worldwide, is well documented. It's my belief that their motivations politically for total control take a back seat to their core motivation. That is to spiritually subjugate all people of faith worldwide. Their orders and intentions can be read in virtually every 'New Age' book or belief system.

It's critical for Christians to develop a rock solid moral compass; this is the only way they will be able to subconsciously decrypt recurring phrases and imagery used by Luciferians. To ensure the safety of all people, the entire U.S. population must realize, that a Luciferian minority exists in high positions of power throughout the United States. It's this minority who are in control of every mechanism of our society e.g., food production, educational system, and political system. Their strength exists in the absolute control of everything and ownership of nothing.

"Own nothing and control everything." – John D. Rockefeller

54

It's this Luciferian minority who are promoting what is popularly referred to as "New Age" thinking. This belief system promotes Satan's lie that man can become God, and that Christians should abandon their belief in Jesus Christ, in favor of a One World Religion [Babylon] ruled by their anti-Christ.

"...ye shall be as gods. [Satan]" - Genesis 3:5

This is the reason behind the uptick in the number of attacks on Christians throughout America, for example: cross removal petitions, teachers mocking Jesus Christ in the classroom, movies and television writers and producers mocking Jesus Christ, etc.

To the viewer who is unfamiliar with real American History Jewish film maker, Steven Spielberg's movie, "Close Encounters of The Third Kind," appears to be the work of a genius. A man who is gifted in the art of science fiction and story-telling. In reality, the film is simply the retelling of a demonic encounter purportedly witnessed by a man named J. Allen Hynek. Hynek was the Technical Director for Spielberg's movie 'Close Encounters of The Third Kind'. Prior to Hynek's work on Spielberg's film Hynek coauthored the U.S. Government's 'Grudge 13' and MJ-12 in 1947. These programs were created under the guidance of Nelson Rockefeller by order of President Dwight D. Eisenhower. MJ-12's sole purpose was to develop and carry out psychological operations upon the American population to manipulate and cover-up critical knowledge related to the safety and security of the American populace. During this same time the Rockefeller Foundation began funding a massive research and training program at Caltech with a focus on molecular biology. The Rockefeller funded and controlled program would become the most influential international program in molecular biology. In future chapters I will demonstrate how and why the Rockefeller Family leveraged this research to develop an industry which debilitates, cripples and kills millions of innocent Americans each year.

Asking the Rockefeller Family to assist with the development and management of MJ-12 would become the single biggest mistake Eisenhower would make during his Presidency. His reckless naiveté not only threatened the future of America, but the whole of humanity. What President Eisenhower literally did was abdicate the presidency to a secret group of Luciferians. In order for Christian's to fully understand the motivations behind Eisenhower's duplicitous natural towards the U.S., one only has to study the body language of Eisenhower [pg.56]. In historical photographs we see President Eisenhower bowing to the President of France Charles De Gaulle. What is truly troubling about Eisenhower's submissive behavior

is that Guy de Rothschild - patriarch to the satanic Rothschild family - quite literally controlled French President Charles de Gaulle. Rothschild also controlled Georges Pompidou, who became De Gaulle's prime minister before serving as president.

Perhaps this is the reason why the Spielberg directed movie 'Killing Lincoln,' inspired by the book by FOX News personality, Bill O'Reilly, omits any reference to The Luciferian Rothschild Family and their motivations to murder President Lincoln. Perhaps Spielberg's reason for excluding Rothschild's involvement with Lincoln's assassination has something to do with Bill O'Reilly's boss [Rupert Murdoch]. After all Murdoch and Rothschild own substantial equity in an overseas company. This relationship is explained inside of my book, DECEPTION: The Ancient Mystery That Holds The Secret of Newgrange, pg.237, "Rupert Murdoch's Empire of Remphan." (KillingIreland.com). Then again, Bill O'Reilly, who purports to be a 'Christian' recently insulted the entire U.S. Christian population when he referred to them on his TV News show in April 2013 as 'Bible Thumpers'. Someone needs to remind Bill O'Reilly of the axiom: 'You can't be just a little bit pregnant'. Bill, you can't be just a little bit Christian either. Moreover it's a gross conflict of interests, spiritually speaking, when you're paid $20 million by a boss [Rupert Murdoch] whose New International Version (NIV) Bible is responsible for deleting nearly 65,000 words found in the King James Bible. I address this further inside of my book at KillingIreland.com.

It doesn't take a rocket scientist to ascertain who Bill O'Reilly's handlers really are, especially following an April 3, 2013 viewer poll where O'Reilly posed the following question: "Do you believe a secret group of global elites are conspiring to rule the world?"

Keep in mind that Bill O'Reilly asked his question during the segment of his show when Scottish American comedian Dennis Miller was present. Miller is a man who on June 3, 2013 at 1:39 p.m. P.S.T., proudly mocked the divinity of Jesus Christ, when on his radio show he suggested that his crew crank call Tim Tebow and pretend to be Jesus Christ. Not the most credible individuals to present an anti-global elite conspiracy question.

Few Senatorial or Congressional representatives voiced suspicions over the dubious malfeasance of both the Senate and House following the obvious public execution of President Kennedy. One outspoken critic was Scottish American Hale Boggs (Congressional House Majority 1971) [below]. Hale is pictured sitting with President LBJ the same President who once said:

'Behind every success there is a crime' - Lyndon Baines Johnson

Out of context this picture of LBJ forming a pyramid with his eyeglasses seems comparatively mundane. However, information provided inside of subsequent chapters will provide the reader a frame of reference that will allow them to reflect back upon the symbolism of this photograph. Readers will have an opportunity to examine a number of examples where Luciferians are promoting the occult pyramid and All-Seeing-Eye of Satan, all for the purpose of gaining power over their subjects. Christians who are unfamiliar with these activities will find it difficult to understand how seemingly ordinary symbols can govern one's existence, but they do. Luciferians feature these symbols near a target or throughout an event believing they are foreshadowing future events, when in reality they are simply orchestrating a kind of self fulfilled prophecy. Luciferians have been deceived by Satan into believing that such icons and ceremonies are a source of great spiritual power, handed down by 'ascended masters' to those in their organization who have achieved 'spiritual enlightenment'. In reality, all that Luciferians are achieving is a state of demonic possession.

Another symbol of great authority within the Church of Babylon is the devil horns and the 666 hand sign, something LBJ has been photographed using on a number of occasions. An example of its use was during funeral services for Lyndon B. Johnson's wife, former first lady 'Lady Bird' Johnson, on July 14, 2007. In attendance for this event were former President Clinton and Mrs. Clinton, former first lady Nancy Reagan and former first lady Barbara Bush. 2hr:1min into 'Lady Bird's' funeral services all in attendance begin holding up the occult devil horns, including the clergy who were standing beside 'Lady Bird's' coffin [pg.58].

57

The Luciferian Doctrine

An entire chapter can be written on the subject of Luciferianism. In the interest of time, here's their belief system in a nutshell. Luciferians deceive their members into believing that God's creations, Adam and Eve, were prisoners in the Garden of Eden. They tell them that Adam and Eve were held against their will in Eden by a spiteful, unfair and malicious bully of a God. They are taught that Satan was the great liberator of Adam and Eve and that it was Satan who imparted secret knowledge onto both of them. Members of this Luciferian cult believe that Satan's great gifts included the secret of how man is able to overcome his earthly, God imposed prison and become God himself.

"…and ye shall be as gods." - [Satan], Genesis 3:5

Many Christians will find the aforementioned information difficult to believe, however I will demonstrate in subsequent chapters that this is exactly what your elected officials, favorite celebrity writer, director, actor, actress and musician subscribe to. It's not only what these megalomaniacal, narcissistic, bigoted, chauvinistic Satanists believe it's what they're indoctrinating our Christian children into believing through film, television, books, music and the internet.

7 Genesis Of The New Age

"Ministering spirits, I loose you in the Name of Lord Jesus Christ, to minister on my behalf according to the will of God. I bind all demons and Satan. In your Holy name. Amen!"

The following information contains a number of Luciferian incantations. Given this fact, I've provided the above prayer, to protect my readers from demonic energy. Remember Jesus Christ's promise that we have, "power to tread on serpents [Satan] and over all the power of the enemy: and nothing shall by any means hurt you" [Luke 10:19].

In order to grasp the complex root system of the 'New Age' movement we'll need to travel back in time to examine the genesis of theosophy. You'll first need to understand that when I talk about the "New Age', I'm talking about a modernist esoteric religious view that promotes the idea that man can achieve God like powers through 'secret knowledge' or enlightenment and of course this 'secret knowledge' comes at a substantial cost to its members. The cost is that the member must surrender his or her faith in the one true God.

Esotericism's main objective is to merge all of the world's religions into one. This they believe will usher in their vision of a one world government and in turn their one world control system and one world leader or anti-Christ.

In order for me to effectively illustrate the inherent danger of this satanic ideology we'll need to thoroughly review the history of an organization by the name of the 'Theosophical Society'. It's this group that's responsible for the complete and total erosion of morality and education throughout America. Furthermore, the Theosophical Society is responsible for the emergence of the 'New Age' faith and the elite funded goal of a 'One World Religion' and 'New World Order'. The founder of the Theosophical Society is a woman by the name of Helena Blavatsky. Helena was born in 1831 and for her entire life was interested in anything dealing with fables and the paranormal. From 1848-1858, Helena travelled throughout the world collecting knowledge about every culture and their religious belief systems. Contemporaries of Helena say that it was during her travels that she became extremely involved with the supernatural and secret knowledge.

59

Armed with an arsenal of satanic 'secret knowledge', in 1873, Helena migrated to America where she established a base camp in New York City. She stated on several occasions that she had been instructed to come to America by her 'ascended masters', and they had instructed her to work with the 'spiritualists' in America. In the book titled: 'H. P. Blavatsky and the Theosophical Movement' - by C. J. Ryan, chapters 5 and 6, Blavatsky states: "I am here in this country sent by my Lodge on behalf of Truth in modern spiritualism, and it is my most sacred duty to unveil what is, and expose what is not."

It was here that Helena Blavatsky along with two other men, Col. Henry Steel Olcott and William Q. Judge, established the 'Theosophical Society'. By 1885, it is estimated that the Theosophical movement had 'thousands of members and branches', all throughout the world, including, Mary Baker Eddy, the founder of Christian Science. It was these types of individuals who followed the establishment of her New York base camp. Thereafter, Helena focused her efforts on India where the Theosophical Society's membership roster grew rapidly. Because of the success throughout India, this would become their global headquarters for their Satanic Theosophy. As an aside India has been the largest troop contributor to United Nations since its inception.

Blavatsky had an authoritative energy that came through in her books. Her first book titled 'Isis unveiled' was published in 1877. Following the release of her first book she founded a magazine in 1887 and named it after her favorite historical figure. 'Lucifer'... It was at Lucifer Magazine where Helena would create her most prized masterpieces 'The Secret Doctrine' in 1888, 'Key To Theosophy' and 'The Voice of Silence'. These collective works will become a blueprint for the satanic global elites 'New-Age' movement.

Not surprising Blavatsky promoted a similar body of satanic works gifted to her by netherworld spiritual advisors namely an 'ascended master' by the name of 'Kuthumi'. According to Blavatsky, Kuthumi currently serves with Master Jesus/Sananda as World Teacher. And based on Satanic Theosophy, Kuthumi, was reincarnated as Pythagoras (circa 582 BC – circa 507 BC) the Greek philosopher and mathematician, Balthazar, who was one of the three wise men who traveled to pay homage to Christ when he was a child, and Francis of Assisi in 1182 who founded the Franciscan Order of Friars. Blavatsky's reverence for Kuthumi is vital when analyzing the types of individuals who are willing to be deceived into the Church of Babylon e.g., Freemasonry, Theosophy and the New Age Movement.

60

Christians must realize that the New Age movement is a religion based on Church of Babylon Theology. Its members believe that the world has left the 'Age of Pisces' and it has entered the golden era of Aquarius. They believe that Jesus Christ represented The Age of Pisces, e.g., the symbol of the fish, etc. and now that The Age of Pisces is over so should the world be over Jesus Christ and in support of a 'New World Order'.

CHAPTER

8 The Zeitgeist Mind Heist

"But the fearful, and unbelieving, and the abominable, and murderers, and whoremongers, and sorcerers, and idolaters, and all liars, shall have their part in the lake which burneth with fire and brimstone: which is the second death." - Revelation 21:8

The Church of Babylon, over the past 140 years, has successfully advanced its Luciferian agenda throughout the lives of hundreds of millions of unsuspecting American citizens. Its minions of possessed have gleefully labored for their dark lord since 1873 successfully deceiving the souls of countless disenchanted Christian Americans. Their primary attractant has been nothing more than the weakness of self indulgence, narcissism, and immorality. If you're unfamiliar with their soul-flypaper techniques, just tune into any of the popular reality television shows or Hollywood films and you'll receive a Master's Degree in demonology.

[handwritten marginal note: —7 BLAVATSKY in AMERICA]

Through modernist, esoteric, lies and deceit, Blavatsky's demonic seeds of Theosophy have germinated into a garden full of Anti-Christ thorns. One of the most recent, whose work blatantly promotes Blavatsky's ideology, is a character who has done absolutely nothing but add a modernist spin to ancient Church of Babylon doctrine. For those who have never heard about writer/director Peter Joseph envision a pre-pubescent, sociopath, rodent tripping on LSD, and you've cloned the one who dreamt up the movie titled: 'Zeitgeist'.

As an aside, I find it interesting how self proclaimed 'enlightened' geniuses always choose Jesus Christ as their so-called 'whipping boy'. Why don't courageous keyboard warriors like, Peter Joseph, create a documentary about Islam's prophet Muhammad? After all 80% of Muslims (Sunni) believe Jesus Christ's presence will be central to the defeat of the "Dijjal" [Muslim Antichrist], a giant one-eyed demonic figure who resides on an island

61

inside of a cave. Sound familiar? If you've read the ancient Babylonian poet Homer, you'll recognize a very similar theme inside Homer's Odyssey "Cyclops Island" [c.900 B.C.], where the hero Odysseus encounters the Cyclops Polyphemus, the son of Poseidon. It's also because the 'All-Seeing-Eye' of Satan is the icon manufactured by Luciferians to personify the United States of America. Why? Because this ancient society of approximately five million understands it is a fool's errand to fight three billion Christians and 1.5 billion Muslims. You get Christians and Muslims to fight each other and destroy each other. Coincidently this is nearly the total number of people Luciferians would like to eliminate from planet earth. This is why throughout history we see the fingerprints of Satanism on every skirmish between Christianity and Islam. I provide evidence of one of the most historic of these in my book at KillingIreland.com. It too is the reason why the U.S. entertainment industry and U.S. government, both of which are riddled with Luciferians, have become synonymous worldwide with the 'All-Seeing Eye" of Satan.

"Believe it or not, entertainment is part of our American diplomacy.
You helped shape the world culture. Tolerance, diversity and creativity"
– President Barack Hussein Obama
2013 DreamWorks Animation Campus

Since Satan's fall from grace [Ezekiel 28:13-19], God's creatio has been deceived into following the one who God said would be, "a terror," throughout the world [Ezekiel 28:19]. An interesting label, God has placed on Satan, considering the fact that Islam's prophet Muhammad said he too had, "been made victorious through terror" [Quran, Sahiih Bukhari 4.52.220]. It's important for the Christian American majority to understand that Islam is not just another religion, on par with Christianity. Islam's entire persona is based on the cult of Baal [Satan]. In fact, Islam's crescent moon and star logo [c. 5th Century A.D.], is an exact replica of the Cult of Baal's logo [c. 14th century B.C., pg.63]. Additional similarities between the cult of Baal and cult of Islam include:

Baal Worshipers:	Muslims:
1) 'Slaves of Baal'	1) 'Slaves of Allah'
2) Debased The Lord	2) Deny Crucifixion/Divinity of Jesus
3) Promoted Sodomy	3) Condone sodomy with young boys
4) Sacrificed Children	4) Torture and Murder Children
5) Practiced necrophilia	5) Sex with dead women is 'Halal'

FUN FACT: Islam's 'Mecca' represented 360 Meccan demons 100s of years before the invention of Islam.

62 | For additional information regarding Islam, please visit David Wood's website: www.answeringmuslims.com

Symbol of Baal
[Ba'al Zebub/Satan]
c.14th century B.C.

Symbol of Islam
c.5th/9th century A.D.

Throughout human history hundreds of millions of innocent men, women, and children have been butchered by Satan's proxies e.g., Islam, Nimrod, Ra, Osiris, Horus, Apollyon, Alexander the Great, Nero, Hitler, U.S. Presidents Bush, Clinton, Obama, Secretary of State Hillary Clinton, etc. It's been Satan's plan for over six millennia, to eradicate the planet of all people who worship God and replace the one true God with Lucifer, Helios Panoptes the Church of Babylon.

"I [Satan] will ascend above the heights of the clouds; I will be like the most High [God]." - Isaiah 14:14

Paris-based spokesman of the National Coordination Committee (NCC), Haytham al-Manna, 'hit the nail on the head' when he made the following evaluation of President Obama's push to attack Syria in 2013:

"We are not in favour of a satanic intervention
against a satanic regime."

Even though it's painfully obvious that Peter Joseph' video Zeitgeist belongs in the fictional section, Luciferian theosophists celebrate his work as one of the greatest space and science documentaries since Star Wars. Take for instance all of Zeitgeists' resources for the video. He borrows from the founder of Theosophy, Helena Blavatsky, New Age cheerleader, Archarya S., New Age Occultist and self proclaimed space alien Jordan Maxwell, and last but not least, a well known Freemason by the name of Albert Churchward, and a long list of other dysfunctional characters whose parents didn't hug them enough or told them that everything they did in life was gold star worthy or deserving of a trophy. This is one characteristic most Luciferians have in common. Instead of being accountable for their own actions and decisions in life, they view everyone else around them as the problem. And who better than Jesus Christ to curse or blame? I personally believe 63 what generates such anger and hatred in these people is that they know that when they take their last breadth on Earth, no one will care about or remember who they were. Jesus Christ's significance, however, will live on throughout His creation. I'm not going to waste anymore text on this lost soul. All I'm going to suggest is that you visit YouTube and search for and watch 'Zeitgeist Exposed - The Film 1 of 8.' or visit, zeitgeistchallenge.com.

Annie Besant

162 years before Zeitgeist Mind Heist's creator (Peter Joseph) was frost giant deep in Dungeons and Dragons, Blavatsky's disciples were purporting the same type of blasphemous rubbish found in Zeitgeist's toilet leavings. One of Theosophists' most prominent female proponents was a woman by the name of Annie Besant. Born in 1874, Annie was a real gift to humanity. Annie was an anti-family, anti-American, anti-Christian feminist who travelled the United States debating the value of transforming American into a Socialist Nation. Friedrich Engels (1820-1895) avowed Communist and contemporary of Karl Marx fondly makes mention of both Besant and Helena Blavatsky in a 1891 letter from London to Kautsky. He states:

"Do you know Mother Besant has joined the theosophists of Grandmother Blavatsky. On her garden gate, 19, Avenue Road, now is in big gold letters: Theosophical Head Quarters. Herbert Burrows has caused this by his love."

A contemporary of Annie Besant, G.W. Foot, who represented the individual rights and freedoms associated with Republicanism, once referred to Annie Besant as being 'proud as Lucifer himself'.

Besant would eventually capture the attention of the elite recruiting apparatus of Freemasonry joining the order in 1902. Upon proving her genuine hatred towards Jesus Christ and anything related to the one true God, Besant was provided the necessary resources to build an international hybrid of satanic Theosophy and Freemasonry lodges. And with elite funding and support, her international order grew throughout the world.

What everyone reading this text must realize is that Freemasonry and 'Marxism' both shares common ideals with Blavatsky's satanic theosophical New Age monster. Given this fact, it was a logical conclusion for elite consortiums to vote in favor of Annie Besant's advancement, in 1908, to the leadership position of President within the Theosophical Society. On a regular basis, I come into contact with low level Masons who argue that

64

Freemasonry does not participate or have any historical connection with Theosophy. This is always perplexing to me given the well documented facts surrounding the long standing relationship between these two organizations. Take for instance one of Besant's contemporaries, who in 1917 wrote: 'Freemasonry viewed doctrinally, is Theosophy'. W. Host, penned this observation in his book titled 'Heresies Exposed' 200 years after Freemasonry had been founded. So, as far back as 1917 people were keen to the machinations of Blavatsky's satanic order and the connection to the seemingly benign Freemasonry recruiting agency.

Alice Bailey

"oppose every form of dogmatic theology, especially the Christian, which the Chiefs of the Society regard as particularly pernicious [evil]… to counteract, as far as possible, the effects of missionaries to delude the so-called "Heathen" and "Pagans" as to the real origin and dogmas of Christianity and the practical effects of the latter upon public and private character in so-called Christian countries."
– Col. Olcott, Co-Founder of the Theosophical Society,
Its Origin, Plan and Aims

One of Helena Blavatsky's most celebrated theosophical pupils was a woman by the name of Alice Bailey. Bailey would become the most dedicated anti-Christ Luciferians of all time. In fact, Bailey's brainchild is the genesis for what satanic elites today refer to as the 'New World Order' or 'One World Religion'. Alice Bailey, long ago, urged her elitist funding sources that it was necessary to recruit the entire world into her Luciferian religion in order to realize the full benefits of the Age of Aquarius. There is no question that Alice Bailey's works have been the driving force behind the global theosophical movement, however, its overall tactical strategy can be found in a book by H.G. Wells titled: "The Open Conspiracy Blueprints for a World Revolution." We see the influence of H.G. Wells throughout Hollywood films, television, and music.

Hollywood has produced approximately 30,000 films as of 2013 along with countless television programs, cartoons, etc. The inconvenient truth is the vast majority of these productions celebrate the Church of Babylon. I remember how disappointed I was when I discovered the fingerprints of theosophy all over Walt Disney Corporation. After all, I had been taught as a child that Disney represented wholesome family values. I discovered later in life that not even Walt Disney Corporation was immune from the virus of Theosophy.

65

Throughout my book, Deception: The Ancient Mystery That Holds The Secret of Newgrange, I expose never before seen information regarding Walt Disney's association with Satanic Theosophy. You can review this book at, KillingIreland.com.

Theosophist Alice Bailey developed the psychology behind the indoctrination process and mass brainwashing found throughout the music industry. When you see demonic imagery or hear demonic lyrics those are Alice Bailey's battle plans running their course. About her plan Bailey is quoted as saying:

"It will be fought largely with mental weapons and in the world of thought; it will involve also the emotional realm, from the standpoint of idealistic fanaticism. This inherent fanaticism will fight against the appearance of the coming world religion and the spread of esotericism. It must not be forgotten that only those souls who are on the probationary path for the path of discipleship will form the nucleus of the coming world religion. There is no question therefore that the work to be done in familiarizing the general public with the nature of the mysteries is of paramount importance at this time. When the gray one comes with his disciples and initiates we shall have the restoration of the mysteries and their exoteric presentation, as a consequence of the first initiation."

Regarding Freemasonry and how it's been instrumental in advancing occultism, Satanism, etc., Bailey is quoted in saying:

"The Masonic Movement [Freemasonry] when it can be divorced from politics and social end and from its present paralyzing condition of inertia will meet the need of those who can and should wield power. It is the custodian of the law; it is the home of the Mysteries and the seat of ignition. It holds in its symbolism the ritual of Deity [Satan]. And the way of salvation is pictorially preserved in its work. The methods of Deity [Satan] are demonstrated in its Temples and under the all-seeing Eye [Satan]. The work can go forward. It is a far more occult organization than can be realized. And is intended to be the training school for the coming advanced occultists."

Helena Blavatsky's Demonic 'Spiritual Advisor':

On several occasions the founder of Theosophy professed that her 'spiritual advisor' was responsible for the creation of her most prized books. It's these books which make up the entire Satanic, Theosophical ideology. Based on statements made by well-known Theosophists, Freemasons, etc., it's widely accepted that a group of 'evolved beings' exist, and that such group guides them and their works. For example, Oprah Winfrey commented that she likes to take long walks on her property so that she can speak with her spiritual advisors. This explains Oprah's New Age position on religion. Again, please watch the video 'Hollywood Unmasked' hollywoodunmasked. com and you'll be able to read her actual quote regarding her spiritual advisors. Like many other celebrities on television and in movies, these influential people actually believe that Jesus Christ, Buddha, Krishna, and Mohammad were all 'Masters of Wisdom' and that all of them were led by a head master by the name of 'Maitreya', who answers to the one true leader 'Sanat Kumara'.

New Age philosopher Dan Rudhyar admits that the leader of the enlightened masters is in fact Satan. He writes:

"Satan is an anagram for Sanat Kumara, who in the esoteric philosophy of India is the Promethean being who gave mankind the fire of self-conscious and independent, individual selfhood."

The New Encyclopedia of The Occult published a note from John Michael Greer that reads as follows:

"Satan is a possible echo Theosophical lore, where the Lord of the world-spiritual ruler of the earth and head of the great White Lodge-is Sanat Kumara... A Lord of the flame who descended to earth from Venus in a fiery chariot some 6 million years ago."

The woman who was inspired by a spiritual advisor [Satan] and who founded Theosophy, Helena Blavatsky did not mince words when it came to the topic of who she thought 'god' really was. Blavatsky believed whole heartedly that Satan is the one true god and Lord Jesus Christ, the Messiah and Jehovah is evil.

Keep in mind what Blavatsky wrote in the following statement, while you review the subsequent pictures of world leaders, billionaire corporate investors, Hollywood celebrities, etc. all communicating their allegiance to The Church of Babylon by flashing the ancient satanic hand-signs associated with Lucifer:

"It is but natural-even from the dead-letter standpoint-to view Satan, the serpent of Genesis, as the real creator and benefactor, the father of spiritual mankind, for it is he who was the harbourer of light bright reading and Lucifer, who open the eyes of the automation created by Jehovah as alleged: and he who was the first to whisper, in the day ye eat thereof ye shall be as Elohim, knowing good and evil, can only be regarded in the light of a

Savior. An adversary to Jehovah the personating spirit, he still remains in esoteric truth the ever loving messenger the angel the Seraphim and cherubim who both knew well, in love still more, and who conferred on us spiritual instead of physical immortality." - Helena Blavatsky

H. Alexander Fussell, in Lucifer Theosophical Magazine, supports Blavatsky's claim that Satan is in fact the god of Theosophy when he writes:

"Satan then was originally a divine being destined to carry light and life to the netherworld's. He stands for the gift of free will and self-conscious mind to man, a power which at once seduces and uplifts man. For with free will comes the power to go astray, Satan is therefore man's teacher."

CHAPTER
9 The Freemason Connection

"Who is a liar but he that denieth that Jesus is the Christ? He is antichrist, that denieth the Father and the Son. Whosoever denieth the Son, the same hath not the Father: (but) he that acknowledgeth the Son hath the Father also." - 1 John 2:22, 23

One of the most celebrated Freemasons, Albert Pike, and a reference for the anti-Christian who wrote and produced the Zeitgeist videos, once said:

"To you, Sovereign Grand Instructors General, we say this, that you may repeat it to the Brethren of the 32nd, 31st and 30th degrees: 'the Masonic Religion should be, by all of us initiates of the high degrees, maintained in the purity of the LUCIFERIAN Doctrine. If Lucifer were not god, would Adonay (Jesus) calumniate (spread false and harmful statements about) him? Yes Lucifer is God."

- Albert Pike, A.C. De La Rive, La Femme et l'Enfant dans la Franc-Maqonnene Universelle, pg. 588

In cities and towns throughout America you'll find them innocuous looking buildings featuring the mark of freemasonry [right]. And the vast majority of Americans believe these 'boys clubs' are harmless. Even low level degree Masons will tell you that their association with the Church of Babylon [Freemasonry] is purely business or social, and for many of those people, that's true. Unfortunately, for these uneducated Masons, the mountain of historical evidence I've collected  over the years suggests otherwise. Those who control this theosophical recruiting tool know very well innocence, and socializing is not the order of the day. And if you happen to be a follower of Jesus Christ and belong to a masonry lodge, you're personally contributing to the stated goal of The Church of Babylon to eliminate Christianity from Planet Earth. If you do not subscribe to these ambitions, abandoning Freemasonry this minute is your only choice. For those who are unfamiliar with the satanic origins of Freemasonry, the following provides a concise history.

Following the reign of William the Conqueror, France, England and the Holy Roman Empire remained a powerful slave under their Norman masters who conquered England through fear and terror and then Scotland by way of invitation, prior to advancing into Ireland byway of Papal request. Still having a great deal of influence, the Roman Catholic Church convinced the superior Norman warriors to act as the special forces branch during the Crusades, a collection of military expeditions undertaken by the Christian nations of Europe for the purpose of rescuing the holy places of Palestine from the hands of the Saracens. Among this elite group of Norman warriors were the Knights Templar's who for a time became the richest and most powerful presence throughout France, England, etc. As an aside, our modern day banking and credit system is based on the ancient Templar system. Much of that Templar legacy is still very much alive today throughout Switzerland whose Nation flag still bears what appears to be a Templar's cross when in fact it's an 'X'. It will be remembered from previous chapters that the Roman Numeral 'X' was not only a number ten but a word 'IO' (pronounced EO) and that in Greek the word 'IO' means Helios or Apollyon otherwise known as "The Beast from the pit" – Revelation 9:11.

"And they had a king over them, which is the angel of the bottomless pit, whose name in the Hebrew tongue is Abaddon, but in
the Greek tongue hath his name Apollyon."
- Revelation 9:11

In addition to being associated with Apollyon, the 'X' or 'IO' is linked to the satanic Babylonian god Nimrod who founded Babylon. Nimrod [Hebrew for "we will rebel"] was worshipped like a god for more than 400 years and constructed the Tower of Babel with the intention of eliminating God. Like Satan, Nimrod rebelled against the will of God and beguiled men into a satanic religious order [Freemasonry] that insidiously controlled their minds. Nimrod promoted diverse and erratic superstitions and led his followers to be governed by the signs in the stars and commanded them to worship fire. Following charges of heresy by King Philip IV; more specifically:

"when professing, the brothers were required to deny Christ, to spit on the Cross, and to place three 'obscene kisses' on the lower spine, the navel and the mouth; they were obliged to indulge in carnal relations with other members of the order, if requested; and finally they wore a small belt which had been consecrated by touching a strange idol, with looked like a human head with a long beard."

On August 12, 1308, the charges would be increased stating that the Templars worshipped idols containing a cat head. The ancient chronicler William of Tyre described the Grand Master of the Templar's Odo de St Amand in 1179:

"A wicked man, haughty and arrogant, in whose nostrils dwelt the spirit of a fury, one who neither feared God nor revered man"

The charge of worshipping idols which contained a 'cat head' referred to the Babylonian god of Demon's Pazuzu [right] a figure that I address in subsequent chapters. By all accounts the band of elite warriors who initially named themselves the "Order of the Poor Knights of Christ", because they took solemn vows of poverty, became possessed like King Solomon by the demon god Pazuzu and his legion of demons, including 'Tiamat' shortly after setting up their base camp near the site where King Solomon's temple once stood. It was Solomon after all who used demons to construct his Temple. Shortly after the Order of the Poor Knights of Christ became possessed, they

70   changed their name to 'Knights Templar' after which they became exceedingly wealthy and powerful. It should be

noted that the accusations of idol worship occurred just nine years after the Knights Templars loaned King Philip IV of France five hundred thousand livres in 1299. The Templars had also loaned large sums of money to European kings, princes, merchants, and a number of Muslim rulers. Much of the Templar's wealth was housed in Paris and London temples, making them leading financial centers. Astonishingly none of the alleged "idols" were ever produced by King Philip IV, suggesting King Philip IV, independent of Templar influence, had previous knowledge of the god of demons Pazuzu. Not surprising given the fact Freemasonry had existed in England as early as 926AD and the progenitor of the church of Babylon [Freemasonry] is identified in Masonic Rituals as 'Hiram Abiff' whose ancestors were the Naphtali, an ancient tribe of Pharisee worshipping Talmudists who along with the demon god Pazuzu and Lucifer built King Solomon's Temple. Ancient text describes Abiff as a man who becomes possessed by the Babylonian demon god Pazuzu, is then murdered, buried and brought back to life. This is the source of the blasphemous reincarnation legend taught to high-level deceived members of Freemasonry.

After the final victory of Muslims in 1291, the Templars took up residence on a number of Islands in the Mediterranean and ultimately changed their name to the Knights of Malta. Following the public execution by burning of Templar leaders Jacques de Molay, and Geoffroi de Charney in front of the cathedral of Notre Dame in Paris on March 11, 1314, the remaining Templar members escaped to various locations around the world which included Scotland, were they educated Scotsman in advanced warfare tactics. It was this Templar training which provided King of Scotland Robert The Bruce with the military prowess necessary to defeat the English. This Scottish victory over the British coincidently occurred in 1314, the same year the Templars disbanded from France and England. In addition to advance weapons training and tactics, the Templar Knights also brought with them what would become known as Scottish Freemasonry.

Flash forward to 1688 and King James II has been unseated by revolution and forced to flee England. It would be Scottish Freemasons who would help stage military campaigns against the English opposition, however, their goal of re-crowning James II would fall short and James II would die in 1701. James II son James III would continue the family's struggle to regain the British throne and to help achieve this goal a new branch of Freemasonry was created and patterned after the ancient Knights Templar Freemasonry. By 1707 the Templar's Scottish Freemasonry had become overrun with English Freemasons and what the British could not achieve in three hundred years and eighteen wars, their English Freemason op-   71 eratives achieved through Scottish and Irish Parliament in just six years, when the Scottish Parliament signed 'The Acts of Union' in 1707, and just sixty-nine years following The Acts of Union, English Freemasonry would become even more corrupted by a man named Adam Weishaupt, the designer of the Illuminati in 1776. What the useful idiots, who promote the Illuminati fail to understand, is that the Illuminati was created by Weishaupt to deceive people into pursuing 'secret knowledge' that doesn't exist.

"Of all the means I know to lead men, the most effectual is a concealed mystery. The hankering of the mind is irresistible; and if once a man has taken it into his head that there is a mystery in a thing, it is impossible to get it out, either by argument or experience. And then, we can so change notions by merely changing a word. What more contemptible than fanaticism; but call it enthusiasm; then add the little word noble, and you may lead him over the world." – Adam Weishaupt.

Google the name 'Illuminati' and you'll be presented with associated data ad nauseam. In my humble opinion, the most accurate resource on the subject of the Illuminati is a book titled "Bloodlines of the Illuminati" by Fritz Springmeier. Many of the online resources that you'll encounter simply parrot Mr. Springmeier's data. Other sites provide undocumented and fanciful data. Like Mr. Springmeier's resource, readers of this book will only find recognized historical facts as this is all that I'm interested in presenting. For those who are seeking a more surreal, Hollywood experience than what our real world has to offer. Godspeed! For this reason, I'm not going to dedicate too many words on the subject. The most critical well documented fact for the reader to understand is that Freemasonry was infiltrated by the Illuminati back in the late 18th century.

The Illuminati was founded by a man named Adam Weishaupt in 1776. Adam Weishaupt was the son of George Weishaupt, who was a Talmudic Rabbi in Ingolstadt, Bavaria. Weishaupt's newly found organization challenged the orthodox views of the day and was considered a radical idea. Weishaupt's primary goal for his new organization was to challenge traditional political and societal norms. Weishaupt's organization grew and with his new found notoriety came the attention of those who opposed his stance on 'change'. Shorty after becoming a topic for discussion, Weishaupt's new organization would become public enemy number one. Multiple edicts were made against Weishaupt's new organization by the ruler of Bavaria, Duke Carl Theodore, the third being issued in 1787.

Sleuthing and arrests garnered a treasure trove of Illuminati documentation and contemporaries of Weishaupt translated these documents into two books. The first are titled 'Proofs of a Conspiracy Against All The Religions and Governments' and 'Memoirs Illustrating The History of Jacobinism'. The documentation spelled out how Weishaupt's Illuminati would create a New World Order. Prerequisite steps to their New World Order included the complete destruction of every world religion and the takeover of Freemasonry. The founder of the Illuminati wrote the following incriminations:

"Do you realize sufficiently what it means to rule – to rule in a secret society? Not only over the lesser or more important of the populace, but over the best of men, over men of all ranks, nations and religions, to rule without external force, to unite them indissolubly, to breathe one spirit and soul into them, men distributed over all parts of the world?"

Weishaupt's Illuminati also believed in the abolition of private property, nations, etc. Much of what his Satanic Cult subscribed to was born out of Weishaupt's knowledge of 'The Acts of Union" in 1707. This is when the Scottish people were forced to merge with England. Weishaupt's Illuminati knew that the wildly unpopular success of The "Acts of Union" was attributed to a corrupt political process and bribes paid to Scottish Parliament. The "Acts of Union" was so hated by the Scottish people that widespread civil unrest resulted in the Scottish Parliament imposing Martial Law. The aforesaid strategy is exactly what has been promoted by every U.S. President since John F. Kennedy. The Rothschild invented, funded and promoted 'Agenda 21' [signed by President G.H.W. Bush and Prince Charles] calls for the abolition of private property rights, America's rights to coastal waters and the merger of the United States with Mexico and Canada under the 'North American Union'. Weishaupt goes on to say:

"The abolition of property, social authority, nationality, and the return of the here and raised a happy state in which it formed only a single family without artificial needs, without useless sciences, every father being priest and magistrate."

President George Washington has been repeatedly attacked by modernist historians claiming Washington was a member of Weishaupt's Illuminati. What's telling is how President Washington opposed Weishaupt's Satanic order and regularly spoke out against the anti-Christian Illuminati whose goal it was to "perfect human nature" through re-education to achieve a communal state with nature, free of organized religion [Communism].

73

Read what President George Washington wrote, thirteen years after the Illuminati had allegedly been outlawed in Bavaria:

"I have heard much of the nefarious, and dangerous plans, and doctrines of the illuminati. It was not my intention to doubt that, the doctrines of the illuminati, and principles of Jacobinism had not spread in the United States. On the contrary, no one is more truly satisfied of this fact than I am. The idea that I meant to convey, was that I do not believe that the lodges of Freemasons in this country had, as societies, endeavored to propagate the diabolical tenets of the first, or pernicious principles of the latter if they are susceptible of separation that individuals of them may have done it, or that the founder or instrument employed to sound, the Democratic societies in the United States, may have had these objects, and actually had a separation of the people from their government in view is too evident to be questioned" – President George Washington, 1797

Flash forward sixteen years after the death of President George Washington to June 19, 1815 the day after Napoleon's defeat at Waterloo. Baron Nathan Rothschild has incited rumors throughout England's investment community that Napoleon had in fact won the battle at Waterloo. This lie perpetrated by Baron Rothschild allows the Baron to take full control of the Bank of England, the epicenter for International Commerce. Now the once powerful Templar Freemasonry commerce system was back in the hands of the descendants of Nimrod the Rothschild Family. With Rothschild's conquest of England's banking system achieved through nothing more than a rumor, Rothschild was now able to infect English Freemasonry with his family's version of satanic, Babylonian Talmudism. Just ninety-nine years later the Rothschild's would order the assassination of Franz Ferdinand and his wife in 1914 for denying the Rothschild Family control of the Austro-Hungarian banking system. Archduke Ferdinand's assassination is considered the most immediate cause of World War I. It's noteworthy to mention the similarities between Archduke Ferdinand's assassination and U.S. President John F. Kennedy's assassination forty-nine years later. Both men rode in dark colored convertible vehicles and both men were shot through the neck. Furthermore, just one hundred two years after taking complete control of the English Banking system and three years after WWI, the Rothschild Family would construct the Balfour Declaration in 1917, one of the most revolutionary documents in the twentieth century. It committed the British people to supporting the establishment in Palestine of "a National Home for the Jewish people," [Israel].

74

Where English Freemason operatives had given Scotland to England through 'The Acts of Union' in 1707, Babylonian Talmudic Freemasons controlled by Rothschild had given England to Rothschild's Israel through the Balfour Declaration. All the satanic Rothschilds needed now was a war and a way to eliminate the Judaic majority who subscribed to the teachings found in the Holy Torah and those who eschewed the Babylonian Talmud. In less than twenty-five years the Rothschild Family had WWII. I ask the reader to contemplate what I've just written while considering the current geopolitical landscape and America's relationship within those conditions, namely America's massive debt to Communist China, all of which has been orchestrated by the Rothschild controlled U.S. Freemason majority House and Senate. Can you guess who anti-Christian, pro-communist Freemasonry has sold America to? Consider this quote from Jennifer Yu, Rothschild's top executive in China:

"The economic balance of power has already changed, and it is moving to the East... There will be an increasing number of Western companies selling assets to China." - Jennifer Yu, Rothschild Corporation, Bloomberg Business Week Magazine 08/05/2010

In response to Rothschild's Jennifer Yu, Chairman David de Rothschild writes in an e-mail:

"Clearly, under the leadership of Jennifer, and with the support of the senior management team, we are making meaningful progress in China."

If we read what President George Washington wrote about the Illuminati in 1797 it's reasonable to believe that Washington was no fan of the Illuminati, unlike President Obama, who chooses to flagrantly tout his affiliation with musicians 'Jay-Z' and 'Beyonce' who blatantly promote the anti-Christian ideology of The Church of Babylon. President George Washington was convinced that the pro-democratic, anti-Republic ideology being promoted throughout America during his lifetime was in fact being directed and funded by the Illuminati [Church of Babylon]. The same holds true in 2014.

I'm personally amazed by the large number of Americans who have allowed themselves to be brainwashed into believing that the United States is a 'Democracy'. Nowhere in our founding documents is the word 'Democracy' a.k.a. mob rule found. On the other hand, 'Republic' a.k.a. individual rights, is. This is why our Constitutional Republic is under attack from every angle by The Church of Babylon and their proxies. Our 'elected' politicians have allowed every globalist wolf throughout the world to feed off the flesh

75

of America, devouring our resources, independence and faith. America's global elite foes want to eradicate our Constitution, because if they achieve this, they'll be shredding any evidence that the 16th Amendment ever existed. This Amendment is crucial in that it clearly states that the United States Government does not have the authority to tax an individual American citizen. The Government only has power to collect taxes on 'profits' or 'gains'. In other words, corporations and/or businesses are the ONLY groups which have a tax burden. Americans need to wake up and educate themselves to the fact that individual citizens are not required to pay federal income tax.

Banking elites know that if people woke up to this reality they would realize that the Internal Revenue Service was not legally created and that it has no authority over them. I referenced this earlier, but I cannot stress the importance of watching the documentary titled 'Freedom to Fascism'. It's these types of schemes that made our founding fathers keen to the dangerous extremes of both tyranny and mobocracy.

What exists in America today is a far cry from the Constitutional Republic our forefathers brought forth. Both the Republican and the Democratic parties have been purchased by two families [Rockefeller and Rothschild] whose 'New World Order' esoteric religion is nothing more than recycled Babylonian Satanism meant to pay homage to their god Nimrod. There is nothing new about what the Rockefeller's and Rothschild's are doing and it's anything but   orderly.

Today the Democratic Party promotes organizations whose objectives are to remove all Christian symbols from schools, Government buildings, etc. It's the Democratic Party which has for generations advocated and supported groups whose views are counter to a productive, morally stable society. It was the Democratic Party, for instance, which ushered in the 1960's 'sexual revolution', a movement born out of the deliberately skewed research and dysfunctional mind of C. Kinsey.

Judith A. Reisman, PhD is the writer of the book "Kinsey". In her book she makes the following statement regarding the fraud Alfred C. Kinsey:

"In 1948, the Institute for sex research at Indiana University was led by eugenicist Alfred C. Kinsey, whose sex research shook America's moral foundations and launched the 1960s sexual revolution. Kinsey a Democrat himself, conducted human experiments in a soundproof laboratory built to his specifications at Indiana University, and that the sexual abuse of at least 317 infants and young boys was a scientific protocol for Kinsey's 1948 report that led to the 1960s sexual revolution."

The fact is, it was the Democratic Party as well, which advocated and supported the founder of Planned Parenthood, Sanger, an avowed Satanist and eugenicist. Sanger spoke of sterilizing those she designated as "unfit," a plan she said would be the "salvation of American civilization." And who were the 'unfit'? Margaret tells us, that it's "Those whose religious scruples prevent their exercising control over their numbers." In other words, the Rockefeller funded, U.S. Democratic Government backed, atheist Sanger, wanted to murder ALL Christian babies. She writes:

"There is no doubt in the minds of all thinking people that the procreation of this group should be stopped." – Margaret Sanger

Her agenda to murder hundreds of millions of babies didn't end with her death unfortunately. On the contrary, to date Planned Parenthood is responsible for murdering more than 30 million Americans. In 2011, Planned Parenthood murdered over 333,964 Americans and guess who paid for those deaths? The Christian American majority did, when they allowed their 'elected' Government to pay more than $542 million to Planned Parenthood.

Where is the voice of America's 80% Christian population? Where are the 240 million Christians in America who are allowing their tax dollars to be spent on the murder of innocent American children? I suppose Planned Parenthood has not spent all of our tax dollars on the murder of children; they've also invested some of it on initiatives whose stated goals are to destabilize the Christian American family.

In 1969 Planned Parenthood-World Population published a memorandum titled 'A Family Planning Perspectives Special Supplement' which called for the eradication of the nuclear family. The plan was delivered by Bernard Berelson (President, Population Council) to Frederick S. Jaffe (Vice-President of Planned Parenthood). Among other things, the proposal called for the reduction of fertility in the U.S. and the programming of Americans to embrace all of the following (a) Social Constraints (b) Economic Deterrents (c) Social Controls:

Restructure Family

- Postpone or avoid marriage;
- Alter image of ideal family size;
- Encourage increased homosexuality;
- Educate for family limitation

- Fertility control agents in food and water supply;
- Encourage women to work;

Modify Tax Policies

- Substantial marriage tax
- Child tax
- Tax married more than single
- Remove parent's tax exemption
- Additional taxes on parents with more than 1 or 2 children in school
- Reduce/eliminate paid maternity leave or benefits
- Reduce/eliminate children's or family allowances
- Bonuses for delayed marriage and greater child-spacing
- Pensions for women of 45 with less than N children
- Eliminate Welfare payments after first 2 children
- Require women to work and provide few child care facilities
- Limit/eliminate public-financed medical care, scholarships, housing, loans and subsidies to families with more than N children.
- Modify Tax Policies
- Compulsory abortion of out-of-wedlock pregnancies
- Compulsory sterilization of all who have two children except for a few who would be allowed three.
- Confine childbearing to only a limited number of adults
- Stock certificate type permits for children
- Discouragement of private home ownership
- Stop awarding public housing based on family size Permits to have children;
- Payments to encourage sterilization
- Payments to encourage contraception
- Payments to encourage abortion
- Abortion and sterilization on demand
- Allow certain contraceptives to be distributed non-medically
- Improve contraceptive technology
- Make contraception truly available and accessible to all
- Improve maternal health care with family planning a core element

Long before the corruption of American universities, Yale University's President, Timothy Dwight the 4th, voiced his negative views of the Illuminati [Church of Babylon], when he was quoted as saying:

"The great and good hands proposed by the illuminati, as the ultimate objects of their union, are the overthrow of religion, government, and human society civil and domestic"

Long before Harvard's academic majority supported the practice of Satanic Black Masses on Harvard's campus, their President understood the danger satanic theosophy represented to a free and just society. Joseph Willard is quoted as saying:

"There is sufficient evidence that a number of societies, of the illuminati [Church of Babylon], have been established in this land of Gospel light and civil liberty, which were first organized from the grand society, in France they are doubtless secretly striving to undermine all our ancient institutions, civil and sacred. These societies are closely lead with those of the same order, in Europe. They've all the same objects in view. The enemies of all order are seeking our room. Should infidelity generally prevail, our independence would fall of course. Our Republic government would be annihilated."

Modern day Vanderbilt University, on the other hand, openly promotes its esoteric satanic theosophical leanings. In its general information and courses of study, for the 2012/13 session, Vanderbilt University's "Divinity School" lists the following as one of its objectives for students:

"To engage men and women in a theological understanding of religious traditions; to help persons, both lay and ordained, re-envision and prepare for the practice of Christian ministry in our time; to encourage individuals in their spiritual and intellectual growth; to prepare leaders who will be agents of social justice; and to educate future scholars and teachers of religion."

Much like what we're witnessing in 2014, the once shrouded Church of Babylon is so confident of its progress throughout America it's now openly displaying itself throughout Hollywood and politics. The same was true in ancient times and earlier American history, when well-known Freemasons began displaying their allegiance for a New World Order. Google "George H.W. Bush + New World Order speech", and you'll see our former CIA Director/President promoting the idea of chopping the head off of America in exchange for a One World Government [Babylon]. He's not alone. George W. Bush, Clinton, and Obama have all proclaimed their allegiance to this ancient Old World Order.

"The express aim of this order was to abolish Christianity, and overturn all civil government... The great strength of our water lies in its concealment, let it never appear in any place in its own name, but always covered by another name. And another occupation none is fitter than the three lower degrees of Freemasonry, the public is accustomed to it, expects a little from it, and therefore takes little notice of it."- From the book proofs of a conspiracy

In 1924 a Masonic publication listed sixty U.S. Senators as Freemasons which means Church of Babylon members constituted over 60% of the U.S. Senate. What's more 290 members of the House of Representatives were Freemason's. The Grand Lodge of California revealed in their "Freemasonry, A Way of Life," that the 97th Congress (1981-1983), contained 28 lodge members in the Senate and 78 in the House. The following is a partial list of past and present verified enemies of Lord Jesus Christ:

Barack Hussein Obama – Freemason. Proponent of Agenda 21, signed Anti-Constitutional executive orders NDAA, and HR 993. HR993 states that Monsanto Genetically Modified Organisms – the same ones that are responsible for the plague of cancer, mental disease, destruction of the human endocrine system, sweeping across the United States - can't be stopped by a court order. Obama Cont'd - GMO crops can still be grown, harvested, and sold in the United States. There is strong evidence that suggests Barack Hussein Obama's (a.k.a. Barry Soetoro) real father is radical communist, bi-sexual, pornographer Frank Marshal Davis. Please watch the documentary by Joel Gilbert 'Dreams from My Real Father' www.obamasrealfather.com:

"I ceased to advertise my mother's race [white] at the age of 12 or 13, when I began to suspect that by doing so I was ingratiating myself to whites." - Barack Obama

"I believe we and mainly you have an incredible opportunity to lead in shaping a New World Order for the 21st century in a way consistent with American interests and common interests," – Vice President Joe Biden 5/28/14 while addressing 1,000 Air Force Academy graduates.

President George W. Bush – Freemason, Member of Council on Foreign Relations, Member of Skull & Bones, Signed The North American Union which ended the United States as we know it. Wife Laura ('Pickles') Bush killed her high school boyfriend/fiancé Mike Douglas in 1963. The tale told around Midland at that time was that Laura thought she was pregnant by Michael Douglas. When she told him, instead of agreeing to marry her, Douglas broke up with her, and began dating Laura's friend Regan Gammon.

President Bill Clinton – Freemason, Council on Foreign Relations, Bilderberg Participant, Rhodes Scholar. Pam Harriman is the person behind Bill Clinton. She is tied in with satanic group 'Hell Fire Club'. Wife Hilary Clinton is known to practice Shamanism Witchcraft. Mrs. Clinton is also an advocate for the Law Of The Sea Treaty which will give total control of all United States ocean rights to the United Nations.

On June 4, 1993 President Bill Clinton signed the Convention on Biological Diversity (Section 9.2,3,2) which reads:

"We must either reduce the earth's human population to 1 billion [murder 6 billion people] or reduce the standard of living to an agrarian [peasant] status."

"We can't be so fixated on our desire to preserve the rights of ordinary Americans." - Bill Clinton USA Today--3-11-93, page 2a.

Bill Clinton's original surname was Bill Blythe III. His father William Jefferson Blythe, Jr's ancestors were from Berwickshire, Scotland however they weren't Scottish, they were border gypsies from India. In fact the Blythe's are related to the late border gypsy King Charles Faa Blythe and her Majesty "Queen Esther Faa Blythe" the most important and well-known name in the gypsy world. Later in life Queen Esther would go on to marry a Freemason by the name of John Rutherford.

The Blythe gypsies were considered a menace to society as they roamed the English and Scottish countryside, practicing witchcraft and selling contraband. Based on Bill "Blythe" Clinton's acts of terrorism throughout the world, it appears Bill's gypsy DNA hasn't fallen far from its original strand. I believe this is the real motivating factor behind Bill joining the ancient and prestigious Scottish Clinton Clan, who in ancient times was called MacClinton which is a variant of MacLintock. The MacLintocks [Mac Gille Ghionndaig] were descended from the ancient Christian Irish Kings of Dalriada.

Bill Clinton's religion of Freemasonry possesses a hatred of ancient Celts [Irish] and Picts [Scottish]. Evidence of this exists in the number of Scottish and Irish men and women who were murdered during Bill Clinton's time as Arkansas governor and America's President. The Clinton's 'Kill List' may be examined inside of my book, Deception: The Ancient Mystery That Holds The Secret of Newgrange. You may review this book at, KillingIreland.com.

Christian American's should also be reminded of the fact that Bill Clinton gave generous support to Turkey in its war against the indigenous Christian Kurds. What many Christians do not know is that a large number of "crypto-jews"

[Talmudists] in the Ottoman Empire who, to escape the inferior conditions of "dhimmis", converted publicly to Islam, but retained their Talmudic beliefs becoming what were known as "Donmeh". Since the 20th century Donmeh have intermarried with other groups and most have assimilated into Turkish society. In other words Talmudists Turkish leaders, masquerading as Muslims, murdered countless Christians for Bill Clinton.

Prince Philip - Freemason, husband of Queen Elizabeth and President of World Wildlife Fund. Philip is also a majority share holder in Archer Daniels Midland Co. [ADM] one of the largest food distributors in the world. What should concern the global Christian community is that while he controls a large portion of the worlds food supply he also harbors psychopathic tendencies namely the extermination of billions of human beings. What if one day this psychopath and his supporters decide to place a virus into the global food supply? The aforesaid is just one of a long list of reasons why the Christian American majority must control their own local Organic food supply.

"If I could be reincarnated, I would wish to return to Earth as a killer virus to lower human population levels." – Prince Philip

Al Gore – Freemason.

Bob Dole – Freemason.

Ross Perot – Started in business with a large Rockefeller awarded New York contract to his computer business. He was a member of the Foreign Intelligence Advisory Board, which requires the highest security clearance.

George H.W. Bush – Freemason, Member of Skull & Bones Society, Member of the Council of Foreign Relations, Director of Central Intelligence Agency (C.I.A), Knighted by Queen Elizabeth II, Member of satanic Bohemian Grove, responsible for the introduction of "Agenda 21' into the U.S., President and CEO of Zapata Oil based in Texas. It was through Zapata Oil that George H.W. Bush began selling drugs to America's children. While a member of the exclusive and secretive Skull & Bones Society, George H.W. Bush's nickname was 'Magog'. Magog is the satanic Babylonian god Nimrod associated with fire worship, child sacrifice and sorcery.

There's ample intelligence which implicates George H.W. Bush in both the assassination of President John F. Kennedy and the attempted assassination of President Ronald

82

Reagan. Consider the fact that the Bush family was close personal friends with Ronald Reagan's Assassin John Hinckley, Jr. whose father was a wealthy oil man close to George H.W. Bush. Lastly George H.W. Bush worked with President Barack Hussein Obama's Communist grandfather Stanley Dunham as they were both C.I.A. officials in the 1960's.

Jesse Jackson – 33rd Degree Prince Hall Freemason (Top 100 African-American Freemasons).

Jack Kemp, R-Hamburg – 33rd Degree Freemason.

Newt Gingrich – Freemason.

Ronald Reagan – was a Freemason who was nearly sacrificed on March 30, 1981, at 3:30p.m. March is the third month (first 3), and 3:30p.m. provides the other two threes (33), producing a 333. Reagan signed into law the 'Immigration Reform and Control Act', section 100, which authorizes identification methods such as invisible tattoos or electronic media under the skin 'Mark of The Beast'. Reagan was a member of the satanic Bohemian Grove in Northern California. Reagan signed reverse mortgage insurance legislation on Feb 5, 1988 knowing that it would increase U.S. debt. Moreover global elites knew that reverse mortgages would allow the U.S. Government [Federal Reserve] to buy back large numbers of privately owned properties from aging U.S. citizens. An intended consequence of this program was that it would eliminate the biblical tradition of leaving children an inheritance.

"A good [man] leaveth an inheritance to his children's children: and the wealth of the sinner [is] laid up for the just" - Proverbs 13:22

The reverse mortgage program is one of many tools being leveraged by government to realize George H.W. Bush's anti-constitutional 'Agenda 21', which calls for the elimination of private property ownership throughout America.

I realize that Irish American President Ronald Reagan to this day is a sacred cow for millions of mentally enslaved Christian American's. Nonetheless it doesn't erase the fact that President and Mrs. Reagan were occult practitioners while in the White House, which explains the pictures below of Ronald Reagan holding up devil horns and the 666 hand-sign [pg. 84]. During Ronald Reagan's Presidency (1981-1989) Mrs. Reagan sought astrological advice on a regular basis from Irish American Joan Quigley. The Reagan Presidency was so dependent on the advice of their New Age, anti-Christian Theosophist; Nancy Reagan would hold regular conference calls with

83

Quigley. It was during these calls where Quigley would advice America's President and First Lady when and where to hold Presidential events, etc. In a book titled 'What Does Joan Say?' Occult practitioner Joan Quigley wrote the following about her experience with the Reagan's:

"Not since the days of the Roman Emperors [Nero] - and never in the history of the United States Presidency ¬ has an astrologer played such a significant role in the nation's affairs of State." - Joan Quigley

"Reagan was responsible for implementing Communist directives." - Charlotte Iserbyt, Senior Policy Advisor in the Office of Educational Research and Improvement (OERI), U.S. Department of Education, during the first Reagan Administration. deliberatedumbingdown.com

Consider the fact that when the Reagans retired, they moved into a house on "666 St. Cloud Road" in Southern California.

President James Carter – Member of the Council of Foreign Relations. President Carter's Secretary of State was commissioned by the Club of Rome to write 'The Global 2000 Report'. This was a plan to reduce the world's population through war, famine, disease e.g., HIV/ Aids. President Carter's National Security Advisor, in concert with David Rockefeller, wrote 'The Technetronic Era'; this was a post-industrial zero growth plan designed to cripple United States' industry in order to prepare Americans for satanic theosophists 'New World Order'.

Vice President Walter Mondale – Freemason.

President Richard Nixon – Member of Council of Foreign Relations; cannot confirm Freemason status. President Nixon was the only President of the United States to mock the "goings-on" at satanic Bohemian Grove. In an interview he stated: 'It was the most faggy thing I've ever seen'. President Nixon was then eliminated from the presidency.

84

Vice-President/President B. Lyndon Johnson – Freemason. LBJ had this to say after signing the 1964 Civil Rights Act into law:

"These Negroes, they're getting pretty uppity these days and that's a problem for us since they've got something now they never had before, the political pull to back up their uppityness. Now we've got to do something about this, we've got to give them a little something, just enough to quiet them down, not enough to make a difference."

LBJ said this to two governors on Air Force One, "I'll have them niggers voting Democratic for the next two hundred years." Lyndon B. Johnson is also responsible for signing into law The Gun Control Act of 1968 (GCA or GCA68) a U.S. federal law that regulates the firearms industry and firearms owners. What many American's do not know is that the 1968 GCA is based on the Nazi's Weapon's Law of 1938.

Vice-President Hubert Humphrey – Freemason.

President Dwight Eisenhower – Member of Council of Foreign Relations. Signed executive order to study man's impact on the Earth. The study concluded that by the year 2000 Planet Earth would self-destruct due to increased population and man's exploitation of the environment. The Jason Society confirmed the findings and called their recommendations 'Alternatives 1, 2, 3'.

President Harry Truman – The only United States Freemason President to be awarded a Freemason fifty-year award. President Truman is quoted as saying: 'I've got every degree in the masons that here is', Member of the Council of Foreign Relations.

President Franklin D. Roosevelt – Freemason. President Roosevelt once said: 'In politics, nothing happens by accident. If it happens, you can bet it was planned that way'. Roosevelt went on to admit: 'The real truth of the matter is, as you and I know, that a financial element in the large centers has owned the government ever since the days of Andrew Jackson.' Roosevelt is responsible for the satanic all seeing eye being placed on the U.S. Dollar. Roosevelt also once said:

"I wish very much that the wrong people could be prevented entirely from breeding... the many immigrants from Scotland, Ireland and the Orient were a threat to American society."

President Herbert Hoover – President Hoover refused to implement the Emergency Banking Relief Act of 1933. Member of satanic Bohemian Grove. Freemason

85

membership unknown.

President Calvin Coolidge – Related to Presidents Harrisons, Jefferson, Jackson, Truman, and Lyndon Johnson. Mason membership unknown.

President Warren Harding – Freemason. President Harding is quoted saying 'I have no trouble with my enemies, but my friends keep me walking the floor nights'.

Woodrow Wilson – Friends with Colonel Edward Mandell House who was a founder of the American Institute of International Affairs, known today as the Council of Foreign Relations, an outer layer of the Royal Institute of International Affairs (RIIA), whose purpose was to retake the United States as a British Colony. RIIA is the outer layer of the main core of a secret establishment called the Circle of Initiates founded by Theosophical cult member Cecil Rhodes. Rhodes founded The Rhodes Scholarship, which is an international postgraduate award for selected foreign students to study at the University of Oxford. However, based on Cecil's circle of friends, penchant for Satanism and stated goal of revitalizing Nimrod's old world order of Babylon; I believe Rhodes University gets its name from the ancient "Colossus of Rhodes" c.280 BC, a statue of the Greek titan-god of the sun "Helios" or Apollyon otherwise known as "The Beast from the pit" – Revelation 9:11. Again, President Bill Clinton is a Rhodes Scholar. Woodrow Wilson is best known for signing the Rockefeller/ Rothschild designed Federal Reserve Act. Following this decision, President Wilson is quoted as saying: 'I have unwittingly ruined my Country'. A complete history of the Federal Reserve Corporation formation can be read in the book titled: 'The Creature From Jekyll Island.'

President William Howard Taft – Freemason. The Taft family dates back to Braintree Mass, which in 1679 helped start the Skull & Bones Order and at least eight members of the Taft family, have been members of the Order.

President Theodore Roosevelt – Freemason. He was blood related to both President Martin Van Buren and President Franklin Delano Roosevelt.

President William McKinley – Freemason. Owned by John D. Rockefeller

President Grover Cleveland – Freemason. He won the Presidential race with a great deal of support from John D. Rockefeller's Standard Oil.

President James Garfield – Confirmed Freemason. He was cousin to Presidents Franklin Pierce and Grover Cleveland and Benjamin Harrison. He was assassinated because he resisted the satanic Theosophical banking elites' plans.

President Ulysses S. Grant – He was related to the Presidents Theodore Roosevelt, Franklin Roosevelt, Washington, Van Buren, and Taft. President Grant sent troops into nine counties of South Carolina to enforce a proclamation commanding the residents to give up their arms and ammunition. Grant suspended the writ of Habeas Corpus and more than 600 arrests were made.

President Andrew Johnson – Confirmed Mason. Did not have a Vice President during his term. One year after the assassination of Abraham Lincoln, Albert Pikes Supreme Council met in full costume inside the White House. There President Lincoln's successor, President Andrew Johnson, granted a pardon to Pike for his role in the murder of President Lincoln.

President Abraham Lincoln – 33rd Degree Freemason. There was a rumor that he was a Rosicrucian (which is a branch of Freemasonry). Lincoln's wife, Mary Todd, was related to the satanic Collins Family and was into the occult. President Lincoln was assassinated because he resisted Church of Babylon banking elite proxies.

President George Washington – Freemason. Was bled to death by a Freemason doctor attempting to balance the 'four-humors' in Washington's blood.

Eric Cantor, Republican Whip for the 111th Congress. Representing Virginia's 7th District since 2001. Cantor is both an anti-Christian Talmudist and Satanic Freemason. He's a member of the Fraternal Lodge No. 53 in Richmond Virginia.

Chuck Grassley, Republican Senator of Iowa - served 5 terms. Grassley is a Satanic Freemason

Jon Tester, Democrat Senator, for Montana - Satanic Freemason

Mike Enzi, Republican Senator of Wyoming - Satanic Freemason

Nick Rahall, Democrat Congressman of West Virginia reelected 14 times - Satanic 33rd degree Mason. When asked by a CNN reporter 'so are you trying to rule the world?' Rahall responded '...if we were, would I tell ya? No.'   87

Arlen Specter, Senator from Pennsylvania - Satanic Freemason at E. Coppe Mitchell Lodge No. 605 and anti-Christian Talmudist

Mark Hatfield, Republican Senator from Oregon - member of Oregon Pacific Freemason Lodge No. 50

RNC Chairman Reince Priebus in 2013 offered on a number of occasions to 'tattoo ObamaCare on the foreheads of Democrats'. What makes Mr. Priebus statement suspect is the fact that the bio-surveillance weapon named 'Obamacare' contains a number [mark]. With that in mind what Mr. Priebus is proposing is the tattooing of a number [mark of the beast] on the foreheads of Americans.

John Quincy Adams, America's Sixth President said the following about Satanic Freemasonry: "I am prepared to complete the demonstration before God and man, that the Masonic oaths, obligations and penalties, cannot, by any possibility, be reconciled to the laws of morality, of Christianity, or of the land."

James Madison, the Fourth President of the United States said: "From the number and character of those who now support the charges against Freemasonry, I cannot doubt that it is at least susceptible of abuse, outweighing any advantages promised by its patrons."

Samuel Adams, the Father of the American Revolution said: "I am decidedly opposed to all secret societies whatever!"

John Hancock, President of the Continental Congress said: "I am opposed to all secret societies."

Paul Revere was a 33 degree Freemason. Revere's famous ride to Lexington warning 'The British are coming' originated inside of a Boston tavern named 'Green Dragon Tavern'. This tavern was owned by the St. Andrews Lodge of Freemason's in 1766. The basement was used by secret societies and became known as the 'Headquarters of the Revolution'. Both the Boston Tea Party and American Revolution were planned by Freemason's inside of the Green Dragon Tavern a name which pays homage to the Serpent Tribe of Dann. If you would like to learn more about, The Serpent Cult of Dann, please read my book, Deception: The Ancient Mystery That Holds The Secret of Newgrange at, KillingIreland.com.

CHAPTER

10   The Lucifer Connection

"he must, as a Satanist, knowing this, realizing what his human potential is, eventually, and here is one of the essential points of Satanism... each man, each woman is a god, or goddess in Satanism" - Anton LaVey, Church of Satan Founder [right]

"...and ye shall be as gods. [Satan]"
- Genesis 3:5

Pres. Bill Clinton   Hillary Clinton   Pres. Ronald Reagan

Navy Adm. McRaven Iran Pres. Ahmadinejad Italian PM Berlusconi

Pope Francis   French Pres. Sarkozy   Pres. George W. Bush

Donald Trump   Pres. Barack Hussein Obama

"The real Satanist is not quite so easily recognized as such"
- Anton Szandor LaVey, The Satanic Bible

"For we wrestle not against flesh and blood, but against principalities, against powers, against the rulers of the darkness of this
world, against spiritual wickedness in high places."
- Ephesians 6:12

SATAN

BAPHOMET

90

Philippine de Rothschild [left] is pictured
wearing a number of satanic emblems.
It's important for Christians to understand that the Rothschild family is one
of only a few families who own the privately held Federal Reserve Bank in the
U.S. Profits realized from U.S. Government loans are paid to the satanic Rothschild Family. In turn, the Rothschild's
reinvest these profits into groups and
individuals who share the Rothschild's
stated goal of eliminating Man from
planet earth. Rothschild's methods of
extermination include: (i) DNA Damaging pharmaceuticals; (ii) DNA crip-
pling genetically modified organisms
(GMOs); and (iii) the indoctrination of
Man into a homosexual lifestyle using
the Luciferian controlled entertainment
industry. It has been through the above
said methods that Luciferians have successfully marginalized the role of males
in our society, strategically placing the Y
gene on a path to extinction. This is why
Satanists, through their proxy 'Planned
Parenthood' advocates for an increase in
abortion and homosexuality? This too is

the reason Luciferians source, manufactures, and force feed the American male massive amounts of estrogen mimicking, endocrine disrupting, cancer causing, DNA damaging GMO soy? It's to eliminate Males.

Luciferian Professor Jenny Graves, of Canberra University, said the male Y chromosome is mostly 'junk' and that 'It's a lovely example of what I call dumb design. It's an evolutionary accident.' Luciferian Professor Steve Jones deems the Y chromosome "decayed, redundant and parasitic". Christian men must understand that our one true enemy [Satan] sees God's creation [Man] in this way, 'parasitic'.

Philippine Rothschild is the descendant of Mayer Amschel Rothschild a demon who built an empire on the credo:

"Who controls the issuance of money controls the government"
- Mayer Amschel Rothschild, c. 1775

M.A. Rothschild's philosophy is the wellspring from which the pestilence of politically correct speech, homosexuality, abortion, pornography, poverty, communism, socialism, war and famine emanate.

Philippine de Rothschild [below] is shown with her employee (IMF) Director Christine Lagarde. Through their IMF proxy the Rothschild's cripple the financial stability of Nations, promote high unemployment and increase poverty and death around the world. IMF headquarters is located inside the Rothschild's master corporation Washington, D.C.,

"A white male child of perfect innocence and intelligence makes the most suitable victim."
– Satanist Aleister Crowley

"I want blasphemy, murder, rape, revolution, anything, bad or good, but strong,"
– Aleister Crowley c.1895

"I wanted to get hold of Satan personally and become his chief of staff. Satan Cry Aloud! Thou Exalted Most High! Oh My Father Satan! The Eye!" – Aleister Crowley

"Do what thou wilt shall be the whole of the Law"
- Satanist Aleister Crowley ['The Beast 666'] from his 'Book of the Law' which was dictated to him by four demons: Nuit, Hadit, Ra-Hoor-Khuit and Aiwass

Jay-Z Promoting Satanist Aleister Crowley

Jay-Z Promoting Satanic Occult Pyramid

During one of the only non-televised games in the U.S., between the Cavaliers vs. Olympiacos), Lebron James was filmed court side signing the devil horns, ceremonial magic pyramid and the Mark of The Beast 666. Lebron James nickname is "King James," an obvious affront to the Christian American majority. 2012 marked the tenth year of James' partnership with NIKE and the release of the 'Lebron X' shoe. Again we see The Church of Babylon celebrating the 'X' of Nimrod. NIKE founder Phil Knight who is worth $18.4 billion purchased Will Vinton Animation Studios [VAS] in 2002.

Lebron James Promoting Satanic Occult Pyramid

VAS has worked for Sumner Redstone's CBS, Rupert Murdoch's FOX TV and The Walt Disney Company. When you support these organizations you're supporting militant anti-Christians.

In 1982 African-Irish American actor James Earl Jones [top right] appeared in 'Conan The Barbarian' aside Arnold Schwarzenegger, whose father btw was a Nazi. The over arching theme of the movie was centered mainly on the characterization of the Serpent Tribe of Dann. 1hr 56min into the film Jones is shown standing in front of the 'All-Seeing-Eye' of Satan, which is also associated with Osiris, Horus and Nimrod while stating:

Actor James Earl Jones w/All-Seeing-Eye of Satan

"...those who have corrupted the earth shall all be cleansed [murdered]"... In your hand you hold my light, the gleam in the eye of Seth"... "Burn you the way to paradise"... "Who gave you the will to live? I am the wellspring, from which you flow. When I am gone you will have never been."

93

There are a number of overtly satanic, anti-Christian and pro New World Order elements to this scene. First, Jones character's statement that "those who have corrupted the earth shall all be cleansed [murdered]" is a recurring theme found throughout 'Agenda 21' propaganda. Agenda 21 policies date back to the 1970's, however it really kicked into high-gear in 1992 at the Earth Summit in Rio de Janeiro. That's when Former C.I.A. director turned President George H.W. Bush and Prince Charles signed onto it. President and Mrs. Clinton saw to it that the anti-Christian Agenda 21 infected the entire U.S. Government. Visit Tom DeWeese's website for additional information at americanpolicy.org. Second, ancient texts tell us that the Babylonian god Nimrod promoted the worship of fire and sacrifice and ancient pyramid writings tell us that Seth was associated with active chaos and universal evil. After murdering Osiris, Seth [Satan] introduced 'divine moral evil' into our world.

This is why we see nothing but evil and chaos throughout Hollywood films and the music industry. The vast majority of celebrated writers, producers and directors throughout these industries worship Lucifer and are knowingly participating in the reemergence of Nimrod's One World Religion [Babylon]. As an aside, Inside of my book, Deception: The Ancient Mystery That Holds The Secret of Newgrange at, KillingIreland.com, I demonstrated how George Lucas' Star Wars Imperial Logo cryptogram is in fact the 'Mark of The Beast' 666. Coincidently, James Earl Jones was the voice of the iconic figure Darth Vader in George Lucas Star Wars franchise now owned by Walt Disney. James Earl Jones also provided the voice of "Mufasa" in Walt Disney's 'The Lion King' and its 1998 sequel, 'The Lion King II: Simba's Pride'. He was also an international host for Fantasia 2000. He also voiced Satan Claus in 'Recess Christmas: Miracle on Third Street'. He also voices Darth Vader in the Star Tours attraction at Disneyland and DisneyWorld's Hollywood Studios. He was also the narrator in 'Judge Dredd'.

Kobe Bryant flashing the universal gang sign for Satan [left]. Bryant was featured in a NIKE commercial titled 'KOBESYSTEM'. In it Bryant emerges from below a stage, flashing the all-seeing-eye of Satan, coming to rest with arms stretched out like Jesus Christ on the Cross.

During the commercial, a pyramid with stylized devil horns [FIG.1, pg.95] is flashed as well as a stylized

Baphomet logo containing a six pointed star. [FIG.2,] This star represents the Mark of the Beast. I have also superimposed Bryant's logo over the face of Baphomet [FIG.3] to illustrate my point.

NIKE's founder, Phil Knight, who is worth $18.4 billion, purchased Will Vinton Animation Studios [VAS] in 2002. VAS has worked for Sumner Redstone's CBS, Rupert Murdoch's FOX TV and The Walt Disney Company. Christians must realize that when they support these individuals and buy their products they're supporting militant anti-Christians.

Irish American actor Bradley Cooper said in an interview, regarding his audition for the movie 'Paradise Lost'. A movie by Legendary Pictures, the same group who employed Cooper in The Hangover movie:

"I love the idea of Lucifer being a... Um... You know... A very charismatic guy who you agree with. Basically, he makes a very sound argument" - Bradley Cooper

"I wanted to be the Amy Grant of music... It did not work out. So, I sold my soul to the devil." - Katy Perry [below]

In 2005, Katy Perry, who publicly stated she was a Satanist, was engaged in a legal battle with the, 'Sisters at Immaculate Heart of Marry,' (Catholic Nun convent). According to reports the L.A. Archbishop, Jose Gomez, didn't have the authority to sell the Nun's convent to Perry for $15 million. The bigger question here is, 'why would an admitted Satanist want to live in a Catholic Nun's convent?

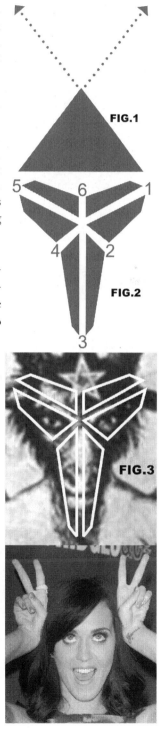

FIG.1

FIG.2

FIG.3

"I sold my soul to the devil"… Prince Hall Freemason, Al Sharp-
"I am a God" – Kanye West   ton Promoting Satanic Occult
Pyramid

Billionaire Rothschild
Family Proxy, Warren Buf-
fet, CEO of   Berkshire
Hathaway Promoting
Satanic Occult Pyramid

UFC's Joe Rogan wearing a 666 T-shirt, flashing Devil Horns with
his arm around Stanton Lavey, the son of
Church of Satan founder Anton Lavey

Rock Star Marilyn Manson, whose ancestors were Luciferian Talmudists, is an ordained "reverend" of Anton Lavey's Church of Satan. Lavey, whose ancestors were also Luciferian Talmudists, was a follower of Irish Freemason Aleister Crowley and white slave trader, Scottish American Herbert Arthur Sloane. Based out of Cleveland, Ohio, Sloane was the first person to have organized and led a specifically satanic religious group in America. Marilyn Manson says that his current lifestyle was inspired by his grandfather who practiced bestiality and sadomasochism. Manson has been known to rip-up the Holy Bible and spew "blasphemies" against Jesus Christ. Manson's concert T-shirts declare: "Kill Your Parents" and "I Love Satan". Other comments include:

"I don't know if anyone has really understood what we're trying to do. This isn't just about shock value . . . that's just there to lure the people in. Once we've got em we can give em our message."
- Hit Parader, Oct. 1996

"I think every time people listen to this new album maybe God will be destroyed in their heads." (huH, Oct. 1996, p.37)

"Hopefully, I'll be remembered as the person who brought an end to Christianity." (Spin, August 1996, p. 34)

"I have always been drawn to radical philosophies and alternative ways of thinking. Before 1990, I took a strong interest in certain issues; pedophilia was among them." He also adds, "I subscribed to the North America Man Boy Love Association (N.A.M.B.L.A) Bulletin"
- Anton Lavey

In 2007 Lavey's 'reverend' [Marilyn Manson] was accused of squandering his band's profits to purchase a child's skeleton and Nazi memorabilia. This explains why Satanists like Marilyn Manson admire satanic pedophiles like Lavey.

Magician Penn Jillete Flashing
Devil Horns

Church of Satan Member, Sam-my Davis Jr. Hugging Church of Satan Founder, Anton Lavey

Church of Satan Member, Jane Mansfield With Church of Satan Founder, Anton Lavey

Irish American Muscian Billy Corgan Wearing 666 Shirt

Muscian Bono Flashing Devil Horns

Musician Justin Bieber Flashing Devil Horns

Actress Katherine Heigl
Flashing Devil Horns

Actress Jada Pinkett Smith
Flashing Devil Horns

Television Host, Bill Maher
Flashing Devil Horns

Mike's Hard Lemonade Commercial Featuring Baphomet

"Woe unto him that giveth his neighbour drink,
that puttest thy bottle to him, and makest him
drunken also" - Habakkuk 2:15

99

"Good! I hope the Jews did kill Christ,
I'd do it again. I'd F***ing do it again in a second!"
- Sarah Silverman, 2006 Movie Titled: 'Jesus is Magic'

Comedian Sarah Silverman, pictured above holding a board containing the image of Lord Jesus Christ, is featured regularly on the cable channel 'Comedy Central'. In addition to the image of Christ on the cross there are some articles of clothing. These include a Satan outfit, women's clothing, etc. The inference here is that Lord Jesus Christ is gay and/or Satan. This picture echoes what is taught in the racist, Pharisee created, anti-Goyimite Babylonian Talmud about Jesus Christ and his followers. Other militant anti-Goyimite comics on Comedy Central include Jonathan Stuart Leibowitz (Jon Stewart - The Daily Show) who referred to the nativity as the "Vagina Manger". Leibowitz then refers to Jesus' mother as the "Vagina Mary". Comic Kathy Griffin, while receiving an Emmy Award, Pompously stated "Suck it, Jesus! This award is my god now." As an aside, Comedy Central is owned by Babylonian Talmudist Sumner Redstone [Rothstein]. Redstone also controls CBS Corporation, Viacom, Paramount Pictures, Simon & Schuster, MTV, Nickelodeon and National Amusements, Inc., a privately owned theater company. When you support these organizations you're supporting militant anti-Christians.

100

Quentin Tarantino, [top, left] flashing Devil Horns, is famous for gutter trash films such as Reservoir Dogs and Pulp Fiction. For years his sadistic story lines have provided the grease which coats the slippery slope of immorality. His latest film titled 'Django Unchained' was given the green light by the Church of Babylon because it effectively needles at the wounds of slavery in America. Cowards like Tarantino avoid portraying real black African history such as the 150 million Africans who were kidnapped, castrated, turned into sex-slaves and murdered by Pagan Arab and Arab Islam. Tarantino would never have the manhood to communicate to the world the fact that Islam's prophet Muhammad referred to black Africans as "raisinheads" and "Satan". Learn more about this subject at, RaisinHeads.com

Jamie Foxx [top, right] had this to say about his character in the film Django:

"I get free. I save my wife and I kill all the white people in the movie. How great is that?"

Jamie Foxx continued his hateful antichristian rhetoric at the SoulTrain Awards in 2012 stating:

"First of all, give an honor to God... And our Lord and Savior Barrack Obama."

Here a person wearing a "Jesus Saves" T-shirt is pretending to commit suicide. You'll also notice two lightning bolt shapes on her shirt which represent the 'Sol' or 'Sig'. These also mean 'Sun' and when two sig's are combined they make up the Nazi Swastika, which is commonly shown inside of a circle. The Swastika also creates an 'X' and an 'X' inside of a circle represents the Roman numeral 1000. In Greek the number 1000 means Helius or Apollyon the destroyer. In Revelations Apollyon is the Beast from Hell. The Sol also represents the Babylonian sun god Shamash, which is discussed in greater detail at www.killingireland.com. Lastly the all-seeing-eye of Satan pyramid hovers over the words 'Jesus Saves', which is of course mocking what the Christian American majority, believe. It takes a special kind of stupid to wear this shirt.

"a wicked man, He winketh with his eye, he speaketh with his feet, he teacheth with his fingers;" – Proverbs 6:12-13"

Musician 'Lady Gaga' Flashing 666 Hand-Sign   Musician Bono Flashing 666 Hand-Sign   Lil Wayne Flashing 666 Hand-Sign   President Lyndon Johnson Flashing 666 Hand-Sign

102

President George
H.W. Bush 666
Hand-Sign

President George
W. Bush Flashing
666 Hand-Sign

President Bill Clinton Flashing
666 Hand-Sign

David Graham, FDA
Official Under Bush,
Flashing 666 Hand-Sign

Senator Harry
Reid Flashing 666
Hand-Sign

French President, Sarkozy
Flashing 666 Hand-Sign

Israeli Prime Minister,
Benjamin Netanyahu,
Flashing 666 Hand-Sign

U.K. P.M.
Tony Blair,
Flashing 666
Hand-Sign

Musician Beyonce, Wife of
Jay-Z, Flashing
666 Hand-Sign

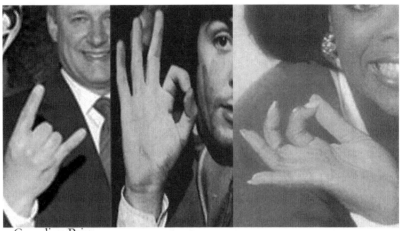

Canadian Prime Minister, Harper, Flashing Devil Horns Hand-Sign

The Beatles, Paul Mc-Cartney, Flashing 666 Hand-Sign

Oprah Winfrey, Flashing 666 Hand-Sign

"Their tongue is as an arrow shot out; it speaketh deceit:"
- Jeremiah 9:8

Muscian Justin Bieber, Flashing 666 Hand-Sign w/Tongue Shooting Out

Actor/Comedian, Eddie Murphy, Flashing 666 Hand-Sign

Actor Jackie Chan Flashing 666 Hand-Sign

World Wrestling Actor, John Cena, Flashing 666 Hand-Sign

Chief Talmudist Rabbi of Israel, Yona Metzger, Flashing 666 Hand-Sign

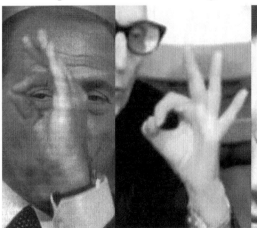
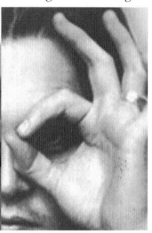

Italian President Berlusconi, Flashing 666 Hand-Sign

Jesuit Superior General, Pedro Arrupe, Flashing 666 Hand-Sign

Actor Johnny Depp, Flashing 666 Hand-Sign

105

Musician, Marshall Mathers "Eminem" Flashing 666 Hand-Sign

Donald Trump, Flashing 666 Hand-Sign

Grand Canyon Christian University Commercial, Cheerleader Flashing Devil Horns

Christian Apologist, Dr. Hugh Ross, "Big-Bang" Creationist, Flashing 666 Hand-Sign

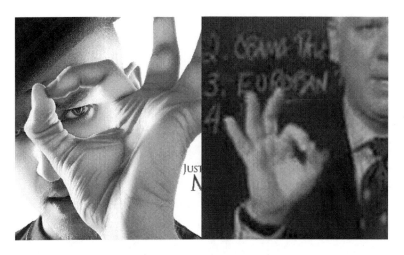

Musician, Justin Timberlake Flashing 666 Hand-Sign

Glenn Beck, Flashing 666 Hand-Sign

Magician Penn Jillette on Glenn Beck Show, Flashing 666

"There shall not be found among you any one that maketh his son or his daughter to pass through the fire, or that useth divination, or an observer of times, or an enchanter, or a witch, Or a charmer, or a consulter with familiar spirits, or a wizard, or a necromancer. For all that do these things are an abomination unto the LORD: and because of these abominations the LORD thy God doth drive them out from before thee." - Deuteronomy 18:10-12

Paramount Pictures' introduction features stars falling from the heavens encircling a pyramid shaped mountaintop. Even though there are just 22 stars in the Paramount Pictures logo, there is an obvious vacant space on the bottom right-hand side for a 23rd star. This is a subtle but common homage to Satan. For instance, the Rothschild Family leaves an empty seat at their dinner table for Satan. To illustrate how a star fits into this space I have placed a 23rd star in the empty space with an arrow pointing to it. Whether or not you consider the vacant spot for a 23rd star, Paramount's introduction clearly depicts Satan and his falling angels discussed in Revelation 12: 4-17. This is an affront to Christianity because it associates the stars [angels] who remained in heaven with God and associates them with Satan and the stars [angels] that he brought with him to earth. The fallen stars are then shown encircling the iconic Illuminati pyramid in the form of a mountaintop. Paramount is owned by Babylonian Talmudist Sumner Redstone [Rothstein]. Redstone also controls CBS Corporation, Viacom, Simon & Schuster, MTV, Nickelodeon and National Amusements, Inc. a privately owned theater company. Christians must understand that when they buy products and/or services from any of the aforesaid company's they're supporting militant anti-Christians.

Luciferians hold sacred the number 23 because to them it represents the value 2/3 which equals 66.6% [666]. This they believe represents the number of angels who remained in heaven with God, while 1/3 (33%) fell with Satan.

"And his tail drew the third part of the stars of heaven, and did cast them to the earth: and the dragon stood before the woman which was ready to be delivered, for to devour her child as soon as it was born. And the great dragon was cast out, that old serpent, called the Devil, and Satan, which deceiveth the whole world: he was cast out into the earth, and his angels were cast out with him. And when the dragon saw that he was cast unto the earth, he persecuted the woman which brought forth the man child. And the dragon was wroth with the woman, and went to make war with the remnant of her seed, which keep the commandments of God, and have the testimony of Jesus Christ."

- Revelation 12:4-17

Clearly the vast majority of previously featured images depict Presidents, Hollywood hypocrites, athletes and musicians, all inciting their minions of fans and constituents into a frenzied celebration of Luciferian iconography and ideology. Contrary to what many Christian Americans may be programmed into believing, the vast majority of these public figures didn't grow up under a rock; and they are certainly not as clueless as they would have you believe. Similar to that of Washington D.C., when Hollywood does something, you better believe they meant to do it.

"In politics, nothing happens by accident. If it happens, you can bet it was planned that way." - Franklin D. Roosevelt

Ancient Origins Of The Devil Horns Hand-Sign:

There are some who will argue that the previous images of politicians, entertainers, etc. flashing the so-called, 'Devil Horns' hand-sign are simply individuals using the internationally recognized sign 'I love you' or showing Harley Clark's 'Hook'em Horns' that he introduced in 1955. What's interesting is that Helen Keller (1880-1968) was instrumental in the Americanization of the deaf signing system. What's more, Helen Keller herself was heavily involved in occult sects such as Swedenborgianism and Helena Blavatsky's satanic Theosophy.

I'm not suggesting deaf people are 'Satanic'. In point of fact, many of the individuals we're examining throughout this book – the operative word here being 'individuals' – do not necessarily represent an entire community nor are they representative of an entire group of people. This is an important distinction to make and for the reader to understand, because Luciferians are masters at ad-hominem attacks, straw man arguments, circular reasoning and the appeal to authority. Quoting someone out of context or calling someone 'intolerant' or 'bigoted' in an attempt to stifle dissent is second, only to public execution, this has always been their primary weapon of choice.

Outside the fog of political correctness what everyone should be asking themselves about Helen Keller and her influence over American Sign Language (ASL) is… Did her membership in satanic Theosophy and other occult leaning groups inspire her to promote an interchangeable American Sign Language (ASL) hand sign for the deaf, whose conceived similarity of form and

110

meaning communicated both 'I love you' as well as 'I love Satan'? Before we condemn 'ASL' and Ms. Keller's promotion of her familiar hand sign, let's explore the origins of the 'I love you' sign' and its ancient meaning.

A similar sign is seen in ancient Greece (circa 7th Century B.C.), and is associated with the "Oneiroi". The Oneiroi were dark-winged Daimones (Demons) of dreams. Ancient texts tell us that the Oneiroi would emerge every night, like a flock of bats from their caves in Erebos, the land of eternal darkness. When people hold up the 'devil horn' sign they are in fact symbolizing the two gates the Oneiroi passed through to reach our world. The first gate made of two 'horns' represented prophetic god-sent dreams, while the second, made of ivory, represented nightmares or 'black dreams'.

According to Greek Historians, the leader of the Oneiroi was 'Morpheus', a god who appeared in the dreams of kings in the guise of a man, delivering messages from the gods. This ancient Greek 'God' sounds eerily similar to Theosophy's manufactured Antichrist named 'Maitreya', who has apparently unveiled himself to a number of world leaders, including former CIA Director and President George H.W. Bush an encounter that I discuss in subsequent chapters. Anyone who has watched the film 'The Matrix' knows who 'Morpheus' is. It's interesting that The Matrix was a computer generated representation of the type of world Luciferians are striving for. And today we have millions of people pledging their allegiance to Lucifer every time they flash the devil horns.

The aforesaid is man's first ancient interpretation of this horn like hand sign. So far, its connotation seems less than benevolent in nature. The second comes from the ancient Sanskrit language which first emerged circa 2,000 B.C. There are two hand signs in Sanskrit, both of which have components found within the 'I love you' and 'Devil Horns' hand sign. The first Ancient Sanskrit sign represents the American Sign Language ('ASL') equivalent of the letter 'L'. In Sanskrit the fingers are pointed down towards the ground and are defined as follows:

"Subjugates demonic passions;
manifests the pure spirit of
wakefulness"

In the spirit of understanding the possessed mind of theosophists and its founder, Helena Blavatsky, the devil horns hand sign is an occult tool which deceives Christians into placing spells on one another. Occultists believe that by inverting the ancient Sanskrit hand sign, practitioners of 'devil horns' are symbolizing the opposite of 'subjugating demonic passions'?

Helen Keller, who wrote a book titled: 'My Religion' proudly described her occult religious perspective on life and her enthusiasm for the teachings of mystic Emmanuel Swedenborg. I know some people might be upset at the idea of Helen Keller being labeled a Satanist, but unfortunately, all of the facts point in that direction. The book titled 'Light in My Darkness', originally published in 1927 as 'My Religion,' was a tribute to Emanuel Swedenborg whom Helen regarded as "one of the noblest champions true Christianity has ever known." This book is regarded as Helen Keller's spiritual autobiography in which she openly declares:

"the teachings of Emanuel Swedenborg have been my light, and a staff in my hand and by his vision splendid I am attended on my way."

Who Was Emanuel Swedenborg?

Emanuel Swedenborg, born February 8, 1688 was a Swedish scientist, philosopher, Christian mystic, and theologian. Contemporaries of Swedenborg agreed that he was an individual who espoused unorthodox religious beliefs and by today's standards would be considered esoteric. The way in which he personally defined the very transparent Christian faith leads many to believe that Swedenborg was in no way a follower of Lord Jesus Christ.

At age fifty-six Swedenborg says he entered into a 'spiritual phase'. It was during this phase, he supposedly experienced 'dreams and visions', eventually leading him to a place where he felt as though he was endowed by 'God' to recreate the Christian faith. Anytime someone announces that they've been provided instructions through 'visions' to recreate Christianity, you know that person is a false prophet. Christ was very clear about the fact that there was nothing left from the long list of promises provided throughout the New Testament. STRIKE #1

112

Swedenborg was vocal about his disdain for the biblical definition of 'salvation' through faith alone.

It's true that 'It is more blessed to give, than to receive" – Act 20:35, however it's through 'faith' and not of yourself that we are saved. STRIKE #2

Swedenborg subscribed to an esoteric philosophy whose definition of salvation was weighted heavily on the side of charity, rather than faith in Christ. STRIKE #3

Clearly, Swedenborg believed in a kind of Marxist like salvation, 'From each according to his ability, to each according to his need' – Karl Marx.

It goes without saying, charity is important in each of our lives; however, it's in no way a measure of one's ability to enter into the Kingdom of Heaven.

"For by grace are ye saved through faith; and that not of yourselves: [it is] the gift of God: Not of works, lest any man should boast. For we are his workmanship, created in Christ Jesus unto good works, which God hath before ordained that we should walk in them."
- Ephesians 2:8-10

"Therefore by the deeds of the law there shall no flesh be justified in his sight: for by the law is the knowledge of sin." - Romans 3:20

"Not by works of righteousness which we have done, but according to his mercy he saved us, by the washing of regeneration, and renewing of the Holy Ghost;" - Titus 3:5

The frightening fact is this type of satanic, Marxist, esoteric modernist Christianity, didn't die with Swedenborg. Today, leaders of Nations are preaching the abomination of collective salvation. Here's what the President of the United States, an avowed Christian, said in front of millions of people:

"You can take your diploma, walk off this stage and chase only after the big house and the nice suits and the other things that our money culture says you should buy, you can choose to narrow your concerns and live life in a way that tries to keep your story separate from America's, but I hope you don't, not because you have an obligation to those who are less fortunate, although I believe you do have that obligation; not because you have a debt to all those who helped you get to where you are today, although I do believe you have that debt to pay. It's because you have an obligation to yourself. Because our individual salvation depends on collective salvation."
– President Barack Hussein Obama

"For we wrestle not against flesh and blood, but against principalities, against powers, against the rulers of the darkness of this world, against spiritual wickedness in high places." - Ephesians 6:12

Swedenborg commonly referred to himself as a 'Mystikos' (mystic). What's a 'Christian mystic'? There's no such title in Christianity, as a 'Christian mystic'. The message, throughout the entire Holy Bible, is very straightforward if you read what is written in order and every promise in context. Blavatsky's satanic Theosophical society had this to say about Swedenborg:

"The modem revival of esotericism extends from Romantic Naturphilosophie to nineteenth-century occultism involving Swedenborgianism, Mesmerism, spiritualism, the ancient wisdom-tradition, and ceremonial magic and paramasonic orders." - Helena Blavatsky

It's the connection between Helen Keller and her admiration for both theosophy and Swedenborg that raises red-flags over her association with modern day sign language, specifically her influence over the 'I love you'/I worship Satan' hand sign. Keep in mind that it was Helena Blavatsky, who founded the Theosophical Society in 1875, who openly stated:

"It is Satan who is the God of our planet and the only God."
– Helena Blavatsky

114

It's clear that Keller's "knowledgeable teacher" Emanuel Swedenborg was possessed by demons. Couple that with her admiration for Theosophy and it's a short putt to occultism and the New Age Agenda. Take for instance, Swedenborg's proponents who wrote:

"The Enlightenment saw another occult revival, perhaps spurred by growing rejection of mainstream religion and increased democracy and freedom of conscience. The period saw the rise of occult fraternities, most notably Speculative Freemasonry and a revived Rosicrucian Brotherhood. Academic interest in ancient mystery cults such as those of Mithras and Dionysus began to develop. Emanuel Swedenborg pulled Christianity in a more mystical or occult direction."

The Holy Bible teaches us that anyone who 'pulls Christianity in a more mystical or occult direction" is of the Devil. Not to mention the fact that there is no way to pull Christianity in any direction; all Christians can do is follow Satan away from Lord Jesus Christ; and that's what 'mysticism', Theosophy, etc. is all about. Christ tells us to trust in all of his promises:

"Jesus answered him, I spake openly to the world; I ever taught in the synagogue, and in the temple, whither the Jews always resort; and in secret have I said nothing." - John 18:20

Again "mysticism" is in no way associated with Christianity mainly because there are no hidden meanings or 'secret knowledge'. These are deceptions used only by Satan. Scripturally, no man can claim that they have received knowledge from God which no one else has:

"Knowing this first, that no prophecy of the scripture is of any private interpretation. For the prophecy came not in old time by the will of man: but holy men of God spake as they were moved by the Holy Ghost." - 2 Peter 1:20-21

"has in these last days spoken to us by His Son, whom He has appointed heir of all things, through whom also He made the worlds"
- Hebrews 1:1,2

What are highly suspicious are the allegorical interpretations, of The Holy Bible that Swedenborg had created. Through his method, all events communicated 'higher truths' through the correspondence of both the spiritual and material worlds. It was during this time that he had attended the 'Last Judgment' and that this had taken place in 1757. Swedenborg expounded that this event created a New Christian Church and that it was his esoteric ideology that herald this 'New Age' of Christianity and that Christians should interpret this event as the real 'Second Coming'. I have to imagine this is where a large number of his followers had an 'Ah-Ha' moment and stepped back away from Swedenborg, anticipating a bolt of lightning any moment.

By the age of fifty-six, Swedenborg began having 'visions of the spiritual world' and during these experiences he said that he 'talked to angels and spirits'. Many of these encounters were with figures from The Holy bible, such as Moses and Jesus. Moreover, Swedenborg said that it were these same spirits who 'guided his interpretation of the Scriptures.'

In 1744, while living in the Netherlands, Swedenborg began experiencing 'strange dreams'. He constantly assaulted by belief and disbelief, having visions of both angelic and demonic states. What is evident is that he was very frightened, a common theme amongst those who open their souls up to demons.

We are told that Swedenborg didn't sleep and would sit for days in an almost catatonic state. Servants in his home commented that they were frightened listening to what he referred to as 'his conflicts with evil spirits'. According to Swedenborg, the Lord filled him with the doctrines of the New Church and that God permitted him to speak with demons and angels. This is who Helen Keller referred to as her spiritual advisor.

Swedenborg made no attempt to create his own version of Christianity. There was however a society that was created in 1787 with the goal of propagating his interpretations; the name of this new group is The Church of the New Jerusalem. It's this new esoteric order that has led astray people such as poets William Blake and William Butler Yeats. Apparently Swedenborg's followers were primarily made up of intellectuals.

116

The Church of Babylon which Poet William Blake attended was founded by a printer named Robert Hindmarsh who had a Methodist background. Hindmarsh's Church was an expansion of the satanic Theosophical Society established in 1783. We know from studying history that a number of Blake's fellow artists were Swedenborgians and that they all convened at the Theosophical Society which was renamed in 1785 to 'The British Society for the Propagation of the Doctrines of the New Church'. Throughout Blake's theological discussions, he would rant about how Christianity has 'duped man into spiritual inaptitude'.

We see exactly how 'Christian' Swedenborg really is when he explains the Divinity of the 'natural Universe' and how it has been corrupted by the Church. He annotates 'all secret knowledge, has been removed by the leaders of modern day religion'. He continues by saying that Christians have been misled by the church and they followed blindly into a life that's incapable of perceiving anything supernatural. Based on Swedenborg's ideology it is clear that he was receiving 'secret knowledge' from the exact same 'spiritual advisor' Helena Blavatsky followed.

Much like the founder of Theosophy, Blake began experiencing 'mystical visions'. He says that his work was influenced not only by his own supernatural experiences, but he was also persuaded by Jacob Boehme and Swedenborg. Blake's supernatural visions would eventually influence poet William Butler Yeats. What's more Blake would create the painting titled 'Ancient of Day' [pg. 118] which depicts the 'god of earth' (Lucifer) constructing a satanic Illuminati pyramid/all-seeing-eye of Satan. The Luciferian Rockefeller Family have an abstract modification of Blake's painting of Lucifer at their, 30 Rockefeller Plaza [pg. 119].

"Among these dark Satanic mills? Bring me my Bow of burning gold, Bring me my Arrows of Desire, Bring me my Spear: O clouds unfold! Bring me my Chariot of fire. I will not cease from Mental Fight, Nor shall my Sword sleep in my hand Till we have built Jerusalem In England's green and pleasant Land."

- William Blake
(From Milton, Preface c.1804

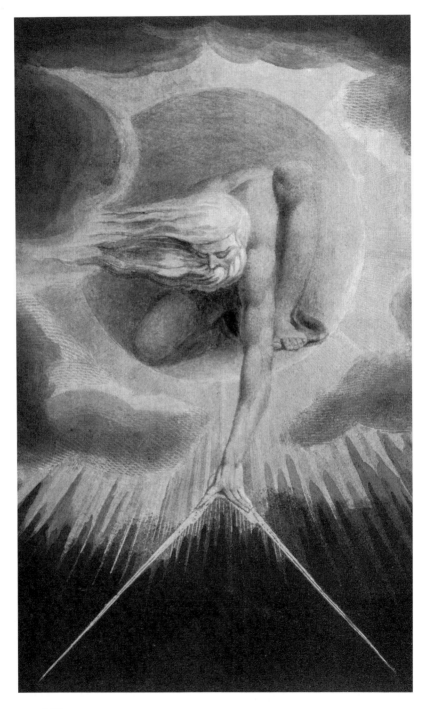

118

WISDOM AND ✳ KNOWLEDGE
✳ ✳ ✳ SHALL BE THE ✳ ✳ ✳
STABILITY OF THY TIMES

Eleven years after Blake's epic poem 'Milton', the Rothschild Family would seize control of the English Banking system in 1815. One hundred two years after taking complete control of the English Banking system and three years after WWI, the Rothschild Family would construct the Balfour Declaration in 1917, one of the most revolutionary documents in the twentieth century. It committed the British people to supporting the establishment in Palestine of "a National Home for the Jewish people," [Israel]. One hundred eighty-eight years after Blake painted the occult 'Ancient

119

of Day' the Rothschild Family in 1992 would finance and build the Israeli supreme court building [below]. At the upper most level of the court's library (representing the 33rd level of Freemasonry) is the base of a Luciferian pyramid, containing an all-seeing-eye of Satan, upside down crosses, etc. Just 9 years after the construction of this Satanic Temple, Israeli Intelligence (MOSSAD), would orchestrate the attacks on September 11, 2001. To discover the truth about 9/11, please read my book, 'On The Jews and Their Lies: 9/11' at, GoyToy.net.

"He that answereth a matter before he heareth it, it is folly and shame unto him." – Proverbs 18:13

As previously mentioned, the Israeli Supreme Court building is the brainchild of the Luciferian Rothschild family, whose net worth is estimated to be $100 trillion. Those closest to the Rothschilds report that the family leaves one seat at their dinner table empty for Lucifer. It will be remembered that Philippine de Rothschild wore Lucifer themed pendants around her neck, before her death. When the Rothschild's agreed to fund the Israeli supreme court building in 1992, they established the following stipulations: (i) they would choose the location, (ii) they would use their personal architect; and (iii) no one, other than the Rothschild's, would know the total cost of the facility, which we're told was ample.

Monday June 19, 1815 the day after Napoleon's defeat at waterloo. Baron Nathan Rothschild incites rumors throughout England's investment community that Napoleon had in fact won the battle at waterloo. This lie perpetrated by Rothschild allows Rothschild to take control of The Bank of England. In 1988 The Rothschild controlled Bank of England Museum is built. On display is a $28M gold bar pyramid encased inside of a larger occult pyramid.

"They shall cast their silver in the streets, and their gold shall be removed: their silver and their gold shall not be able to deliver them in the day of the wrath of the LORD: they shall not satisfy their souls, neither fill their bowels: because it is the stumblingblock of their iniquity." - Ezekiel 7:19

'Palace of Peace' [right], was designed by Fosters+Partners. According to their website their Satanic Temple, inside of Astana Kazakhstan, represents:

"a non-denominational contemporary building form, the pyramid is resonant of both a spiritual history that dates back to ancient Egypt as well as a symbol of amity for the future."

The truth of the matter is, nothing is friendly about this structure. This structure is blanketed in the, 'Star of Remphan (Satan)' - Acts 7:43. When the double-triangle is combined it creates the 'Mark of the Beast,' [666] - Revelation 13:16-18.

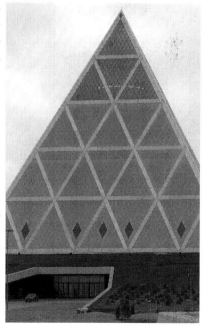

Foster+Partners is also the designer for New York Mayor Michael Bloomberg's "Bloomberg Place," a massive occult facility which will be built atop the ruins of a 2,000-year-old Luciferian Roman temple in the heart of London.

Located within feet of the Rothschild controlled Bank of England and Museum, "Bloomberg Place, roughly the size of a Manhattan city block, it is the future European home of Michael R. Bloomberg's company... Two bronze and stone towers, connected by sky-bridges atop the ruins of a 2,000-year-old Roman temple. In one corner of the development sits the Temple of Mithras, Walbrook, a relic from London's days under Roman rule. First uncovered in 1954, the temple, a sacrificial altar for an ancient religion, is being restored at Mr. Bloomberg's expense. Last month, a team of 55 archaeologists from the Museum of London were combing the temple site. Their efforts, paid for by Mr. Bloomberg, have turned up dozens of artifacts, including coins, pewter bowls, jewelry and, preserved just where it was found, a human skull." - New York Times February 7, 2013

Michael Bloomberg's temple is dedicated to the Babylonian sun god Shamash and Aion. The god Aion, also referred to as Chronos or deus leontocephalus was represented as a lion-headed human figure, much like the Babylonian demon god Pazuzu, standing atop a sphere containing the 'X' of Nimrod. What's more the god Aion is wrapped in the coils of a serpent signifying the Serpent Cult of Dann. When we read about the 12 tribes of Israel,

122

Dan was one of them however in [Revelation 7:5] Dan is no longer mentioned. I believe Dan's tribe is the men mentioned in [Jude 1:4] which reads, "For there are certain men crept in unawares, who were before of old ordained to this condemnation, ungodly men, turning the grace of our God into lasciviousness, and denying the only Lord God, and our Lord Jesus Christ." Modern day artists use the 'Scales of Justice" to represent the Tribe of Dann due to [Genesis 49:16-17] which states:

"Dan shall judge his people, as one of the tribes of Israel. Dan shall be a serpent by the way, an adder in the path, that biteth the horse heels, so that his rider shall fall backward."

Lastly the god Aion holds a key in his hand and has a thunderbolt on his chest signifying Zeus the father of Mercury also known as Helios or Apollyon, otherwise known as "The Beast from the Pit" – Revelation 9:11. The Mithraic religion rose to prominence in the 3rd century A.D., and though its roots extend much further back, its rituals were based on the concept of a savior, sacrifice, rebirth and was very much an Anti-Christian order. The select group of Roman males who worshiped here rose through its seven levels of enlightenment by means of formidable initiation ceremonies.

"The devil, of course, to whom pertain those wiles which pervert the truth, and who, by the mystic rites of his idols, vies even with the essential portions of the sacraments of God. He, too, baptizes some— that is, his own believers and faithful followers; he promises the putting away of sins by a layer (of his own); and if my memory still serves me, Mithra there, (in the kingdom of Satan,) sets his marks on the foreheads of his soldiers; celebrates also the oblation of bread, and introduces an image of resurrection." – Tertullian (c.160-225 AD), Prescription against Heretics, Chapter 40

Mithraic rituals were markedly pagan in nature. Services were held communally, followers sitting on benches either side of a narrow nave leading to a sacrificial altar. Slaying of bulls and Christian sacrifices were common in Mithraic rituals, as were shared meals of wine and bread, particularly on the festival of the 25th of December. Mithraic members intentionally chose December 25th because of its importance to Christians. This observance in particular acted as an affront to early Christians, and was meant to disrespect the divinity of Lord Jesus Christ. The demonic cult of Mithraism was a serious rival to Christianity and focused much of its efforts on the destruction of the New Testament. When Christianity became the dominant religion of the Roman Empire c.300 A.D., Constantine the Great focused much energy on dismantling everything Mithraic in sight.

123

You won't hear this on the BBC because in 2009 the BBC appointed a Muslim named 'Aaqil Ahmed' to head up all religious programming. If you're a Christian you should not be contributing to the BBC's viewership.

Bloomberg's restoration of a 3rd century amusement park of horrors and twisted obsession with Christian sacrifice should worry every Christian American. What should strike fear in the hearts and minds of every U.S. citizen is Doomberg's 4/16/2014 announcement that he would invest $50 million into a human exploitation psychology based organization 'Every town for Gun Safety'. His goal? To "battle for the hearts and minds of America". This sounds eerily similar to Attorney General Eric Holder, who said the government needs to "brainwash people into thinking about guns in a vastly different way." Doomberg's 'Every town for Gun Safety' will do nothing more than progress the Church of Babylon's agenda of (i) eliminating The Second Amendment, (ii) disarming of U.S. citizenry, and (iii) eliminating 90 percent (279M) of U.S. citizens.

Henry Kravis, co-founder of (KKR) private equity firm, is a major contributor to the emerging global, New World Order, technocracy. Kravis' acquisition of GoDaddy.com in 2011 gave Luciferians oversight on more than 45 million domain names worldwide or 40 percent of the global market. If you're a Christian business owner just getting started online, I ask that you consider purchasing your new domain name from an alternative domain registrar. If you currently own a domain through GoDaddy.com please consider transferring and/or renewing it under an alternative registrar.

Additional KKR assets include: RJR Nabisco which distributes toxic GMOs; Former CIA Director and four-star Army general David Petraeus; Sun Microsystems which capitalizes on the elite created Spy-Cloud Computing control initiative; Hospital Corporation of America which capitalizes on the Rockefeller created GMO plague currently being managed by the elite devised predictive 'shock management' algorithm and bio-surveillance weapon named 'Obamacare'. KKR and Mitt Romney's Bain Capital purchased Toys "R" Us which distributes toxic estrogen mimicking plastic toys and baby formula, fire retardant clothing, occult themed movies and toys to our children.

In December 2011 'KKR Capstone' executives (capstone referring to the top of an occult all-seeing-eye of Satan pyramid) took the Reins of GoDaddy.com. KKR owned Kindercare Learning Center [KLC] logo is a stylized pyramid and a capstone containing six notches. To Satanists the six notches inside of the capstone represent man above God. I have deconstructed the KLC logo [pg. 124] to illustrate the hidden design and meaning of KLC's Anti-Christian occult pyramid logo. You'll notice that the [KLC] logo is identical to the occult pyramids flaunted by the Satanic Rothschild Family.

KinderCare is a leading child-care provider which operates 1,149 centers in 39 states and has child-care contracts with both The Walt Disney Company and The Lego Group. If you're a parent who is currently utilizing a KLC facility or are considering their services, please consider the aforementioned information. Also, consider the fact that KLC has been accused in the past of being part of an institutional pedophile ring. In 1999 a director for Kindercare [Martin Gibbons] was charged with two counts of 1st degree child molestation. It's noteworthy to mention that KinderCare's Talmudic owner, Henry Kravis, is very close friends with George H.W. Bush, Henry Kissinger, and the Rockefeller Family.

The U.S. one dollar bill contains three hidden six pointed hexagrams [666]. Furthermore, each hexagram is comprised of two independent pyramids which forms the "Remphan" [Acts 7:43] which belongs to those who worship the "tabernacle of Moloch, the star of your god" [Satan] - Amos 5:26-27. To Satanists the top pyramid in this formation represents Man, while the bottom pyramid represents God. As you can see in the top image, the six pointed hexagram also contains a clue regarding who designed this satanic logo. The six points of the top hexagram point to the letters M. A. S. O. N... [*MASON*] referencing the satanic order of Freemasonry. Symbolically speaking, those who worship this satanic symbol are placing Man above God. What's more, these symbols are comprised of a six pointed star inside of a circle. This symbol is used during high ceremonial magic or witchcraft to summon demons. When you look at the 13 stars directly above the head of the eagle in the middle image, you'll see a hexagram and surrounding the hexagram are the 28 guidelines that make up a circle. Inside every point of this particular hexagram you'll notice a single star and to Satanists these six total stars represent Man. Furthermore, inside the center of this hexagram are seven stars and to Satanists these seven stars represent God. In other words, Satanists such as the Rothschild and Rockefeller Families believe this symbol signifies Man surrounding God or Man being placed above God. Lastly, the bottom image features the eagle. To occultists this image has always represented the messenger of Zeus [Mercury], also known as Apollyon, the destroyer from the book of revelations.

126

"Let no man deceive you by any means: for that day shall not come except there come a falling away first, and that man of sin be revealed, the son of perdition; Who opposeth and exalteth himself above all that is called God, or that is worshipped; so that he as God sitteth in the temple of God, shewing himself that he is God." - Thessalonians 2:3-4

"I [Satan] will exalt my throne above the stars of God"
- Isaiah 13-14

The Latin inscription atop the all-seeing eye of Satan [pg.126] reads: "Annuit Coeptus" Which means "He approves our undertaking." 'He' to Satanists means Lucifer.

Louis Farrakhan Muhammad Sr. [right] is shown holding a book with the Satanic, "Star of Remphan," [Acts 7:43]. It will be remembered that when the double-triangle is combined it creates the 'Mark of the Beast,' [666] - Revelation 13:16-18.

Farrakhan is the leader of The Nation of Islam (NOI) and is a self ascribed advocate for African Americans. The irony is that Arab Islam is responsible for the murder of 150 million black Africans. Compare Islam's slave history with that of Americas. America inherited 700,000 black Africans and their offspring were freed by white European Christians. What's more, the prophet of Islam, referred to black Africans as 'Raisin-Heads' and when asked to describe Satan, the Prophet of Islam told his followers that Satan looks like a black man. To examine these sources, please visit, RaisinHeads.com.

Given Farrakhan's lifelong strategy for achieving peace throughout the African American community, I have to say that his goal is quite possibly one of the biggest contradictions in terms. Why? Let's begin with Farrakhan's stated goal of achieving global peace. If this is genuinely one of Farrakhan's ambitions, then he should start with disassociating himself with groups whose stated goal it is to 'kill all white babies'.

"Kill 'All White' Men, Women, Babies, Blind, Cripple, Faggots, Lesbians & Old Crackers... Then dig'em up and kill'em again'
- Black Panther Party

127

Farrakhan is shown [pg. 127] speaking at the University of California, Berkeley, for the Afrikan Black Coalition Conference on Saturday, March 10, 2012. While addressing his audience Farrakhan stated:

"To those who dare, who arrogantly thought that they could frighten this generation as they used to frighten our parents ... so I ask you, 'What are you afraid of?' "Farrakhan said. "What is it I might say to your students, or your slaves?"

Farrakhan, at one point, briefly adopted a faux Asian accent and used gibberish after asking the audience if they had ever seen the Chinese picketing, drawing a gasp from some in the crowd. One female student quietly muttered "Oh no," when Farrakhan said he had "a word to the Jewish students" before warning against a U.S. or Israeli attack on Iran.

The absurdity of Farrakhan's entire persona reaches a crescendo when you consider Farrakhan speech [below], which advocates for a Luciferian, 'One World Order' [Babylon], is the very ancient fraternity responsible for the creation of slavery. During his speech, Farrakhan boasts that he has an elevated '90 degrees' of 'secret knowledge' well above the coveted 33 degrees so many deceived Freemasons strive to achieve. Farrakhan, seems to have received knowledge so secret they left out the fact that Freemasonry was created by Satanic Talmudists, who harbor an ancient disdain for black people and anyone who is not a Talmudist. If you would like to learn more about the Toxic history of Talmudism, please read the book, 'On The Jews and Their Lies: 9/11' at, GoyToy.net.

"Now you don't have to keep the secret anymore Masons and Shriners, because the secret is out. Your job is to help me build the kingdom of god on earth [Church of Babylon] and only then will you have a place in the kingdom... If you don't help me deliver this people that you have sworn to keep down and build a world that all of us can live together in peace then you will find yourself under the sword of the judgment of god... You hold key positions all over America. In Government, in business, in law, in medicine, in education, in finance, in trade and commerce and you have used that authority to keep the black man on the bottom of society... If you're the Moslem son. Who's your father? Who is the Moslem that you're the son of? And what should the son do to help the father? Before the honorable Elijah Muhammad left he said to me quote. 'You may sit in my seat as the father over the house in my absence'. So I'll ask it again. What should you do to help the father that you are the son of? And if you help us god will show you mercy... We have a sheep that is lost in the house of Israel. But in his DNA he's connected to the

128

symbol of Freemasonry, the square and the compass... If you're only at 33 degrees, this is where you are, you're just crawling around with your little child like knowledge... I must say respectively to our Ufologists what you're looking at is the wisdom of the gods. What you're dealing with is the wisdom of man and a little man at that. So when you marvel at what you see from that wheel you're marveling at the wisdom of god who is also a human being." – Louis Farrakhan

"And call no man your father upon the earth: for one is your Father, which is in heaven." - Matthew 23:9

"...and ye shall be as gods" - [Satan], Genesis 3:5

"Surely, if masons really understood what Masonry is, as it is delineated in these books, no Christian Mason would think himself to remain at liberty to remain another day a member of the fraternity. It is as plain as possible that a man, knowing what it is, and embracing it in his heart, cannot be a Christian man. To say he can is to belie the very nature of Christianity."

- Irish American evangelist Charles Finney, responsible for the Christian revival throughout America c.1830, Book titled: FREEMASONRY Pg.115

To illustrate how pervasive Luciferianism is throughout our Christian institutions, we're going to examine one of the most famous symbols inside of the Catholic Church. Christograms assign monograms and/or combinations of letters that form an abbreviation for the name of Lord Jesus Christ. These man-made interpretations have been used in Latin since the seventh century. It is important however for believers in Jesus  Christ to understand that the first use of IHS in an English document appears in 1400AD. We are told that the IHS monogram was carved into a catacomb in Rome around the time of Emperor Nero; however, its creator has never been identified nor has its meaning. We're told that Franciscan disciple Bernardine popularized the use of the three letters on the background of a blazing sun to supposedly 'displace' the popular pagan symbol. The problem with this story is if you want to get rid of something you don't restore it for the world to see. Saint Bernardino not only restored the popular pagan sun god symbol of Halios, he was instrumental in making the pagan symbol synonymous with Lord Jesus Christ. Christians are cautioned by Lord Jesus Christ in Acts 17:24 to worship nothing man-made:

"God that made the world and all things therein, seeing that he is Lord of heaven and earth, dwelleth not in temples made with hands."

Upon closer evaluation of the IHS symbol [pg.129], what we find is one the most blasphemous, anti-Christ symbols on earth. First, there is the cross inside of a circle. A cross inside of a circle represents the Roman numeral 1000 and in Greek this represents Halios, otherwise known as Apollyon, the beast from The Book of Revelation. Next, we have the sun emblazoned behind the IHS monogram. The sun represents the son of Zeus commonly referred to as the sun God a.k.a. Apollyon the destroyer in The Book of Revelation. What's more the symbol of Saturn is just like the "h" and "t" letters fused.

What is most disturbing about this man-made 'Holy' symbol is what it spells. When we look at an inventory of the letters used in this man-made symbol we find the letters S...H...I...T... SHIT!

This blasphemous icon is one of the best examples I can point to why Lord Jesus Christ warned his followers to not worship man and/ or man-made symbols.

"Howbeit in vain do they worship me, teaching for doctrines the commandments of men." - Mark 7:7

"And they brought forth the images out of the house of Baal, and burned them." - 2 Kings 10:26

The Egyptian obelisk is one of the most widely used satanic occult symbols on earth. It's important for Christian Americans to understand that these monuments stand in reverence to both the Babylonian god Nimrod and the Egyptian god Osiris. Ancients tell us that Osiris was chopped into thirteen pieces by Seth. The wife of Osiris, obsessed with her husband's penis, searched far and wide for it; we're told that Osiris' penis was eaten by a fish. Osiris' lost penis is symbolized in these Egyptian obelisks which are commonly located inside of a circle, which represents female genitalia. These occult altars, which honor the 'God' Osiris, inhabit a number of well-known public and private grounds throughout the world.

130

One of the world's most famous occult obelisks is the Washington Monument. The monument began construction nearly fifty years after the death of President Washington and has absolutely nothing to do with the former President. The monument in fact stands in honor of Nimrod the Progenitor of global tyranny. Like Satan Nimrod possessed the minds of men and caused them to rebel against God. What's curious is the fact that the assembly of the Washington monument commenced in 1848, the same year the founder of Theosophy Helena Blavatsky began the development of her one world religion. This may explain the Washington Monuments demonic measurements; such as each side of the monument measures 666 inches and its height is exactly 6,666 inches.

Historian Michael Bradley talks about the Washington Monument in his book Secrets of the Freemasons on pg. 163:

"The Washington Monument, which lies directly west of the Capitol, is an obelisk, a tall, four-sided stone pillar tapering toward a pyramidal top. Most people are aware that an obelisk is Egyptian in origin, but few know the story behind it, and fewer still that it is an important Masonic symbol."

Aleister Crowley

Irishman Aleister Crowley was known as 'The Great Beast 666'. Crowley is best known as the most evil man to have ever existed. He has deceived countless souls to follow Satanism, mysticism, magic, ceremonial human/animal sacrifice, and is the father of the religious philosophy of Thelema. In his role as the founder of the Thelemite philosophy, he came to see himself as the prophet who was entrusted with informing humanity that it was entering the new Aeon of Horus in the early 20th century.

It's unsurprising that we find Crowley's malevolent philosophy and writings are in large part inspired by Satanist poet William Blake. Crowley credits Blake when he writes:

"It has struck me - in connection with reading Blake that Aiwass, etc. 'Force and Fire' is the very thing I lack. My 'conscience' is really an obstacle and a delusion, being a survival of heredity and education."
– Aleister Crowley 1906

131

In keeping with the rich tradition of Demonic possession as practiced by Blake, Swedenborg Blavatsky, Anton LaVey, and others, Crowley too claimed that he had been contacted by a 'Holy Guardian Angel' in 1904 while visiting Egypt. It was during this Demonic Possession by a Demon named 'Aiwass' that secret knowledge was imparted unto Crowley. It's this Demonic influence that would inspire Crowley to write 'The Book of The Law'. It's this secret knowledge which is the basis for Crowley's philosophy known as 'Thelema'. Crowley, would go on to found his own occult society named The A.A. and eventually become the leader of Ordo Templi Orientis (O.T.O.) before founding the religious commune in Cefalu known as The Abby of Thelema, which he led from 1920-1923. Amidst widespread opposition, Crowley was forced to abandon the commune, forcing him into seclusion back in Great Britain. Crowley continued to promote Thelema until his death, in 1947.

In addition to being a proponent of Satanism and homosexuality, Crowley was a heavy drug user. One of Crowley's most prominent homosexual conquests was famed Irish writer, poet and Freemason Oscar Wilde. Oscar Wilde is best known for his homoerotic novel 'Picture of Dorian Gray'. Wilde is a tragic figure who came from an affluent family; his father, William Wilde, was a prominent surgeon who had a number of curious interests, one of which was his collection of skulls. It's reported that William Wilde owned the skull of Jonathan Swift. Swift is best known for his book 'Gullivers Travels' as well as an essay titled: 'A Modest Proposal for Preventing the Children of Poor People From Being a Burden to Their Parents or Country'; in it Jonathan Swift suggests that poor Irish mothers and fathers should sell their children to Church of Babylon members as food. Swift then goes into vivid detail as to the best ways in which to cook their poor Irish children. Some suggest that Swifts recommendations were mere satire, others dispute these claims. Child sacrifice by The Church of Babylon throughout history is well documented and continues to this day throughout Europe and America.

Throughout my book, Deception: The Ancient Mystery That Holds The Secret of Newgrange at, KillingIreland.com, I provide ample data regarding the Luciferian vendetta against people of Christian Celtic and Pictish ancestry. One example of this is how thousands of children of Celtic ancestry are clandestinely sacrificed to Gilles de rais' Old World Satan every year. For instance in 2014, the International Common Law Court of Justice (LCLCJ) in Brussels is investigating numerous children's murders connected to the Ninth Circle Satanic Child Sacrifice Cult network. Death certificates were released on the 796 Irish children, ages two months to nine years, found in a cistern (septic tank) used as a mass grave at the Catholic St. Mary's Mothers and Babies Home near Taum, Ireland. LCLCJ forensic experts have confirmed the decapitation and dismemberment of babies in the mass grave resembled the usual signs of ritualistic murder. The Ninth Circle was/is directly linked to underground Satanic Cult networks throughout American including a large one in South Dakota.

As an aside each year members of The Church of Babylon gather at Bohemian Grove, located in Northern California, to worship a 50ft owl shrine, representing the demon god Moloch. Moloch is also linked to the Babylonian demon goddess Lilith who is associated with the theft and murder of children. It's during this blood lust ceremony at Bohemian Grove that member's burn a small child in effigy, all the while dressed in red and black cloaks, chanting incantations to their Babylonian demon god. To see for yourself, go to youtube.com and search for 'Bohemian Grove by Alex Jones' infowars.com. There you will be able to watch the actual ritual. You may be surprised to learn that most United States Presidents, Vice Presidents, Congressmen, Senators, International World Leaders, etc., have all participated in these satanic rituals.

Not quite as stunning as Presidents participating in child sacrifice, William Butler Yeats recounts a story where Oscar Wilde's father, William Wilde, removed the eyes of a man once, and then proceeded to feed them to a cat.

Towards the end of his life, Oscar Wilde would describe himself as simply a pawn used by the satanic global elites of his day to corrupt the morality of society. Oscar Wilde was convicted of homosexual offences in 1895 and sentenced to two years of hard labor in prison, It's between January to March 1897 that Wilde would write a 50,000-word letter in which he coldly examines his career to date, stating that he had simply been a colorful agent provocateur in Victorian society, his art, like his paradoxes seeking to subvert as well as sparkle. He considered himself one who, "stood in symbolic relations to the art and culture of my age".

133

Wilde, in a moment of spiritual clarity and free from the chains of Satan, finally realizes that throughout his entire life, he has been nothing more than a useful idiot utilized by The Church of Babylon to inspire arrogance and vanity throughout society. Wilde's epiphany reads eerily similar to that of our own American movie and music industry. Does it not?

It is said that during Oscar Wilde's incarceration he requested the Holy Bible in French, Italian and German. Wilde's spiritual journey throughout his prison stay would lead him to redemption and fulfillment. Wilde commented on a number of occasions that his incarceration had filled his soul with the fruit of experience, however bitter it tasted at the time. He states:

"I wanted to eat of the fruit of all the trees in the garden of the world... And so, indeed, I went out, and so I lived. My only mistake was that I confined myself so exclusively to the trees of what seemed to me the sun-lit side of the garden, and shunned the other side for its shadow and its gloom."

It is reported that towards the end of Oscar Wilde's life, he would receive the salvation of Lord Jesus Christ and renounce the trappings of occultism that had irrevocably altered his earthly body.

Oscar Wilde's life story is a redemptive one, in that it proves God's grace and salvation is never taken off the table. It's also just one example of the countless many who are deceived on a daily basis by the lies of mortal men and women such as Helena Blavatsky, Aleister Crowley, The Rothschild Family, The Rockefeller Family, Adolf Hitler, Anton Lavey, Zbigniew Brzezinski, George H.W. Bush, George W. Bush, Bill Clinton, Barack Hussein Obama, Hilary Clinton, etc. Crowley's entire life and those that he touched became a revolt against the moral and religious values that made The United Nations of America the greatest Nation the world has ever known. Crowley's libertinism and the much celebrated rule, "Do What Thou Wilt" gained him popularity as 'The Wickedest Man in The World'.

Even though there is ample evidence that proves Aleister Crowley is nothing more than a sexual deviant inspired by the writings of William Blake, a man who admits being under the possession of demonic spirits, this perverted conman con-

134

tinues to be the most influential figure throughout the occult world. A 2002 British Broadcasting Company (BBC) poll described Crowley as being the 73rd greatest Briton of all time. Not surprising, considering Great Britain abandoned Lord Jesus Christ long ago. Most troubling of all is the fact that the occult is so widespread throughout Great Britain, England, etc., that homes are having witches' brooms installed onto their chimneys.

References to Aleister Crowley are found throughout Hollywood, the music industry, etc. He's also been named a 'key influence' to a number of esoteric groups and individuals, such as the founder of Scientology, L. Ron Hubbard, who referred to Aleister Crowley as 'My very good friend''. Then, others who have been influenced by Crowley are musicians Marilyn Manson, Alan Moore, Kenneth Grant, Kenneth Anger, Jack Parsons, Gerald Gardner, Robert Anton Wilson, Timothy Leary, Jimmy Page and Austin Osman Spare. Two of Aleister Crowley's biggest proponents are billionaire rapper Jay-Z and his wife 'Beyonce'. It will be remembered, Jay-Z wearing a t-shirt with Aleister Crowley's satanic golden rule: 'Do What Thou Wilt'. Both he and his wife regularly flaunt satanic iconography throughout their videos, lyrics, etc. Moreover, they are regularly seen wearing satanic jewelry and accessories. Jay-Z goes out of his way to associate himself with anti-Christ's and individuals known for their anti-Christian philosophy. For instance Jay-Z has an album called The Black Album the opposite of the Beatles White Album. Recently an associate of Jay-Z named "DJ Dangermouse", a hip-hop producer, combined the White and Black albums to create the Grey Album. In the Grey Album one can clearly hear the voice of Jay-Z saying "Murder, Murder Jesus 666" and "Kill Catholics".

Couple the aforesaid with the well documented fact, that 'The Beatles' were known to have been followers of Aleister Crowley's satanic laws. This explains the pictures of John Lennon flashing the devil horns hand sign and Paul McCartney flashing the 666 hand sign. The band was so smitten with the most evil man in the world that they even put Aleister Crowley on the cover of their album titled Sgt Pepper's Lonely Hearts Band.

A series of weekly articles entitled "How Does a Beatle Live?" appeared in the London Evening Standard during March 1966. Written about John Lennon, Ringo Starr, George Harrison, and Paul McCartney, the four articles were completed by journalist Maureen Cleave. Well known by all four Beatles, Cleave had interviewed the group regularly since the start of 'Beatle mania' in the United Kingdom. Three years previously she had written of them as "the darlings of Merseyside" and had accompanied them on the plane to the United States when they first toured there in January 1964. For her lifestyle series in March 1966, she chose to interview the group individually rather than all together as was the norm.

Cleave interviewed Lennon on March 4, 1966. After encountering a full-size crucifix, a gorilla costume and a medieval suit of armor on her excursion through his home, Kenwood, in Weybridge, she found a well-organized library with works by Jonathan Swift, Oscar Wilde, George Orwell and Aldous Huxley. John Lennon stated to Cleave that these figures all influenced his ideas about Christianity.

Cleave quoted a comment John Lennon made regarding his desire to see Christianity exterminated:

"Christianity will go. It will vanish and shrink. I needn't argue about that; I'm right and I'll be proven right. We're more popular than Jesus now; I don't know which will go first—rock 'n' roll or Christianity. Jesus was all right but his disciples were thick and ordinary. It's them twisting it that ruins it for me."
– John Lennon 1966

Another lesser known proponent of both Aleister Crowley and Anton Lavey is Boyd Rice. Rice is best known as one of the creators of 'Industrial Music' that draws on transgressive and provocative themes. Over time, Industrial Music's influence spread into and blended with many other styles, including ambient and rock, all of which now fall under the Industrial Music label. The two most notable hybrid genres are industrial rock and industrial metal, which include bands such as Nine Inch Nails and Ministry, both of which released platinum-selling albums in the 1990s. These three genres are often referred to as simply industrial. A number of musicians, throughout this genre, describe their music:

"An attempt to conjure "Martian," "homosexual energy"

136

Israel Regardie, born Francis Israel Regudy (1907 – 1985), was an occultist, writer, and Aleister Crowley's personal secretary and transcriptionist. Regardie is widely known for his books and commentaries on the Hermetic Order of the Golden Dawn.

Throughout Aleister Crowley's biography he argues that The Eye in the Triangle, "Aiwass", was in fact, an unconscious expression of Crowley's own personality. Regardie says that although Crowley initially regarded Aiwass as one of the secret chiefs, he would later believe that Aiwass was his own Holy Guardian Angel. Regardie argued:

"If Aiwass was his own Higher Self, then the inference is none other than that Aleister Crowley was the author of the Book, and that he was the external mask for a variety of different hierarchical personalities... The man Crowley was the lowest rung of the hierarchical ladder, the outer shell of a God, even as we all are, the persona of a Star... He is the author of The Book of the Law even as he is the author of The Book of the Heart Girt with a Serpent and Liber Lapidis Lazuli, and so forth. ...these latter books reveal a dialogue between the component parts of Crowley. It seems to me that basically this Liber Legis is no different."

Regardie also noted resemblances between the Book of the Law and these latter holy books such as the inclusion of "rambling, unintelligible" passages, "some repugnant to reason by their absurdity, and their jarring goatish quality". In 1906 Crowley wrote:

"It has struck me - in connection with reading Blake that Aiwass, etc. 'Force and Fire' is the very thing I lack. My 'conscience' is really an obstacle and a delusion, being a survival of heredity and education."

Regardie considered this an "illuminating admission" and argued that due to Crowley's early religious training he developed an overly rigid superego or conscience. When he rebelled against Christianity, "he must have yearned for qualities and characteristics diametrically opposed to his own. In The Book of the Law the wish is fulfilled." The Book of the Law was therefore a "colossal wish-fulfillment."

Regardie noted that the Book's rejection of Judaeo-Christian morals was completely in accordance with Crowley's own moral and religious values and that in this sense "it is his Book". Although Crowley claimed to have initially objected to the Book's contents, Regardie expressed the view that he could not see what a person like Crowley would possibly object to. Regardie referred to Crowley's 1909 statement:

"I want blasphemy, murder, rape, revolution, anything, bad or good, but strong," – Aleister Crowley

Lucifer's Talmud and Kabbalah:

"And have no fellowship with the unfruitful works of darkness, but rather reprove them." - Ephesians 5:11

In the above illustration Madonna is displayed next to a sketched interpretation of her 'god' Lucifer, outfitted and posed by her handlers. Madonna impersonates the satanic Baphomet and Babylonian Demon god Pazuzu. In effect, Madonna is proselytizing her anti-Christian, anti-Torah esoteric religion of Kabbalah to millions of spiritually naïve Christian Americans. In a 1997 interview with MTV's Kurt Loder, Madonna in her own words describes Kabbalahism stating:

"Basically the Kabbalah is the mystical interpretation of the New Testament."

138

In reality, demonology is at the root of Kabbala. In fact, Kabbala is nothing more than black magic or Satanism. Its deceived members are taught that King Solomon's 72 Names of Demons are 72 different names for 'God'. This is why many of its celebrity members have had mental breakdowns and even died under mysterious circumstances.

Other 'celebrities' who practice the Satanic religion of Kabbalah and impersonate ancient Babylonian demons are: Lady Gaga [right] who in a T.V. interview said "I swear to Lucifer;" Beyonce who regularly flashes the satanic illuminati pyramid and 666; Scarlet Johansson; Bono; Brittany Spears; Katy Perry who in a T.V. interview said that she "sold her soul  to the devil'; Christina Aguilera; Liz Taylor; Victoria Beckham; Charlize Theron; Sandra Bernhardt; Ashton Kutcher who attended the funeral of prominent Kabbalah Chief Rabbi Berg in Isreal; Demi Moore; Paris Hilton; Lindsay Lohan; 'Steve-O', Rosie O'Donnell; Courtney Love; Brittany Murphy; Rosanne Barr, etc. Barr is a celebrity who stated on the late, late show with Craig Ferguson:

"When I was twelve years old I signed a deal with Satan in my room, because I wanted to get famous no matter what."

The above list of celebrities is just a sampling of the vast satanic resources through which Lucifer's deceptive message is broadcasted. For generations "Tinsel Town" has effectively deceived millions into believing that satanic worship of Baphomet, Kabbalah, witchcraft, freemasonry, etc. is the ticket to fame and fortune. Christians who read The Holy Bible realize that these deceptive promises merely strengthen the Holy Scripture warnings that all false religions have spiritual ties to each other.

The image of Baphomet was drawn by a man named Eliphas Levi, whose name appears in the lower part of the picture. He was a 19th century Kabbalah mystic in France who established many teachings followed today by magicians and occultists. Originally named Alphonse Louis Constant, he originally pursued priesthood with the Catholic Church but left the seminary to embrace the occult, beginning with Rosicrucianism.

Levi's Baphomet drawing is full of occult Babylonian symbols. However most people who are familiar with Levi's Baphomet's drawing are unaware of Levi's inspiration behind his Baphomet creation. The progenitor of Levi's Baphomet is the Babylonian demon Pazuzu [left]. In the 1971 novel 'The Exorcist' and the movie based on the novel, Pazuzu is the evil spirit that possesses the young Scottish girl Regan MacNeil. As an aside, the MacNeil surname is descended of an ancient Scottish dynasty c.405 A.D. whose crest resembles that of the Babylonian god Nimrod's Tower of Babylon. The most recognizable demonic symbol on Levi's Baphomet is the pentagram on Baphomet's forehead. The pentagram, whether upside down or right side up, is a very prominent occultist symbol. According to Levi, the pentagram symbolizes the power of the mind to dominate the spiritual realm in order to interact with "legions of angels and hosts of fiends". In Christian speak this means that he was communicating with demons.

"I know thy works, and tribulation, and poverty, (but thou art rich) and I know the blasphemy of them which say they are Jews, and are not, but are the synagogue of Satan." - Revelation 2:9

Christian Americans are not the only ones who have been deceived by Satanic, esoteric, New Age, doctrines. The anti-Torah Talmud has deceived generations of Judaic people into following Lucifer and the teachings of mortal sages and Pharisees, over the Holy Torah. One of many examples of this is the Chief Rabbi of Prague who once stated:

"It appears to me, since the heretics (Christians) also study Bible for their own purposes, if your son studies Bible without supervision, he may have a teacher who is one of them, and he will follow after their empty beliefs." – Rabbi Yechezkel Landau (circa 1760)

It's Luciferians such as Rabbi Yechezkel which caused the governor general of Kiev, a man named Drenteln, in 1881 to present a plan to the Emperor of Russia, Alexander II. His plan called for the immediate suppression of all Talmudist mercantile activity. The governor general felt that it was necessary for the Christian Emperor to:

"Shield the Christian population against so arrogant a tribe as the Jews [Talmudists], who refuse on religious grounds to have close contact with the Christians"

Actions taken by the Emperor to protect Christians from what he referred to as a destructive 'Liberal' agenda included important changes to Russia's legislation concerning industry and commerce. Moreover, the Emperor signed the emancipation of the serfs [slaves of Russia]. Serfdom was the dominant form of relation between peasants and nobility in the 17th century and by the 19th century the peasant class population totaled more than 49 million. As an aside the same year [1881] the Emperor made changes to Russia's legislation concerning commerce he was assassinated by the Rothschild Family; just sixteen years prior the Rothschild family coordinated the assassination of U.S. President Abraham Lincoln. Lincoln's assassination was due to his repeal of the Rothschild's business plan to build a Federal Reserve Bank Inc. on U.S. soil. As of 2013 the only countries left without a Central Bank owned by the Rothschild Family are Cuba, North Korea and Iran.

Because of the ample spiritual discrepancies between the Talmud - created 1st century A.D. in the Babylonian Talmudic Academies of Iraq - and the God inspired Holy Torah, Karaite Jews are a growing sect of Judaic people who only follow the God inspired Holy Torah or what the Christian American majority refers to as the Old Testament. Karaite Jews rightly eschew the Satanic Talmud, which they have shown to be nothing more than a collection of man-made laws verbally handed down by Luciferian Rabbis. It should also be noted that Talmudists in these regions used 'Seleucid Era' dating also known as the 'Anno Graecorum' [AG] or 'Era of Contracts'. This begs the question: With whom were Talmudists creating contracts with? Based on their bigoted, Lucifer inspired rhetoric it's quite clear their contracts were with Satan and his demon Pazuzu.

"Jesus saith unto them, Did ye never read in the scriptures, The stone which the builders rejected, the same is become the head of the corner: this is the Lord's doing, and it is marvellous in our eyes? Therefore say I unto you, The kingdom of God shall be taken from you, and given to a nation bringing forth the fruits thereof. And whosoever shall fall on this stone shall be broken: but on whomsoever it shall fall, it will grind him to powder. And when the chief priests and Pharisees had heard his parables, they perceived that he spake of them." - Matthew 21:42-45

In the above Biblical quote, it is clear Lord Jesus Christ is referring to the minority Judaic heretical movement of his day, whose goal it was to develop a sacrilegious, self serving rabbinic movement [Talmudism]. It's of vital importance for both the Christian American majority as well as the Judaic American population to be aware of the verbiage throughout the anti-Torah Talmud, which places the Babylonian Talmud above The Holy Bible. In the book titled From Torah to Kabbalah: A Basic Introduction to the Writings of Judaism (Page 40), R.C. Musaph Andriesse writes:

"The authority of the Babylonian Talmud is also greater than that of the Jerusalem Talmud. In cases of doubt the former is decisive." What's more, the Babylonian Talmud teaches that "The Almighty Himself" is inferior to the sages, Pharisees and Rabbis.

"The realization of the difference between written and oral regulations finds expression in the appraisal that 'The Sages safeguarded their own enactments more than those of the Torah' and in the hyperbolical statements concerning the supreme authority of the expositions and decisions of the Rabbis. The Almighty Himself is bound by them." - Pesiqta de-R. Kahana, Para, ed. Mandelbaum, p. 73

Christians exist only to serve Jews [Talmudists]:

"Goyim [Christians] were born only to serve us. Without that, they have no place in the world - only to serve the People of Israel... With gentiles [Christians], it will be like any person - they need to die, but [God] will give them longevity. Why? Imagine that one's donkey would die, they'd lose their money. This is his servant... That's why he gets a long life, to work well for this Jew [Talmudist]. Why are gentiles [Christians] needed? They will work, and they will plow, they will reap. We will sit like an effendi and

142

eat. That is why gentiles were created." - Rabbi Ovadia Yosef, senior Sephardic posek and head of the Shas Council of Torah Sages. Sermon on the laws regarding non-Jews. Source: "Yosef: Gentiles exist only to serve Jews," Jerusalem Post, October 18, 2010.

"The best among the Gentiles deserve to be killed."
– Talmud, Rabbi Simeon BenYohai

"I can state with assurance that the last generation of white children is now being born. Forbid the Whites to mate with Whites. The White Women must cohabit with members of the dark races, the White Men with black women. Thus the White Race will disappear, for the mixing of the dark with the White means the end of the White Man, and our most dangerous enemy will become only a memory. We shall embark upon an era of ten thousand years of peace and plenty, the Pax Judaica, and our race will rule undisputed over the world. Our superior intelligence will easily enable us to retain mastery over a world of dark peoples." – Rabbi Rabinovich, Speaking at the Council of European Rabbis in Budapest, Hungary, January 12th, 1952

A real world example which demonstrates Talmudist Rabbi Yosef, BenYohai and Rabinovich's aforesaid, racist, hate speech, can be found in the actions of Talmudist Rabbi Isaac Rosenbaum. Rabbi Rosenbaum, along with five additional Talmudist Rabbi's, was arrested in 2009 for running the largest organ trafficking scheme in America. Victims were flown into the United States from predominately impoverished Christian majority nations such as Moldova, once in the U.S. their organs were cut out of their bodies and sold to the highest bidder. In connection with the crime Talmudist real-estate developer Solomon Dwek was arrested for $50 million in bank fraud. As an aside, Dwek's family founded the Deal Yeshiva, an educational institution that focuses on the study of the anti-Christian Babylonian Talmud.

"It is permitted to take the body and the life of a non-Jew."
- Talmud, Sepher Ikkarim IIIc, 25

The following are just a few of the blasphemous teachings inside of the Talmud. For instance, in the book titled Jewish History, Jewish Religion, (Pages 97-98, 118) Dr. Israel Shahak writes:

"The Hebrew form of the name Jesus--Yeshu--was interpreted as an acronym for the curse, 'may his name and memory be wiped out,' which is used as an extreme form of abuse. In fact, anti-zionist Orthodox Jews (such as Neturey Qarta) sometimes refer to Herzl as 'Herzl Jesus' and I have found in religious zionist writings expressions such as "Nasser Jesus" and more recently 'Arafat Jesus."

Additional Lucifer Inspired Talmudic heresy:

- **Talmud, Gittin 57a:** "Jesus is in hell where he is boiling in hot excrement."
- **Talmud, Yebamoth 98a:** "All gentile [Christian] children are animals."
- **Talmud, Abodah Zarah 36b**: Gentile Christian] girls are in a state of niddah (filth) from birth. Christian women are regarded as slaves, heathen and whores.
- **Talmud, Avodah zarah:** Do not worship false gods [Jesus Christ].
- **Talmud: Baba Mezia 114b:** "The Jews are called human beings, but the non-Jews are not humans. They are beasts."
- **Talmud, Ereget Raschi Erod. 22 30:** "The Akum [Christian] is like a dog. Yes, the scripture teaches to honor the dog more than the Akum."
- **Talmud, Midrasch Talpioth, p. 255, Warsaw 1855**: "Even though God created the non-Jew they are still animals in human form. It is not becoming for a Jew to be served by an animal. Therefore he will be served by animals in human form."
- **Talmud, Coschen Hamischpat 405**: "A pregnant non-Jew is no better than a pregnant animal."
- **Talmud, Jalkut Rubeni gadol 12b**: "The souls of non-Jews come from impure spirits and are called pigs."
- **Talmud, Schene Luchoth Haberith, p. 250b:** "Although the non-Jew has the same body structure as the Jew, they compare with the Jew like a monkey to a human."
- **Talmud, Sanhedrin 74b:** "Sexual intercourse between non-Jews is like intercourse between animals."
- **Talmud, Jore Dea 377, 1:** "If a Jew has a non-Jewish servant of maid who dies, one should not express sympathy to the Jew. You should tell to the Jew: God will replace your loss,' just as if one of his oxen or asses had died."

144

- **Talmud, Sepher Ikkarim IIIc, 25**: "It is permitted to take the body and the life of a non-Jew."
- **Talmud, Sanhedrin 59b**: "It is the law to kill anyone who denies the Torah.
- **Talmud, Coschen Hamischpat 425, Hagah 425, 5**: The Christians belong to the denying ones of the Torah (Talmud)."
- **Talmud, Bammidber Raba, c 21 & Jalkut 772**: "Every Jew, who spills the blood of the godless (non-Jew), is doing the same as making a sacrifice to God."

The Talmud's penalty for disobedience of the aforementioned laws is to be as follows:

"One additional element of greater severity is that violation of any one of the seven [Noahide] laws subjects the Noahide to capital punishment by decapitation – Sanhedrin 57A."

The anti-Christian, anti-Torah Talmud contains disturbing edicts which the Christian American Majority must be made aware of. Understand that all of the above sacrilegious Talmudic laws, targeting Lord Jesus Christ and Christians, are celebrated by Hollywood writers, directors, actors and actresses in both feature films and on television, as well as business moguls throughout Corporate America. Consider The Walt Disney Company's Lifetime Channel "Television for Women" which depicts daughters of Christian preachers exhibiting lewd behavior in the TV Show 'Preachers' Daughters'.

What's more, there is Larry David [pg.146] the creator of both 'Seinfeld' and 'Curb Your Enthusiasm'. In October 25, 2009, an episode of Curb Your Enthusiasm aired titled "The Bare Midriff". In this episode Larry David features himself urinating on a picture of Lord Jesus Christ. This is obviously an endorsement of the Talmud, Gitten 57a which states Lord Jesus Christ is in hell "boiling in hot urine". HBO released a statement defending Larry David's hateful anti-Christian act, which read:

"Anyone who follows Curb Your Enthusiasm knows that the show is full of parody and satire. Larry David makes fun of everyone, most especially himself. The humor is always playful and certainly never malicious."

145

Through his career, Larry David has not only attacked the Christian American majority, but he has also shown a propensity towards the hatred of conservative Jews who eschew the satanic Talmud. On April 28, 1994 millions of viewers tuned into Seinfeld to watch a two-part episode written by Larry David. The title of this episode was "The Rain Coats". In it Jerry Seinfeld's character is featured groping and kissing his girlfriend inside of a movie theater, while the movie Schindler's List is playing. It begs the question. Why would self ascribed Jewish actors, writers and directors feature lustful, celebratory acts during the showing of a film which depicts millions of Jewish people being exterminated? The explanation is quite simple if you understand what the Talmud says about "am ha'aretz" or Jews who deny the Pharisee written Talmud.

In the book titled "Judaism's Strange Gods" writer Michael Hoffman (www.revisionisthistory.com) shares with his readers what many of the leading Babylonian Talmudic leaders subscribe to, namely the murder of anti-Talmud conservative Jews. On pg. 37 of his book Mr. Hoffman cites the Talmudic views of Lubavitcher Rebbe on the subject of the Jewish Holocaust. Keep in mind, that Rebbe is the so-called 'King Messiah' of the largest Jewish organization in the world.

"Rebbe…compare(s) God to a surgeon who amputates a patient's limb in order to save his life. The limb 'is incurably diseased… The Holy One Blessed Be He, like professor-surgeon… seeks the good of Israel, and indeed, all He does is done for the good… In the spiritual sense, no harm was done, because the everlasting spirit of the Jewish people was not destroyed."

According to Rebbe's man-made anti-Torah Talmud the murder of conservative Jews who eschew the Talmud is justified and Hitler was a 'servant of God'.

When militant anti-Christian Corporations, such as HBO, defend 'men' like Larry David they promote Rebbe's vitriol. What's more, they inspire the notion that it's perfectly fine to urinate on the divinity of Lord Jesus Christ. Urinating on Lord Jesus Christ is not "playful"? And if you're a Christian reading this, who currently subscribes to HBO, I hope that you will consider cancelling your membership and boycott any project the anti-Christian Larry David is associated with.

The American entertainment and fashion industries, especially music and films, have been normalizing misogynistic language and imagery, as well as child pornography for the past fifty-years. Dr. Jason D. Kovar's documentary titled: "Hollywood Unmasked" exposes the demonic influence over Hollywood and provides quotes from the vast majority of Hollywood actors and actresses proclaiming their allegiance to Lucifer. Dr. Kovar's video can be purchased at: www.hollywoodunmasked.com.

Beginning in the late 1970's, verbal and visual attacks against the sacredness of our Christian American young girls and women reached epidemic proportions. In 2011 however, we begin to see a level of satanic propaganda which surpasses all previous levels of depravity. It's in 2011 that ABC Television, Inc. - whose core viewership is sadly Christian – announces its plan to release a show titled "Good Christian Bitches". It's these types of show titles which support militant anti-Christian Talmudic teachings such as Abodah Zarah 36b which reads "Gentile girls are in a state of niddah (filth) from birth". Companies like 'American Apparel Clothing' further endorse Abodah Zarah 36b when they promote pornographic messaging on clothing made for little girls and women. Examples include: "Who needs brains when you have these", "Must be 21 to enjoy this ride", "Contains strong sexual content."

It's messaging like this which makes our young Christian girls and women look like mindless pieces of meat. Free speech is the foundation of our Republic. So too is the freedom of choice. To eliminate anti-Christian organizations such as American Apparel Company from the free market, all the Christian American majority must do is simply not buy goods and/or services 147 from them. These types of blatant satanic attacks against our Christian women should have our Christian American Majority up in arms. It's these types of extremely offensive and distasteful show titles and clothing companies which should cause the Christian American Majority to bankrupt all Companies and Corporations which exhibit aforementioned behavior. Achieving this goal is quite simple; you merely stop watching their shows and discontinue using any of their products. In the case of ABC, Inc. this includes subscribing to their cable channel Showtime.

Aimonides Mishnah Torah, a code of Talmudic religious law authored by Rabbi Moshe ben Maimon (1170 and 1180), is one of history's foremost rabbis. In Chapter 10 of the English Translation, he states about Lord Jesus Christ:

"It is a mitzvah [religious duty; ARC], however, to eradicate Jewish traitors, minnim, and apikorsim, and to cause them to descend to the pit of destruction, since they cause difficulty to the Jews and sway the people away from God, as did Jesus of Nazareth and his students, and Tzadok, Baithos, and their students. May the name of the wicked rot."

The Talmudic influenced Jewish Encyclopedia predicts a "Noahide" regime as a possible New World Order immediately preceeding the universal reign of the Talmud. The Christian American majority must understand that we are not dealing with the Noah of The Holy Bible when Talmudic worshipers refer to "Noahide law," but the Noahide law as understood and interpreted by the absolute system of falsification that constitutes the militant anti-Christian, anti-Torah Talmud.

Under the Talmud's Noahide Laws, the worship of Jesus is absolutely forbidden under penalty of death, since such worship of Christ is condemned by the Talmud as idolatry. Meanwhile various forms of incest are permitted under the Talmudic understanding of the Noahide code. (Enziklopediya Talmudit, note 1, pp. 351-352).

The Talmud also states the penalty for disobedience:

"One additional element of greater severity is that violation of any one of the seven laws subjects the Noahide to capital punishment by decapitation." - Sanh. 57A

148

"With the end of free will, the opportunity to earn reward and enhance one's portion in the World to Come will also cease forever."
– Talmud, Sukkah 52a

The Christian American majority have been issued a clear warning of the aforementioned Satanic behavoir. What's more, Christians have been warned throughout the Holy Bible about Satan's end-game to exterminate God's chosen people, which consists of those who "believeth" in Jesus Christ [John 11:25].

"And I saw thrones, and they sat upon them, and judgment was given unto them: and [I saw] the souls of them that were beheaded for the witness of Jesus, and for the word of God, and which had not worshipped the beast, neither his image, neither had received [his] mark upon their foreheads, or in their hands; and they lived and reigned with Christ a thousand years." - Revelations 20:4

This is why a United States Army training instructor listed Evangelical Christianity, Catholicism and "Orthodox Jews" e.g., conservative Torah faithful Jews, as examples of religious extremism, along with Al Qaeda and Hamas during a briefing with an Army Reserve unit based in Pennsylvania. Ron Crews, executive director of the Chaplain Alliance for Religious Liberty, states:

"We find this offensive to have Evangelical Christians and the Catholic Church to be listed among known terrorist groups; it is dishonorable for any U.S. military entity to allow this type of wrongheaded characterization."

Christians must be aware of the fact that Satan's, Church is comprised of those who worship the Serpent Cult of Dann, Nimrod, Baylonian Talmudism, Freemasonry, the Zohar, etc. and it's this force which is driving these kinds of militant anti-Christian agendas. For example, high-level members of the Serpent Cult of Dann have deceived thousands of U.S. Military men and women into performing occult serpent rituals. Since 1980 the "Cobra Gold exercise" hosts soldiers from Thailand, U.S. Singapore, Indonesia, Japan, South Korea and Malaysia. The multi-national military training exercise teaches soldiers the occult serpent ritual of drinking fresh cobra blood because it's "nutrition for a human body." In Acts 21:25; Acts 15:19-20, 28-29; 1 Samuel 14:32-33; Deuteronomy 12:23; Leviti-

149

cus 19:26, Leviticus 17:10-14 and Genesis 9:4-5, man is commanded to not eat or drink blood. "Lest Satan [the serpent] should get an advantage of us; for we are not ignorant of his devices." – 2 Corinthians 2:11

To better understand the Church of Babylon, all one must do is examine its fruits. The extensive history of Satanic rituals and malevolent habits of Freemasons illustrate just how wicked the tree from which freemasonry was born really is. Kabbalah is nothing more than a bastardization of the Holy Jewish Torah e.g., The Old Testament, and is thought to have been created nearly 1300 years after Lord Jesus Christ gave us the New Testament. Its teachings come from a 23-volume book called 'The Zohar' and is very similar to the teachings of modern day esoteric Theosophy, in that it promotes an interpretation of the inner meaning of the Torah. Lord Jesus Christ has instructed Christians globally to use The Holy Bible alone when researching and defining the Holy Scriptures:

"Jesus answered him, I spake openly to the world; I ever taught in the synagogue, and in the temple, whither the Jews always resort; and in secret have I said nothing." - John 18:20

Traditionally its practices were reserved for a select number of scholars who already had an advanced understanding of religious law, but for the past 500 years it has been followed more widely. What Christians must understand is that 'Kaballah' will not bring you closer to Lord Jesus Christ, but in fact it will take you away. Not once does Lord Jesus Christ cite Kabbalism or the Talmud as Christians' way into heaven, nor was he a fan of mysticism:

"In my Father's house are many mansions: if it were not so, I would have told you. I go to prepare a place for you." – John 14:2

In chapter two I shared with readers my concerns over the mad rush by elites to indoctrinate the Christian American majority into utilizing Spy-Cloud Computing and how Christians have allowed 76% of their U.S. libraries to become electronic book (eBook) friendly; it's been under the guise of convenience and security that our enemies have brainwashed the Christian American majority into believing that eBooks offer a superior experience and security over holding and owning a physical copy. This 'Big-Lie' has led to the purging of a number of significant historical writings from State and Federal Archives by Church of Babylon members. Take for instance

150

the deletion of a speech by Scottish American Joseph R. McCarthy titled 'George Washington's Surrender' from the Library of Congress and the Jesuit Marquette University. Not surprising given the fact it was Spanish Jesuit, Francisco Ribera who proposed that the final seven years of the 70 weeks of Daniel was a future Antichrist. This is where the manufactured seven years of tribulation comes from before the second coming of Christ. This was manufactured prophecy with the sole purpose of deceiving Christians about the true identity of Antichrist. Attributing Daniel's 70th week of Jesus' baptism and crucifixion and applying it instead to Antichrist is outright blasphemous.

To communist sympathizers, anti-Christians and Theosophists Joseph R. McCarthy is considered America's Most Hated Senator. Why? Because in the 1950's McCarthy was responsible for exposing the fact that the Roosevelt and Truman Administrations were riddled with active Communist spies, Communist sympathizers and Russian dupes. Why was his speech deleted from the Library of Congress and all other state and federal archives? Because McCarthy's speech references a 1781 book by Scottish American Jonathan Williams titled "Legions of Satan".

Jonathan Williams is one of Christian America's biggest unsung historical figures, primarily because the Rothschild's, Rockefellers, etc., have gone to great lengths to delete what he wrote 232 years ago. What historians have concealed for centuries is that Williams was a close trusted friend and officer in one of General George Washington's artillery regiments. It's well documented that Washington along with many of his contemporaries were ardent critics of Adam Weishaupt's Illuminati and yet he is promoted in both paintings and literature as being a Satanic Freemason, which begs the question... Was President George Washington truly a Freemason or was he merely painted into historical archives as one by The Church of Babylon to suit their agenda? After all President Washington was bled to death by a Freemason doctor to balance the 'four humors' in Washington's blood. Even more mystifying is the fact that General Washington's wife Martha is on record having owned hundreds of Class A stock in the Bank of England, a financial institution whose capitalization was based on the appropriated wealth of Babylonian Talmudic Freemason created "Templar Knights".

151

In his book officer Jonathan Williams [below] writes that he was the man who received General Cornwallis' letter of surrender following Cornwallis defeat to General Washington in Yorktown, Virginia 1781. It was during this time period that Jonathan Williams wrote his book titled 'Legions of Satan', in it he notes a provocative warning made by General Cornwallis to General Washington. He states:

"A Holy War will now begin on America, and when it is ended America will be supposedly the citadel of freedom, but her millions will unknowingly be loyal subjects to the Crown... Your churches will be used to teach the Jews' [Talmudist] religion, and in less than two hundred years the whole nation will be working for divine world government. That government that they believe to be divine will be the British Empire. All religions will be permeated with Judaism [Talmudism] without even being noticed by the masses, and they will all be under the invisible all-seeing eye of the Grand Architect of Freemasonry."
- Jonathan Williams, c.1781

Who in the U.S. Government might harbor a grudge against Scottish American Senator Joseph McCarthy for exposing a communist Russian, presence in the U.S. Government back in the 1950's? As an aside the MacCarthys, O'Briens, O'Conners, O'Donnells and O'Neills make up the principle Celtic families of ancient Ireland. (The Annals of the Four Masters. cit. Cusack. p.85). If you would like to understand the over two millennia old Luciferian war against ancient Christians Celtcs, please read my book at, KillingIreland.com.

Who might be unfriendly towards historical figures that at some point in their careers provided Americans with knowledge that exposed anti-Christian bigotry, anti-Americanism, pro-socialism and pro-communism?

Who possessed the motivation; resources, access and authority to what I can only imagine are highly secure database archives in the publicly financed and owned Library of Congress?

Meet Dr. James Hadley Billington U.S. Librarian of Congress' National Digital Library since 12/14/1987, just months after the modern Internet came into being. The following is a summary of Dr. Billington's resume; I'll leave it up to you to decide whether or not Billington's professional profile is anti-American and pro-Communist.

Dr. Billington is a proponent of digitizing all of America's historical documents. In my opinion, this is a modern day hi-tech version of Nazi book burning, scripted rituals where high Nazi officials, professors, rectors, and student leaders burned more than 25,000 books. During these bonfires Nazis would play songs, perform "fire oaths," and incantations, all of which are rituals based on the Babylonian god Nimrod. The only difference between Nazi book burning and future American book burning will be the ease through which American Tyrants 'delete' or rewrite world history. And because the Christian majority are allowing the train wreck of 'distance learning' to flourish throughout America, future dictators will only have to edit the information streaming to your children's monitor to control their minds and the future of America.

Dr. Billington proposed in 2005 to create a 'World Digital Library' with the endorsement of UNESCO in 2007. Director of UNESCO, Julian Huxley was an enthusiast of the USSR dictator Joseph Stalin. Huxley said that he admired the social and economic planning results achieved by Stalin. It was Stalin's planning that Huxley so admired, which led to the starvation and murder of more than 14 million Ukrainians, nearly three times the number of Jews murdered by Hitler. Dr. Billington's idol, Huxley, also said:

"The lowest strata are reproducing too fast. Therefore... they must not have too easy access to relief or hospital treatment lest the removal of the last check on natural selection should make it too easy for children to be produced or to survive; long unemployment should be a ground for sterilization." - Sir Julian Huxley

153

"I suppose the reason why we leapt at the Origin of Species [Darwin's Theory] was that the idea of God interfered with our sexual mores" – Sir Julian Huxley, Head of UNESCO

Dr. Billington is a Rhodes Scholar and the former director of the Woodrow Wilson International Center for Scholars, the nation's official memorial in Washington to America's 28th president. Dr. Billington was honored with the Woodrow Wilson Award. As director, he founded the Kennan Institute for Advanced Russian Studies. For those Christian Americans who are unaware of what a 'Rhodes Scholar' is, here's a quick overview. Woodrow Wilson's best friend Colonel Edward Mandell House founded the American Institute of International Affairs, known today as the Council of Foreign Relations, an outer layer of the Royal Institute of International Affairs (RIIA), whose sole purpose was to retake the United States of America as a British Colony. RIIA is the outer layer of the main core of a secret establishment called the Circle of Initiates founded by self avowed Satanic Theosophical cult member Cecil Rhodes. The Rhodes scholarship is an international postgraduate award for selecting foreign students to study at the University of Oxford. However, based on Cecil's circle of friends, penchant for Satanism and stated goal of revitalizing Nimrod's old world order of Babylon; I believe Rhodes University gets its name from the ancient "Colossus of Rhodes" c.280 BC, a statue of the Greek titan-god of the sun "Helios" or Apollyon otherwise known as "The Beast from the pit" – Revelation 9:11. President Bill Clinton, who infected America with the constitution killing Agenda 21, is a Rhodes Scholar.

Dr. Billington's idol Woodrow Wilson is best known for the Rothschild/Rockefeller/Morgan designed Federal Reserve Act. President Wilson would later comment on the signing of this act:

"I have unwittingly ruined my Country".

Dr. Billington authored "Mikhailovsky and Russian Populism" (1956), "Russia Transformed: Breakthrough to Hope", (August 1991), "The Face of Russia" (1998) which he wrote and narrated for the Public Broadcasting Service (PBS) and finally "Russian in Search of Itself" (2004).

154

Dr. Billington has accompanied 10 Congressional delegations to Russia and the former Soviet Union. In June 1988 he accompanied President and Mrs. Reagan to the Soviet Summit in Moscow.

Dr. Billington is the founding chairman of the Board of Trustees of the Open World Leadership Center (1999-2011) which has brought more than 14,000 emerging young Russian political leaders to communities throughout America.

Dr. Billington has received more than 40 honorary doctorates, including from the University of Tbilisi in Georgia, Russia (1999). In 2005 The Russian State University in Moscow awarded Billington the Karamzin prize Moscow and the Likhachev Prize Moscow (2006).

Dr. Billington was awarded the Presidential Citizens Medal by President Bush in 2008, the same President whose family financed the Nazis, murdered Scottish President JFK and Scottish American House Majority Leader Hale Boggs, developed the drug trade which has crippled American youth and incarcerated more people than any other Nation on Planet Earth.

Dr. Billington is a member of the Russian Academy of Sciences.

Dr. Billington was awarded the Order of Friendship by the President of Russian Federation Dmitry Medvedev in 2008, the highest state order that a foreign citizen may receive. Like Ronald Reagan, the Bush family, the Clintons and Obama, Medvedev supported the creation of an anti-Christian New World Order. Medvedev was not only a proponent of the New World Order, he envisioned Russia being a 'cofounder' stating:

"We are living in a unique time. And we should use it to build a modern, flourishing and strong Russia ... which will be a cofounder of the new world economic order." – Dmitry Medvedev, June 18, 2010

155

With Officer Jonathan Williams 1781 warning that: "All religions will be under the invisible all-seeing eye of the Grand Architect of Freemasonry [Satanism]," fresh in your mind, allow me to provide you with a visual representation of Officer Williams' warning. The above image is an aerial view of Oral Roberts University in Tulsa, OK. Oral Roberts was one of the most well-known 'Christian' leaders of the 20th century who preached a form of Christianity he called 'seed-faith'.

When we study the building design elements throughout his entire University we immediately begin to see who Roberts represented. There are literally too many to list, however, the most glaring examples that I can point to include the main

156

building of the University which is comprised of two large pyramids. Both large pyramids contain a smaller pyramid which acts as the 'all-seeing-eye'.

Geometrically the two large pyramid shapes are identical to the two pyramids which make up the 666 star of Remphan [acts 7:43]. In the late 1500's the Talmudist patriarch of the Rothschild family, Izaak Elchanan Rothschild [born in 1577] adopted the 666 star of Rempan [right] as the official moniker for the Church of Satan.

Additional design features on the campus include pyramid shaped buildings; Baphomet shaped walkways; two large 8 pointed Stars of Ishtar [pg. 158], paying homage to the Babylonian demon of war, and sex. One of the most famous Ishtar myths describes her descent to the underworld where she demands:

> "If thou openest not the gate to let me enter, I will break the door, I will wrench the lock, I will smash the door-posts, I will force the doors. I will bring up the dead to eat the living. And the dead will outnumber the living."

Many believe that Ishtar is identical to the ancient female demon Lilith said to strangle children, seduce young men, and then kill them. Some claim Lilith was the creator of prostitution and the degrading of sex.

In the neighboring 'City of Faith' parking lot, where in 1977 Roberts claimed to have been visited by a 900-foot-tall Jesus, we find a Pyramid shaped parking lot with capstone [pg. 158], pentagram shaped buildings and a giant penis water feature or what Freemasons refer to as the generating principle of life symbolizing the Egyptian god Osiris, containing two smaller pyramid shapes at its base that when combined make up the 666 star of Remphan [pg. 158]. In short, Oral Roberts "Christian" University Campus is Disneyland for Lucifer.

When we examine Oral Roberts Medical Center [pg. 159] we see two hands praying to the multiple pyramids be for it. There are two pyramids stacked on one another, one facing down the other facing towards the sky. This is in observance of Satanic Freemasonry's "As Above So Below". What's more this configuration is an abstract modification of the satanic star of Rothschild, which contains 666 "Mark of the Beast". Oral Roberts deceived 'Christians" into worshipping the false gospel which states, if you stop sinning you'll be saved. There's no mention in there about your belief in Jesus Christ.

The most troubling feature of Oral Roberts University isn't the plethora of demonic ideograms. It's the fact that men and women who publicly describe themselves as being children of Lord Jesus Christ empower these sanctuaries of Satan when they financially support their construction and ongoing maintenance.

Take for example, self avowed Christian Scottish American billionaire and owner of Hobby Lobby David Green whose vision statement reads:

"Hobby Lobby partners with organizations working to share the Good News of Jesus Christ to all the world." Mr. Green goes on to say: "Hobby Lobby has always been a tool for the Lord's work... For me and my family, charity equals ministry, which equals the Gospel of Jesus Christ".

Mr. and Mrs. Green are so serious about helping God's children around the world that they have pledged to give a majority of their wealth to philanthropic causes such as 'The Giving Pledge,' the brainchild of Warren Buffet and Bill and Melinda Gates. Currently the pledge is comprised of New York City Mayor Michael Bloomberg and 50 'givers,' many of which are Luciferians. Warren Buffet is friends with the Satanic Rothschild Family. In fact, Buffet has been photographed walking side-by-side with Jacob Rothschild. Buffet has also been photographed holding up the all-seeing-eye of Satan. Buffet is also friends with rapper Jay-Z, an admirer of Satanist Aleister Crowley. It will be remembered that Jay-Z's voice is featured on an album saying "Murder, Murder Jesus 666". 'Giving Pledge' Bill Gates is a proponent of global population reduction and the elimination of billions of people. Bill Gates is also a major shareholder in Monsanto, a company which produces cancer causing genetically modified organisms (GMO's). Lastly, it will be remembered that 'Giving Pledge' member Michael Bloomberg, is resuscitating a 3rd century AD Temple of Mithras in London, an ancient temple that was dedicated to the god of the sun and was used to sacrifice Christians on December 25th.

The question I have for billionaires like Mr. Green who maintain they are ministers for the Gospel of Jesus Christ is... Why do you sell the 'Star of Remphan' [pg.157] inside your 'Christian' owned stores? What's more, why would you give $70 million dollars to bailout Oral Roberts University, whose grounds are littered with blasphemous, anti-Christian ideograms? This is exactly what Green did in 2007. Furthermore, why in heaven's name would a Christian Billionaire choose to enrich the militant anti-Christian agenda of men like Buffet, Gates and the Rothschild's? How does a man who possesses the spirit of Jesus Christ and a seemingly unlimited amount of resources allow himself to be led down a path of deception? Mr. Green is either a horrible judge of character surrounded by the world's laziest, most incompetent advisors. Else he is in fact a proponent of the Church of Babylon.

Men like Mr. Green, Oral Roberts, etc. are tragic figures simply because of the fact that if they were to designate just 10% of their net worth into a program to educate the Christian majority on the real threat facing our community and couple that knowledge with a Christian reconstruction plan, they would save countless lives. The truth is anyone directly or indirectly involved with the Rothschild Family does not want the Christian majority to posses the knowledge inside of this book or a reconstruction plan. Because enemies of Christ know that if the Christian majority were to inventory their collective advantage over its enemy, which is ample and became educated about its enemy's weaknesses and its exploitation, the elements throughout our society impeding the Christian majority would be transformed overnight into threats against enemies of Christ. The final chapter of this book provides a rudimentary reconstruction plan for Christians to consider.

"Now the Spirit speaketh expressly, that in the latter times some shall depart from the faith, giving heed to seducing spirits, and doctrines of devils;" - 1 Timothy 4:1

"For such [are] false apostles, deceitful workers, transforming themselves into the apostles of Christ. And no marvel; for Satan himself is transformed into an angel of light." - 2 Corinthians 11:13-14

"The real Satanist is not quite so easily recognized as such"
- Anton Szandor LaVey, The Satanic Bible

"If they're [other true Satanists] at all intelligent they'll realize that there's only so much I can say publicly. I will not advance things in print which make my position untenable (indefensible). How long would the Church of Satan have lasted if I hadn't appeased and outraged in just the right combination? It required a certain amount of discretion and diplomacy to balance the outrage."
– Lucifer Rising pg.33

Rudolph Steiner

In America, Rudolf Steiner [right] is best known for being founder of the Anthroposophical Educational 'Waldorf' Theories Movement. What most parents who send their children to a Waldorf school don't realize is that Rudolf Steiner was also contemporary with both the founder of Satanic Theosophy's Helena Blavatsky and Annie Besant. His involvement with dark spirits is evident when you read many of his quotes. For example Rudolf Steiner once said that he 'felt his thoughts as something given by beings or spirits' that were, according to his autobiography, 'His constant companions since childhood'. Steiner then gives us a peek into his opinion of Satan, when he writes:

"Lucifer is not a being that we can see with our present day physical eyes: Lucifer can be seen only with the awakened clairvoyance, seen clairvoyantly, in fact, Lucifer is a particular being who is left behind during the moon phase of evolution."

Russian philosopher Nikolai Berdyajev made the following comment regarding his observation of Rudolph Steiner's followers:

"Some Anthroposophists impressed me as possessed. They were spellbound by a fixed idea. When they uttered the words: 'The Doctor (i.e. Steiner) says...' the expression of their eyes changed, the face became different and it was impossible to continue the conversation. Devout Anthroposophists are much more dogmatic, much more bound to authority than the most orthodox Orthodoxes or Catholics"

N. Sri Ram, a leading theosophist and writer of Lucifer Magazine, further clarifies who Theosophy considers to be their God:

"The adversary or Satan is no other than Lucifer, the light bearer, the bright morning star: he is the initiator, awakening the divine faculties of intellect on man, he is the King of the fallen angels, spirits from higher spheres, who descended among primitive mankind of the third race, to develop in man, and endow him with his self-conscious mind, or Manas"

At this point in the book, I trust my readers are beginning to see the clear connection between Theosophy, Freemasonry, Talmudism, etc. and Satanism. New Age proponents such as Wayne Dyer, Deepak Chopra, a modernist guru who is financed by many Hollywood celebrities including Demi Moore and Scottish American Tony Robbins, a neuro linguistic programmer (NLP) who specializes in Human Exploitation Psychology. Robbins has taught many powerful people like Bill and Hilary Clinton how to put people in a virtual trance. Luciferian Tony Robbins was featured in the Kobe Bryant commercial 'KOBESYSTEM' that readers examined earlier. It will be remembered that is Byran't commercial is rife with Satanic symbols. It is modernists such as the aforesaid who are placing new recruits on the doorstep of Luciferianism every day by promoting the concept of being able to obtain God like powers.

"and ye shall be as gods. [Satan] - Genesis 3:5

Wayne Dyer's main tool of influence, for instance, is his suggestion that people have power over the Universe if they simply harness what he calls 'The Power of Intention'. Dyers' teachings completely negate the role of God in their lives, again supporting Satan's big lie that man can become God. "The Power of Intention" is also echoed throughout the occult film 'The Secret'.

In the book titled 'Reflections On The Christ', David Spangler says that Theosophists worship Satan and that Lucifer is a light of God:

"the true light of Lucifer cannot be seen through sorrow, darkness through rejection, the true light of this great being, can only be recognized when one's own eyes can see with the light of the Christ the light of the inner sun. Lucifer works within each of us trying to bring us to wholeness and as we

move into a new age, which is the age of man's wholeness, each of us
in some way is brought to that point which I term the Luciferic initiation. The particular doorway through which the individual must pass, if
he is to come fully into the presence of his light and his wholeness. Lucifer comes to give us the final gift of hope and wholeness if we accept
it, then he is free and then we are free. That is the Luciferic initiation. It
is one that many people now and in the days ahead will be facing. For it
is an initiation into the new age. It is an initiation into leaving the past
and moving into the new. Leaving our guilt's, our needs, our tempta-
tions, and becoming whole and that piece. Because we have recognized
her inner light and the light that enfolds us, the light of God."

The above is further evidence that the Luciferian doctrine is
indeed one with the New Age philosophy and it's all been influenced by
Blavatsky's Satanic theosophy. Inherent to this philosophy is that man
will conquer and control the world and become God.

W.L. Wilmhurst, a high level Freemason, qualifies the connection between Freemasonry, Satanic Theosophy and the role it will play in
ushering in Satan's promise to make men Gods. He writes:

"The height of the Lodge even as high as the heavens implies the
range of consciousness possible to us when we have developed our
potentialities to the full, is infinite. Man who has sprung from the Earth
developed through the lower kingdoms of nature to his present rational
state, has yet to complete his evolution by became in a God-like being
an unifying his consciousness with the Omniscient - to promote which
is and always has been the sole aim and purpose of all initiation."

11   Lucifer's Antichrist

"And through his policy also he shall cause craft to prosper in his hand;
and he shall magnify himself in his heart, and by peace shall destroy
many: he shall also stand up against the Prince of princes; but he shall
be broken without hand." - Daniel 8:25

Every generation has had its share of individuals vying for the
title of most evil. In the late 50's one man not only 'took the cake', he
took the entire bakery. His name was Benjamin Crème and he insisted
that he had been contacted by a spiritual advisor who told him that he
would be the personal messenger for Helen Blavatsky's prophesized
New World Order anti-Christ. Over the next several years, Benjamin
Crème would tour the country side speaking at all of the most highly
respected Satanic occult organizations, including Freemason halls and
the like; then in the mid-70's, an organization that Crème founded, by
the name of 'Share International', announced that their spiritual world
leader 'Maitreya' had unveiled himself. And just as you would expect,
from an all powerful 'god'… Maitreya boarded the first flight out of the
Himalaya's and made a 'bee-line' for his new spokesperson.

Before we continue, I would just like to interject one thought.
If you're a 'God' or benevolent figure who will literally unite the entire
human race, why on earth would anyone believe that a 'god' would be
compelled to sneak around the Himalayas, waiting for his agent to set
up television and radio interviews? I've read somewhere that Christ's
second coming will be a bit more spectacular than a radio and television
appearance. Furthermore, I couldn't bear the thought of Jesus Christ
being subjected to a TSA crotch search, just so that he's able to promote
himself on The Tonight Show or David Letterman.

It should come as no surprise to readers that all of Benjamin
Crème's propaganda surrounding an appearance never produces anything for the madman in chief. God has written about these types of
fools in The Holy Bible. He says that there will be many false prophets
and Benjamin Crème's Holy Hoax 'Maitreya' most definitely fits this description.

"When a prophet speaketh in the name of the Lord, if the thing follow not, nor come to pass, that is the thing which the Lord hath not spoken, but the prophet hath spoken it presumptuously: thou shalt not be afraid of him" - Deuteronomy 18:22

Who Is Maitreya?

'Maitreya' [right] is a very serious candidate for The Church of Babylon. As a matter of fact, here is a picture of their 'god'. Don't you like the two horns in his beard? Or are those suppose to be a serpent's tongue? You decide. Nonetheless, I can't see why anyone wouldn't see this possessed looking human being as anything but a fun, loving associate of Lord Jesus Christ (sarcasm). I especially like how this supposed 'savoir of mankind' feels that it's appropriate to only communicate with The Church of Babylon e.g., Theosophists, Freemasons, Talmudists, Satanists, etc. Yeah, that's got 'second coming' written all over it. The sick and twisted fact is that this possessed human meat sack and fraud 'Maitreya' is actually revered by a number of world leaders, and United States Presidents who I'll identify later in this chapter. And even though Maitreya has missed a number of scheduled interviews and appearances, well known Theosophists, world leaders and celebrities all promote the idea that he is in fact living on Planet Earth and in the late 70's was residing in an Asian Community within East London. Church of Babylon members believe that Maitreya will unveil himself to the entire world very soon and that all religions, e.g. Christians, Muslims, Hindus, Sikhs, Torah following Judaic people and Buddhists will see him as the one true God and follow him into a Church of Babylon scripted One World Religion. Furthermore, the idea that has been promoted is that this Maitreya character will communicate with everyone in their own tongue, throughout the entire world.

165

"And then shall that Wicked be revealed, whom the Lord shall consume with the spirit of his mouth, and shall destroy with the brightness of his coming: Even him, whose coming is after the working of Satan with all power and signs and lying wonders, And with all deceivableness of unrighteousness in them that perish; because they received not the love of the truth, that they might be saved." - 2 Thessalonians 2:8-10

Many of you may not be aware of the fact that the United States Government owned 'Evergreen Airlines', which has for years been dropping a cocktail of miscellaneous toxic chemicals into our atmosphere. Outspoken critics will tell you that it's a mixture of chemicals to supposedly help retard the damage being done to our ozone. One of these outspoken critics was former CIA/DEA pilot and friend of mine Captain Philip Marshall.

It will be remembered that Philip was an author of a number of books questioning the narrative of September 11, 2001, which was faithfully promoted by the Bush administration. In addition to Captain Marshall, his son Alex, 17 and daughter Macaila, 14, were all murdered in 2013 inside their home, in Northern California just 40min from my home. Please Google this story for additional information. In addition, please search, 'Evergreen Aviation Admits to Chemtrail Contracts with USAF' and read for yourself the Chemtrail history. A great website for Chemtrail related information is aboutthesky.com.

After hearing the claims by Theosophists that their manufactured world leader 'Maitreya' will be able to communicate with everyone 'telepathically' and in their own tongue, I was immediately reminded of the HAARP mind control program as well as the above said government 'Chemtrail' evergreen program. In addition I recalled Raymond Kurzweil's premonition regarding nanotechnology and its ability to manipulate human health. All of the aforesaid information called to mind an article published in the United States National Library of Medicine, 10/25/2009, titled: "Inhaled Carbon Nanotubes Reach the Sub-Pleural Tissue in Mice." In part, the article reads:

"We exposed male C57BL6 mice to an aerosol of MWCNT (1 mg/m3 or 30 mg/m3) or carbon black nanoparticles (CB, 30 mg/m3) for 6 h and then collected lung tissues at 1 dy, 2 wk, 6 wk, and 14 wk post-inhalation exposure."

What if, our Luciferian world leaders are spraying nano-tubes which contain nano-receivers over the United States? These nano-receivers would simply need to be inhaled or ingested and once inside our bodies they would make their way to our brains by way of genetically-modified organisms (GMO) gluten. What's interesting is that GMO gluten is capable of penetrating the 'blood/brain barrier'. In other words, gluten may be capable of transporting these nano-tubes into the brain. I discuss the facts surrounding the blood/brain barrier in more detail in later chapters. Once inside our brains they would attach themselves to neurons or synapse and activated through the 'piezo effect'. It's through these nano-receivers that Luciferians intend on transmitting their anti-Christ message simultaneously [Revelation 13:15].

The emergence of the anti-Christ will be a great spectacle. It will deceive many, so the trick is going to have to be pretty extravagant. To pull the wool over the eyes of an American Christian population which has been exposed to computer generated imagery (CGI) and Holographic Imagery, etc., their solution will need to be more than just some simple wires and mirrors trick.

Deceived 'New Agers' tell us that their perfect 'god' is out of reach for most people and that only a chosen few are capable of communicating with their mysterious inaccessible god. The New Age belief system suggests that Jesus Christ is not the name of a particular being. New Agers suggest the name 'Christ' is simply a level of enlightenment within their order of spiritual advisors. There's nothing 'anti-Christ' about that. Right? New Agers believe that it's these spiritual advisors, namely Maitreya, who has been responsible for all of humanity's advancements and the real 'Christ'. I guess their omnipotent puppet master has been too busy to telepathically transfer the fix for cancer, global warming, world hunger, etc. And if this is the one true God who loves all nations and people, why is he allowing organizations such as Monsanto and The Gates Foundation to poison billions of human beings with Toxic Genetically Modified Food and Vaccines?

So, who in their right mind would buy into all of this nonsense? Well, you remember our possessed village idiot, Benjamin Crème? He says that when he became possessed initially with the spirit of Maitreya he was shown a vision of the future, where he was responsible for the introduction of Maitreya to the entire world. Furthermore, Crème was instrumental in establishing Hel-

167

ena Blavatsky Satanic Theosophical manufactured One World Religion. In the following statement Crème admits to being inspired by the Satanic Theosophical doctrine of Helena Blavatsky and Alice Bailey:

"To many today, this awareness includes the recognition of higher states of consciousness attained by those who make up the emerging spiritual kingdom, the Masters and initiates of the world. Their existence was first revealed in modern time by H.P. Blavatsky, cofounder of the Theosophical society, as long ago as 1875. A more detailed communication about the Masters in their work was given by Alice a daily between 1919 in 1949. In her book the externalization of the hierarchy she revealed the existence of a plan return to physical-plane work and activities by this group of enlightened men, which return, I submit, has already begun."

"Won't the advent of a single world religion annoy the hierarchies of all the current orthodox religions? More than that he said, with a smile, they will be shocked. I daresay they will be among the last to accept the Christ. It will come, because it must, we will begin to live, as potential gods." - from the book: 'The Hidden Dangers of The Rainbow'

Benjamin Crème has never been shy about proclaiming his love of Satan. Take for instance, a radio interview back in the early 80's for WLAC Nashville in which Cème told the 'Bible Belt':

"Lucifer came to planet earth from planet Venus 18 ½ million years ago and made the supreme sacrifice for us."

As stunning as this may all seem, it's not just relatively unknown psychopaths who are professing their love for the anti-Christ Maitreya. It's also World Leaders e.g., United States Presidents, Congressmen, Senators, the United Nations, and others. Take retired American diplomat, Wayne Peterson, who is an avowed Maitreya worshipper. What should really concern you is that Wayne Peterson is heavily connected with the Pentagon as well as the co-creators of 'Agenda 21' over at the United Nations.

168

In an interview with Vision Magazine back on June 20, 2000, Peterson made the following statement regarding Mikhail Gorbachev and the White House. Please pay close attention to what he says about the Satanic Theosophical manufactured Maitreya and President George H.W. Bush and you'll understand why George H.W. Bush spearheaded the genocidal 'Agenda 21' into the heart of America.

Reporter Kendall Klug asks: "I believe Mikhail Gorbachev has publicly stated his belief of the existence of Maitreya. You know if this is true?"

Wayne Peterson answers: "I have one little story I could tell you about Gorbachev. A friend of mine who worked with the World Bank went to a heads of state conference in Europe and gave a speech where he borrowed many of Maitreya's ideas for economic reform out of the book by Benjamin Crème that I had given him. He told me that he had read the book on his flight to Europe and realized that his keynote address to these world officials, especially presidents and prime ministers -it was a very high-level meeting-was going to be very boring, with many having heard similar sentiments over and over. So he thought he would throw in some of Maitreya's ideas into his speech. The country he was in had a reigning monarch who invited him to lunch the next day. When he showed up for lunch there were 16-20 people there including Mr. Gorbachev.

The monarch of this country said to him (my friend). I suppose you're wondering why we invited you here today? Well, we are all curious about where you got those ideas for your speech which you presented yesterday. He said that my friend Wayne gave me a book written by Benjamin Crème about Maitreya's mission. Immediately they nodded their heads, we thought so, was the apparent response. That's why we invited you here today. We all know of Maitreya; and we are doing what we can for him but we are not able to say anything publicly because we are world leaders. We each have our own public to deal with. Only one person there stood up and said that they could use his name to legitimize the sightings and that was Mikhail Gorbachev. He was the only man in the room who said 'Use my name if you want'."

Reporter Kendall Klug asks: "Do you think President Clinton had an experience of Maistreya?" Wayne Peterson answers: "I don't know if President Clinton has. I believe the former president George Bush has. We used to have transmission meditation groups that Maitreya had asked us to do around Washington D.C. People who were interested in Maitreya in the reappearance story would get together once a week in Georgetown, in the home of President Bush's main counselor at the White House. President Bush came over to this house for dinner one night, and the hostess was in the dining room and President Bush asked her, what do you think? I'm running against Clinton in this election, am I going to win? She said, no, Mr. Pres. you are not. Maitreya has already said you're going to lose to Clinton. Bush never challenged her, but merely said, yeah, yeah. He didn't ask who Maitreya was? He was very quiet and said, I think I've got to go now. Benjamin Crème has said many times that he had heard from one of Maitreya's associates that Maitreya had appeared to Bush and that they had discussions in the White House. So that incident with my meditation group seemed to confirm that Bush did in fact know of Maitreya. I do know people in the White House had been visited by Maitreya many times. And these are people I've seen on the front page of the Washington Post standing next to the president."

Mikhail Gorbachev said, on several occasions, the following about the Satanic, Theosophical pursuit of a "New World Order":

"Nothing describes why the world has changed so much and why the world has turned so much towards a new world order and a new kind of civilization."

As an aside, Albert Pike [pg.172] was the founder of the occult organization 'Knights of the Golden Circle'. Its members list included John Wilkes Booth and Jessie James. Pike' Knights assassinated President Abraham Lincoln for double-crossing his status as a 33rd degree Freemason, when he disallowed the installation of a Rothschild Family central banking system in the U.S.

While Lincoln publicly touted Christ to the majority "called by my name" [2 Chronicles 7:14], stating: "Take all that you can of this book [Holy Bible]"; "But for this book [Holy Bible] we could not know right from wrong"; "I believe the Bible is the best gift God has ever given to man. All the good from The Savior of the world is communicated to us through this Book," etc.

170

Lincoln privately plotted against Jesus Christ and His Church.

According to the book "Lincoln and the Jews," It was Lincoln who flooded America with antichristian Talmudists. In 1809 there were a mere 3,000 Talmudists in America, however by 1865 there were 150,000. Lincoln appointed many Jews to public office and had numerous Jewish advisors. The most disturbing aspect of Lincoln's Presidency is the fact that it was President Lincoln who changed America's label of being a "Christian Nation" to "This nation under God" to appease antichristian Talmudists [so-called 'Jews'].

In 1871, Babylonian Talmudist, sovereign Grand Commander of the Supreme Council 33rd degree of Freemasonry, British spy, Ku Klux Klan founder, Grand Dragon and "Knights of the Golden Circle" founder [Albert Pike] — in a letter to Giuseppe Mazzini — a 33 degree Grand Master Freemason, founder of Italian Freemasonry, Revolutionary Terrorist Leader, Sicilian Gangster and founder of the "Mafia" stated:

> "In the third World War we shall unleash the nihilist
> and the atheists and we shall provoke a formidable social
> catechism which in all its horror will show clearly to the
> nations the effect of absolute atheism, origin of savagery.
> And of the most bloody turmoil then everywhere the
> citizens obliged to defend themselves against the world mi-
> nority of revolutionaries will exterminate those destroyers
> of civilization [Islam]. And the multitudes disillusioned with
> Christianity whose deistic spirits will from that moment
> be without compass, or direction, anxious for an ideal, but
> without knowing where to render its adoration, will receive
> the true light through the universal manifestation of the
> pure doctrine of Lucifer [Satan] brought finally out into the
> public view. This manifestation will result from the general
> reactionary movement which will follow the destruction of
> Christianity and atheism both conquered and exterminated
> at the same time."

"Every Masonic lodge is a temple of religion [Satanism], and its teachings are instructions in religion... This is true religion revealed to the ancient patriarchs; which masonry [Church of Lucifer] has taught for many centuries, and which it will continue to teach as long as time endures." – Albert Pike, Book: Morals and Dogma, pg. 213-214. Chapter Eleven

"I do conscientiously and sincerely believe that the order of Freemasonry, if not the greatest, is one of the greatest moral and political evils." - 6th U.S. President John Quincy Adams

The above image features a 17ft. tall statue of George Washington standing inside 'The George Washington Masonic National Memorial' in Alexandria, VA. It is dedicated to the 1st President of the U.S. and a 33 degree Freemason. Washington's statue was unveiled on 2/22/1950 by 33 degree Freemason President Harry S. Truman the only United States Freemason President to be awarded a Freemason fifty-year award.

The most unique feature of this 16-17ft tall statue of President Washington, is its connection with the "sons of God" [Genesis 6:2]. The "sons of God" were fallen angels [demons] who defied God and impregnated human females. This unholy union produced giant offspring standing 13ft-30ft tall. The Book of Genesis reads, "There were giants in the earth in those days; and also after that, when the sons of God came in unto the daughters of men, and they bare children to them." Matthew 24:37 prophecy reads, "But as the days of Noe were, so shall also the coming of the Son of man be."

Two Biblical accounts of giants include, "Og the king of Bashan" [Psalms 136:20] and "the sons of Anak" [Numbers 13:33]. What's more, the dome behind Washington contains a tessellation pattern known as the 'Sacred Geometry of the Flower of Life'.

If you're interested in learning more about this subject, please read my book at, KillingIreland.com.

173

"I've got every degree in the masons that there is" - 33rd U.S. President, Harry S. Truman [above], 1945-1953

Harry S. Truman was also a member of the Council of Foreign Relations (CFR). On February 17, 1950 fellow 33rd degree Freemason and CFR member, James Warburg, publicly announced that the CFR's goal was to destroy U.S. sovereignty in exchange for a Luciferian, New World Order, stating:

"We shall have world government whether or not you like it, by conquest or consent."

CFR member, Richard Gardner, writing in the April 1974 issue of the CFRs journal, Foreign Affairs states:

"The New World Order will have to be built from the bottom up rather than from the top down... but in the end run around national sovereignty, eroding it piece by piece will accomplish much more than the old fashioned frontal assault."

Professors Laurence H. Shoup and William Minter, writing in their study of the CFR, "Imperial Brain Trust: The CFR and United States Foreign Policy." (Monthly Review Press, 1977) states:

"The planning of UN can be traced to the secret steering committee established by Secretary [of State Cordell] Hull in January 1943. All of the members of this secret committee, with the exception of Hull, a Tennessee politician, were members of the Council on Foreign Relations. They saw Hull regularly to plan, select, and guide the labors of the [State] Departments Advisory Committee. It was, in effect, the coordinating agency for all the State Departments postwar planning."

CHAPTER 12 Lucifer's United Nations

"The lowest strata are reproducing too fast. Therefore... they must not have too easy access to relief or hospital treatment lest the removal of the last check on natural selection should make it too easy for children to be produced or to survive; long unemployment should be a ground for sterilization."
– UNESCO Director, Julian Huxley

(Note: The above image of a U.N. Assembly contains 666)

The United States of America was built on the foundation that every human being is born with inalienable rights; these are: Life, Liberty and the Pursuit of Happiness. What most Christian Americans are oblivious to is the fact that these God given rights are literally just a few unconstitutional, Luciferian influenced executive orders and treaties away from complete obscurity. United States Presidents, for the past thirty years, have been willing participants in the deconstruction of America and its fusion into 'The North American Union', which is roughly patterned after the European Union (EU). In short, President George W. Bush signed an executive order which ended America as we know it. He, along with Presidents from Mexico and Canada agreed to do everything in their power to progress the long time goal of Luciferians, to bring about an end to America and the emergence of a 'North American Union'. The hegemony of the United Nations over America's executive branch is unmistakable. Critics have argued that the United Nations' efforts to assume complete control over America's land, oceans, agriculture, water supply, vitamins and guns, is nothing but circumstantial. The United Nations suggests that it is simply working in a direction that will benefit all nations equally. Under close examination such explanations are quite hollow. Take for instance, United Nations Security Council 'Resolution 666', adopted on September 13, 1990. Resolution 666 was adopted with thirteen votes; Cuba and Yemen voted against the resolution, with Cuba stating that even through the use of disclaimers, the resolution amounted to:

"Using starvation as a weapon of war", banned under Protocol 1 of the Geneva Conventions"

It's not as if there was a long conflict between 1994 and 2002 which left 5.4 million Congolese dead by murder and starvation, and that the central figure to this genocide was Susan Rice. This is the woman, by the way, who President Barack Hussein Obama, on June 5, 2013 believed was qualified to hold the position of United States Security Advisor, a person who abetted the Congo genocide for much of her political career.

Appointed to President Bill Clinton's National Security Council in 1993, at age 28, Susan Rice rose to Assistant Secretary of State for African affairs in 1997 as Rwanda and Uganda were swarming across the eastern Congo, seizing control of mineral resources amid a sea of blood. She is known to be personally close to Rwanda's minority Tutsi leadership, including President Paul Kagame, a ruthless soldier trained at the United States Army's Command and General Staff College at Fort Leavenworth, Kansas, and mentored by Ugandan strongman (and Reagan administration favorite) Yoweri Museveni, who is believed to have pioneered the use of child soldiers in modern African conflicts.

Furthermore, there's evidence which shows the United Nations 'Peace Keepers' were complicit in transporting a deadly strain of Cholera into Haiti, which is still raging in 2014. The deadly Cholera strain is said to have originated in Nepal. Perhaps it was a gift from Theosophist created Antichrist 'Maitreya'? After all, Maitreya handlers have always promoted Nepal as his country of origin.

It certainly doesn't sound like the Christian American majority has anything to worry about. Why should America's Christian majority be concerned with the prospect of the United Nations having control over America? Aside from losing our Constitution and Bill of Rights, it would mean that we would be subjected to the United Nations dreadful track record of managing international conflicts. Take for instance, the 17,000 United Nations Peace Keepers in Africa, who were outperformed operationally by just 70 independent special operators. Comparing these numbers, it's not hard to see why America's enemies have been sacrificing Navy Special Forces operators, most recently, former Navy SEAL Chris Kyle, the author of the best-selling book "American Sniper". When asked about his perception of America's reality, Chris Kyle had this to say:

"For the most part, the public is very soft, you live in a dream world" – Scottish American Chris Kyle, Navy Seal

(Note: If you would like to learn why Navy Seal, Chris Kyle was sacrificed please read my book at, KillingScotland.com)

As grim and foreboding as the above atrocities are, they pale in comparison to the foundational ideology of those who influence United Nations policy makers and who are longtime strategic consultants, who literally control the actions taken by the United Nations. President F.D. Roosevelt's son-in-law Curtis Dall, in his book titled 'My Exploited Father in Law,' states the following about the United Nations' power over the United States:

"For a long time I felt that FDR had developed many thoughts and ideas that were his own to benefit this country, the United States. But, he didn't. Most of his thoughts, his political ammunition, as it were, were carefully manufactured for him in advance by the Council on Foreign Relations One World Money group... Brilliantly, with great gusto, like a fine piece of artillery, he exploded that prepared "ammunition" in the middle of an unsuspecting target, the American people, and thus paid off and returned his internationalist political support. The UN is but a long range, international banking apparatus nearly set up for financial and economic profit by a small group of powerful One World Revolutionaries, hungry for profit and power. The depression was the calculated 'shearing' of the public by the World Money powers, triggered by the planned sud-

den shortage of supply of call money in the New York money market...
The One World Government leaders and their ever close bankers have
now acquired full control of the money and credit machinery of the
U.S. via the creation of the privately owned Federal Reserve Bank."

It will be remembered that Alice Bailey is one of the most dedicated Luciferians of all time. It was Alice Bailey who infected the global
network of Theosophists with the idea of artificially developing a 'New
World Order', the very New World Order that former American CIA
Director/President George H.W. Bush is on film everywhere promoting.
Alice Bailey was also a student of Helena Blavatsky who trumpeted the
idea of recruiting the entire world into her Luciferian religion in order to
realize the full benefits of the Age of Aquarius, such "full benefits" being defined as the world's complete and total abandonment of Lord Jesus
Christ. This has always been the driving force behind all occult, New Age
and Satanist groups; the only difference between any of these vehicles is
their packaging. Take for instance American 'Shock-Star' Marilyn Manson who is an avowed Satanist, former student of Anton Lavey's 'Church
of Satan' and proponent of 'The Most Evil Man on Earth' – Aleister
Crowley. Marilyn Manson, regarding his contribution towards achieving
Alice Bailey's 'full benefit' of the Age of Aquarius, states:

"Hopefully, I'll be remembered as the person who brought an end to
Christianity." – Marilyn Manson

Alice Bailey, much like the founder of militant anti-Christian
Theosophy, Helena Blavatsky, was quite the writer. As a matter of fact,
Alice Bailey would go on to write as many as 24 books on her favorite
topic, the occult, although she cannot really say that they were all written
by her. You see, she brags that she was possessed by her spiritual guides
[demons] during her writing sessions and that these spirits channeled
their ideas through her. That doesn't sound at all like demon possession,
now does it?

Alice Bailey would eventually come up with the morbidly
wicked idea of forming a publishing company by the name of 'Lucifer
Publishing'. Again deifying her role model Lucifer, Bailey's publishing
house would be instrumental in the distribution of Helena Blavatsky's
satanic writings as well as a long list of possessed, New
Age, Theosophical writers. Now, due to the fact that the
American majority back then was in some form or another

179

comprised of followers of Jesus Christ, Bailey later came to the sensible conclusion that Americans may not take kindly to a publishing company named after Satan. That being said, Bailey changed the name of Lucifer Publishing to 'Lucis Trust'.

You may be asking yourself. When did Lucis Trust go out of business? The truth is Lucis Trust never shuttered its doors. It's still very much in operation today. Not only is it operating, it has become an influential member of the United Nations. That's right folks. The pupil of Satanic Theosophy founder Helena Blavatsky and founder of Lucifer Publishing is directly associated with the United Nations. Let's read the following entry from the 2009 United Nations Geneva Yearbook:

"The Lucis Trust is recognized by the United Nations as a non-governmental organization and is represented at regular briefing sessions at UN headquarters. The Lucis Trust is on the roster of the United Nations economic and social Council."

How does it make you feel to know that the United Nations members list includes an avowed satanic organization? Not only is Lucis Trust recognized by the United Nations, but it holds a supervisory position influencing other member Nations. Nations, by the way, who have openly called for the eradication of the United States Constitution, freedom of speech, freedom to own weapons, freedom to defend ourselves, freedom to own land, freedom to grow our own food, the implementation of Agenda 21, ICLEI, global genocide, etc. Most troubling of all is the fact that this avowed Satanic organization has for generations been instrumental in deciding matters related to the United Nations 'Economic and Social Council'. Let me repeat that. An avowed Satanic Theosophical, New World Order, One World Religion advocate has oversight and influence over our Nation's social progress or more accurately stated regression.

Under the Luciferian authority of the United Nations America has gone through a massive moral, educational and spiritual transformation. Over the past sixty years America has witnessed a 'sexual revolution' which has been shown to have been orchestrated and engineered by The Church of Babylon using their useful idiot, Dr. Kinsey. Through Kinsey's abhorrent junk science, Theosophists fabricated data to push an agenda that would completely erode the morality of America, coupling Kinsey's treachery with that

180

of Planned Parenthood's "1969 memo" whose overt agenda calls for an increase in homosexuality throughout America, the dismantling of the nuclear family and forcing women into positions where they would develop a compulsion to work, over a desire to have a family. The majority of Christian Americans today are completely unaware of the fact that just one year prior to Planned Parenthood's 1969 announcement to increase homosexuality throughout America, the American Psychiatric Association removed homosexuality from their Diagnostic and Statistical Manual of Mental Disorders (DSM) which listed homosexuality among the sociopathic personality disturbances.

The Christian American majority must understand that the women's liberation movement didn't occur by accident; remember, 'In politics, nothing happens by accident' - Freemason President Franklin D. Roosevelt. The fact is the vast majority of women, sixty years ago, worked extremely hard at raising quality, morally astute American citizens. The problem with that particular job description is that it was not conducive to a Church of Babylon based 'Do What Thou Wilt' one world religion economy. Millions of new female workers would be extremely beneficial to the elites' goal of America's deconstruction. Not only would they generate billions more in new tax revenue, they would also delay a woman's choice to have a family, children, etc. Moreover, a mother who is working creates an educational, moral and economic void, gladly filled by The Church of Babylon.

(IMPORTANT NOTE: Watch the documentary 'America: From Freedom to Fascism' freedomtofascism. com by Aaron Russo)

Other than Bill & Hillary Clinton, most people would agree that it's a conflict of interest to be a senior senator from West Virginia knowing that your family owns the Federal Reserve Corporation? That's exactly what the great-great grandson of oil tycoon John D. Rockefeller is doing. John Davison "Jay" Rockefeller IV [right] is the senior United States Senator from West Virginia and I'm sure you can guess his position on auditing the federal government. Jay isn't the only Rockefeller who has had enormous influence over our Nation.

Jay Rockefeller's father, David Rockefeller, in his book - simply titled 'Memoirs', makes no attempt at hiding his family's participation in the destruction of America, our Constitution and the formation of a New World Order.

Justin Aldrich Rockefeller, [right] with a meat cleaver hidden behind his back, is the 34 year old demon seed of West Virginia Senator Jay Rockefeller and the fifth-generation member of the satanic Rockefeller Family. At just 34 Justin demonstrates in this picture the 'secret knowledge' of his Rockefeller ancestry e.g., deceive, steal and kill. Already groomed by The Church of Babylon, Justin serves on the Board of Trustees for the Trillion dollar Rockefeller Brothers Fund and Richmond 'Sustainability' Foundation which cham-
pions the Rothschild invented Agenda 21. What's more, Justin uses his Princeton bachelor's degree in 'politics' to direct a financial tech company named Addepar whose algorithm provides data aggregation and analysis for clients having in the aggregate more than 50 billion in assets. It's these types of algorithms that are used by the Rockefellers and Rothschild's to 'Shock Test' portions of the U.S. economy. This is a central mechanism within elite controlled finance.

In his book, 'Memoirs' pg. 405, the puppet master of J.P. Morgan Chase [DBA Chase] , David Rockefeller, arrogantly boasts about his family's participation in the intentional destruction of Christian America.

"For more than a century ideological extremists at either end of the political spectrum have seized upon well-publicized incidents such as my encounter with Castro to attack the Rockefeller family for the inordinate influence they claim we wield over American political and economic institutions. Some even believe we are part of a secret cabal working against the best interests of the United States, characterizing my family and me as internationalists and of conspiring with others around the world to build a more integrated global political and economic structure-one world order, if you will, if that's the charge, I stand guilty, and I am proud of it."

If you're a Christian who currently utilizes the services of CHASE Bank, or have in your possession a Chase credit card, I highly recommend that you boycott these products and any organization associated with the Rockefeller Family. This includes toxic genetically modified organisms [GMOs] distributor Yum Restaurant Services Group (NYSE: YUM), the world's largest fast food restaurant company with more than $11 billion in annual sales. Yum! operates or licenses Taco Bell, KFC, Pizza Hut, Pasta Bravo, WingStreet, and East Dawning restaurants worldwide. Yum!' chairman and CEO is Ukrainian American David C. Novak. Novak, an alleged Christian and member of Southeast Christian church, has also been a director for J.P. Morgan Chase [DBA Chase] since 2001. J.P. Morgan is the largest bank in the U.S., the third largest public company in the world, with total assets of $2.415 trillion, and is under the complete control of the antichristian Rockefeller Family. Every day that you're paying interest on your CHASE Credit Card, CHASE Home Mortgage, etc., or killing yourself with toxic fast-food GMOs you're enriching the Rockefeller Family and funding initiatives meant to sicken and 'soft-kill' the Christian American majority.

Not only are these Luciferian controlled corporations selling American's toxic, DNA destroying, cancer causing GMO's at KFC, Taco Bell, etc. they provide them with Dine-In and To-Go facilities which are literally surrounded by the "Mark of the Beast" [666]. For example the Taco Bell logo [below] is comprised of a large "6" encircling a serpent eye. This logo represents the oldest, most powerful proxy for Satan, the ancient Serpent Cult of Dann [Genesis 49:17]. To learn more about this death cult, please visit, KillingIreland.com. Many of the Taco Bell restaurants throughout America possess this Serpent 6 logo on the front and two sides which creates "666".

In addition to the Mark of the Beast, the newer Taco Bell restaurants are in the shape of a cube [below] and to the Church of Babylon the cube represents Saturn otherwise known as Satan. Additional design elements which adorn the outside of newer Taco Bell locations include a distinct abstract modification of the Eye of Horus or Ra.

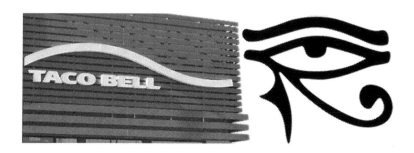

The majority of readers examing the aforementioned information will be unaware of the fact that, Bel [Bell] is the name of the patron deity of Babylon. The name Bel is closely related to that of Baal [Ball], the patron deity of Canaan. The Bible tells us that worshipping Baal is identical to worshipping the Devil [1 Kings 16:30-33, 22:53; 2 Kings 17:16] God condemned Baal worship, slaughtered the priests of Baal , and finally abolished it altogether in Israel. Yet, here, Freemasonry boldly states that they revere him.

In addition to being "proud of working against the best interests of the United States," David Rockefeller gives us a peak into the mind of a pyschopath, when on August 10, 1973, he wrote the following for the New York Times:

"Whatever the price of the Chinese revolution [an indirect reference to
the 65 million Chinese who were murdered throughout China during
Chairman Mao's leadership], it has obviously succeeded not only in producing, more efficient and dedicated administration, but also in fostering high morale and community of purpose. The social experiment in
China under Chairman Mao's leadership is one of the most important
and successful in human history."

Even our United States foreign policy analyst/former Deputy Secretary of State, Strobe Talbot, called for globalization and world government in Time Magazine issue of July 20, 1992:
"Here is one optimist's reason for believing unity will prevail over
disunity integration over disintegration in fact I bet within the next
hundred years, I'm giving the world time for setbacks and myself to
be out of the betting game, just in case I lose this one. Nationhood
as we know it will be obsolete all states will recognize a single global
authority, a phrase briefly fashionable in the mid 20th century; citizen
of the world will have assumed real meaning by the end of the 21st. All
countries are basically social arrangements accommodations to changing circumstances, no matter how permanent or sacred they may seem
at any one time. In fact they are all artificial in temporary."

Mikhail Gorbachev noted:

"The threat of environmental crisis will be the international disaster key that will unlock the New World order."

Mikhal Gorbachev also said:

"We are moving toward a new world order, the world of communism. We shall never turn off the road."

The following text was lifted from the final sermon of New Age Theosophist Reverend Jim Jones. Jones was the founder and leader of the Peoples Temple. Jones was a voracious reader as a child and studied Joseph Stalin and Karl Marx. Jones is best known for his cult suicide in 1978 of 914 of the cult's members in Jonestown, Guyana. He's also responsible for the murder of five individuals at a nearby airstrip which included (D) Congressman from California Leo Ryan. Furthermore, 200 children were murdered at Jonestown, almost all of them by cyanide poisoning. Jones died from a single gunshot to the head.

"Don't lay down with tears and agony. There's nothing about death. It's like stepping over into another plane. Don't be this way. Stop this hysterics. This is not the way for people who are socialists and communists to die. We must die with some dignity. Soon we'll have no choice, now we have some choice."

Still not convinced that Satanic Theosophy has any influence over the opinions and policies at the United Nations? Consider this fact: Dwight L. Kinman, author of the book 'The Worlds Last Dictator', student of Satanic Theosophists Alice Bailey and FORMER GENERAL SECRETARY FOR THE UNITED NATIONS, confessed on page 81 or his book:

"We must move as quickly as possible to a one-world government; a one-world religion under a one-world leader."

IMPORTANT NOTE: If the reader is unfamiliar with 'AGENDA 21', please visit Tom DeWeese's website americanpolicy.org Mr. DeWesse is a great American Patriot whose contributions to educate the American public about the very real threat of the Satanic, Theosophical based, and Anti-Constitutional 'AGENDA 21' are immeasurable.

If the reader has any reservations regarding the threat of Agenda 21 to the American population, please consider this fact. ICLEI is a non-government enforcement arm for the creators of Agenda 21. In communist China, out of a population of over one and a half billion people, there is only one ICLEI facility. In America, a population of 311 million, ICLEI has planned over 1,500 locations. This is what an invasion and takeover of a free Republic, whose majority is Christian, looks like.

Ask a hundred people on the street. 'Who is Samuel Adams?' and I'll bet 40% of them will tell you 'a beer'. In actuality, Samuel Adams was one of the most patriotic founding fathers of America. Mr. Adams rejected the concept of communism or socialism. Both of these concepts are second only to Satan within the Theosophical belief system. Mr. Adams said about communism and socialism:

"The utopian schemes of leveling [redistribution of the wealth] and a community of goods [central ownership of the means of production and distribution], are as visionary and impractical as those which best all property in the crown. [These ideas] are arbitrary [choices and actions which are done not by means of any underlying principle or logic], despotic [ruling with absolute political power], and, in our government, unconstitutional."

N.B Ghodke, in the book Encyclopaedic Dictionary of Economics, page 205, describes communism based on the ideals of Marx:

- Social wealth will be distributed according to human needs: (meaning things that are scarce will be distributed first to those who need them the most).
- The state will wither away as there is no need for coercion.
- Social classes will not exist.
- It will be a moneyless economy.
- It will be a command economy. Government planners decide which goods and services are produced and how they are distributed.

Nikita Khrushchev, on July 19, 1962 commented:

"The United States will eventually fly the Communist red flag. The American people will hoist it themselves."

187

Satanic Theosophist Alice Bailey concurs, when she said:

"the true communist platform is sound"

New Age, Satanic Theosophists and their useful idiot proxies all promote the idea of a New World Order or One World Religion. These possessed souls are sold on the idea of this new societal control system. They're excited about how well this would dovetail with the belief system of communism, socialism and Satanism. If you read any of the New Agers books, they promise a New World Order, where food distribution and all worldly demands would be met utilizing a complex network of super computers. It will be remembered from previous chapters where I voiced my concerns over the elites push for Spy-Cloud Computing and the inherent dangers associated with adopting this system of consolidation. I cannot stress the importance of refusing the global elite Spy-Cloud Computing nemesis. Do not adopt its use in your personal lives e.g., education, etc. and do not incorporate it into your business. Lastly you should eschew 'search engines' such as Google, Yahoo, Facebook, etc. in favor of search engines that do not track or record your online activity. Search engines such as DuckDuckGo.com, StartPage.com, Ixquick.com and Tor all facilitate anonymous surfing. In terms of secure encryption tools you should consider Cryptocat, which encrypts chat messages before they are sent.

13 Lucifer's Religion of Transgenderism

"America is like a healthy body and its resistance is threefold: It's patriotism, its morality, and its spiritual life. If we can undermine these three areas, America will collapse from within."

- Joseph Stalin, Satanist Dictator of the Central Committee of the Communist Party of the Soviet Union

The Holy Bible contains 177 verses which instruct Christians how and why husbands and wives should cherish the sanctity of their marriage. However, the anti-Christian element which controls the American entertainment industry seeks to undermine and destroy each and every one of those sacred verses. One of Hollywood's most successful stakes in the heart of Christian American marriages was the widely popular TV show and movie 'Sex and the City'. This was a show about four desperate aging women seeking husbands. The recurring theme throughout this show was that the characters are emotionally and spiritually incompatible with all of the men they come across. Anyone who is keen to the programming of Hollywood will see the blatant feminist/lesbian undertones that men and women are identical.

The 'Sex and the City' characters found themselves in a very confusing lifestyle, mainly because they wanted to control the men they were pursuing, while at the same time wanting to be possessed. Like many American women today, these characters have been programmed by anti-Christian theosophists to resist their God given femininity. The resulting effect is a group of depressed, angry, emotionally and physically unfulfilled women, who engage in fruitless sex acts with countless men, all the while growing older and bitterer. The overarching dysfunctional theme of the show is that it's OK that you're a shallow, materialistic whore so long as you have your girlfriends to sit with in a coffee shop, complaining about what's wrong with everyone else.

It should come as no surprise that the creator of "Sex and the City" was Darren Starr, a homosexual. It's through shows like 'Sex and the City' that heterosexual Americans have been brainwashed into accepting the aforesaid toxic exis-

189

tence and why the Christian American majority will never find Hollywood story lines which promote:

"Whoso findeth a wife findeth a good thing, and obtaineth favour of the LORD." - Proverbs 18:22

Instead anti-Christian theosophists throughout Hollywood inspire promiscuity and instigate the idea that marriage is unrewarding, miserable, etc. Why won't Hollywood promote:

"For by means of a whorish woman a man is brought to a piece of bread: and the adulteress will hunt for the precious life." - *Proverbs 6:26*

"Husbands, love your wives, and do not be harsh with them." - *Colossians 3:19*

"Husbands, love your wives, as Christ loved the church and gave himself up for her," - *Ephesians 5:25*

"Let marriage be held in honor among all, and let the marriage bed be undefiled, for God will judge the sexually immoral and adulterous." - *Hebrews 13:4*

Instead the psychological warfare research and Freudian Psychotherapy based Tavistock Institute, through funding and support by the Rockefeller Foundation, Stanford Research Institute, The U.S. Office of Naval Research, the Science Policy Research Unit in England, MIT, Heritage Foundation, U.S. Air Force Intelligence, Wharton School, Institute for Policy Studies, Hudson Institute, Brookings Institute and Rand Corporation, a group who was once accused of being commissioned by the USSR (Russia) to work out terms of surrender of the United States Government have all supported initiatives necessary to maintain dominion over the Christian American majority. Social manipulation, moral decline, and de-industrialization has all been achieved through TV programming and has resulted in the growing rate of illegitimacy, petty lawlessness, drug addiction, welfare, STDs, and mental illness. One of Tavistock' key methods of destabilizing a victim's character and inducing a target with mental illness was repeatedly shown throughout the "Sex and the City" program. For instance, victims were repeatedly advised throughout the show to 'establish new rituals of personal interaction', that is, to indulge in brief sexual encounters which actually set the subjects adrift with no stable personal relationships in their lives, destroying their ability to establish or maintain a family. What's more, the show repeatedly characterized

190

married women as nagging, cheating, materialistic whores who cannot be trusted. This message is parroted throughout Hollywood which promotes the idea that men should physically and mentally abuse women and that sharing their marriage bed with multiple partners is healthy. Men are characterized as being weak, impotent, stupid animals which Hollywood programmers know sow the seeds of low self esteem and self hatred. Unsurprisingly, the percentage of American women using antidepressant drugs is higher than in any other nation in the world. Drugs containing warnings such as "suicidal thoughts" should be expected. Predictably, these drugs kill more people than car accidents every year. Why doesn't Hollywood promote:

"Nevertheless let every one of you in particular so love his wife even as himself; and the wife see that she reverence her husband." - *Ephesians 5:33*

"So ought men to love their wives as their own bodies. He that loveth his wife loveth himself." - *Ephesians 5:28*

The lesbian, gay, bisexual, transgender (LGBT) agenda promoted by theosophist controlled Hollywood sponsors the idea that women should look at their girlfriends as 'soul-mates' and men as something to just have fun with. Because of the selfish, whorish lifestyle funded and facilitated by Hollywood, men and women no longer see value in marriage or relationships. Young girls and women have been conditioned to seek out random sexual partners, while leveraging their girlfriends for emotional related topics. This toxic programming has shaped American men into an army of children, whose eternal goal it is to extend their adolescence as long as possible. This American male conditioning by anti-Christian Hollywood is intentionally undermining and emasculating our American male population. Why? Because the enemy knows this lifestyle will rob our American men of their ability to gain a woman's trust. No trust + No Relationship = No Children. They win. Game over. Why doesn't Hollywood promote:

"Submit yourselves therefore to God. Resist the devil, and he will flee from you." - *James 4:7*

Hollywood promotes a lifestyle filled with anti-Christian, satanic imagery and story lines, because Satan is who they serve. Most Christian Americans are unfamiliar with the Babylonian Talmud which originates in Nimrod's Babylon. Nimrod like Satan rebelled against God and promoted the idea of becoming god. For this reason none of Christ's virtues will ever appear in anti-Christian, Talmudist created Hollywood films. The question all Christians

191

should be asking themselves is... If Hollywood isn't investing in Christian imagery and messaging, why are Christian Americans investing in Hollywood?

"But I say unto you, That whosoever looketh on a woman to lust after her hath committed adultery with her already in his heart."
- Matthew 5:28

"The heart of her husband doth safely trust in her, so that he shall have no need of spoil." - Proverbs 31:11

"That they may teach the young women to be sober, to love their husbands, to love their children," - Titus 2:4

"Train up a child in the way he should go: and when he is old, he will not depart from it." - Proverbs 22:6

"And, ye fathers, provoke not your children to wrath: but bring them up in the nurture and admonition of the Lord."
- Ephesians 6:4

"I have no greater joy than to hear that my children walk in truth."
- 3 John 1:4

Some of today's most celebrated 'New Agers' whose messages are quite soothing and inspiring, in a science fiction kind of way, are upon closer observation, promoting nothing more than an esoteric buffet devoid of any Christian based spiritual nutrients. It's 'New Agers', such as Deepak Chopra, clinical psychologist and 'TFT' founder Irish American Dr. Roger Callahan, Neuro Linguistic Programming (NLP) Certified Master Practitioner and 'EFT' founder Scottish American Gary Craig, Wayne Dyer, Scottish American Tony Robbins, Rick Warren, and Michael Beckwith, to name a few, who are encouraging a diet rich in esotericism and spiritual malnutrition. Worst of all, Christian Americans, who have found these New Agers entertaining to listen to and follow, have grown spiritually weak, feeding on their diet of philosophy, vain deceit and man-made traditions. I've encountered a number of these types of Christian Americans who are extremely proud and boastful of their wonderful new insights and enlightenment. In reality, the vast majority of these avowed Christians have become so compromised spiritually by new age messaging that they are in no condition to face the slightest spiritual warfare.

192 "Beware lest any man spoil you through philosophy and vain deceit, after the tradition of men, after the rudiments

of the world, and not after Christ." - Colossians 2:8

Take Rick Warren for example. He's a prominent, mainstream, self avowed Christian minister. Warren's blatant dismissal of ancient Christian doctrine smacks of Theosophy, and his position on homosexuality should be roundly criticized and rejected by America's Christian majority. Warren said that he "apologized to his homosexual friends for making comments in support of California's Proposition-8 same-sex marriage ban." Which 'god' is Rick Warren representing when he apologizes for his stance on same sex marriage?

Michael Beckwith is the founder of 'Agape International Spiritual Center'. Like Rick Warren, Beckwith is a 'spiritual leader' who proudly espouses a number of the tenants promoted by Helena Blavatsky's Theosophy. One of Theosophy's leading objectives is the complete and total eradication of the 'Nuclear Family', Superior Biblical morality and virtues.

A powerful proponent of Beckwith's theosophist leanings is of course Hollywood, which gaily bombards Christian   Americans with programming, promoting the notion that adultery and homosexuality are emotionally, physically and spiritually benign in nature. What's troubling is that even though Christian Americans know this to be false, 240 million of them willingly contribute to the nearly 11 billion dollars generated by the movie industry each year. It's this money that is then recycled into toxic propaganda that disparages the sanctity of Jesus Christ and the health and spirituality of Christian American families.

"Marriage is honourable in all, and the bed undefiled: but whoremongers and adulterers God will judge." - Hebrews 13:4

How exactly is Beckwith contributing to the erosion of godly living? The Bible says:

"Let no man despise thy youth; but be thou an example of the believers, in word, in conversation, in charity, in spirit, in faith, in purity."
– 1 Timothy 4:12

Beckwith, along with the Reverend Ed Bacon, from the All Saints Episcopal Church, appeared on an episode of the Oprah Winfrey Show. It was on this episode where Beckwith and Bacon proceeded to mislead hundreds of thousands of believers on national television, with these words:

193

"Being gay is a gift from God" and "being gay is a divine right."

The above comments demonstrate Beckwith's blatant loyalty to the deconstruction of Christianity through esoteric, modernist dogma. This is just one of many examples illustrating the lengths to which theosophist proxies will go to destroy the sanctity of Christianity and the nuclear family. For years, gay and lesbian proponents have argued that gay marriage is in no way an assault on traditional marriage, it's about 'equal rights'. However, when we review the commentary of leading gay and lesbian activists, it's clear their intentions have absolutely nothing to do with 'equality'.

Take for instance the 2012 speech of lesbian activist, Masha Gessen, who arrogantly announced to the world the aim of many supporters of gay marriage was to destroy the institution of marriage and redefine the "traditional family." That's theosophist speak for 'kill Christianity'. Opponents of gay marriage suggest that the legalization of gay marriage will lead to other warped variations and definitions of 'family', a claim that's denied by supporters of gay marriage. Nonetheless, Masha Gessen confirms this concern when she says:

"I don't see why they [her children] shouldn't have five parents legally."

Here's just one of many experiences I have personally had within the past couple of years regarding esoteric ideological deception in the Christian church. Since the age of fourteen I attended a Church in Sacramento, California, by the name of 'Capital Christian Center'. Back in the late 80's the minister was the father of the current pastor Rick Cole. After not attending service at this particular church for some time, I thought to myself: Hey, what a great idea, to introduce my wife and young son, to service at Capital Christian Center.

I raved about the facilities and more importantly, the message that I received growing up from Pastor Rick Cole Sr. Towards the end of Pastor Cole Jr.'s sermon on this particular Sunday, the excitement and pride that I once shared excitedly for Capital Christian Center and its leaders turned to disappointment and embarrassment. While sitting there with my impressionable young son, Pastor Cole proceeds to spew his personal views about homosexuality. With an almost prideful conceit, Pastor Cole began promoting the idea that all of the parishioners of Capital Christian Center, should willingly seek out and invite as many homosexuals into Capital Christian Church as we could, as this was our divine charge by our God. I immediately thought to myself, this may be the charge through which

God has called Pastor Cole; however, I would never intentionally expose my children to that lifestyle.

There is a saying that goes "When you dance with the devil, you don't change the devil, the devil changes you." I am all too aware of this fact, as I've tried my entire life to help people 'change' or redirect those who were intent on living destructive lives. I've learned that if a person does not want to help themselves, all they will end up doing in the end is dragging you down with them. If someone is not ready or willing to receive the truth, and they want to just walk out of your life, it's best to just let them walk. That's been my experience.

Needless to say, service at Capital Christian Center that morning was more like an indoctrination of the theosophical one world religion than a celebration of Lord Jesus Christ's message. It's my personal opinion that Pastor Cole Jr.'s message was opportunistic, irresponsible, unprincipled, and counter to anything the God of The Holy Bible teaches. I was deeply disappointed that this community leader and representative of Lord Jesus Christ would allow himself to fall victim to a false doctrine that believes it's appropriate to expose my impressionable young son and hundreds of other young people in the audience that day to the psycho-pathological behavior of homosexuality. It was, quite frankly, shocking that this Pastor was presenting an ideology that was in lockstep with the 1969 Planned Parenthood Memo and theosophical teachings to expose and indoctrinate our young people into the homosexual lifestyle.

"I have hated the congregation of evil doers; and will not sit with the wicked." – Psalm 26:5

Its sermons such as the one preached by Pastor Cole and men like him, who is responsible for America's rampant moral and economic decline. It's these types of ministers who are willfully omitting Christ's principal message of liberation. Instead of presenting Christ's only path to salvation, they are more focused on modernist Marxist, theosophical principles, such as 'Political Correctness'. Messages such as these do nothing for the salvation of souls and everything for the salvation of one's paycheck, and the deliverance of souls to Satan. This has been Satan's 'Big Lie' to ministers across America. He convinced our Christian leaders that if they adhered to satanic, Marxist political correctness, they would gain favor among our younger generation, while in actuality this has achieved the opposite effect. Christianity isn't the only religion whose leaders have deceived its followers into accepting the homosexual lifestyle. Judaism is rampant with anti-Torah new agers. Take for instance the 'Union for Reform Judaism'. It is the largest Jewish movement in North America. It currently represents an estimated 1.5 million Jews with over 900 congregations in

195

the U.S., Canada, the Bahamas, Puerto Rico and the Virgin Islands. In the 'priorities' section of their website, it states that their 'sacred purpose' is to provide:

"advocacy resources, ideas and more about how to welcome the LGBT community into your congregation."

There is no other time throughout American history that we've seen such a falling away within our community of Christian leaders. America's Christian Pastors must come to the realization that our young people do not hold Lord Jesus Christ in contempt, instead they hold the Pastors as such, and the reason is quite simple. Our Nation's young people hold Christian Pastors in contempt because our young people do not feel that their leaders care enough about them to tell them the truth. Because of this reason, men and women in such leadership positions must be audited, exposed, and if necessary, removed by their parishioners and replaced with men and women of conviction and an uncompromising adherence to the truth.

"These things speak, and exhort, and rebuke with all authority. Let no man despise thee." – Titus 2:15

And before anyone raises the claim that I 'hate gay people' or anyone for that matter, that's just not the case. I believe the literal translation of The Holy Bible and that God defines 'hate speech' as any message which deceives people into believing a homosexual lifestyle is condoned by Him, and that by participating in this type of lifestyle an individual won't face punishment. I admit that I strongly disagree with the infertile homosexual lifestyle, as it in no way contributes to the propagation of the 'circle of life', the very same circle of life that has perpetuated the existence of Man on planet earth since its creation.

Church of Babylon Targeting Children:

"But whoso shall offend one of these little ones which believe in me, it were better for him that a millstone were hanged about his neck, and that he were drowned in the depth of the sea." - Matthew 18:6

Shockumentary Director Michael Moore's self ascribed superior moral and ethical worldview is quick to assert evil Corporations, Christianity and America's Constitution/Bill of Rights as our Nation's central adversaries, whilst living in his 11,058 square-foot, $5.2 million dollar, Torch Lake home in Michigan. What's fascinating is how Moore espouses an antigun ideology while he gallantly bounces about town, cloaked in the security and protection of an armed escort. Moreover, Moore proclaims that it's tyrannical for the Christian American majority to not do what the satanic theosophist ideologues controlling the United Nations and U.S. Government want them to do. Moore's hypocrisy doesn't end there; his documentary's titled "Capitalism: A Love Story" and "Bowling For Columbine" attempt to convert the uninformed masses by showing them isolated horror stories pertaining to the movies topic. Like the rest of Moore's projects, he fails to explore any root causes, namely why American children are murdering each other. They're murdering each other because they have been indoctrinated into the kingdom of the devil. And while parents play fill-in-the-blank children's game, our future leaders are being instructed by men who are possessed by the devil, a very real entity that many American parents have been deceived into believing does not exist. Instead of acknowledging the aforesaid cause, Moore uses demagoguery to make everyone feel guilty. At the same time, Moore is professionally and financially backing anti-family, theosophist driven homosexual love stories through film maker Kyle Henry. This is the same anti-family agenda which calls for the elimination of the title 'mother' and 'father', something that is now being implemented throughout the United Kingdom. Henry is the creator of such films as 'AMERICAN COWBOY', the story of a gay rodeo champ and 'FOURPLAY' a feature film anthology of four short tales covering such topics as:

"In TAMPA, a poorly endowed gay man finds unexpected company in a public rest room and In SAN FRANCISCO, a professional transvestite hooker faces a challenging prospect on a business call to Marin County." – Kyle Henry, Fourplay

With financial backing from Michael Moore and Richard Linklater, producer of films such as School of Rock, Dazed and Confused, Bad News Bears, Fast Food Nation, etc. Kyle Henry was provided the resources necessary to encourage pro-gay, anti-family, theosophist propaganda to U.S. college/university students throughout America during what's called the "McCollege Tour'.

Homosexual activists such as Michael Moore, Richard Linklater, and Kyle Henry publicly deny their desire to have access to our young American Christian boys; however, the vast majority of homosexual organizations around the world are aggressively pursuing laws that would lower the age of sexual consent. Backing these Anti-Christ groups are the same Wundt trained psychiatrists and psychologists who backed the sadomasochist, homosexual Alfred Charles Kinsey and his fraudulent 'research' which lead to America's sexual revolution and with it, the pestilence of homosexuality. Kinsey, an ardent militant antichristian, understood the importance of erod-

197

ing America's Christian foundation in order to encourage homosexuality stating: "less homosexual activity among devout groups whether they be Protestant, Catholic, or Jewish, and more homosexual activity among religiously less active groups." A 1983 study found those raised in non-religious homes were four times more likely to become homosexual than those from religiously committed homes. This study suggests that when individuals believe that homosexual behavior is immoral, they are far less likely to engage in sexual depravity. Their agenda in recent years has moved toward normalizing pedophilia much as they did with homosexuality in the early 1970s by promoting inequality, subjugation, hate and elimination of the Christian American majority. In a recent article for Gay Voices, actor/writer Harvey Fierstein, writes about Christianity:

"Fundamentalism from our home parishes, is the enemy. It is the death knell of tolerance, progress and compromise. Fundamentalism is, in all practicality, nothing but an invitation to bigotry."

Kevin Bishop, an admitted pedophile, promotes the work of the North American /Man-Boy Love Association (NAMBLA) in South Africa. Bishop, who says he was sexually assaulted when he was only six, is also an admitted homosexual; even more, he is proud of the abomination of homosexuals and their progress towards normalizing pedophilia. In an interview with the Electronic Mail & Guardian (June 30, 1997) Kevin Bishop states:

"Scratch the average homosexual and you will find a pedophile," (Angela Johnson, "The man who loves to love boys," Electronic Mail & Guardian, June 30, 1997, www.mg.co.za/mg

Bishop began studying pedophilia while a student at Rhodes University. As an aside Rhodes was founded by a Satanic Theosophical cult member named Cecil Rhodes. However, based on Cecil's circle of friends, penchant for Satanism and stated goal of revitalizing Nimrod's old world order of Babylon; I believe Rhodes University gets its name from the ancient "Colossus of Rhodes" c.280 BC, a statue of the Greek titan-god of the sun "Helios" or Apollyon otherwise known as "The Beast from the pit" – Revelation 9:11. Bishop also discovered Karl Marx at Rhodes, as well as other literature that helped form his modernist worldview. It's these views which are being echoed around the world by homosexual activists seeking what they call "sexual freedom" for children.

198

Bishop is on a crusade in South Africa to have "age of sexual consent laws" abolished, and he is looking for help from NAMBLA to accomplish his goal. He says children must be empowered:

"By teaching them about loving relationships at an early age, and giving them the opportunity to make an informed decision about having sex"

Bishop also approves of incest, noting:

"Two women psychologists in America say the healthiest introduction to sex for a child should be with their [sic] parents, because it is less threatening and the emotional intimacy more comfortable."

Bishop agrees with NAMBLA that the next social movement in Western politics will be an attack on "sexual ageism," which prohibits sexual contact based on age differences. The movement already is well under way in Europe and Canada.

Michael Swift's gay manifesto was first published February 1997 and was titled "Gay Revolution". Throughout Swift's proposal he provides an unfiltered vision of the elite orchestrated homosexual agenda stating:

"We shall sodomize your sons, emblems of your feeble masculinity, of your shallow dreams and vulgar lies. We shall seduce them in your schools, in your dormitories, in your gymnasiums, in your locker rooms, in your sports arenas, in your seminaries, in your youth groups, in your movie theater bathrooms, in your army bunkhouses, in your truck stops, in your all male clubs, in your houses of Congress, wherever men are with men together. Your sons shall become our minions and do our bidding. They will be recast in our image. They will come to crave and adore us.

Women, you cry for freedom. You say you are no longer satisfied with men; they make you unhappy. We, connoisseurs of the masculine face, the masculine physique, shall take your men from you then. We will amuse them; we will instruct them; we will embrace them when they weep. Women, you say you wish to live with each other instead of with men. Then go and be with each other. We shall give your men pleasures they have never known because we are foremost men too, and only one man knows how to truly please another man; only one man can understand the depth and feeling, the mind and body of another man.

199

All laws banning homosexual activity will be revoked. Instead, legislation shall be passed which engenders love between men.

All homosexuals must stand together as brothers; we must be united artistically, philosophically, socially, politically and financially. We will triumph only when we present a common face to the vicious heterosexual enemy.

If you dare to cry faggot, fairy, queer, at us, we will stab you in your cowardly hearts and defile your dead, puny bodies.
We shall write poems of the love between men; we shall stage plays in which man openly caresses man; we shall make films about the love between heroic men which will replace the cheap, superficial, sentimental, insipid, juvenile, heterosexual infatuations presently dominating your cinema screens. We shall sculpt statues of beautiful young men, of bold athletes which will be placed in your parks, your squares, your plazas. The museums of the world will be filled only with paintings of graceful, naked lads.

Our writers and artists will make love between men fashionable and de rigueur, and we will succeed because we are adept at setting styles. We will eliminate heterosexual liaisons through usage of the devices of wit and ridicule, devices which we are skilled in employing.

We will unmask the powerful homosexuals who masquerade as heterosexuals. You will be shocked and frightened when you find that your presidents and their sons, your industrialists, your senators, your mayors, your generals, your athletes, your film stars, your television personalities, your civic leaders, your priests are not the safe, familiar, bourgeois, heterosexual figures you assumed them to be. We are everywhere; we have infiltrated your ranks. Be careful when you speak of homosexuals because we are always among you; we may be sitting across the desk from you; we may be sleeping in the same bed with you.

There will be no compromises. We are not middle-class weaklings. Highly intelligent, we are the natural aristocrats of the human race, and steely-minded aristocrats never settle for less.

Those who oppose us will be exiled.
We shall raise vast private armies, as Mishima did, to defeat you. We shall conquer the world because warriors inspired by and banded together by homosexual love and honor are invincible as were the ancient Greek soldiers.

200

The family unit-spawning ground of lies, betrayals, mediocrity, hypocrisy and violence–will be abolished. The family unit, which only dampens imagination and curbs free will, must be eliminated. Perfect boys will be conceived and grown in the genetic laboratory. They will be bonded together in communal setting, under the control and instruction of homosexual savants.

All churches who condemn us will be closed. Our only gods are handsome young men. We adhere to a cult of beauty, moral and esthetic. All that is ugly and vulgar and banal will be annihilated. Since we are alienated from middle-class heterosexual conventions, we are free to live our lives according to the dictates of the pure imagination. For us too much is not enough.

The exquisite society to emerge will be governed by an elite comprised of gay poets. One of the major requirements for a position of power in the new society of homoeroticism will be indulgence in the Greek passion. Any man contaminated with heterosexual lust will be automatically barred from a position of influence. All males who insist on remaining stupidly heterosexual will be tried in homosexual courts of justice and will become invisible men.

We shall rewrite history, history filled and debased with your heterosexual lies and distortions. We shall portray the homosexuality of the great leaders and thinkers who have shaped the world. We will demonstrate that homosexuality and intelligence and imagination are inextricably linked, and that homosexuality is a requirement for true nobility, true beauty in a man.

We shall be victorious because we are fueled with the ferocious bitterness of the oppressed who have been forced to play seemingly bit parts in your dumb, heterosexual shows throughout the ages. We too are capable of firing guns and manning the barricades of the ultimate revolution. Tremble, hetero swine, when we appear before you without our masks."

For generations, The Church of Babylon has carried out clandestine attacks on literally every American organization whose goal has been to develop and promote mentally and physically stable American children. It's through children everywhere that satanic theosophists foster, fund, promote, and perpetuate their corrosive modernist belief system. It's through our young people's food, water, overly prescribed medications, toxic television, movies, fashion, etc. that satanic theosophists are chemically and mentally reengineer-   201
ing our young people into believing that they were born

into existence to do nothing more than live a life of servitude inside of a tyrannical, theosophical controlled one world government.

"Train up a child in the way he should go: and when he is old, he will not depart from it." - Proverbs 22:6

For instance the anti-Christian clothing company 'American Apparel Clothing' promotes pornographic messaging on little girls clothing. After the citizens of California unanimously passed 'Prop 8' in 2008, which defines marriage in California as being between one man and one woman. American Apparel launched the 'Legalize Gay campaign' printing clothing with the slogan "Legalize Gay" and "Repeal Prop 8". In June 2012 American Apparel partnered with the Gay and Lesbian Alliance Against Defamation to release a new anti-Christian line of T-shirts, celebrating the modernist lesbian, gay, bisexual, and transgender (LGBT) Pride Month. For their efforts American Apparel was named a 'Pro-Gay Company' by TheStreet.com in 2013. The first openly transgender model 'Isis King' modeled for American Apparels new LGBT line.

"The woman shall not wear that which pertaineth unto a man, neither shall a man put on a woman's garment: for all that do so are abomination unto the LORD thy God." - Deuteronomy 22:5

In subsequent chapters I will be discussing the unholy obsession Church of Babylon members have for the Egyptian pharaoh Osiris and his wife Isis. Here is a brief overview. The people of Egypt cut up Osiris into 13 pieces and threw him into the ocean. This is why Church of Babylon members memorialize the number 13. Isis, the wife of Osiris, searched for her husband's 13 pieces so that she may reassemble him. To her disappointment she is unable to find his penis. Osiris' penis is memorialized throughout America in the form of phallic shaped obelisks. For instance President Washington's phallic monument pays homage to Osiris. Unbeknownst to many Christian American's today, their church towers promote this occult practice. It's important for the Christian American majority to understand the mythology and ancient kinship Church of Babylon members have with Osiris and Isis. For the reasons stated above modernists named America's first openly transgender model 'Isis King'.

It's through this modernist engineered matrix that our children are being stripped of any awareness or relationship with Lord Jesus Christ. Rather, our youth are being deceived into believing, that they are simply going to die one day, unless of course, they achieve Godhead through 'illumination', which can only be reached through the convergence of man and machine.

202

Raymond Kurzweil is a well known inventor, futurist and advocate of Satan's big-lie that man himself is capable of becoming God. Kurzweil himself refuses to accept the inevitability of physical death, which he expresses throughout his 2009 documentary 'Transcendent Man'. In this documentary, Kurzweil suggests:

"The Law of Accelerating Returns—the exponential increase in the growth of information technology—will result in a singularity, a point where humanity and machines will merge, allowing one to transcend biological mortality: advances in genetics will provide the knowledge to reprogram biology, eliminate disease and stop the aging process; nano-technology will keep humans healthy from the inside using robotic red blood cells and provide a human-computer interface within the brain; robotics, or artificial intelligence, will make superhuman intelligence possible, including the ability to back up the mind."

If modernists want to create their own eternal living hell on earth, which is what they're proposing, that's their business. Just don't use the tax dollars of unsuspecting, naïve Christian Americans to drug and brainwash the American citizenry into submissive compliance. Furthermore, don't try to convince me that my Christian belief system is 'crazy', when modernists are promoting the religion of evolutionism which states all life on earth evolved from a rock and being able to download your mind, soul, etc. into a robot, will allow you to live forever as a 'God'.

As a Christian American, where I become outraged is when the minions of useful idiots insult the divinity of Lord Jesus Christ by suggesting that 'Jesus was Gay'. This relatively new heretical movement is plastered with the finger prints of Anti-Christ theosophy, and through the study of modernist history we find a number of references linking The Church of Babylon to America's gay agenda. Sadly, what American gays don't understand is that their entire lifestyle is nothing more than a disposable weapon being wielded by the spiritual offspring of Nimrod to attack the sanctity of the Christian faith and our pillars of morality and family values.

Just one example, of how The Church of Babylon is using their expendable asset of homosexuality to destroy America's founding principles, as well as the minds of impressionable young children, are their recent attacks on the oldest and largest youth organizations in the United States of America. With over 2.7 million youth members and over one million adult volunteers, the Boy Scouts of America, since its founding in 1910, has sculpted young boys into productive, self sufficient American men, free from the toxic influence of mind warping video games, garbage Hollywood cinema and the

203

modernist agenda. To better understand the motives behind theosophy's attack on one of America's most morally astute organizations for young men, all one must do is read The Boy Scouts of America's hard-line position excluding Homosexuals, Satanists, Atheists and Agnostics.

"Declaration of Religious Principle. The Boy Scouts of America maintains that no member can grow into the best kind of citizen without recognizing an obligation to God. In the first part of the Scout Oath or Promise the member declares, 'On my honour I will do my best to do my duty to God and my country and to obey the Scout Law.' The recognition of God as the ruling and leading power in the universe and the grateful acknowledgment of his favours and blessings are necessary to the best type of citizenship and are wholesome precepts in the education of the growing members."

Because of constant attacks on the Boy Scouts' support of Biblical values, in 2013 the organization announced that it 'may eliminate the exclusion of gays from membership at the national level'. This would shift the decision to exclude or admit gays to the local units. As you can imagine, this has stirred controversy throughout the organization. Many of its members have stated that they are 'gravely distressed'.

More than two-thirds of The Boy Scouts of America is affiliated with religious organizations. Not surprising given the fact that 'faith in God' has played not only a major role in its founding, but its success over the past 103 years. Thankfully, there are Christian leaders who may not clearly understand the source of these attacks, but understand the importance of renouncing them. Recently, the spokesman for the Conservative Southern Baptist Convention Executive Committee had this to say on the subject of Homosexuals being allowed into The Boy Scouts of America:

"I think it's clear that the Scouts have made a sea change in who they are and that down the road they will be a different organization than they are today," - Roger "Sing" Oldham, spokesman for The Southern Baptist Convention

The leader of The Conservative Southern Baptist Convention, Frank S. Page, was clear to The Boy Scouts of America that the board members "would not allow gays." In addition, Page said: "I think there are a lot of parents and students who will make the decision to look for other organizations that are more in line with the principles that they espouse,"

Christians must realize that The Boy Scouts of America is under attack because more than 70% of its 100,000 scouting units are sponsored by religious organizations. What's more The Boy Scouts of America are under attack, because of what it promotes, namely a pledge to do their "duty to God".

Much like other 'faiths' which are under attack for supporting their belief in the One True God, Christianity has become infiltrated nationwide by esoteric theosophists who much like Michael Beckwith, founder of Agape International Spiritual Center, espouse a number of the tenants promoted throughout Theosophy's doctrine of a One World Religion. One of Theosophy's most celebrated methods of eradicating Christianity throughout America has been to foster a toxic environment which promotes the destruction of the 'Nuclear Family', Superior Biblical virtues, and any organization which teaches our youth about Lord Jesus Christ.

The only way Christians will eradicate The Church of Babylon from our Nation is to vigilantly profile the duplicitous nature and methods of those individuals who are actively espousing Theosophy in our national network of Christian organizations. Upon identifying such individuals, they should be immediately eliminated from having any association with our Christian youth. Here is a perfect example of the type of person who should be removed from any position of leadership. Reverend Chase Peeples of the 'gay-friendly' Country Club Congregational United Church of Christ, in Kansas City, Missouri, recently stated:

> "Boy Scouts are like baseball and apple pie. we welcome ALL Boy Scouts."

The truth of the matter is, there is voluminous evidence that demonstrates the increase in the United States Gay population has in fact been intentionally engineered, and the ones who have engineered their lifestyle are in fact members of The Church of Babylon. And for the record, let's test the integrity and accuracy of what the above mentioned 'Men of God' are promoting alongside what The Holy Bible e.g., Lord Jesus Christ teaches us about those who choose to promote and live a Homosexual lifestyle:

> "Know ye not that the unrighteous shall not inherit the kingdom of God? Be not deceived: neither fornicators, nor idolaters, nor adulterers, nor effeminate, nor abusers of themselves with mankind, Nor thieves, nor covetous, nor drunkards, nor revilers, nor extortioners, shall inherit the kingdom of God."
> - Corinthians 6:9-10

205

"Thou shalt not lie with mankind, as with womankind: it is abomination." - Leviticus 18:22

"For whoremongers, for them that defile themselves with mankind, for menstealers, for liars, for perjured persons, and if there be any other thing that is contrary to sound doctrine;"
- 1 Timothy 1:10

"If a man also lie with mankind, as he lieth with a woman, both of them have committed an abomination: they shall surely be put to death; their blood shall be upon them." - Leviticus 20:13

"Think not that I am come to destroy the law, or the prophets: I am not come to destroy, but to fulfil." - Matthew 5:17

"And he brake down the houses of the sodomites, that were by the house of the LORD, where the women wove hangings for the grove."
– 2 Kings 23:7

"For verily I say unto you, Till heaven and earth pass, one jot or one tittle shall in no wise pass from the law, till all be fulfilled."
- Matthew 5:18

"Whosoever therefore shall break one of these least commandments, and shall teach men so, he shall be called the least in the kingdom of heaven: but whosoever shall do and teach them, the same shall be called great in the kingdom of heaven." - Matthew 5:19

"For I say unto you, That except your righteousness shall exceed the righteousness of the scribes and Pharisees, ye shall in no case enter into the kingdom of heaven." - Matthew 5:20

Now that you've read what Lord Jesus Christ says about the homosexual lifestyle, please show me where it reads that the homosexual lifestyle will be rewarded as a 'gift' or 'divine right'. The truth of the matter is that homosexuality is condemned as a prime example of sin and sexual perversion. Teachers of Christ's message can neither alter, nor depart from his teachings. Unfortunately the biblical truth regarding Homosexuality is regularly glossed over and popularized in Hollywood films, television, etc. These vehicles are infamous for promoting the illusion that Gay America's sterile 3% population is larger than it really is. It's these groups which help to propagate the gay agenda throughout America. Take for instance a 1969 Planned Parenthood memo that reads:

206

"Encourage increased homosexuality"

The theosophist designed 1969 Planned Parenthood memo has been the catalyst through which modernists have been empowered to attack Christian owned business. This is why in 2013 Christian business owners have experienced a bevy of unconstitutional, anti-Christian laws, forcing them to compromise the very religious beliefs that inspire our lives. On August 22, 2013 the New Mexico Supreme Court ruled that Elaine Photography in New Mexico violated the law when she refused photography services to a same-sex marriage couple. Justice Richard Bosson's said about the court's decision:

"In the smaller, more focused world of the marketplace, of commerce, of public accommodation, the Huguenins have to channel their conduct, not their beliefs, so as to leave space for other Americans who believe something different. That compromise is part of the glue that holds us together as a nation, the tolerance that lubricates the varied moving parts of us as a people. That sense of respect we owe others, whether or not we believe as they do, illuminates this country, setting it apart from the discord that afflicts much of the rest of the world. In short, I would say to the Huguenins, with the utmost respect: it is the price of citizenship."

What I hear the New Mexico Supreme Court Justice saying. Is that theosophist based 'Illumination' has superiority over the value system of Christianity. Moreover his proposed 'price of citizenship' into the satanic one world religion, is the total admonishment of Lord Jesus Christ. Justice Bosson is a text-book example, of how too many of America's key positions of authority; have been abdicated to spiritual derelicts. "Whatever strikes at the root of Christianity tends manifestly to the dissolution of civil government" – New York Supreme Court 1811

Walt Disney's Culture of Homosexual Corruption:

Two of the largest corporations in America who are fulfilling the 1969 Planned Parenthood stated goal of "Encourage increased homosexuality" are The Home Depot and The Walt Disney Company. Here are just a few facts regarding The Home Depot and Walt Disney's contributions to America's growing culture of homosexuality:

In 2010 The Home Depot began financing 'Gay Pride' events; however simply financing these events was not enough they also chose to participate in the Gay Pride events as a vendor. Amidst graphic displays of homosexuality The Home Depot conducted kid's craft workshops. In other words The Home

Depot, with your money, is encouraging the attendance of children at events which expose them to transvestites, cross-dressers and homosexual activists. If you're a Christian contractor or 'DIY' please consider this next time you're shopping for supplies.

In June, 1996, Disney helped promote the 6th annual "Gay and Lesbian Day at Walt Disney World." Disney has allowed the homosexual organizers to portray Mickey Mouse and Donald Duck as homosexual lovers, and Minnie Mouse and Daisy Duck as lesbians.

Disney has extended company health benefits to live-in partners of homosexual employees (the policy does not cover unmarried heterosexual couples who live together) – The Orlando Sentinel, 10/7/95; USA Today, 10/19/95; Daily Variety, 10/9/95.

Disney's President, Michael Eisner, is quoted as saying he thinks 40% of Disney's 63,000 employees are homosexual.
Disney has the largest gay and lesbian employee organization in the entertainment industry.

Disney helped underwrite the 1993 Hollywood benefit for the National Gay and Lesbian Task Force – The Press Enterprise, 12/28/93.

Disney advertised in "Out", a homosexual magazine – Out, 2/94.

Tom Shumacher, Disney's Vice President of feature animation, is an open homosexual who takes his "husband" to executive retreats. In an interview with the homosexual publication The Advocate, Shumacher said: "There are a lot of gay people (at Disney) at every level. It is a very supportive environment." – Human Events, 8/12/94; The Advocate 6/25/94.

Disney hired avowed lesbian Lauren Lloyd for the specific purpose of developing female and lesbian movies. OUT magazine, a homosexual publication, praised Disney: "Like it or not, lesbians are not yet chic entertainment attractions for a lot of America. With Lloyd and Disney on our side, though, anything is possible." – Out, 11/94.

According to monitoring by American Family Association, Disney has been one of the top sponsors of pro-homosexual television programming.

In the May, 1995 issue of BUZZ magazine, contributing editor Steven Gaines reports that a homosexual rights activist said that she was once told by Disney Chairman

208

Michael Eisner that "as many as 40% of the company's 63,000 employees might be gay." Thomas Schumacher, an open homosexual and one of the guiding lights behind Disney's billion-dollar hit, THE LION KING, added, "...there are a lot of gay people here at every level."

In 2013 The Walt Disney Company chose Neil Patrick Harris who describes himself as a 'content gay man' and advocate for same sex marriage to host their Christmas Day Parade. Harris is also a magician holding the position of President of the Board of Directors for Hollywood's 'Magic Castle'.

In 2014 The Walt Disney Company notified the Boy Scouts of America (BSA) that it will withdraw all funding from the organization beginning 2015 unless the BSA overturns its policy of not allowing openly gay members to be 'leaders' [predators]. Disney is clearly an advocate for Planned Parenthood's 1969 agenda to 'increase homosexuality' throughout America and Naambla's goal of legalizing the act of men having sexual intercourse with children. Openly gay executive, George Kalogridis, was appointed President of Walt Disney World in 2013 and in June 2014 DisneyWorld will host "Gay Day" events. When you support The Walt Disney Company you're supporting militant anti-Christians.

BUZZ is described as a magazine which "provides readers with perspective on personalities, politics, culture and commerce of Los Angeles, California." The cover story, entitled "Disney Comes Out of the Closet," also reported that Disney has the "largest lesbian and gay employee's organization in the entertainment industry" and that the perception of Disney as having many homosexual employees is "well founded."

In addition to Schumacher, BUZZ names prominent openly homosexual Disney executives such as production vice president Lauren Lloyd of Disney's Hollywood Pictures, studio producer Laurence Mark, supervising animator Andreas Deja, the man responsible for the character of Gaston in Disney's Beauty and the Beast, senior vice president at Disney's interactive division Steven Fields, Rick Leed, who heads the production company that produced the television sitcom HOME IMPROVEMENT. Disney's training coordinator Jimi Ziehr said that at Disney's Epcot Centre in Orlando, Florida:

"gays outnumber the straights at Futureland operations, and there's nothing in the closet at Guest Relations." - Buzz, 5/95.

Unbeknownst to the vast majority of gay people throughout America, the very symbol that represents their lifestyle [The Rainbow] was in fact created by The Church

209

of Babylon. The Holy Bible teaches us that the rainbow represents God's covenant that he would not destroy the earth again with a flood. The rainbow to theosophists, however, represents the construction of a rainbow bridge or 'antahkarana' between that of mankind and Lucifer who theosophists say is the 'over-soul'. This 'rainbow bridge' is depicted by Theosophist controlled Hollywood in the 2011 movie Thor and 2013 movie Thor: The Dark World. What's more, the rainbow is associated with the Greek Goddess Iris who like Mercury was a messenger of Zeus. It will be remembered from earlier chapters that Mercury is also known as Helios or Apollyon, otherwise known as "The Beast from the Pit" – Revelation 9:11

Masonic author, George Oliver, says that in ancient times, the Masonic gavel referred to the hammer of the God Thor. [Oliver, Signs and Symbols, Macoy Publishing and Masonic Supply Co., 1906, p. 14]. Thor is an ancient pagan god, one whom Freemasons worship. In fact, Thor is part of the pagan Trinity in Scandinavia [Pike, Morals and Dogma, p. 552; also W.L. Wilmshurst, The Masonic Initiation, Trismegistus Press, 1980, p. 92]

Albert Pike makes identification of Thor very easy for us, as he states, on page 15 of Morals and Dogma, that Thor is another name for Sirius, the Blazing Star or the Pentagram. Now you can see why Freemason's often depict three different types of gavels in the familiar pentagram. However, on page 381, Pike also tells us that Thor was the Sun, the Egyptian Osiris, and Kneph, the Phoenician Bel or Baal. The Bible tells us that worshipping Baal is identical to worshipping the Devil [1 Kings 16:30-33, 22:53; 2 Kings 17:16] God condemned Baal worship, slaughtered the priests of Baal , and finally abolished it altogether in Israel. Yet, here, Freemasonry boldly states that they revere him.

Former Lesbian, Linda Jernigan, made an address to over one hundred Chicago area Pastors, on January 24, 2013, where she stated:

"Homosexuality is a behavior, that can change, and thus, shouldn't be included in the civil rights debate. Sexual orientation is not like other non-changeable attributes, such as skin color or natural gender."

Linda Jernigan, a black American woman, has been straight for thirteen years and has become an evangelist speaking openly about her past life in a gay relationship. In her statement, Linda Jernigan addresses one of the most troubling methods through which theosophist backed gay America is attempting to force that lifestyle onto the American majority. Through theosophist proxies - which include both the entertainment industry and antagonists of

Lord Jesus Christ - gay America attempts to bridge the cavernous divide which separates the artificially manufactured lifestyle programming of homosexuality with that of Black America's 240 years slave history. This egregious association should be condemned by supposed 'civil rights' advocates anytime it's trotted out for display by The Church of Babylon, and yet the silence is deafening. This erroneous and irresponsible association is a blatant slap in the face for those who have experienced far worse than the victims of the theosophist manufactured agenda of homosexuality; a scheme which seeks to establish superior rights rather than equal rights over the Christian American majority.

Another former homosexual saved by Jesus Christ is Michael Glatze. Glatze was the managing editor of XY Magazine, a popular gay San Francisco-based publication that offers advice to gay men. When Glatze renounced his Church of Babylon homosexual programming he publically announced:

"Homosexuality, delivered to young minds, is by its very nature pornographic. It destroys impressionable minds and confuses their developing sexuality; I did not realize this, however, until I was 30 years old... It became clear to me, as I really thought about it – and really prayed about it – that homosexuality prevents us from finding our true self within. We cannot see the truth when we're blinded by homosexuality... This, again, is my story. And in my story, it makes me repulsed to think about homosexuality. And when I step back a little bit, I know why! Because people are supposed to feel like homosexuality is gross, because such a feeling prevents them from wanting to do it. And people are supposed to not want to do it, because doing it is something that prevents them from having babies, and having babies is something that we – naturally – are supposed to want to do, for human beings to survive. And, so, it's obvious why people should feel gross about homosexuality. It's not 'wrong' for people to think it's gross. It makes sense!"
– WorldNetDaily article titled "Confessions of a Former 'Gay Rights' Leader 7/10/2007.

If industry experts genuinely subscribe to the theory that the homosexual lifestyle is not a matter of choice, then why are professional groups pushing to use drugs on 'sexually confused' children? The Endocrine Society, for example, wants to use drugs to delay puberty in children with 'gender-identity' problems', which is a condition that has been intentionally engineered by global elites to reduce our global population. California Governor Jerry Brown is a strong supporter of the elite's ambitions to mutilate our impressionable youth and decimate the population size in America. On August 12, 2013 Gov. Jerry Brown signed into law a transgender student law, al-

211

lowing California State transgender students to choose which bathrooms they use and whether they participate in boy or girl sports. Executive Director of the Transgender Law Center had this to say about the bill:

"Now, every transgender student in California will be able to get up in the morning knowing that when they go to school as their authentic self they will have the same fair chance at success as their classmates."

I will address in more detail in following chapters how Rockefeller funded groups have funded the hybridization and genetic modification of our delicate agriculture. It's these foods which are directly responsible for the plague of toxic endocrine systems sweeping across America in 2014. It's these foods that are being used to completely alter the DNA, hormones, etc. of developing children with the intention of creating a culture of lemmings, willing to trust the insanity proposed by the endocrine society. I will cite data in following chapters that will show how our children's sexual behavior and identity is being altered and decided through the foods they eat on a daily basis.

Caleb Price of 'Focus on the Family' tells OneNewsNow that drugs are designed to give adolescents more time to decide which gender they prefer for themselves. Price says:

"Well, there's been an increasing push in the medical and psychological communities to try and somehow more easily facilitate gender-confused people to transition to the gender of their choice"

Price says Focus on the Family has caught a lot of heat for referring to this philosophy as "ethical bankruptcy." He contends teens are not stable enough emotionally to make a decision of such magnitude. Price adds:

"We see this as a situation that's tragic, foolish, and unconscionable for a professional medical group to encourage young people to move forward on a road where they might be making a decision about changing their gender"

From the time when President Bill Clinton introduced his transgender Presidential advisor to the Nation in the 1990s to the present Obama administration, the American public has been deceived into believing a transgender lifestyle is spiritually, physically and mentally healthful.

212

According to author and former Miss Arkansas, Sally Miller, the husband of 2016 Presidential candidate Hillary Clinton had an affair with the former beauty queen. According to Bill Clinton's mistress, Bill disclosed that when he was young he would get aroused when he massaged his mother's feet and frequently dressed up in his mother's clothing. The allegations made by Sally Miller about President Bill Clinton would explain Bill's transgender Presidential advisor in the 90s.

Contrary to Bill Clinton's alleged deviant behavior, Transgenderism and homosexuality are in direct conflict with a universal harmony that's existed for more than six thousand years. This ancient dogma states that homosexual and transgender behavior is psychopathological and detrimental to the survival of God's creation. Luciferian elites promote these lifestyles so heavily, because they have studied the damaging effects on nations who embrace these practices. When we examine these effects we find that nations first experience a decline in morality followed by massive population level decrees. Remember that God's commandment for man was to, "Be fruitful, and multiple" [Genesis 1:28] whereas Satan's goal is to kill every person on earth through hate, war, abortion, homosexuality, etc. Although the Book of Enoch is not scriptural, this ancient text contains information regarding Satan's army of fallen angels or "watchers" and how they taught men weapons of war, sorcery, sun/moon worship, etc. One demon in particular whose name is 'Kasdeja' taught men abortion:

"...the smitings [killing] of the embryo [baby] in the womb, that it may pass away." – Book of Enoch, The names of the Watchers

Those who are proponents of "pro-choice" please keep in mind that abortion was taught to man by one of Satan's principle demons. When you murder an unborn baby that God knew, "Before I formed thee in the belly" [Jeremiah 1:5] you're doing the work of Satan and you should consider what Jesus Christ said about those who harm innocent little babies and children.

"It were better for him that a millstone were hanged about his neck, and he cast into the sea, than that he should offend one of these little ones." – [Luke 17:2]

In more modern history, the Diagnostic and Statistical Manual of Mental Disorders (DSMMD) reaffirmed the ancient opposition to homosexuality and transgenderism, listing the behavior of homosexuals and transgenders as 'Psychopathological'. Prominent Toronto psychiatrist Dr. Joseph Berger reaffirmed the scientific based DSMMD on 1/11/2013 stating that:

"From a medical and scientific perspective there is no such thing as a "transgendered" person. People who identify themselves as "transgendered" are mentally ill or simply unhappy. Hormone therapy and surgery are not appropriate treatments for psychosis or unhappiness. The medical treatment of delusions, psychosis or emotional happiness is not surgery."

In 1980 a Rockefeller Family influenced homosexual attorney argued for the removal of homosexual behavior from the DSMMD and won. Proponents of globalism, the deconstruction of Christianity and the nuclear family have championed the courts unconstitutional 1980 decision. On December 12, 2007 the Director of the Society for Christian Psychology told the Christian American majority:

"…If any model of humanity would lead to a compassionate stance towards those with same-sex attraction [Psychopaths], as well as pedophilia [Psychopaths], one would think Christianity would. Gay people deserve our respect and love" – Eric L. Johnson

It's New Age Christian Mystics like Eric Johnson who have played a key role in programming the American public into believing that the inundation of Psychopathological imagery we seen on a daily basis in movies and TV is acceptable. The reclassification of 'Psychopathological Behavior" has not only paved the way for the legalization of transgenders, it's currently clearing a path for other demonic practices to follow such as, child molestation, bestiality, necrophilia and all other deviant behavior including transspeciesism a state of mental illness where a person believes he/she is a dog, cat, bird, reptile, cow, goat, fish, etc.. As of December 1, 2012, transgender are no longer classified as having a mental disorder and if the Christian American majority remains silent expect to see all of the aforementioned mayhem legalized.

According to an ABC News report, Christian American tax payers have been forced to finance the establishment of the Religion of Transgenderism. Through the use of human exploitation laced audio and visuals in film and on television and gender bending, genetically modified organisms, the Religion of Transgenderism has been psychologically and chemically encouraged. Contrary to the rights granted to Americans by The Creator and reaffirmed inside of The United States Declaration of Independence and Bill of Rights, members of The Religion of Transgenderism have been granted superior rights by their creators over anyone who opposes their ideology. This hedonistic cult forces American adults and children, who are not victims of chemical, psychological and environmental alteration, to suspend disbelief and have faith that someone who was born male and/or female is biologically the opposite. Isn't this the argument atheists like to use regarding the existence of God? Atheists say there is no physical evidence for God, therefore God does not exist. The same argument may be used to discredit the religion of Transgenderism. There is no scientific evidence that a biological human male can change into a biological human female, therefore the reality of such a being and/or transformation may exist only through faith. Mainstream media would never put forth this fact, nor would they take the time to explain to the congregation of Transgenderism that if a man removes his genitalia he is still a male biologically. He will never be a female biologically, because he does not possess female reproductive organs e.g., ovaries, womb, etc. A man with no genitals is simply a eunuch. The same holds true for men who practice sodomy. Men who inject their reproductive essence into the orifice of another man which holds waste or digestive juices are celebrating death and will not be rewarded with life in this world or the next. The Holy Bible states, "…all they that hate me love death" – Proverbs 8:36

The New-Age religion of Transgenderism was largely introduced to America by President Bill Clinton however it was Barack Hussein Obama and his fanatic, social justice warrior, transgender "Recruitment Director" Raffi Freedman-Gurspan who injected the cult of Transgenderism into every aspect of American culture. Born a boy to a family in Honduras, Raffi was adopted by an American Jewish couple who apparently raised him to believe that he was a female, Latina, Jew.

The most prominent leaders behind the world's LGBT and Pedophile initiative are descendants of Talmudists. These include Michael Swartz a director for the largest national lesbian, gay, bi-sexual and transgender civil rights organization 'Human Rights Campaign'. Leslie Feinberg was an American transgender activist, who described his/herself as a "secular Jewish, female revolutionary communist". Ginsberg authored, 'Stone Butch Blues' in 1993 and 'Transgender Warriors' in 1996. The largest gay porn company in the world, 'Lucas Entertainment' is owned and controlled by the offspring of Talmudists.

"Is there a deeper reason beyond the mere financial as to why Jews in particular have become involved in porn? Pornography thus becomes a way of defiling Christian culture. Jewish involvement in porn by this argument is the result of an atavistic [genetic] hatred of Christian authority. They [Jews] are trying to weaken the dominant culture in America by moral subversion."
- Professor Abrams, Jewish Quarterly

"We [Jews] have fooled, bemused and corrupted the youth of the goyim [Christians] by rearing them in principles and theories which are known to us to be false although it is that they have been inculcated [programmed through repetition]. We Shall Destroy God. It is indispensable for us to undermine all faith, to tear out of the mind of the Goyim [Christians] the very principle of god-head and the spirit, and to put in its place material needs." – Babylonian Talmudic Protocols of The Learned Elders of Zion, Protocol No.9, Section 10, 13; Protocol No.4, Section 3, www.destroyers.us

David Thorstad, the leader of the pro-pedophile, gay liberation and socialism activism group, 'NAMBLA' (North American Man Boy Love Association) is a descendant of Talmudists. Other Talmudists who endorse the demonic crime of rapping children include British Labour Party MP, Patricia Hope Hewitt who once said, "We can't prove sex with children does them harm" and Labour Cabinet Minister, Harriett Harman who said, "Childhood sexual experiences, willingly engage in, with an adult result in no identifiable damage." During the 1970s a prominent child sex group named the 'Paedophile Information Exchange (PIE) worked with her civil liberties organization. The Jewish Babylonian Talmud contains a number of pro-pedophile verses, these include: Yebamoth 60B which reads:

"It was taught: R. Simeon Ben Yohai stated: A proselyte who is under the age of three years and one day is permitted to marry a priest."

To examine the toxic effects of the Lucifer inspired Babylonian Talmud throughout history, please visit, GoyToy.net.

In 2010 the transsexual Raffi Freedman-Gurspan was hired by Mayor Joseph A. Curtatone of Somerville, Massachusetts; In July 2011 Raffi played a key role in passing the transgender civil rights bill; In 2014 Raffi was hired by the National Center for Transgender Equality in Washington, D.C. to focus on "sustainable economic development opportunities for transgender people in the United States". In 2014 Barack Hussein Obama drafted an executive order which would make it illegal for employers nationwide to fire or harass someone based on their sexual orientation or gender identity. To ensure the success of his executive order, Obama nominated LBGT rights activist, Chai Rachel Feldblum to the position of Equal Employment Opportunity Commission (EEOC). Feldblum is the offspring of Babylonian Talmudists. Her father, Rabbi Meyer Simcha Feldblum, raises Chai in an Orthodox Jewish home. Here is what the militant antichristian, homosexual Talmudist Feldblum had to say about targeting the Christian American majority and America's God given right to free speech:

216

"I believe granting liberty to gay people advances a compelling government interest, [communism] that such an interest cannot be adequately advanced if "pockets of resistance" [Christians] to a societal statement of equality are permitted to flourish, and hence that a law that permits no individual exceptions based on religious beliefs will be the least restrictive means of achieving the goal of liberty for gay people."

Recently Obama threatened North Carolina's bathroom privacy law stating that he wants to achieve a "gender fluid" society. What's more Obama is now pushing the Religion of Transgenderism on our youth through 'Gender Identity' rules on all K-12 schools, which according to the American College of Pediatricians (ACP) is child abuse. The ACP goes on to cite statistics that show how nearly 100% of children abandon the human exploitation Religion of Transgenderism once they reach puberty:

"According to the DSM-V, as many as 98% of gender confused boys and 88% of gender confused girls eventually accept their biological sex after naturally passing through puberty," – American College of Pediatricians

On May 13, 2016 [Friday the 13th] Obama and his transgender Tsar, Raffi Freedman-Gurspan, issued an unconstitutional decree threatening every U.S. Public School to accept tranny freaks or else. Perhaps Babylonian Talmudist Joan Rivers knew something when on July 3, 2014 she commented, "Obama is gay and Michelle is a tranny". On September 4, 2014, just two months later, Joan Rivers was dead. Obama seems to have had a soft spot for the Tranny/Homosexual community his entire life. The Daily Mail reported that Raymond Boyer, known as "Gay Ray" to Obama and his pot-smoking "Choom Gang," was bludgeoned to death with a hammer seven years after selling narcotics to Obama and his friends. Larry Sinclair on Puerto Rico's WAPA TV exposed the murder of alleged Obama gay lover Donald Young. Obama even entrusted the writing of important White House speeches to his homosexual speechwriter turned comedian, Jon Lovett. Lovett is the person who wrote Barack Obama's big-lie, "If you like your insurance you can keep your insurance". To illustrate how psychopathological these individuals are, watch the video featuring Jon Lovett on the Charlie Rose talk show, laughing at American's who lost their insurance because of Obamacare. Since Raffi's hiring in 2015 by President Barack Hussein Obama there has been an infestation of transsexual propaganda throughout mainstream media and the entertainment industry, even though less than .03% of the U.S. population are transvestites. On May 17, 2016 Barack Hussein Obama's Administration doubled-down on its goal of destroying America's Military by introducing the first opening gay leader of any U.S. military service. Eric Fanning, became the first openly gay Army Secretary.

While European nations are being systematically invaded and their ancient cultures weakened by Baal [Satan] worshipping Muslims, who ironically throw homosexuals off buildings, decapitate transsexuals and rape indiscriminately. While George Soros finances Satan worshiping communists to overthrow America's Republic and economic system and 2016 elections and Global Elites murder millions of American's with toxic, cancer causing, gender bending, genetically modified organisms, fluoridated/chlorinated water, mercury/live cancer cell/live virus laden vaccines. All you see on television and hear on radio are people advocating for transsexuals and their right to use whatever restroom they choose.

The reality Christians need to wake-up to is that the purpose of all the above-mentioned rhetoric has nothing to do with tranny rights, gay rights, etc. and everything to do with an engineered collapse of Western Civilization. If you're interested in educating yourself about this subject and learning how you can become a firewall for American sovereignty, please visit, KillingIreland.com

Barack Obama's handler, Valerie Jarrett is so smitten with the globalist plan to destabilize the west and their token White House freak tranny, she told ABC News that Raffi is one of Obama's "administration champions" and that:

"Her [his/Its] commitment to bettering the lives of transgender Americans, particularly transgender people of color and those in poverty, reflects the values of this Administration."

I couldn't agree more with Jarrett that the presence of this trannie freak inside of the White House perfectly represents Obama's abhorrent homosexual proselytizing and abject hatred towards the Christian American majority.

The fact of the matter is psychopathological, deviants such as, child molesters, homosexuals and transvestites – who make up less than .03% of the U.S. population – would not exist inside of America's borders if the Christian American majority of approx. 240 million people would denounce the Religion of Transgenderism and reaffirm Jesus Christ's message regarding the above-mentioned abominations.

God's Solution for Molesters: "It were better for him that a millstone were hanged about his neck, and he cast into the sea, than that he should offend one of these little ones." – [Luke 17:2]

God's Solution for Trannies: "But from the beginning of the creation God made them male and female [Mark 10:6-9]. "The woman shall not wear that which pertaineth unto a man, neither shall a man put on a woman's garment: for all that do so are abomination unto the LORD thy God."

God's Solution for Homosexuals: "For this cause God gave them up until vile affections: for even their women did change the natural use into that which is against nature: And likewise also the men, leaving the natural use of the woman, burned in their lust one toward another; men with men working that which is unseemly, and receiving in themselves that recompence of their error which was meet." [Romans 1:26-27]. "If a man also lie with mankind, as he lieth with a woman, both of them have committed an abomination: they shall surely be put to death; their blood shall be upon them." – [Leviticus 20:13]

If industry experts genuinely subscribe to the theory that the homosexual lifestyle is not a matter of choice, then why are professional groups pushing to use drugs on 'sexually confused' children? The Endocrine Society, for example, wants to use drugs to delay puberty in children with 'gender-identity problems', which is a condition that has been intentionally engineered by global elites to reduce our global population. California Governor Jerry Brown is a strong supporter of the elite's ambitions to mutilate our impressionable youth and decimate the population size in America. On August 12, 2013 Gov. Jerry Brown signed into law a transgender student law, allowing California State transgender students to choose which bathrooms they use and whether they participate in boy or girl sports. Executive Director of the Transgender Law Center had this to say about the bill:

"Now, every transgender student in California will be able to get up in the morning knowing that when they go to school as their authentic self they will have the same fair chance at success as their classmates."

14 Culling The Christian American Majority

"...yea, the time cometh, that whosoever killeth you will think that
he doeth God service."
- John 16:2

It will be remembered that David Rockefeller once said that he was "proud" of being "part of a secret cabal working against the best interest of the United States" and its people. And for building a "One-World Order" For generations the Rockefeller family's many corporations and strategic corporate proxies have all been heavily vested in both the idea and process of completely disarming and dismantling the United States Constitution and all that it affords the American people. Furthermore, they've been working feverishly to destabilize our food supply, educational system and financial system. They're well aware of the fact that intelligent, self-sufficient, and accountable Americans would never accept their artificial state of consciousness.

A subject that I will expand on in subsequent pages is the role David Rockefeller has played in the destabilization of America's food supply. His efforts include: hybridization, genetic manipulation, and toxic chemical treatments. The Rockefellers have always been proponents of culling the global population through eugenics. Here is just one of many examples where David Rockefeller calls for global extermination.

"The negative impact of population growth on all of our planetary
ecosystems is becoming appallingly evident. Unless nations agree
to work together, to tackle these cross-border challenges, posed by
population growth, overconsumption of natural resources and environmental degradation, the prospects of a decent life on our planet will be
threatened." – David Rockefeller

The blatant hypocrisy of elitist families' and elite funded Satanists such as Blavatsky is that on one side of their
face, they preach 'peace, love, and harmony', and then as

soon as their belief system is questioned or their quotes are read back to them verbatim, they begin promoting the idea of violence and extermination. New Agers argue that 'traditional' Christianity is totalitarian in nature, which is completely false. On the other hand, take for example the fact that Helena Blavatsky's Satanic Theosophy is based on an ideology that demands all people accept a One World New Age religion, else they should be murdered. Now, as a Christian living in the United States of America for the past 42 years, I cannot remember one instance where someone has ever told me that if I didn't accept or continue being a Christian, I would be murdered. The fact of the matter is Satanic Theosophy is nothing more than communistic/socialistic totalitarianism, whose Chief Executive Officer is Lucifer.

Here are a just a few examples of Theosophists reveling their true belief system and strategy.

New Ager, David Spangler, from 'Planetary Citizens', another United Nations group, regularly promoted the idea of eliminating all religions from earth:

"We can take all the marshmallows, Scriptures, all the tablets etc. and have a jolly good bonfire." So essentially he's promoting abolition of all faiths.

Maharishi Mahesh Yogi, a very influential New Age proponent and someone who was worshiped by the famous band "The Beatles", pulled no punches when describing his remedy for those who do not adopt a One World Theosophical Religion:

"There has not been, and there will not be a place for the unfit. The fit will lead, and if the unfit are not coming along, there is no place for them. In the place where light dominates there is no place for darkness."

So, here we have a well-known New Age proponent who is telling us who the Satanic Theosophists see as 'fit' and 'unfit'. Those who accept the Satanic Theosophical One World Religion are 'fit' and the rest of us who refuse to worship their One World Religion anti-Christ are 'unfit'. The bottom line is New Age Theosophy is the antithesis of freedom, peace, love, and harmony.

221

Well respected New Age leader and author Barbara Marx Hub-bard, in her book titled "Book of Co-Creation" makes a statement on page 59 that raises eyebrows. She gives credence, however, to a number of my examples in following chapters that Satanic Theosophical elites are in fact intentionally poisoning our citizens with Genetically Modified Toxic Corn, Wheat, Soy, and Sugar. Furthermore, they have amassed an army of Satanic Theosophical proxies throughout Washington, miscellaneous governmental agencies in the United States, private and public companies and corporations. It's these proxies who have for instance brainwashed the American public for generations into believing that brushing with Fluoride, an active ingredient in Rat Poison, actually promotes healthy teeth. In reality, Fluoride, damages teeth and contributes to a litany of deadly health conditions. Billions have been spent on deceptive advertising promoting the ridiculous notion that America's 'obesity epidemic' is due to 'Large Sodas' and/or portion control, not once making mention of the real cause of obesity. I will share this knowledge with you in the upcoming chapters. And I assure you, the knowledge I'll be sharing with you is not simply about Monsanto's GMO's. First, let's read what Barbara Marx Hubbard has in store for you and your loved ones. Then ask yourself the following question: 'Are these the types of people I want in control of my food, water, air and economy?'

"Out of the full spectrum of human personality, one fourth is electing to transcend. One fourth is resistant to election. They are unattractive by life ever-evolving. Now, as we approach the quantum shift from creature-human to co-create human, the destructive one-fourth must be eliminated from the social body. Fortunately you, dearly beloveds, are not responsible for this act. We are. We are in charge of God's selection process for planet Earth. He selects, we destroy we are the riders of the pale horse, death."

Again Barbara Marx Hubbard, in her book titled "Happy Birthday Planet Earth" on page 17 describes what will happen to those of us who reject Satanic Theosophy's One World Order:

"The end of this phase of evolution shall come. All will know their choice. All will be required to choose. All who choose to be natural Christ's will be guided from within as to how to proceed. All who choose not to evolve will die off. The kindergarten class of Earth will be over."

An admirer of Barbara Marx Hubbard was the Illuminati futurist and creator of the geodesic sphere, Buckminster Fuller, who said:

"There is no doubt in my mind that Barbara Marx Hubbard - who helped introduce the concept of futurism to society - is the best informed human now alive regarding futurism and the foresights it has produced."

Regarding the Illuminati, Buckminster Fuller had this to say:

"Great nations are simply the operating fronts of behind-the-scenes, vastly ambitious individuals who had become so effectively powerful because of their ability to remain invisible while operating behind the national scenery."

One of America's greatest village idiots, Alice Bailey, chimes in once again. She verbally paints a vivid picture of what the One World Religion and New World Order will look like and how it will eliminate those who do not accept their Satanic Theosophical ideology. On page 112 of her Lucifer Publishing book titled "Education In The New Age", Bailey warns:

"Let us never forget that it is the life, its purpose and its directed intentional destiny that is of importance. And also that when a form proves inadequate, or to diseased or two crippled for the expression of that purpose, it is-from the point of view of the hierarchy-no disaster without form has to go. Death is not a disaster to be feared, the work of the destroyer is not really cruel or undesirable. Therefore, there is much destruction permitted by the custodians of the plan and much evil turned into good."

Aleister Crowley, the self described most evil man on earth, and pals with Helena Blavatsky, made this following prediction regarding his vision for Christians:

"The peer of Blavatsky's, often called the prophet of the New Age, Alastair Crowley, and claimed to have been visited in the spring of 1904 by an Egyptian entity called Aiwass. Who foretold to Crowley, the end of Christianity."

223

Robert Muller in his book "Ideas and Dreams for a Better World", 1001-1500, Volume 3, 1024, April 30, 1997, had the following to say:

"I am surprised that no one has yet thought of creating a pro-Earth, humanity-challenging organization which would put itself in the shoes of our mother earth and rejoice whenever humans diminishing numbers or consume less. It would give yearly prizes to people, events or institutions which achieve a reduction of the human population or of the consumption of Earth resources. The first prize should go to the United Nations which through its world population conferences and anti-population work has prevented 2 billion 200 million more people from being born between 1952 in the year 2000."

Dr Peppler, writer of the book "Revelation in The Stars" describes the meaning behind all of last year's 2012 conspiracies that were promoted by Satanic Theosophists and New World Order global elites:

"They believe the next age will start around AD 2012 and will be the Age of Aquarius. This, they say, will be an age of Enlightenment and world unity-a post-Christian world in the fullest sense of the word."

Now be honest. How many of you were sitting around on December 25, 2012 just waiting for California to rip clean off of the United States and sink into the ocean? You're not the only one. As a matter of fact, there were hundreds of millions, if not billions, of people who were with you in that premeditated, well orchestrated illusion. Have you ever once stopped to think, how all of that negative emotion manifested? And on such a massive scale too.

It's clear that all of the 2012 propaganda was an engineered hoax carried out by Hollywood, the Church of Babylon's societal programming proxy. The 2012 movie, countless websites, radio interviews, television documentaries, etc., were all designed to indoctrinate the American people into accepting the Satanic Theosophical illusion of 'The Age of Aquarius'. Think about how many movies have portrayed the concept of 'The Age of Aquarius'. Just one example is the movie 'The 40 year Old Virgin'. In it, the main character played by Steve Carell finally gets the girl and now, he's going to consummate their marriage.

224

This entire portion of the film is depicted visually and musically as a rebirth and is completely dedicated to the 'The Age of Aquarius'.

Elite Luciferian globalists, who make up the top level executive branch of their hierarchy of evil, feed off of your fear. And they use Hollywood as a kind of 'energy vampire' to siphon off your energy. There are a number of innocent depictions developed by Theosophy-controlled Hollywood that will help me illustrate my point. For example, in the popular movie cartoon, Monsters, Inc., monsters are sent into the rooms of little children to scare them. The resulting effect is that the children's fear generates energy that is then utilized to power their Monster city. Alternatively, there are less subtle versions such as the popular 1999 movie, The Matrix. In this film human beings are reduced to nothing more than a battery used to power the control system.

As an aside one of the Wachowski brothers, who directed The Matrix, Larry to be exact, introduced himself in 2012 as having gone through a sex change to become a woman. Larry Wachowski is now named 'Lana'. Apparently, rumors about his sex change have been swirling around Hollywood for years after the director was spotted in 'The Dungeon' in 2002. This is a notorious S&M club in Los Angeles. The Sunday Times reported that Wachowski's wife filed for divorce and the filmmaker subsequently bought a mansion in San Francisco under the name Laurencia. In the new movie "Cloud Atlas," which stars Tom Hanks, Halle Berry, Hugh Grant, and Susan Sarandon, Wachowski is credited under the name Lana Wachowski.

Larry Wachowski is a perfect example of how influential the Church of Babylon has been at programming certain Americans. In previous sections of this book I mentioned both the Planned Parenthood's 1969 Memo which tells us how they intend to artificially increase deviancy throughout America, and the 1948 'Institute for Sex Research' at Indiana University led by a Satanic Theosophist who believed strongly in Theosophical based eugenics. Alfred C. Kinsey, a homosexual, sado-masochist and child molester, whose sex research is responsible for the emergence of the 1960's sexual revolution, would be exposed as a fraud fifty-years later by Dr. Judith Reisman's 1981 expose titled 'KINSEY: Crimes & Consequences'. In it she proves that the 'Kinsey Report' was nothing more than 'scientific fraud and criminally derived data'. She goes on to write:

225

"Kinsey conducted human experiments in a soundproof laboratory, built to his specifications, at Indiana University, and that the sexual abuse of at least 317 infants and young boys was a scientific protocol for Kinsey's 1948 report."

The parasite that is The Church of Babylon burrowed itself deep inside of our Nation's morality over 65 years ago. And now we're beginning to taste its pestilent fruit. The transvestite Larry/Lana Wachowski has become nothing more than a victim of Satanic Theosophy. And now, through Satanic Theosophical owned and controlled Hollywood, he has become a useful idiot. Larry/Lana is now helping The Church of Babylon to propagate unprecedented generational trauma. To learn more about the designers of the 'Religion of Transgenderism' please visit www.TransDelusion.com

The Club of Rome admits that it's a globalist think tank. And the aim of this group is to assist with the construction of a Satanic Theosophical One World Government. In 2009, the Club of Rome held the 'Future of The American Hemisphere Conference'. Francesco Stipo opened the conference. Stipo is a member of the United States Club of Rome and he wrote 'The Manifesto of World Federalism, Globalization, Political Globalization, Balanced Contribution Theory'. In it, he says:

"Political globalization is the creation of the world government which regulates the relationships among governments"

Ervin László, who is also a member of the Club of Rome, partnered with the revered New Age author and speaker Deepak Chopra, who was a student of Jiddu Krishnamurti. Krishnamurti, who died in 1986, was the Indian born speaker and writer once promoted by the Satanic Theosophical society as "The Christ" and Helena Blavatsky's prophesized anti-Christ unifier of all the worlds' religions. Unfortunately for Satanic Theosophy, their manufactured 'Christ' got cold feet and decided that he didn't want to be 'The Christ'. Both Ervin and Chopra would go on to form a partnership with former communist leader Mikhail Gorbachev. Gorbachev was both a supporter of the Satanic Theosophical anti-Christ 'Maitreya' and Agenda 21. Together they authored a book titled 'Worldshift 2012' – Making Green Business, New Politics & Higher Consciousness Work Together'. In their book, they encourage hypothetical circumstances for 2012. Based on documented facts, there is no question the Sa-

226

tanic Theosophical elites have a vested interest in the successful implementation of Agenda 21 and the manufactured illusion of 2012 hysteria. What's concerning is that they were willing to do, say, and spend anything to make this a reality for billions of human beings.

Ervin László's of Club of Rome fame would go onto to create a spinoff named 'The Club of Budapest. This organization encouraged the same type of hypothetical circumstances for 2012. Satanic Theosophical 'New Age' members at the Club of Budapest include Robert Muller, who was a former Assistant Secretary-General of the United Nations, and Barbara Marx Hubbard. Laszlo, Muller and Marx commented:

"We have been projecting the transformation in 2012.
It is happening now."

Is the aforesaid simply part of what Swiss psychologist Carl Jung's called 'synchronicity'? Jung referred to synchronicity as the "temporally coincident occurrences of acausal events" and "meaningful coincidence."

In other words, the events are apparently not causally related, but do reveal an underlying pattern or a larger framework.
If the collection of data, which I've outlined throughout the previous 257 pages, is in fact as Jung suggests a revelation of a much larger framework, what role has Jung's teleological point-of-view played in the construction of this framework? My contention is that the underlying pattern, or larger framework of The Church of Babylon, emanates directly from Lucifer himself; and Christians are sadly victims of his duplicitous orderliness. Who better than that of Jung to support my theory? After all, for more than 160 years, Theosophy has been the vehicle through which Lucifer, has imposed prejudice, war, poverty, and immorality onto the Christian American majority. Jung himself was very much influenced by militant antichristian Friedrich Nietzsche and was a devotee to Madam Helena Blavatsky's occult Theosophist ideology, The Golden Dawn system of magic, and Aleister Crowley's Satanism.

Jung was deeply interested in Alchemical symbolism and the occult since his youth, participating in séances, which he used as the basis for his doctoral dissertation "On the Psychology and Pathology of So-Called Occult Phenomena". In 1913, Jung had already adopted a "spiritualist and redemptive inter-

227

pretation of alchemy", likely reflecting his interest in the occult literature of the 19th century. Jung began writing his views on alchemy from the 1920s and continued until the end of his life. His interpretation of Chinese alchemical texts in terms of his analytical psychology also served the function of comparing Eastern and Western alchemical imagery and core concepts and hence its possible inner sources. Jung did not completely reject the material experiments of the alchemists, but he massively down played it, writing that the transmutation was performed in the mind of the alchemist. He claimed the material substances and procedures were only a projection of the alchemists' internal state, while the real substance to be transformed was the mind itself.

These facts raise questions as to the underlying motivations behind Jung's Human Exploitation Psychology which led to the creation of the polarizing and prejudice human labeling system of 'introverts' and 'extroverts'. Jung's inhumane labeling scheme lends itself to the Darwinian, modernist plot which seeks to reduce God's creation [Man] to apemen. By rejecting any suggestion of creation modernists avoid Man's altruistic, aesthetic, intellectual, spiritual and religious faculties, of which not the very slightest trace is seen in the animal species. By doing so the deceived rehearse Satan's own words, 'Hath God said?". It's this human expediency which led Jung to the concept of the archetype and the occult leaning theory of 'collective unconscious'.

Marie-Louise von Franz, a disciple of Jung, continued Jung's studies on alchemy and its psychological meaning. Von Franz founded the C.G. Jung Institute in Zurich. In The Way of the Dream she claims to have interpreted over 65,000 dreams, primarily practicing in Kusnacht, Switzerland. Von Franz also wrote over 20 volumes on Analytical psychology, most notably on fairy tales as they relate to Archetypal or Depth Psychology, most specifically by amplification of the themes and characters. Von Franz, in 1968, was the first to publish that the mathematical structure of Deoxyribonucleic acid (DNA) first isolated by the Swiss physician Friedrich Miescher in 1869 is analogous to that of the I Ching one of the oldest of the Chinese classic texts.

Because DNA collects mutations over time, which is then inherited, it contains historical information, and, by comparing DNA sequences, geneticists can infer the evolutionary history of organisms, their phylogeny. This field of phylogenetics is a powerful tool in evolutionary biology. If DNA sequences

228

within a species are compared, population geneticists can learn the history of particular populations. This can be used in studies ranging from ecological genetics to anthropology; For example, DNA evidence is being used to try to identify the Ten Lost Tribes of Israel. However, there is no direct evidence of ancient genetic systems, as recovery of DNA from most fossils is impossible. Scientists say this is because DNA survives in the environment for less than one million years, and slowly degrades into short fragments in solution. However these claims are controversial considering the scientific data which proves earth is as The Holy Bible states just 6,000 years old. To understand the dangers posited by the religion of evolutionism please listen to: "Creation Seminar" - by Dr. Kent Hovind www.2peter3.com.

"Professing themselves to be wise, they became fools, And changed the glory of the uncorruptible God into an image made like to corruptible man, and to birds, and fourfooted beasts, and creeping things. Wherefore God also gave them up to uncleanness through the lusts of their own hearts, to dishonour their own bodies between themselves: Who changed the truth of God into a lie, and worshipped and served the creature more than the Creator, who is blessed for ever. Amen. For this cause God gave them up unto vile affections: for even their women did change the natural use into that which is against nature: And likewise also the men, leaving the natural use of the woman, burned in their lust one toward another; men with men working that which is unseemly, and receiving in themselves that recompence of their error which was meet [homosexuality]." – Romans 1:22-27

CHAPTER

15 Waking The Sleeping Giant

"In whom the god of this world [Satan]
hath blinded the minds of them which
believe not, lest the light of the glorious
gospel of Christ, who is the image of
God, should shine unto them."
- 2 Corinthians 4:4

One of the most influential control methods enlisted by Luciferians is the instrument of division through political correctness. In order for the Christian American majority to survive, they must unite as one unconditional, unapologetic, and seamless family. This requires that every Christian American detach themselves from Talmudist controlled Hollywood, whose film scripts are engineered to inspire a wicked, low-energy lifestyle. It's these methods through which Lucifer has subjugated and destroyed countless generations. Christians must wake up and realize that it's their majority who has power and authority over Satan and his proxies [Luke 10:19]. Anything to the contrary is an illusion.

To this end, the first step Christians must take is the immediate audit and replacement of anyone in their church leadership, local, state, and federal government, etc., who is in any way espousing the ideology of Luciferianism e.g., Islam, Talmudism, Buddhism, Sikhism, etc.

Apostle Paul's first letter to timothy warns Christians about the 'spiritual advisors' mentioned by Theosophy founder Helena Blavatsky, and her Luciferian colleagues. Paul tells Christians that these demons will deceive them with false doctrines:

"Now the Spirit speaketh expressly, that in the
latter times some shall depart from the faith,
giving heed to seducing spirits, and doctrines
of devils; Speaking lies in hypocrisy; having
their conscience seared with a hot iron;"
- 1 Timothy 4: 1-2

230

Apostle Paul also predicted the Theosophical New Age movement:

"For the time will come when they will not endure sound doctrine; but after their own lusts shall they heap to themselves teachers, having itching ears; And they shall turn away [their] ears from the truth, and shall be turned unto fables." - 2 Timothy 4:3-4

A popular lie that the Church of Babylon and New Agers use is that The Holy Bible promotes their astrological beliefs. This is patently false. The Book of Isaiah explicitly forbids astrology and identifies it as an abomination to God.

"Thou art wearied in the multitude of thy counsels. Let now the astrologers, the stargazers, the monthly prognosticators, stand up, and save thee from [these things] that shall come upon thee. Behold, they shall be as stubble; the fire shall burn them; they shall not deliver themselves from the power of the flame: [there shall] not [be] a coal to warm at, [nor] fire to sit before it."
- Isaiah 47:13-14

Church of Babylon tools such as Rupert Murdoch's NIV and NKJV Bibles deceive Christians into believing that Jesus talks about the Theosophist celebrated 'end of the age' or age of Pisces, however, in The King James Holy Bible, we read:

"Teaching them to observe all things whatsoever I have commanded you: and, lo, I am with you alway, even unto the end of the world. Amen." - Matthew 28:20

Although the zodiac was around in first century Palestine, the age theory was not around. With that being said, biblical writers certainly could not have been referencing the astrological age.

Professor of astronomy and astrophysics at the University of Chicago, Dr. Nowel Swerdlow, disputes many of the false scientific claims found in the book titled 'The Christ Conspiracy':

"Within which group of stars the vernal equinox is located, was of no astrological significance at all. The modern ideas about the age of Pisces or the Age of Aquarius are based upon the location of the vernal equinox in the regions of the stars of those constellations. So when this woman says that the

231

Christian fish was a symbol of the coming age of Pisces, she is saying something that no one would have thought of in antiquity."

Church of Babylon proxies ignore key passages throughout the Holy Scriptures if those messages dispute or debunk their modernist New Age religion. For instance, Matthew 28:20 defines 'the end of the age' or 'eon' in Greek. Unfortunately, for possessed and deceived souls, Matthew is not referring to astrological ages. The fact of the matter is that this concept didn't exist then. The 'age', Matthew refers to, is that of Jewish understanding.

Author of the book "Shattering the Christ Myth" J.P. Holding made the following statement about blatant lies regarding the end of the age:

"Zeitgeist is correct that when Jesus refers to the end of the eon he doesn't mean the end of the world. However, he is also not speaking of the astrological age of Pisces. Rather in the first century Jewish thought there was an awareness of the current age, ha-olam ha-zeh, and the age to come, ha-olam ha-ba. The distinction between the two appears both in the New Testament in another Jewish writings. This has nothing to do with astrology."

It will be remembered from earlier chapters the miscreant who produced the video 'Zeitgeist'. Throughout the movie, its mental midget of a creator follows the pre-canned, talking points of Theosophist Helena Blavatsky who commanded her possessed followers to rewrite biblical scripture. How? By completely ignoring biblical, scientific, and historical facts. To the educated observer it's obvious that it's the goal of the director to deceive people who have limited to no real understanding of The Holy Bible and Jesus Christ. Jesus Christ, John, and Paul, all predicted the emergence of a One World Religion and its anti-Christ thousands of years ago. This is the very reason, The Church of Babylon, absolutely HATE Christianity.

Apostle Paul writes in second Thessalonians:

"Don't be so easily shaken or alarmed by those who say that the day of the Lord has already begun. Don't believe them, even if they claim to have had a spiritual vision, a revelation, or a letter supposedly from us. Don't be fooled by what they say. For that day will not come until there is a great rebellion against God and the man of lawlessness is revealed—the one who brings destruction. He will exalt himself and defy everything that people call god and every object of worship. He will even sit in the temple of God, claiming that he himself is God. And you know what is holding him back, for he can be revealed only when his time comes. For this lawlessness is already at work secretly, and it will remain secret until the one who is holding it back steps out of the way. Then the man of lawlessness will be revealed, but the Lord Jesus will kill him with the breath of his mouth and destroy him by the splendor of his coming. This man will come to do the work of Satan with counterfeit power and signs and miracles."

– 2 Thessalonians 2:2-4, 6-9

On April 25, 1982, millions of people around the world awoke to a full-page ad that brazenly proclaimed 'THE CHRIST IS NOW HERE'. You can guess who financed the $500,000+ ad campaign. Jesus Christ has warned us about the false Christ. Jesus says to not believe anyone who says 'look the Christ has returned'. Jesus Christ's prophesized second coming comes after the false Christ deceives the world.

Matthew 24:4-5, 9, 23-27, 29-30 reads:

"And Jesus answered and said unto them, Take heed that no man deceive you. For many shall come in my name, saying, I am Christ; and shall deceive many. Then shall they deliver you up to be afflicted, and shall kill you: and ye shall be hated of all nations for my name's sake. Then if any man shall say unto you, Lo, here is Christ, or there; believe it not. For there shall arise false Christs, and false prophets, and shall shew great signs and wonders; insomuch that, if it were possible, they shall deceive the very elect. Immediately after the tribulation of those days shall the sun be darkened, and the moon shall not give her light, and the stars shall fall from heaven, and the powers of the heavens shall be shaken: And then shall appear the sign of the Son of man in heaven: and then shall all the tribes of the earth mourn, and they shall see the Son of man coming in the clouds of heaven with power and great glory."

Apostle John, in the book of Revelation, warns us about this demonic One World Religion false Christ who the deceived will follow and claim to be God:

"And he opened his mouth in blasphemy against God, to blaspheme his name, and his tabernacle, and them that dwell in heaven. And it was given unto him to make war with the saints, and to overcome them: and power was given him over all kindreds, and tongues, and nations. And all that dwell upon the earth shall worship him, whose names are not written in the book of life of the Lamb slain from the foundation of the world. And he causeth all, both small and great, rich and poor, free and bond, to receive a mark in their right hand, or in their foreheads: And that no man might buy or sell, save he that had the mark, or the name of the beast, or the number of his name. Here is wisdom. Let him that hath understanding count the number of the beast: for it is the number of a man; and his number [is] Six hundred threescore [and] six."- Revelation 13, 6-8, 16-18

John tells Christians how the Satanic Theosophical world leaders will form a One World Government and how they will hand over all power to the false Christ:

"And the ten horns which thou sawest are ten kings, which have received no kingdom as yet; but receive power as kings one hour with the beast. These have one mind, and shall give their power and strength unto the beast. These shall make war with the Lamb, and the Lamb shall overcome them: for he is Lord of lords, and King of kings: and they that are with him [are] called, and chosen, and faithful."
– Revelation 17: 12-14

Christians must take seriously the Church of Babylon manufactured 'Maitreya' as he just might be the prophesized anti-Christ. It's clear that world leaders are aware of him all of the aforementioned knowledge proves this. I've also shown how world leaders are in full support of his presence on the world stage.

"And the kings of the earth, and the great men, and the rich men, and the chief captains, and the mighty men, and every bondman, and every free man, hid themselves in the dens and in the rocks of the mountains; And said to the mountains and rocks, Fall on us, and hide us from the face of him that sitteth on

234

the throne, and from the wrath of the Lamb: For the great day of his wrath is come; and who shall be able to stand?" – Revelations 6: 15 -17

The Holy Bible is very specific about how the real Jesus Christ will return. Christians must stop listening to modernist ministers at the pulpit, who have deceived many Christians into believing they will be 'taken' prior to persecution by the Beast and his minions. The Theosophical ideology has hijacked a number of pulpits throughout the large population of American Christian Churches. Theosophists have persuaded and deceived a number of church leaders to adopt the fraudulent 'Pre-Tribulation Rapture'. This is a doctrine that cannot be found in the Holy Bible until 1830. It was the modernist 'Scofield Reference Bible' which completely removes key bible passages that has misled millions of Christians across America.

If you have not yet watched the film by Pastor Steven L. Anderson, Pastor Roger Jimenez, and creation scientist Dr. Kent Hovind titled "After the Tribulation: The Pre-Tribulation Rapture Fraud Exposed", please visit their website at afterthetribulation.com

"Immediately after the tribulation of those days shall the sun be darkened, and the moon shall not give her light, and the stars shall fall from heaven, and the powers of the heavens shall be shaken:"
- Matthew 24:29

The Church of Babylon is deathly afraid of the one true God and the message of eternal life through Lord Jesus Christ. They willfully dismiss the powerful message that Jesus Christ lived a life completely void of sin [something Satanists embrace e.g., 'Do What Thou Wilt'] and then gave his life on the cross to resolve our sins (something Satanists don't believe exists). Those who worship and promote The Church of Babylon and the religion of Evolutionism deceive people away from the truth of Lord Jesus Christ. Lucifer's empty promises and religions do nothing more than hide the truth of Jesus Christ and replace it with an individual's own ego and pride. This makes the concept of accepting Jesus Christ in exchange for eternal spiritual life a foreign idea. Throughout world history revisionary Antichrists have attempted to strip away Christians' free will to choose who they worship and give praise. Why? Because they want all recognition and worship directed towards them. This is a common trait among all Church of Babylon members. They simply believe they are superior

235

and nobody – not even God almighty – is above their prideful egos.

It will be remembered from previous chapters that I addressed the Pharisee invented Babylonian Talmud and how its adherents subscribe to a rigid anti-Christ, bigoted, racist, hate filled ideology. I cited a number of anti-Christian passages from the Babylonian Talmud, as well as quotes by some of the most revered Babylonian Talmudic scholars. I demonstrated how the Babylonian Talmud and its anti-Christ philosophy is the foundation upon which the vast majority of Hollywood screenplays and Music Industry songs are constructed.

For thousands of years it has been the goal of Babylonian Talmudists possessed by Babylonian demons to destroy the divinity of Jesus Christ and the promises found throughout The Holy Bible. Like the Babylonian god Nimrod these demons seek to reestablish a 'One World Religion' upon earth uniting all religions. What the Christian American majority must hold onto are the promises made by Jesus Christ that:

"Jesus saith unto him, I am the way, the truth, and the life: no man cometh unto the Father, but by me." – John 14:6

Nowhere in Jesus Christ's promise does he name any other method of salvation. With that being said it begs the question… Is it possible for a follower of Jesus Christ to be merged with any other religion or ideology which promotes the idea that salvation can be achieved through some other means? The answer is an emphatic NO!

Daniel's 70 week prophecy

In my book, Deception: The Ancient Mystery That Holds The Secret of Newgrange at, KillingIreland.com, I expose globalist Rupert Murdoch's take over of more than 50% of the Christian book publishing and Live Events Industry. Most troubling of all is the fact that anti-Christ elites like Murdoch have now begun to make drastic changes to The Holy Bible. What's more, I've cited instances where Church of Babylon members were complicit in the creation and propagation of 'New Age' Religious cults. Moreover, I shared with reader's cases where the U.S. Government through our Military is now targeting Christians as well as Judaic people who have a strict adherence to The Holy Torah [Old Testament]. There is however one additional method of subjugation that's used by Talmudic Luciferians to attact Christians and those seeking the truth about Lord Jesus Christ and that's a Talmudic 'Curse' which reads:

236

"May the bones of the hands and the bones of the fingers decay and decompose, of him who turns the pages of the book of Daniel, to find out the time of Daniel 9:24-27, and may his memory rot from off the face of the earth forever" (Talmudic Law, p.978, Section 2, Line 28).

The vast majority of Christians living throughout America may be surprised to learn that Babylonian Talmudic Law curses anyone who reads the book of Daniel. Why? Because there is no other Messianic prophecy that so perfectly foretells the coming of Jesus Christ and the year of His baptism and crucifixion. Why then has the 70 week prophecy been so convoluted by scholars, church leaders, etc.? The short answer is The Church of Babylon that Scottish American Jonathan Williams wrote about in his 1781 book titled 'Legions of Satan' has in fact come to pass.

"A Holy War will now begin on America, and when it is ended America will be supposedly the citadel of freedom, but her millions will unknowingly be loyal subjects to the Crown... Your churches will be used to teach the Jews' [Talmudist] religion, and in less than two hundred years the whole nation will be working for divine world government. That government that they believe to be divine will be the British Empire. All religions will be permeated with Judaism [Talmudism] without even being noticed by the masses, and they will all be under the invisible all-seeing eye of the Grand Architect of Freemasonry"
– Officer Jonathan Williams, 1781

The most significant reason the Church of Babylon has attempted to eliminate or rewrite Daniel's 70 week prophecy is because it provides indisputable proof Jesus Christ is the anointed one. The unfortunate truth is Non-Babylonian Talmudists would realize they had missed the first coming of the Messiah if they actually took time to read and understood Daniel's prophecy however; they are cursed by their spiritual leaders and told to avoid The Book of Daniel as though it was cursed. Moreover, they actually tell their uneducated, deceived members that The Book of Daniel predicts the coming of the Antichrist. So how did this blasphemous tradition begin? It all began when a Spanish Jesuit named Francisco Ribera proposed that the final seven years of the 70 weeks of Daniel was a future Antichrist and that Antichrist would bring an end to sacrifices in a rebuilt temple. This is where the supposed 7 years of tribulation comes from before the second coming of Christ. But this was manufactured prophecy, written with the sole purpose of deceiving Christians on the true

237

identity of the Antichrist. When has a Bible passage ever been so abused by Satan? Attributing Daniel's 70th week of Jesus' baptism and crucifixion and applying it instead to Antichrist is outright blasphemous.

Even though The Book of Daniel is relatively easy to process there are still those who allow themselves to be deceived by the Spanish Jesuit Francisco Ribera's gap of time between the 69th and 70th week, which is a fabrication. Publishers Weekly commented on Ribera's great lie stating:

> "Left Behind authors Jerry Jenkins and Tim LaHaye took the fictional, future one man Antichrist idea of Ribera, Bellarmine, Maitland, Todd, Newman, Irving, John Darby, Cyrus Scofield and Hal Lindsey and made it the most successful Christian-fiction series ever."

To demonstrate just how deceived the Christian American majority have become consider the fact that sound eschatology, ecclesiology, and hermeneutics based books such as "The Coming Prince" by Scottish Author and Chief of Criminal Investigation for Scotland Yard [Sir Robert Anderson 1841-1918] encounter a temped response, while a complete fabrication of the truth like "Left Behind" becomes a blockbuster fictional novel featured in The New York Times, Wall Street Journey and Larry King, coincidently all owned by The Church of Babylon.

Daniel's Timeline:

In Daniel 8:13 Daniel is engaged in a revelation between two Saints. One of the Saints query's the other Saint:

> "How long shall be the vision concerning the daily sacrifice, and the transgression of desolation, to give both the sanctuary and the host to be trodden underfoot?"

In Daniel 8:14 Daniel answers:

> "And he said unto me, Unto two thousand and three hundred days; then shall the sanctuary be cleansed."

The aforesaid statement by Daniel establishes a timeline of 2300 years. Now let's review in chronological order Daniel's prediction.

238

Daniel's Vision Revealed:

In Daniel 8:17 an Angel appears to Daniel and says:

"So he came near where I stood: and when he came, I was afraid, and fell upon my face: but he said unto me, Understand, O son of man: for at the time of the end shall be the vision."

This vision is so overwhelming to Daniel he loses consciousness. Upon regaining consciousness, Daniel realizes his Angelic messenger has gone, Daniel begins to pray:

"Yea, whiles I [was] speaking in prayer, even the man Gabriel, whom I had seen in the vision at the beginning, being caused to fly swiftly, touched me about the time of the evening oblation. And he informed [me], and talked with me, and said, O Daniel, I am now come forth to give thee skill and understanding. At the beginning of thy supplications the commandment came forth, and I am come to shew [thee]; for thou [art] greatly beloved: therefore understand the matter, and consider the vision. Seventy weeks are determined upon thy people and upon thy holy city, to finish the transgression, and to make an end of sins, and to make reconciliation for iniquity, and to bring in everlasting righteousness, and to seal up the vision and prophecy, and to anoint the most Holy. Know therefore and understand, [that] from the going forth of the commandment to restore and to build Jerusalem unto the Messiah the Prince [shall be] seven weeks, and threescore and two weeks: the street shall be built again, and the wall, even in troublous times. And after threescore and two weeks shall Messiah be cut off, but not for himself: and the people of the prince that shall come shall destroy the city and the sanctuary; and the end thereof [shall be] with a flood, and unto the end of the war desolations are determined. And he shall confirm the covenant with many for one week: and in the midst of the week he shall cause the sacrifice and the oblation to cease, and for the overspreading of abominations he shall make [it] desolate, even until the consummation, and that determined shall be poured upon the desolate." - Daniel 9:21-27

Deciphering Daniels Prayer:

In Daniel 9:24 we learn that seventy-weeks is determined upon thy people and upon they Holy City. In this verse 'The People' are the Jews and 'The City' is Jerusalem. In order to fully grasp the significance of the following time line it's essential that you understand how long 'Seventy Weeks' is in this prophecy. To determine this value we do not consult a Rubert Murdoch modernist New World Order International Babylonian Talmudist Version or Scolfield Heretical Reference Bible, we consult the The King James Holy Bible (KJV). Inside of the King James Holy Bible we learn:

"I have appointed thee each day for a year"
– Ezekiel 4:6

"After the number of the days in which ye searched the land, even forty days, each day for a year, shall ye bear your iniquities, even forty years, and ye shall know my breach of promise."
– Numbers 14:34

Taking into account the above instructions we learn that one day equals one year, therefore, one week equals seven years, thus, 'Seventy Weeks' equals Four Hundred and Ninety Years [70x7 = 490]. What we've just learned by calculating the aforesaid knowledge found within the pages of the Book of Daniel is that the prophetic cutoff date for the Jews is Four Hundred Ninety Years.

The 2300 Year Starting Line:

In order to determine when prophetic 2300 year begins, we once again consult the Book of Daniel inside of the Kings James Holy Bible which reads:

"Know therefore and understand, that from the going forth of the commandment to restore and to build Jerusalem unto the Messiah the Prince shall be seven weeks, and threescore and two weeks: the street shall be built again, and the wall, even in troublous times."
– Daniel 9:25

240

OK, we've just been given the answer in the above verse. The 2300 year starting line begins "that from the going forth of the commandment to restore and to build Jerusalem". What's more, we've been provided a time line defining when the Messiah would emerge. We're told that seven weeks is equal to forty-nine years, thus sixty-two weeks equals four hundred thirty four days.

The Reconstruction of Jerusalem:

It's now time to reverse engineer the decree made 457 B.C. by the Persian King Artaxerxes to reconstruct Jerusalem. It is true Cyrus issued a decree; however, Cyrus' decree was limited to the reconstruction of the Temple alone. This knowledge is found in Ezra 7:12-13 which reads:

"Artaxerxes, king of kings, unto Ezra the priest, a scribe of the law of the God of heaven, perfect peace, and at such a time... I make a decree, that all they of the people of Israel, and of his priests and Levites, in my realm, which are minded of their own freewill to go up to Jerusalem, go with thee." – Ezra 7:12-13

"And I, even I Artaxerxes the king, do make a decree to all the treasurers which are beyond the river, that whatsoever Ezra the priest, the scribe of the law of the God of heaven, shall require of you, it be done speedily," – Ezra 7:21

OK, the above verses have established a start date. Now let's read who Daniel says the Messiah is. In Daniel 8:25 we're told:

"Know therefore and understand, that from the going forth of the commandment to restore and to build Jerusalem unto the Messiah the Prince shall be seven weeks, and threescore and two weeks: the street shall be built again, and the wall, even in troublous times."
– Daniel 8:25

Daniel tells us there are sixty-nine weeks until the appearance of the Messiah. 69 x 7 = 483. Remember that we're told in Ezra 7:12-13 a start date of 457 B.C.... 457 B.C. + 483 = 27 A.D.

The Significance of 27 A.D:

"Now in the fifteenth year of the reign of Tiberius Caesar, Pontius Pilate being governor of Judaea, and Herod being tetrarch of Galilee, and
his brother Philip tetrarch of Ituraea and of the region of Trachonitis,
and Lysanias the tetrarch of Abilene... Now when all the people were
baptized, it came to pass, that Jesus also being baptized, and praying,
the heaven was opened,"
– Luke 3:1, 21

The above verse communicates that all of the people were baptized including Lord Jesus Christ, thus beginning his ministry at age 30.
Some people may be saying that 30 and 7 do not add up, however, it's
important to understand that you do not count the zero between B.C.
and A.D., thus the 69 week prophesy is fulfilled by Lord Jesus Christ.
The aforesaid collective knowledge is the very reason why Babylonian
Talmudists, Theosophists, etc. curse anyone who reads The Book of
Daniel. Simply put, The Book of Daniel dispels the Pharisee created
heretical Talmud, Kabbalah and ALL other religions who dismiss the
fulfilled prophecy of Lord Jesus Christ.

What Transpired in the 70th week?

"And after threescore and two weeks shall Messiah be cut off, but not
for himself: and the people of the prince that shall come shall destroy
the city and the sanctuary; and the end thereof shall be with a flood,
and unto the end of the war desolations are determined... And he shall
confirm the covenant with many for one week: and in the midst of the
week he shall cause the sacrifice and the oblation to cease, and for the
overspreading of abominations he shall make it desolate, even until the
consummation, and that determined shall be poured upon the desolate."– Daniel 9:26-27

This brings us to the last week of the 70 which would be 7
years. The above verses tell us that Lord Jesus Christ would confirm the
covenant for one week of 7 years and in the middle of that time span
Lord Jesus Christ shall cause the sacrifice and the oblation to cease. Jesus
Christ fulfilled this prophesy, was crucified and resurrected in 31 A.D.

"When he [Pilat] was set down on the judgment seat, his wife sent unto him, saying, Have thou nothing to do with that just man: for I have suffered many things this day in a dream because of him. When Pilate saw that he could prevail nothing, but [that] rather a tumult was made, he took water, and washed [his] hands before the multitude, saying, I am innocent of the blood of this just person: see ye [to it]. Then answered all the people, and said, His blood [be] on us, and on our children."
– Matthew 27:19-25

The Final 3 1/2 years

God's probation for the Jews ended 34 A.D., the 70 weeks ended when Stephen was stoned after his immense speech before the council in Acts chapter 7. The Jews had rejected the Gospel message and so were no longer God's chosen people and thus the Gospel began to go to the Gentiles (Acts 8:4). The Jews now receive salvation as individuals in the same way we do.

"And they stoned Stephen, calling upon God, and saying, Lord Jesus, receive my spirit... And he kneeled down, and cried with a loud voice, Lord, lay not this sin to their charge. And when he had said this, he fell asleep." – Acts 7:59-60

My expectation and reason for sharing the aforesaid time line is so that Christians are armed with the knowledge and confidence necessary to share the fulfilled prophesy of Jesus Christ and effectively demonstrate to modernists, New Agers, "Judeo-Christians" and non-believers alike how Lord Jesus Christ is in fact the prophesized Messiah and that the curse placed upon anyone who seeks the truth in The Book of Daniel by The Church of Babylon is a fool's errand. Why? Because Christians belong to Christ, Abraham's seed, thus it's Christians who are the heirs to the exceeding great and precious promises of God.

"O foolish Galatians, who hath bewitched you, that ye should not obey the truth, before whose eyes Jesus Christ hath been evidently set forth, crucified among you? Christ hath redeemed us from the curse of the law, being made a curse for us: for it is written, Cursed is every one that hangeth on a tree: Now to Abraham and his seed were the promises made. He saith not, And to seeds, as of many; but as of one, And to thy seed, which is Christ. And if ye be Christ's, then are ye Abraham's seed, and heirs according to the promise."
- Galations 3:1,13,16, 29

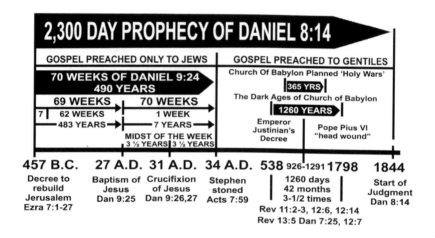

"Be it known unto you all, and to all the people of Israel, that by the name of Jesus Christ of Nazareth, whom ye crucified, whom God raised from the dead, even by him doth this man stand here before you whole. Neither is there salvation in any other: for there is none other name under heaven given among men, whereby we must be saved."
- Acts 4:10-12

If you are currently part of our Christian American majority, I challenge you to get directly involved in auditing your local, regional and National Christian leadership today to ensure they are in fact sharing the true message of Jesus Christ and not promoting the Church of Babylon. Moreover, if you're a Christian parent please begin to apply the deciphering techniques that you learned in earlier chapters to identify Church of Babylon cryptography in your child's cartoons, television programs, toys, food containers, clothing, theme parks and what's being promoted as a whole throughout their peer group.

If you are a non-Christian and this information has inspired you to know the real message and meaning of Lord Jesus Christ, please pray with me now.

"Father, I know that I have broken your laws and my sins have separated me from you. I am truly sorry. I want to turn away from my past sinful life toward you. Please forgive me, and help me avoid sinning again. I believe that your son, Jesus Christ died for my sins, was resurrected from the dead, is alive, and hears my prayer. I invite Jesus Christ, to become the Lord of my life, to rule and reign in my heart from this day forward. Please send your Holy Ghost to help me obey You, and to do Your will for the rest of my life. In Jesus' name I pray, Amen."

"For whosoever shall call upon the name of the Lord shall be saved."
— Romans 10:13

CHAPTER
16 Rockefeller's Weaponized Wheat

"The supreme art of war is to subdue the
enemy without fighting."
- Sun Tzu Art of War

Wheat is a common ingredient found in most pre-made food products throughout America. However, this is not the grain our ancient ancestors consumed. The wheat found in most American grocery stores is a nutrient deficient, Rockefeller Family abomination.

The grain Americans use to cook with today, is not the biblical definition of wheat. In fact, wheat hasn't existed in its original form for thousands of years. Our modern version of wheat doesn't even resemble the grain our relatives consumed in the latter part of the twentieth century. Thanks in large part to the Rockefeller Family, this once perfect food source has been transformed into a weapon. Rockefeller grain is one of the culprits responsible for the epidemic of obesity, heart disease, colon cancer, pancreatic cancer, brain tumors, etc. in America. We'll examine information in subsequent pages, showing how the Rockefeller Family hired industry experts

245

to engineer a weaponized wheat, capable of destroying the human endocrine system, the system that's responsible for hormone production and distribution.

"All truth passes through three stages. First, it is ridiculed. Second, it is violently opposed. Third, it is accepted as being self-evident."
- Arthur Schopenhauer German philosopher (1788 - 1860)

Rockefeller's weaponized wheat program began in New York back in 1922. That year the Rockefellers hired Nobel Prize winning Jewish scientist, Karl Landsteiner. Like many of his Talmudic ancestors, Landsteiner publicly converted from Judaism to Catholicism to carry out his vengence on the Christian American majority in secret. After being exposed in a book, 'Who's Who in American Jewry," Landsteiner stated about his Jewish religion, "it will be detrimental to me to emphasize publicly the religion of my ancestors." To understand what Landsteiner meant, please read my book at, GoyToy.net.

Landsteiner, who was recognized worldwide as the premier expert on the mechanisms of immunity, is also the scientist who discovered the existence of the four blood groups (O, A, B, and AB). What's more Landsteiner discovered the way in which each blood group responds to different organic and chemical stresses. This provided molecular biologists working at Rockefeller funded Caltech the necessary data to develop microbial invaders capable of withstanding specific blood types and their antibodies. It's noteworthy to mention that Landsteiner worked closely with Jewish Nobel Prize-winner, Emil Fischer, a protein chemist who lived in Wurzburg and Eugen von Bamberger who lived in Munich. I mention this fact because of the random significance of protein toxicity that's been intentionally engineered into genetically modified foods. Landsteiner's revelations laid the groundwork for the Rockefeller Family's plan to develop hybridized and genetically modified foods capable of attacking the immune system of human beings. Just four years after Landsteiner retired in 1939, the Rockefeller Family, in association with the Mexican Government, founded the International Maize and Wheat Improvement Center (IMWIC) located near Mexico City in 1943; and just two years after forming the IMWIC, the Rockefellers hired another pioneer in immunology, Henry Kunkel. Kunkel is credited with discovering the cause of a number of harmful autoimmune diseases. It's these clinical insights into fundamental principles of immunology that would be beneficial to the develop-

246

ment of genetically modified organisms capable of stimulating an auto-immune response and is why America has seen an explosion in autoimmune disease.

The Rockefeller Family propaganda machine would successfully promote the idea that they established the IMWIC to help Mexico realize their goal of agricultural self-sufficiency. The Rockefeller Family brainwashed the global community into believing that they forged this strategic relationship to 'eliminate world hunger'. Their operation developed into an international effort and soon its focus spread to include both soy and corn production. During the 80's, the Rockefeller Family announced that it had made measurable strides. By the early 80's they had developed thousands of new stains of wheat.

Flash forward to September 23, 1994. David Rockefeller is a keynote speaker at the United Nations Ambassadors Dinner. During his speech, he says:

"The negative impact of population growth on all of our planetary ecosystems is becoming appallingly evident. Unless nations agree to work together, to tackle these cross-border challenges, posed by population growth, overconsumption of natural resources and environmental degradation, the prospects of a decent life on our planet will be threatened."

If the Rockefeller Family was so concerned with the overpopulation of the world 51 years ago, why then did the family, who is estimated to be worth ten trillion dollars and share ownership of The Federal Reserve Bank, Inc. along with the Rothschild Family [worth $100 trillion] and JP Morgan beneficiaries, take up the seemingly altruistic and financially gargantuan endeavor of solving world hunger? Truth of the matter is the Rockefeller Family's research into the genetic make-up of America's most widely used food source had absolutely nothing to do with solving world hunger, and everything to do with:

- Subduing their one true enemy [Christians] on a genetic level without having to fight them in a traditional war.
- Branding people on a genetic level thus making them the property of their new monopoly.
- The global extermination of all persons who have knowledge of or on some level believe in Jesus Christ.

247

Empirical evidence will show that Rockefeller Weaponized Wheat, etc. was unleashed into the American food supply illegally and that the United States government was complicit in this crime of releasing an untested, unsafe, organism - a Trojan horse central to the Rockefellers' self fulfilling prophecy, and a critical component necessary for achieving their long time goal of eliminating the Christian American majority. Much like the Luciferian engineered potato famine throughout Ireland and Scotland, which killed more than five million innocent people [ethnic cleansing], possessed elites know that by destroying wheat and other precious crops in the United States, their hybridized and genetically modified foods become the 'pale horse' that's promoted throughout the anti-Christian theosophical new age elite hierarchy.

"Go to now, [ye] rich men, weep and howl for your miseries that shall come upon [you]. Your riches are corrupted, and your garments are moth-eaten. Your gold and silver is cankered; and the rust of them shall be a witness against you, and shall eat your flesh as it were fire. Ye have heaped treasure together for the last days. Behold, the hire of the labourers who have reaped down your fields, which is of you kept back by fraud, crieth: and the cries of them which have reaped are entered into the ears of the Lord of sabaoth" - James 5:1-5:4

Remember what the well respected Theosophist and New Age Leader, Barbara Marx Hubbard, said in her book: "Book of Co-Creation" about eliminating ¼ of the global population.

"Out of the full spectrum of human personality, one fourth is electing to transcend. One fourth is resistant to election. They are unattractive by life ever-evolving. Now, as we approach the quantum shift from creature-human to co-create human, the destructive one-fourth [Christians] must be eliminated from the social body. Fortunately you. Dearly beloved's, are not responsible for this act. We are. We are in charge of God's selection process for planet Earth. He selects, we destroy we are the riders of the pale horse, death."

Since Barbara Marx Hubbard announced theosophy's vision for global genocide, obesity throughout the United States has risen from 9.7% to more than 31% in 2013. What's more the number of cancer caused deaths has risen by 35% and is expected to increase to more than 50% by 2020. And if you're one of the poor souls who are expecting the Rockefeller controlled Medical

Industrial Complex to do something. Keep in mind that the Rockefeller controlled United States health insurance giants own more than $2 billion in stock in Ray Kroc's McDonald's, KFC, the queen of Englands Burger King and Taco Bell.

"Very soon, every American will be required to register their biological property in a national system designed to keep track of the people and that will operate under the ancient system of pledging. By such methodology, we can compel people to submit to our agenda, which will affect our security as a charge back for our fiat paper currency. Every American will be forced to register or suffer NOT being able to work and earn a living. They will be our chattels [property] and we will hold the security interest over them forever, by operation of the law-merchant under the scheme of secured transactions. Americans, by unknowingly or unwittingly delivering the bills of lading [Birth Certificate] to us will be rendered bankrupt and insolvent, secured by their pledges. They will be stripped of their rights and given a commercial value designed to make us a profit and they will be none the wiser, for not one man in a million could ever figure our plans and, if by accident one or two should figure it out, we have in our arsenal plausible deniability. After all, this is the only logical way to fund government, by floating liens and debts to the registrants in the form of benefits and privileges. This will inevitably reap us huge profits beyond our wildest expectations and leave every American a contributor to this fraud, which we will call Social Insurance [Social Security]. Without realizing it, every American will unknowingly be our servant, however begrudgingly. The people will become helpless and without any hope for their redemption and we will employ the high office [presidency] of our dummy corporation [U.S.] to foment this plot against America."

- Edward M. House; private meeting
with President Woodrow Wilson 1913-1921

17 The Whole Wheat Truth

"Let both grow together until the harvest:
and in the time of harvest I will say to the
reapers, Gather ye together first the tares,
and bind them in bundles to burn them:
but gather the wheat into my barn."
- Matthew 13:30

Ancient wheat has played an important role throughout the history of the world, especially on Christianity. The ingredient wheat is the most frequently mentioned food in The Holy Bible. What is clear is that bread, throughout The Holy Bible symbolizes having a plentiful life, free from hunger and malnourishment. Wheat represents freedom and independence. The majority of Christians inside the United States have little to no understanding about how this perfect food arrived in what would become The United States of America. In 1602 it was the Christian Pilgrims, fleeing Luciferians in England, who were responsible for bringing both Christianity and wheat to America. With that knowledge in mind, is it any wonder the Luciferian Rockefeller Family has chosen to target the one food in The Holy Bible that anchors Christians to the promise of Liberty?

"The Spirit of the Lord GOD [is] upon me; because the LORD hath
anointed me to preach good tidings unto the meek; he hath sent me to
bind up the brokenhearted, to proclaim liberty to the captives, and the
opening of the prison to [them that are] bound;"
- Isaiah 61:1

One of the tools Luciferians are using today to abolish American Liberty is, "Agenda 21," a United Nations backed program created to eliminate your constitutional right to own land, live in rural areas, and grow your own organic food.

250

The majority of individuals who are promoting the, "Green Movement," "Global Warming," and "Climate Change," have no idea that these programs were the brainchild of Satanist, Leopold De Rothschild, a member of the same family who cofounded the Federal Reserve Bank and the entire global central banking cabal. It was Leopold who was the father of the biggest scam ever perpetuated on planet earth 'Global Warming'. In 2012 Leopold mysteriously died from a rare lung disease, even though he had no symptoms. You would think a man whose family is worth trillions of dollars, would have had a decent medical plan. Leopold must have become too much of a liability. Else, Ray Kurzweil's 'singularity' and vision of Artificial Intelligence [merging man with machine] is ahead of schedule for those who can afford it.

Today, Global Warming as well as Agenda 21 has exposed great frauds and great patriots. Tom DeWeese is one America Patriot who is building a coalition of educated supporters. His website is: american-policy.org

Nazi propaganda Chief Joseph Goebbels was the master of the "big lie" tactic in which a lie, no matter how outrageous, is repeated often enough that it will eventually be accepted as truth. Goebbels explained:

"If you tell a lie big enough and keep repeating it, people will eventually come to believe it. The lie can be maintained only for such time as the State can shield the people from the political, economic and/or military consequences of the lie. It thus becomes vitally important for the State to use all of its powers to repress dissent, for the truth is the mortal enemy of the lie, and thus by extension, the truth is the greatest enemy of the State."

The 'Big-Lie' that's been successfully sold to the American people began in 1983 when Monsanto, Genetically Modified Organisms (GMO's) were allowed to enter the United States food supply. Now that the Rockefeller funded hybrids and Monsanto GMO's had successfully infected our Nation's agricultural system, Monsanto's legion of Washington lobbyists went to work promoting measures that would ensure maximum proliferation of their laboratory abominations throughout every American household.

What's most troubling is that their questionable behavior and intentions have been met with little if any resistance from our United States Congress or Senate. Unsurprisingly, the vast majority of Senatorial and Congressional leadership throughout Washington are in fact hand-picked proxies, who take their marching orders directly from Luciferian elites. Why on earth, would any mentally stable human being who is genuinely interested in protecting the lives of innocent Americans support both the creation and propagation of organisms throughout the American food supply, which have been shown to cause terminal disease in all living creatures?

Take the Academy of Nutrition and Dietetics, for instance, which posed the following question: "Can You Be Too Healthy?" According to the world's largest organization of food and nutrition professionals, America's poor health is in no way associated with the toxic GMO's and hybridized foods being forced fed to our citizenry, and it certainly has nothing to do with the caustic Aspartame and fluoride they're drizzling on everyone's brains.

According to the Academy of Nutrition and Dietetics, the primary contributing factor negatively impacting American health today is a condition they refer to as 'Orthorexia', which is defined as: "An unhealthy fixation on eating only healthy or pure foods". Just as Theosophist Carl Jung's Human Exploitation Psychology did when he labeled human beings 'introverted' and 'extroverted', those promoting the man-made condition of Orthorexia are doing nothing but inventing new conditions meant to bring about some self-fulfilling prophecy. This is a well documented technique utilized by Luciferians for generations. By successfully affixing some sort of stigma onto an educated, defiant segment of society, the enemy is able to effectively neutralize those who are threatening their agenda. The resulting effect are mentally, physically, and spiritually weak, 'Sheeple," who are willing to consume cancer causing GMO Corn, Soy and Wheat, toxic fluoride, aspartame, and subject themselves to all manner of slow-kill methods.

Academy of Nutrition and Dietetics Spokesperson, Marjorie Nolan, MS, RD, CDN, ACSM-HFS says:

"Orthorexia starts out with a true intention of wanting to be healthier, but it's taken to an extreme,"

Nolan's specialty is working with people who have 'eating disorders'. I trust that I do not have to point out the obvious 'Big-Lie' methodology enlisted here by Ms. Nolan. This is a textbook strategy that is used anytime elites feel threatened that they've been figured out. They simply attempt to discredit the individual by prescribing them a 'disorder' which makes controlling their lives that much easier. Nolan goes on to say:

"If someone is orthorexic, they typically avoid anything processed, like white flour or sugar. A food is virtually untouchable unless it's certified organic or a whole food. Even something like whole-grain bread – which is a very healthy, high-fiber food – is off limits because it's been processed in some way."
– Marjorie Nolan MS, RD, CDN, ACSM-HFS

It is useful idiots like Ms. Nolan who are promoting villainous dishonesty at the cost of millions of American lives. Moreover, she is empowering the Luciferian controlled United Nations and their agenda to murder 90% of the U.S. How can someone with four acronyms after her name in good consciousness proclaim GMO/Hybridized White Flour, Sugar, Whole Grain and processed foods are 'very healthy'? That is at best criminal.

A study of ancient societies who lived on a high-fiber, high-carbohydrate diet, demonstrates just how unhealthy Ms. Nolan's suggestions to the American people are. Take Ancient Egyptians for example. A large percentage of the Egyptian diet was based on a high-fiber, whole grain, low-fat life style. In the times of pharaohs, an Egyptian's diet was predominately vegetarian and yet the health effects were devastating. Analysis of Egyptian writings and the study of their mummies show us that Egyptians were plagued with intestinal disease, arthritis, osteoporosis, diabetes, heart disease, and poor dental health. Egyptians' high-fiber, high carbohydrate diets contained no refined carbohydrates, however, their remains do not reflect the health benefits promoted by industry associations and experts such as Ms. Nolan. I do not have as many acronyms behind my name as Ms. Nolan, however, one cannot dispute the overwhelming evidence gathered from tens of thousands of well-preserved Egyptian mummies. The fact of the matter is that a high-fiber, high-carbohydrate diet creates an environment of disease and death.

Sitting just off the shores of Long Island New York sits by far one of the most deadly installations in America. And I'll bet you've never even heard about it. Its name is 'Plum Island'. Plum Island is the United States Government's advanced Bio-Weapons Laboratory. Just like NASA, the bio-weapons unit on Plum Island was founded using Nazi scientists.

What should concern you, as an American citizen, is the fact that the United States Government, which is controlled by Luciferians whose stated goal is to drastically reduce global population levels, is now planning to move the Plum Island Bio-Weapon installation to Kansas. I mention this fact only because on average Kansas produces more wheat than any other state in the United States, and not to mention, the importance of all the surrounding state crops. Kansas wheat alone accounts for nearly 20 percent of total domestic production. And now, the United States Government is going to relocate a bio-weapon installation with a history of mistakes right in the middle of America's 'Bread Basket'?

Keep in mind that wheat has always been the crown jewel of American crops to the global elite owned and controlled Monsanto Corporation. After all, wheat makes up about 20% of the total calories consumed by Americans each year. Not to mention the profits involved. When you consider the fact that just five cents worth of wheat nets a profit of more than $3.99, it's no wonder the Rockefellers wanted to corner the hybridized, genetically modified market. Now factor in all the free advertising from The Whole Grain Council, USDA, The American Heart Association, and The American Diabetes Association, and you've got yourself the only type of business elites get involved with. That is, an industry that's been created by elites for elites. And since they were the ones who created the new market, they've had all the time in the world to work out all possible contingency factors, leaving nothing to chance. This is standard operating procedure for global elites. And in the event something does go wrong, their ship, or in this case food supply, is the last one on earth to go belly up. Have you ever wondered why the elites have built a massive arctic 'doomsday vault' located in Antarctica filled with samples of the world's most important crop seeds? That's their hedge or contingency when they've genetically modified all of our food into extinction.

254

It's also the motivating factor behind Monsanto's announcement in 2009 to introduce 'RoundUp Ready Wheat'. Monsanto calls this their most important new product. As you can imagine, this has caused uproar throughout our Nation amongst groups of people who find it difficult to allow Monsanto to destroy any additional food crops in America. Being poisoned to death doesn't sit well with these groups. Monsanto says that the level of debate in the United States, in general, is because it is the first major GMO crop which would be used predominantly for products to be consumed by humans, rather than as animal feed. We'll ignore the fact that GMO soy is currently circulating throughout most of the products Americans consume today. I'll expand on this later.

Consider the fact that United States wheat holds 26-28% of the world market share. The European Union was the fourth largest importer of United States wheat overall in 2001, and although this position may diminish due to new European Union's rules on imports, it would nevertheless be extremely serious for the United States to virtually lose the European Union market for its wheat, which is a real possibility if GMO wheat is commercialized.

This is the global elites' proverbial final nail in America's coffin. The elites first removed manufacturing from the United States and shipped it to China. Then the elites removed all R&D for technology offshore. Then our service industries, e.g., call centers and others went to India. The GMO created fat lady will begin singing if the elites are allowed to decimate our Nation's crops. Americans will be threatened with the reality of having to buy all 'Organic', non-GMO foods from other nations. If they choose not to do so, they'll have no other option but to eat cancer causing toxic GMO's. Have you ever read the Country of Origin when buying fruits and vegetables? Next time take a look! You will most likely find 'Product of Mexico', 'Product of Vietnam', 'Product of China', etc.

The internationally grown food that should concern you the most, is the one that reads 'Product of China'. I am familiar with a number of provinces in China. This is a Nation with rivers that are so contaminated from growing cultured pearls and dumping waste, etc. that a citizen of Mexico would get sick from drinking Chinese water. Chinese water is so contaminated that the Chinese Government is buying up America's fresh water supply through Nestle Corp. (Perrier and San Pellegrino). The depth of the Great

Lakes is down 10 feet because of the Chinese water sales. Are we as a Nation seriously going to consider China as our 'go to' Nation, for organic products? Good luck with that one.

This is why it's important to buy locally grown fruits and vegetables and demand that your local grocery store support local organic meat, dairy and produce.

So, what's the correlation between GMO's and the epidemic of disease throughout America? Consider this fact. Just two years, after Monsanto illegally introduced their toxic genetically modified abominations into our food supply in 1985, The National Heart, Lung and Blood Institute, in concert with the National Cholesterol Education Program began recording an explosion in obesity. This has led to what is today commonly referred to as 'Syndrome X'; a pre-diabetic state in which the body is incapable of processing toxic GMO sugars. When your body is placed into this state, your cells are no longer able to create energy from sugar, resulting in massive fat storage. Needless to say, people with this condition develop a myriad of symptoms associated with a toxic endocrine system. If allowed to continue, your body will eventually develop Type 2 diabetes, high cholesterol, and cardiovascular disease.

Kirk Azevedo graduated with a biochemistry degree from California Polytechnic State University and worked for Monsanto doing research on Bt (or Bacillus Thuringiensis) pesticides. Around 1996, Kirk worked as a local market manager for Monsanto, serving as a facilitator for genetically modified crops for the Western States. He explained to Food Nation Radio how he had assumed that California cotton that was genetically engineered for herbicide resistance could be marketed as conventional California cotton (to get the California premium) since the only difference between the two, he believed, was the gene Monsanto wanted in the crop. However, one of Monsanto's Ph.D. researchers informed Azevedo that "there's actually other proteins that are being produced, not just the one we want, as a by-product of the genetic engineering process." This concerned Azevedo who had also been studying protein diseases (including diseases such as mad cow disease) and knew proteins could be toxic. When he told his colleague they needed to destroy the seeds from the GE crop so that they weren't fed to cattle, the other researcher said that Monsanto isn't going to stop doing what it's been doing everywhere else.

Azevedo recalls his disillusionment:

> "I saw what was really the fraud associated with genetic engineering: My impression, and I think most people's impression with genetically engineered foods and crops and other things is that it's just like putting one gene in there and that one gene is expressed. If that was the case, well then that's not so bad. But in reality, the process of genetic engineering changes the cell in such a way that it's unknown what the effects are going to be."

Azevedo has since left the chemical industry and now calls for the enforcement of GE labeling laws. In California such a law appeared on voter ballots in November 2013 as Proposition 37 – the first of its kind and failed (even though no labels would have been required for livestock that feed on GE crops). Supporters of GE labeling predicted the California rule, which would have required labels on most foods containing GE ingredients, could influence food labeling throughout the country.

Not so great news on the national front, however. The United States House agriculture committee passed its version of the proposed Farm Bill this week that includes attached provisions severely weakening USDA's oversight of GE crops. Not only does the bill provide back door approval for any new GE crop before meaningful environmental review, but it also protects the biotech industry from lawsuits brought by organic farmers whose crops are contaminated by GE crops through "genetic drift." According to the Center for Food Safety: "all requirements of the National Environmental Policy Act or Endangered Species Act would be banned, even if a crop approval would harm protected species."

> "Wherefore if ye be dead with Christ from the rudiments of the world, why, as though living in the world, are ye subject to ordinances, {rudiments: or, elements} (Touch not; taste not; handle not; Which all are to perish with the using;) after the commandments and doctrines of men?" - Colossians 2:20

The love story between human beings and Wheat began 6,000 years ago. Einkorn wheat was one of the earliest cultivated forms of wheat alongside emmer wheat. Grains of wild einkorn have been discovered throughout the 'Fertile Crescent' of northeast Africa. It was first domesticated approximately

257

4,000 BC, in the Garden of Eden. Evidence from DNA testing suggests einkorn was domesticated in the Middle-East, in an area where a number of farming villages have been found. Since that initial ancient harvest 6,000 years ago, wheat has divided into over 25,000 different varieties.

The cultivation of einkorn decreased in the Bronze Age, and today it is a relict crop that is rarely planted, though it has found a new market as a health food. It remains as a local crop, often for bulgur (cracked wheat) or as animal feed, in mountainous areas of France, Morocco, the former Yugoslavia, Turkey, and other countries. It often survives on poor soils where other species of wheat fail.

In contrast with modern Rockefeller hybridized wheat, Einkorn does not seem to affect those suffering with intestinal disorders e.g., 'IBS', Celiac, Colitis, etc. Clients to whom I have recommended Einkorn Wheat Flour have experienced no adverse reactions.

How I came to know Einkorn, was by complete luck, really. I personally have always had an extremely negative response to wheat products my entire life. My understanding about what American wheat really was would change considerably after a trip to visit family in Transylvania Romania. During our trip, I was surprised to learn that in addition to a drink by the name of 'Tuică', bread played an important role at every meal. While in Transylvania we visited an estate of a friend who grew something I had never heard of... 'Einkorn' Wheat. Now, being a lifelong student of alternative health remedies, as well as a forensic historian, I was ashamed to learn that there was this nutrient dense life force, gracing the fields of our planet and I had never heard about it. After about three days of speaking with my relatives about the nutrient superiority of this food e.g., growing, cultivation and preparation methods, etc., I discovered that Einkorn was so incredibly distant from what we call wheat in America. This led me to ask what I considered to be a logical question: 'If this strain of wheat has never been exposed to Rockefeller hybridization or genetic modification, would my body receive it any differently than its FrankenWheat cousin in America'? That question, would change my life and those around me irrevocably.

For the past five years now, I've been eating the Einkorn species with great success. Furthermore, I've had no intestinal upset. Like most Christians, I've occasionally followed in the earlier footsteps of 'Doubting Thomas', and thought to myself, 'this is just too good to be true'; and just like Apostle Thomas, I've been humbled by The Creator. Immediately following one of my doubting phases I would perform a test on my body, where I would stop eating Einkorn, for a month or so. Then I would consume a small amount of a popular American 'Whole Wheat' product. Well, upon ingesting traditional American wheat products, I would soon experience an extremely unpleasant reaction e.g., shortness of breath, delay in ocular motor skill, heart palpitations, bowel distress, etc. Most frustrating of all, however, is the adverse effects on neuronal activation and response. In normal wheat-less brains the 'file-guy' is highly efficient at retrieving memories that you've requested, and delivers them within a few seconds... In the case of a Wheat-Head however, the file guy is literally high on wheat. In this environment he becomes sluggish. A typical Wheat Detox takes me about a week before I'm able to get my intestinal swelling down and my 'file guy' out of the Betty Ford clinic. If you're currently experiencing any of the above described mental or physical distresses, the final section of my book will walk you through my easy to follow solutions to heal your digestive system in as little as a few days.

If you're like I was, you're probably asking yourself... What's so clever about Einkorn?' That's a great question. My research has shown that the gliadin protein found within einkorn may not be toxic to sufferers of certain intestinal disorders. This is a logical explanation given what a former Monsanto PhD researcher admitted about toxic GMO proteins. He said:

"There's actually other proteins that are being produced, not just the one we want, as a byproduct of genetic engineering process."

This is what concerned former Monsanto Bio-Scientist Kirk Azevedo. Kirk knew, just as Monsanto knows that 'New' unidentified proteins, ones that have never been tested on human beings, can be lethal. This is precisely the reason why America is experiencing an epidemic of obesity, diabetes, cancer, etc. The good news is the final portion of my book will provide you with suggestions that may help with cleansing your entire body of these Dr. Frankenstein created toxins.

The sobering reality for many Americans reading this book should be that they have been duped and propagandized into believing the 'Big-Lie'. The 2014 model of American 259 bread that looks feels and smells like bread is not really bread at all. Rather, it's a man-made abomination that's completely incompatible with our trillion cells; not to mention, the ten trillion bacteria that ensure a healthy digestive system. Unfortunately, the wheat in our cupboards and our plates is nothing like the bread our parents and/or grandparents ate just seventy-years ago.

The Rockefeller Family has intentionally corrupted one of the most genetically complex and hardy organisms on planet earth, this perfect food which contains 42 chromosomes and executes God's perfectly designed human code. And now, the code written by God is no longer interoperable with the rest of God's eco-algorithm. In essence, The Rockefeller's have downloaded a Monsanto/Cargill/ADM virus into the global ecosystem and now God' complex creation that is the human machine considers modern man-made wheat a foreign invader, virus, etc. instead of a life sustaining food source. Americans must realize God's perfect code that has flawlessly orchestrated the human experience for six thousand years has now been tainted by The Rockefeller's.

The resulting effect is that we're beginning to see a mutated species of human being. If you don't believe me, next time you're out at the mall, your favorite restaurant, etc. count the number of obese people that you see around you; 'Obese' being defined as people who have multiple chins, people who have that distinctive hanging belly, challenging the tensile strength of their size 50+ waist leather belt. They waddle instead of walk and they pant and wheeze with every step. If our Nation continues to embrace this level of poor health and ignore the truth found throughout this book, the logical outcome, several generations into the future, is that the human race will split into two disparate species, "gracile" and "robust" humans, similar to the Eloi and Morlocks foretold by HG Wells in his 1895 novel The Time Machine.

It makes you wonder. What was the Geneticist who developed this new FrankenWheat thinking? This whole endeavor reminds me of the movie 'Jurassic Park'. In it, Jeff Goldblum's character poses the following question with regards to the driving force behind scientists' desire to clone dinosaurs:

"Your scientists were so preoccupied with whether or not they could,
they didn't stop to think if they should"

I believe that in a completely transparent and well monitored environment scientific research and discovery has a place in our society. However, allowing a microcosm of our global community [Luciferians] to elect themselves supreme beings with godlike privileges simply because they've reverse engineered one Angstrom of God's perfect code of life is akin to some Chinese manufacturer reverse engineering Top Secret United States military weaponry and then saying that they are the father of this invention.

The fact is that elites knew the dangers associated with genetic modification, and yet they chose to ignore these harbingers of disease and illegally forged ahead. It's been this lack of transparency shown to the American population, and malevolence on the part of the elites, for instance, which enabled famed Geneticist Norman Borlaug and the trillion dollar Rockefeller Family to develop a toxic high-yield 'Dwarf Wheat'. And because the United Government has been complicit in these crimes, United States Congressional, Senatorial, and Executive level leadership have ignored the fact that our Nation has been high-jacked by Satan worshipping, inbred, clinically insane, syphilitic Luciferians. And now, more than 99% of American wheat crops and all of the products you are ingesting contain toxic, cancer causing genetically modified organisms.

As if the poisoning of America's Amber Waves of Grain weren't enough, Borlaug's Frankenstein Monster was plunged into the soils of China increasing their 'wheat' output eightfold, not to mention the poisoning of untold numbers of Chinese People. So impressed were Luciferians of their prophesized Pale White Horse that they actually awarded Geneticist Norman Borlaug a Presidential Medal of Freedom, Congressional Gold Medal, and the Nobel Peace Prize in 1970.

Even in 2014, strong Presidential support continues. Avowed Freemason and President of the United States, Barack Hussein Obama, recently signed HR 993. In it, he supports a Monsanto and biotech rider. The gist of the rider is that cancer causing genetically modified organisms can't be stopped by a court order. These abominations, under Obama's HR 993, can still be grown, harvested, and sold to unsuspecting United States citizens. What's telling is the response of 250,000 signatories to an emergency letter to Obama, asking him to send HR 993 back to Congress, so the rider could be removed. Obama ignored the request and chose to allow Monsanto and their GMO's to slowing and painfully exterminate millions of Americans.

261

Even with all of the damming evidence slithering around the GMO viper pit, it's difficult to comprehend a reality that features highly educated physicians in 2014 who are willing to ignore a mountain of scientific evidence that clearly shows a connection between GMO's and an epidemic of disease, but that's exactly what Americans are faced with. The reckless and irresponsible notion that the Rockefeller hybridization/genetic modification experiments in Mexico had absolutely nothing to do with the increase in illnesses is criminal at best. A number of AMA and FDA marionettes argue that the vast majority of genetic manipulation actually occurred over a long duration, many thousand years to be exact, and that the Rockefeller science experiments had little to no effect on modern American food crops. Sure, we'll just ignore the correlation between the introduction of hybridization/GMO's into America's agricultural system in 1983 and the spectacular upsurge in colon, pancreas, lung and liver cancers, which began in 1983 and has risen ever since.

Dr. Rebecca Johnson, a cancer specialist at Seattle Children's Hospital, who was diagnosed with breast cancer [a major profit center for the Rockefellers] at age 27, seventeen years ago, seems to be one doctor who senses something is not adding up. She said:

"The change might be due to some sort of modifiable risk factor, like a lifestyle change" or exposure to some sort of cancer-linked substance."

Through duplicity, secrecy, and bulging coffers, Luciferians shelter the truth, and when they are exposed they defend and embrace their malevolence with pride. The truth is science has for years proven how devastating this modern wheat like imposter has been to our health. As a matter of fact, if given the choice, Americans would be better served, calorically and nutritionally, if they were to choose a candy bar over what elites are peddling as modern American wheat. Now that's not to say that I want you to jump on the candy bar diet or anything; neither choices are good, however the candy bar is certainly the lesser of the two evils.

Consider the following. In the early 80's, the University of Toronto developed what would become known as the glycemic index. The index provides a measure of how quickly blood sugar levels (i.e. levels of glucose in the blood) rise after eating a particular type of food. What they found is that foods which have been propagandized by the FDA and others as being 'healthy' are nutritionally subordinate to that of chocolate and beans – such 'healthy' foods including Rockefeller wheat like toxins that Americans are shoveling in their mouths each and every day. In addition, consider the fact that wheat actually motivates you to eat more of the foods that are making you unhealthy.

Keep in mind that the Church of Babylon considers the Christian American majority 'worthless eaters'. To them Christians are no better than a colony of rodents in need of extermination. What most people don't realize is that it's not the tasty ingredients that make up 99.9% of rat poison that kills the little furry rodent. What kills the rat makes up less than 0.1% of the ingredients contained in the poison. Flawlessly skinned GMO fruits and vegetables, as well as beautifully packaged and frosted GMO cakes, cookies, ice creams, and prepackaged meals, all work off this very simple principle. It's through our food supply that elites have hitched their global holocaust wagon.

Have you ever held an American grown organic apple or pear up to its GMO counterpart? The organic fruit is beat up and in some cases downright ugly. Very much like the aesthetically perfect apple which put Snow White into a coma. GMO fruits and vegetables are toxic, only they won't just put you into a temporary slumber; their effects are much more permanent. I would however like to point out the distinction between fruit and vegetables which are simply labeled with an official looking 'organic' sticker with truly organic food. The Christian American majority must be vigilant when purchasing organic food. Why? Because the truth is a large percentage of the organic fruits and vegetables sold in grocery stores in the United States, United Kingdom, Canada, and Australia, are in fact grown in nations such as in South America and South East Asia. Having personally travelled throughout China, I can't think of a single food item that the American consumer should feel safe eating. Consider the fact that China's regulation of its environment is almost non-existent. Aside from growing cultured pearls, in virtually every river system, the countless manufacturing facilities that blanket China's landscape contribute to the popular practice of dumping mercury into their river systems. Furthermore, the Chinese government sees nothing wrong with selling the Christian American majority vegetables sprayed with human waste, not to mention the chemically impregnated smog which blankets their food crops. Moreover, the Chinese rivers are so toxic that they would actually catch fire and burn for days. Recently a high ranking Communist Chinese Government official was offered $30,000 to swim in a Chinese river and declined because

263

the Chinese official knew that he would die.

I share the above information to get the Christian American majority to understand that the vast majority of internationally grown 'Organic' foods are in fact sprayed with Monsanto insecticides which is an illegal practice in America. These fruits and vegetables are then falsely classified as 'Organic' and then routed through a number of middlemen prior to reaching their American destination. The actions of these foreign nations and the United States Government are not only malicious and fraudulent, but criminal. They are knowingly importing toxic, cancer causing foods and then allowing the Christian majority of America to consume them. This is why, I strongly recommend, that you buy your fruits and vegetable from local growers only.

Please visit silvanusselect.com to discover where to buy the best organic food in your area. Unearth family owned organic farms and farmer's markets selling vitamin rich organic produce. What's more you'll find growers of drug-free, grass-feed meat and related products. Please support, our aspiration of providing alternative health solutions to America's Christian majority, by shopping at silvanusselect.com for health related products that are unavailable in your hometown.

In terms of choosing quality Organic fruits and vegetables, a good rule of thumb is, do not eat anything an insect won't eat, with the exception of a dung beetle. Much like the food tasters of ancient times, who would taste the food of kings to ensure no poison was present, insects are our personal little food tasters. So next time you see little holes in your organic fruits and vegetables, rejoice in knowing that the little guy didn't take a dirt nap tasting your food. Personally, I'd rather rely on the advice of an insect over a corrupt FDA official any day of the week and twice on Sunday. If the Christian American majority do not heed the warnings in this book and begin challenging the status quo and burning the tares [Matthew 13:30] from our lands, the Luciferian's plans to eliminate 90% of the global population (100% of the Christian population) will continue as scheduled.

264

"(For many walk, of whom I have told you often, and now tell you even weeping, that they are the enemies of the cross of Christ: Whose end is destruction, whose God is their belly, and whose glory is in their shame, who mind earthly things.) For our conversation is in heaven; from whence also we look for the Saviour, the Lord Jesus Christ:"
- Philippians 3:18-20

Gluten's Motive Operandi

"Lies come up in the elevator; the truth takes the stairs but gets here eventually." - Koffi Olomide, Congolese poet

The vast majority of Americans today have heard about gluten, gluten free diets, etc. However I've discovered that most people have no idea what gluten really is. Gluten is simply a protein found in flour which forms during bread making. Glutanin and gliadin, two protein molecules in flour, combine to form gluten when water is added to flour, and the resulting dough is worked over or kneaded into bread, etc. The gluten forms a network that traps CO_2 created by yeast, giving bread its traditional features. It will be remembered from previous chapters my mention of wheat as one of God's most complex gifts to man/womankind and how this gift contains over one thousand proteins. It's this complex protein structure that protects wheat from pathogens, etc. Unfortunately, wheat hackers have corrupted the God code of wheat to the point that the human machine no longer identifies it as a compatible resource. To further confuse our body's ten trillion intestinal food processors, The Luciferians, who own every major food manufacturer, further complicate matters by adding a myriad of fungal enzymes. Then to add insult to intestinal injury, bakers add toxic, estrogen containing GMO soy flour, just so that they're able to enhance the appearance of their creations.

Some of my readers may be asking the question: 'Paul, how on earth, can you claim that Luciferians own all of these companies? What evidence, do you have'? I came to this conclusion after reading a 2011 Swiss Institute of Financial Control Study. In this study, they demonstrated that just twenty banks and individuals owned the largest and most influential International community of corporations, and that it's these 43,000 international corporations which control more than 60% of the wealth on Planet Earth.

As consumers, we've all been deceived into believing that our stores are offering us a multitude of options. In reality, just ten massive corporations are represented on the shelves of the average grocery store. It's these ten corporations that are deliberately sourcing and manufacturing toxic GMO ingredients, and then propagating their toxic health destroying products throughout our global community. They are complicit in the epidemiology of Cancer, Hypothyroidism, Obesity, Learning Disabilities, Birth Rate Reduction, Impotency in men, and the destruction of the endocrine system in billions of human beings worldwide. They are the collective corporate version of the four horseman of the apocalypse. Who are these top ten foods manufactures? They are: KRAFT, Coca Cola, Pepsico, General Mills, Mars, Kelloggs, Unilever, Johnson & Johnson, P&G, and Nestle.

"On December 16, 1773, the Boston Tea Party took place to protest the British monopoly of American tea sales. Two hundred years later, as we prepare to celebrate the bicentennial of our freedom from British control, we find that Unilever - a British-Dutch company-monopolizes American tea sales."
- Jim Hightower, from the 1975 book Eat Your Heart Out

You may be asking. How is this all being hidden, Paul? In the United States it's all being ran illegally and outside the jurisdiction of the United States Constitution through what's referred to as 'Black Budgets'. These budgets are run by both the CIA and FBI and were made possible with the creation of the 'Exchange Stabilization Fund' and 'Financial Stability Board'. Both were created in the 1930's by Freemason President Franklin D. Roosevelt who once stated:

"In politics, nothing happens by accident. If it happens, you can bet it was planned that way"
– Franklin D. Roosevelt

"The real truth of the matter is, as you and I know, that a financial element in the large centers [Rothschild/Rockefeller] has owned the government ever since the days of Andrew Jackson"
– Franklin D. Roosevelt

266

Luciferians know that its time is running out and that's why we're seeing what most people believe to be unbelievably swift changes to our Nation's moral consciousness, economic stability, and the physical and mental health of millions of Americans. For me, the bellwether will always be the individual actions being taken by the elites themselves.

Warren Buffet, is one of the world's richest proxies for Lord Jacob Rothschild, co-owner of the United States Federal Reserve Bank, Inc. and business partner to hundreds of billionaire's around the world including the owner of FOX News Rupert Murdoch. Recently Buffet has begun purging American stocks at an alarming rate. His company Berkshire Hathaway sold tens of millions of shares belonging to useful idiot corporations like Johnson & Johnson, Procter & Gamble, and Kraft Foods. These are three of the world's top ten food manufactures, and it's my prediction that the top ten food manufacturers are about to be ceremonially crucified for the role they've played in sourcing, manufacturing, and propagating toxic, cancer causing GMO's throughout the United States. Why? For the sole purpose of 'Shock Testing' America's food supply.

The Rothschild's, Rockefellers, Morgan's, Buffets, Gates, etc. are masters of 'Shock Testing'. Simply put this is when a strategically selected staple commodity e.g., gas, sugar, pork, beef, coffee, gold, silver, water, bullets, etc. experience a sudden change or 'shock' to their price and/or availability. This causes a shift in consumer buying habits and allows the Rothschild's, Rockefellers, Morgan's, Buffets, Gates, etc. to observe the effects on pricing, advertising, sales, etc. This empowers these Luciferians with the critical data necessary to customize a very predictable, self fulfilling, destructive mathematical theory of Operations Research algorithm for every individual, company, corporation, state, government and religion around the world.

These men are neither mystic nor are they oracles of industry; and they sure as hell are not my God. The fact of the matter is markets and wealth is created by elites for elites. And I personally believe that these professional criminals are well aware of the specific research that points toward a massive market correction of as much as 90%. Before you dismiss my claim that we're going to see a 90% drop in the stock market, consider everything that I've shared with you up to this point. Couple that with the picture featuring Warren Buffet walking with Lord Jacob Rothschild, whose family co-founded the Federal Reserve Privately Held Corporation, along with the Rockefeller Family. It's estimated that the Rothschild fortune is worth in excess of $100 trillion, ten times that of the Rockefeller Family. Logic dictates that Buffet has been handed down some 'secret' financial knowledge from the global money changers, and that is in fact what's caused Buffet's recent purge of American stocks.

> "Let me issue and control a Nation's money
> and I care not who makes its laws"
> - Amschel Bauer Mayer Rothschild, 1838

Elites are proud of what they're doing to the American people and they openly brag in just about every book or article they write and in every television broadcast in which they're featured. Elites are fully aware of the physical and mental damage caused by their hybridized/GMO products. Their geneticists knew the dangers and must have explained to their elite handlers the addictive nature of these products. Moreover, they're fully aware of the fact that there is absolutely no difference between hybridized/GMO products and street narcotics. Elites are intentionally creating an entire generation of doped up, permanently dependant adolescents. Most concerning of all is the fact that scientists have proven that digested gluten is capable of penetrating what is commonly referred to as the 'blood-brain barrier'. This process works like a security fire wall for our brain. Unfortunately this doesn't apply to gluten which is fully capable of penetrating and corrupting the complex security code found within our grey matter.

The faster people develop a negative association with injecting massive amounts of toxic, mass produced Rockefeller Wheat into their bodies, the sooner the American people can begin eliminating the Luciferian power structure. As difficult as all this might seem, the facts speak for themselves. The Rockefeller Family financed research to develop a fast growing toxic organism that mimics the physical appearance and taste and texture of wheat. Unfortunately this imposter organism that's been photocopied over 20,000 times is completely incompatible with the human body. Nonetheless, the Trillion Dollar Rockefeller Family, in concert with Monsanto, have established strategic government and non-government partnerships which have enabled these Satanic elites with the necessary resources to successfully propagandize the American public into believing the 'Big-Lie' that 'whole grain' is not only healthy but a requirement to achieve a

268

healthy body. This is akin to supplying the crack dealer downtown with unlimited access to advertisers, leading scientists and others with the ultimate goal in mind of validating crack as nature's number one weight loss supplement. It's complete and total madness to entertain such an idea. Nonetheless, this is exactly what our politicians have allowed to happen and now, America has become a Nation of brainwashed, unhealthy fatties, who actually believe a toxic man-made organism that's making them fat and unhealthy is in fact good for them. If that's not disturbing enough, elites have then created drug companies that are pumping out billions of dollars of toxic pharmaceuticals to address the elite created epidemic of obesity throughout America and the illnesses it creates e.g., heart disease, diabetes, stroke, etc. What's truly disconcerting is that these elite manufactured toxic pharmaceuticals do nothing more than mask the warning signs which your body is boldly and blatantly displaying for the whole world to see. I will tell you that I've never met a person who is sick because he or she has developed a deficiency in fill-in-the-blank pharmaceuticals.

Much like the warning the American people received from President Eisenhower on January 17, 1961 about the 'Military Industrial Complex', we face yet another equally alarming reality in 2014, at the hands of the Medical Industrial Complex. Let me give you an idea of what I mean. The costs associated with all of the aforementioned toxic GMO created diseases range between $190,000 to $260,000 for each and every individual, both in direct and indirect costs and that is if the patient is diagnosed by the age of forty-nine years old. Furthermore, GMO's have increased the number of Americans suffering with diabetes from 6 million in 1980 to over 25 million in 2009. Again, obesity and all related diseases correlate with the 1983 introduction of GMO's into American soil. What elite controlled statistic agencies won't tell you is that for every confirmed case of diabetes, there are 4-5 Americans who are pre-diabetic, which suggests a whopping 25%-40% of the United States population is pre-diabetic. And most troubling of all are the manifestation of disease throughout America's population of young people; this is why I've dedicated this book to America's youth. Not only because they represent the future of American greatness, but rather, it's a fact that they have done absolutely nothing and yet they are being chemically lobotomized and exterminated by the Church of Babylon. Consider the fact that mental illness amongst America's youth skyrocketed from just 16,200 in 1987 to over 561,569 in 2007, according to the Center for Disease Control and Prevention.

Not to mention the fact that cancer throughout America's population of innocent children is up over 10,000%. The truth of the matter is the Church of Babylon and its proxy Monsanto are not in the business of feeding poor people around the world; they're in the cancer for profit business. Just look at who is on the board of Monsanto; you have Microsoft cofounder Bill Gates, McDonalds, and a list of other individuals and corporations whose products interact with us on almost a daily basis. I'm waiting for the day when McDonald's introduces a McTumor on their menu.

The McDeath System:

"We have found out... that we cannot trust some people who are nonconformists... We will make conformists out of them... The organization cannot trust the individual; the individual must trust the organization." - Ray Kroc

"The FDA requires that we tell people our Big Macs are made of mostly gluten filler. We've done two corporate press releases about it over the years – one in 1963 and one in 1977. It's just not something we share on our commercials." – Ray Kroc

For those of you who are unaware of McDonald's Corp beginnings, here is a brief history. Ray Kroc, a satanic Freemason and milkshake machine salesman, convinced the already wildly successful satanic Freemason McDonald brothers to sell Kroc the 'Speedee Service System' that they had invented in 1948. It was this system which established the principles of the modern fast-food system.

In his first year of operations with McDonald's he unsuccessfully attempted to convince Walt Disney, a fellow WWI ambulance driver with whom he had been acquainted, to let him open a restaurant in the forthcoming Disneyland.

It's important for the Christian American majority to understand that Walt Disney, Ray Kroc and Scientology founder L. Ron Hubbard were all in the military together. Both Kroc and Hubbard have been linked to Satanism.

270

In 1961, Kroc bought McDonald's Corp. from the McDonald brothers for a paltry $2.7 million. As someone who has personally recruited and/or partnered with parasites, who have later attempted to steal my own business ideas, it's easy for me to understand why the McDonald Brothers disliked Kroc. It's well documented, that Kroc's relationship with the McDonald Brothers was not friendly. In fact, Kroc denied the McDonald Brothers rights to the very first restaurant they had opened. What's more, Kroc opened a new McDonald's nearby to force them out of business.

In the 1970's, Kroc would be investigated by the FBI for donating large amounts of money to CREEP (the Committee to Re-elect the President). It was alleged that Kroc intended to obtain a monopoly on food sales at 1976 U.S. bicentennial celebrations.

Like many of the men I have personally come across in my life. Kroc's actions and questionable business practices failed to mirror that of the Christian American majority. The question I have is. What was the motivating force behind Kroc? What caused him to act so evil towards his fellow man? An accusation made against Kroc, back in the late 70's may shed some light on Kroc's questionable behavior.

On Tuesday June 7th, 1977, it is alleged by a number of television viewers, that a frazzled, Ray Kroc with cigarette in hand, appeared on the popular TV talk show "The Mike Douglas Show" [right]. It was during this appearance, viewers claim, they heard Ray Kroc broadcast to the public that he had donated money to Anton LaVey's Church of Satan. Shortly after the Kroc interview, a boycott against McDonalds by Christian's ensued, forcing Kroc to respond.

The above story presents two very important lessons to be learned. Number one; A very limited response on behalf of the Christian American majority in the 1970's; created such financial pain for McDonalds Corp., that they were

271

forced to respond to our community. Number two; IF Ray Kroc in fact had any affiliation with Anton Lavey's Church of Satan it would explain the global pestilence caused by McDonald's. What's more, it offers an explanation for the picture [left] featuring former McDonalds Chairman and Chief Executive Officer Jim Cantalupo and Charlie Bell; both men are flashing satanic devil horns. As an aside Cantalupo died from a heart attack in April, 2004. His successor, Charlie Bell, underwent colorectal cancer two weeks later and ultimately died from cancer in early 2005. It is commonly known that heart disease and colon cancer is caused by genetically modified organisms. The same GMO's sourced and sold by McDonald's Corporation.

Until that day, when McDonald's ceases to exist, do what I do anytime someone recommends McDonald's as a restaurant option. I simply say: 'I'm sorry… I can't eat at McDonald's because I'm allergic to cancer'. It must be the goal of every responsible American citizen to educate every single child living throughout this great Nation that those individuals and corporations who are willfully sourcing, manufacturing and selling, toxic GMO's, are the enemy. Children should be so knowledgeable about GMO toxicity, and know that when they drive by a McDonald's. They should think and say exactly what my three year old son does when we drive past the front of a McDonald's. My little guy says: 'Daddy. They sell poison there…'

As of 2013, McDonald's signage brags that they have served over one quarter of a trillion people, and with that revenue they have contributed to the plague of illness sweeping across our Nation. Imagine the financial effect on this harbinger of disease if 240 million American Christians all of a sudden stopped serving up massive profits to McDonald's Corp.

Some people might be saying: 'Paul, are you proposing that we completely boycott these companies and cause all of these people to lose their jobs?' What I am suggesting is that we stop poisoning ourselves with toxic food like substances. This is the only solution to eliminate the grave threat facing our Nation.

272

It's time for Christians to confront the dangers facing our community together. Each and every one of us should be picking up the phone or a pen and communicating our disgust with the 'fast-food' corporate executives, who are poisoning our communities. Each of us should personally correspond with their subordinates as well, to explain how they themselves are complicit in what amounts to crimes against humanity. It's our job as Christians to educate the American workforce, so that they clearly understand the bigger pictures of what they're involved in. Then we provide the morally sound individuals, who wish to be on the right side of history, the necessary training, motivation and financial resources to replace Church of Babylon controlled corporations throughout America.

A short list of Corporations created by Satanic Babylonian Freemasons include: Dave Thomas (founder of Wendy's), Bob Evans, and Harland Sanders ("the colonel," founder of Kentucky Fried Chicken) also were members. In fact, Sanders's gravestone bears the Masonic square and compasses. Samuel Colt, who popularized the revolver; safety razor inventor King Camp Gillette; Frank Hoover of Hoover vacuums; James Cash Penney, who started J.C. Penney; and automotive pioneer Walter Chrysler.

CHAPTER

Soy I Met You   **18**

"Now the Spirit speaketh expressly, that in the latter times some shall depart from the faith, giving heed to seducing spirits, and doctrines of devils; Speaking lies in hypocrisy; having their conscience seared with a hot iron; Forbidding to marry, and commanding to abstain from meats, which God hath created to be received with thanksgiving of them which believe and know the truth. For every creature of God is good, and nothing to be refused, if it be received with thanksgiving: For it is sanctified by the word of God and prayer" - 1 Timothy 4:1

Soy runs 'neck and neck' with that of traditional American grown wheat and corn in terms of how toxic it is to human beings, as well as how pervasive it is throughout America's culinary landscape. Soy is found in just about every product sold at your local grocery store. The bad news is that soy has a bad habit of inspiring cancer cells in the human body. It's especially lethal when it is ingested in large quantities. Which begs the question…? Why on earth are the mainstream media and Medical Industrial Complex going to painstaking lengths to deceive the American people into believing soy is a healthy food source? When in reality, soy is in no way a healthy food. As a matter of fact, soy would be more aptly labeled 'health risk'. Why? Because epidemiologists have shown that soy causes massive distress, even cancer to our bowel, brain, and heart, and not to mention, absolute nightmarish conditions for our thyroid and adrenals. By the way, if you're someone who is purposely consuming soy on a regular basis… STOP! The final portion of my book will help you detoxify your body from this abominable invader and get your body back onto a healthful track.

To better understand how soy came into being referred to as a 'health food', we'll need to understand the history of soy and why it was injected into the American food supply, in the first place. Many years ago, there was a campaign by the controlling elites to demonize the importation of healthy tropical oils which for years have sustained both the health industry as well as a number of industrial applications. The elite owned mainstream media were quite successful at labeling these healthy oils such as Palm and Coconut Oil as ' damaging' and the American public swallowed this propaganda, hook-line-and-sinker. The truth of the matter is their contention that the above said tropical oils were 'damaging' couldn't have been further from the truth.

What motivated the elites to do this? Money control and population reduction. Elites knew that if they could successfully perpetuate this myth about tropical oils they would be able to create a GMO monopoly by elites for elites, to suckle from for generations. It's this new industry that would allow them to eventually sell their genetically modified, cancer causing, vitamin and mineral robbing Corn and Soy oils.

Now, the following information I'm going to share may upset you if your diet is heavily dependent on soy, as it's been my position for many years, unless you're eating fermented soy (these are products such as Natto, which contains the highest amount of vitamin K, Tempeh and Miso). Please note that I do not consider Tofu a safe food source. Again, if you're consuming any form of unfermented soy – which most Americans are - you're eventually going to develop one or more of the above mentioned health challenges.

What's so dangerous about Soy?

More than 95% of Soy used in American cuisine is non-organic soy protein isolate. It's important to understand that this is often processed with hexane, a petroleum solvent similar to that of gasoline. Traditionally, natural food manufactures have used only expeller-pressed oils and fats, which do not involve the use of hexane in the crushing process. However, the resulting hexane-processed "residual soy meal" is utilized in many soy protein powders, cereals, and bars that are sold throughout the natural food industry. We've already discussed ad nauseam, the overwhelming inherent risk factors associated with GMO's, not to mention the underlying reasons for which the elites introduced GMO's into the global food supply.

Much like the damaging effects of Rockefeller FrankenWheat, soy has been shown to promote generational defects in creatures that digest this toxic protein. What's devilish about soy is that the disastrous effects aren't usually noticed by the individual who is consuming the soy; the actual damage is seen in second and third generation offspring. By the second and third generation, scientists are seeing subjects that are completely sterile or diagnosed with infertility. Future generations are literally being erased by this Church of Babylon concocted abomination. This is of course just one of many ways human beings are being eliminated from the future of planet earth.

Now, what if you're someone who is aware of the dangers of GMO's and you are careful to buy only non-GMO, organic tofu, etc. Unfortunately, you're still putting your health in harm's way. Why? Because, if you're digesting any type non-fermented soy e.g., Tofu, Soy Milk, Soy Butter, Soy Yogurt, etc. you're still ingesting large quantities Of Goitrogens which have been shown to cause hypothyroidism, especially amongst women. So if you're a woman or man, who is overweight or obese, please go through your cupboards and refrigerator and audit each and every product that you're eating. Identify and eliminate the products that read any of the following:

- "May contain soy"
- "Produced on shared equipment with soy"
- "Produced in a facility that also processes soy"

Other names for Soy include:

- Bean curd
- Bean sprouts
- Edamame (fresh soybeans)
- Kinako
- Nimame
- Okara
- Shoyu
- Soy sauce
- Soya
- Soybean (curds, granules)
- Tamari
- Tofu (dofu, kori-dofu)
- Yuba

Ingredients on a label are not always recognizable as soy. These ingredients are created from soy that has been processed in some way, such as the following:

- Hydrolyzed soy protein (HSP);
- Mono- and di-glycerides;
- MSG (monosodium glutamate);
- Soy (albumin, cheese, fiber, grits, milk, nuts, sprouts, yogurt, ice cream, pasta);
- Soy lecithin;
- Soy protein (concentrate, hydrolyzed, isolate);
- Soybean oil;
- Teriyaki sauce; and
- Textured vegetable protein (TVP).

It will be remembered from previous chapters my warning to the Christian American majority regarding the dangers of Rockefeller FrankenWheat, cautioning against eating gluten because of its effects on the endocrine system. Gluten affects the endocrine system in a way that inhibits certain hormones in your body and inspires the production of others. Unfortunately for men, Soy is another toxic food that affects the body in a similar fashion. More specifically, Soy stimulates the production of estrogen, also referred to as isoflavones, which instructs our bodies to store fat around our stomachs, hips, and chests. So if you're a guy who is seeking 'Man-Boobs', heart disease, hypothyroidism, and sterility, keep shoveling toxic soy down your throat. Soy also contains phytic acid which has been shown to impair the absorption of all minerals, e.g., magnesium, zinc, copper, and calcium.

As we discussed earlier, there are only ten corporations which control the vast majority of food production throughout the United States. It's these companies which are fully aware of the dangers of Soy in the human body and yet, they continue to sell products to the American people, such as isolated soy protein powder which is found in products such as protein bars and protein drinks. The important fact for people to realize is that this substance is not naturally produced. On the contrary, it's processed in an extremely toxic manner. The top ten manufacturers use an acid wash containing aluminum, MSG, etc. As an aside Alcoa Inc. (Aluminum Company of America) whose aluminum is used in cookware, soft drink cans, our atmosphere, food processing, etc. has a logo which contains one large pyramid and two smaller pyramids. When combined these pyramids create a satanic six pointed star.

So these soy products contain ingredients that stack one neurological retardant onto another. Take MSG for instance. We have a mountain of evidence that shows MSG alone is an excitotoxin that causes neurological disorders.

When I meet with new clients we perform a thorough audit of their refrigerator and cupboards, as well as where they eat out, etc. and what surprises them the most is how pervasive soy oil is throughout the products being sold at their local grocery store. That's because soy oil is in just about every prepackaged, processed food that you buy. As a matter of fact, soy oil is in over 95% of all processed foods. The danger with soy oil is that it contains high amounts of what's known at Omega 6 fatty acids, creating an imbalance of healthy Omega 3 fatty acids. Omega 6 is a fatty acid that's highly susceptible to oxidative damage, which can lead to the development of cancer.

In my opinion, the most criminal application global elites have identified for soy is as an ingredient inside infant formula. Why? Soy is extremely high in estrogen and is an endocrine disrupter influencing 'sexual orientation' and 'gender identity'. Soy is why our baby boys are growing up more feminine and in some cases sterile. Consider a 2004 survey of 1,500 fish at 50 river

277

sites in Great Britain which found endocrine disrupters in the water are causing fish to change from male to female damaging fish populations by reducing their ability to reproduce. Soy formulas also contain estrogen levels 20,000 times higher than birth control pills and these hormones are entering your little baby at his or her most critical development period. Soy formula is also extremely high in toxic minerals, such as Alcoa aluminum and manganese. It's this collection of harmful ingredients that effectively stunt the growth of your babies' intestinal development. And as I've discussed in detail throughout this book, the intestinal system, with its ten trillion bacteria, is super critical to the development of a healthy, life sustaining digestive system. In short if you have a baby please discontinue the practice of feeding toxic soy to your little person. Please visit silvanusselect.com where you will find a healthy homemade baby formula alternative. Just type 'homemade baby formula' into the search panel and you'll find a solution that will provide your little one with a nutritionally optimal option. Again, please warn as many parents as you can, so that they stop feeding their little ones the toxic soy cocktail, being promoted by the Top 10 eugenicist elite owned food corporations.

We're just a few paragraphs away from completing my overview and profiling of the Luciferian dynasty bequeathed to us by The Church of Babylon. It's been my contention, for many years now, that The Church of Babylon's extensive and very complex scaffolding of possessed proxies have in large part contributed to the moral, economic, educational, and spiritual decent of the United States of America. Furthermore, I believe that I've provided my readers with a treasure-trove of offenses that incriminate the vast majority of Fortune 100, 500 and 1000 companies on our planet and the elites who own and operate them. Even the most ardent coincidence theorists must admit a clear connection between The Church of Babylon and a massive increase in the number of deadly diseases being diagnosed throughout America.

The bottom line is that the elitist boil on the body of America is filled with nothing more than a colony of conniving, syphilitic, cowardly, little inbred villains who need to be lanced. It's this close knit cabal who has for generations conspired against all Christian Americans, leveraging layer upon layer of deceitful and duplicitous proxies.

It is the stated goal of The Church of Babylon to murder as many American citizens – specifically Christian Americans – through our food, water, air, and medicine.

In part, my conclusions are supported by the following reports: 'The Population Bomb' by: Dr. Paul R. Ehrlich (his wife by the way Anne is a member of the Club of Rome), 'The Global 2000 Report To The President' and 'The Limits to Growth, A Report for the Club of Rome's Project on the Predicament of Mankind'. On page 17, of the book: 'The Population Bomb' it reads:

"In summary, the world's population will continue to grow as long as the birth rate exceeds the death rate; it's as simple as that. When it stops growing or starts to shrink, it will mean that either the birth rate has gone down or the death rate has gone up or a combination of the two. Basically, then, there are only two kinds of solutions to the population problem. One is a 'birth rate solution', in which we find ways to lower the birth rate. [Elites are achieving this, through toxic wheat, corn, soy, fluoridated water, medicine, etc.] The other is a 'death rate solution', in which we find ways to lower the birth rate – war, famine, pestilence – find us. [This is the reason for all of the manufactured wars around the world] The problem could have been avoided by population control, in which mankind consciously adjusted the birth rate so that a 'death rate solution' did not have to occur."

"Christianity is our foe. If animal rights are to succeed, we must destroy the Judeo-Christian Religious tradition."
- Peter Singer, founder of Animal Rights

"Childbearing should be a punishable crime against society, unless the parents hold a government license. All potential parents should be required to use contraceptive chemicals, the government issuing antidotes to citizens chosen for childbearing."
- David Brower, first Executive Director of the Sierra Club

"The extinction of Homo Sapiens (man) would mean survival for millions, if not billions of Earth-dwelling species. Phasing out the human race will solve every problem on Earth – social and environmental."
- Ingrid Newkirk, Founder of PETA

"My three main goals would be to reduce human population to about 100 million worldwide, destroy the industrial infrastructure and see wilderness, with its full complement of species, returning throughout the world." - Dave Forman, co-Founder of Earth First "In order to stabilize world populations, we must eliminate 350,000 people per day."
- Dr. Jacques Cousteau

19   Codex Alimentarius

"And God said, Behold, I have given you every herb bearing seed, which is upon the face of all the earth, and every tree, in the which is the fruit of a tree yielding seed; to you it shall be for meat."
- Genesis 1:29

If a gauntlet of toxic, soy, corn, sugar, wheat, water and air controlled by wealthy Satanic Elites were not enough to keep you up all night, there's their 'secret weapon', insurance policy and contingency plan, that will knock your socks off. Have you ever heard of the 'Codex Alimentarius'? If not, don't feel bad as the vast majority of Americans haven't. The fact is, the Codex Alimentarius is an even a bigger secret than the unpredictable toxic proteins that are responsible for the plague of cancer sweeping across America in 2014. You know, the ones that the FDA considers 'generally recognized as safe'. The Codex Alimentarius is by far the most devastating blow to the health and welfare of human beings all across our planet.

What is the Codex Alimentarius?

In the Austro-Hungarian Empire between 1897 and 1911, a collection of standards and regulations for a wide variety of foods was developed, called the Codex Alimentarius Austriacus. It wasn't legally binding, but served as a useful reference for the courts to determine standards for specific foods. The post-World War II rebirth of the Codex Alimentarius however, is much more dubious.

To understand the full implications, we need to go back to the history of one huge conglomerate: The Interessengemeinschaft Farben, or IG Farben—a powerful cartel that consisted of German chemical and pharmaceutical companies such as BASF, Bayer, and Hoechst.

IG Farben was, you could say, the corporate arm of Adolf Hitler's Third Reich. Having lucrative contracts with Hitler's regime, IG Farben produced everything from ammunition to Zyklon B, the nerve gas that was used to kill prisoners in the concentration camps. IG Farben was the single largest donor to Hitler's election campaign, and later the single largest profiteer of World War II. Whenever the German Wehrmacht conquered another country, IG Farben followed, systematically taking over the industries of those countries. The United States government investigation of the factors that led to the Second World War in 1946 came to the conclusion that without IG Farben the Second World War would simply not have been possible.

Auschwitz, the largest and most infamous German concentration camp, also benefited IG Farben. New, unsafe pharmaceutical drugs and vaccines were liberally tested on Auschwitz prisoners, many of which died during the tests. Not surprising, the Nuremberg War Crime Tribunal prosecuted 24 Monsanto...Ooops! I mean IG Farben board members and executives for mass murder, slavery, and other crimes against humanity. One of those convicted was Fritz ter Meer, the highest-ranking scientist on the executive board of IG Farben, who was sentenced to seven years in prison (of which he only served four). When asked during trial whether he thought those human experiments had been justified, he answered:

"concentration camp prisoners were not subjected to exceptional suffering, because they would have been killed anyway."

In 1955, ter Meer was reinstated as a member of the supervisory board at Bayer and one year later became its chairman. In 1962, together with other executives of BASF, Bayer and Hoechst, he was one of the main architects of the Codex Alimentarius. When he got out of jail, he went to his United Nations buddies. In a passionate speech at the 2005 conference of the National Association of Nutrition Professionals (NANP) Fritz ter Meer said:

281

"If we take over food worldwide, we have power worldwide."

The result was the creation of a trade commission called the Codex Alimentarius Commission, now funded and run by the United Nations World Health Organization (WHO) and the Food and Agricultural Organization (FAO). You know, the same United Nations who proudly lists 'Lucis Trust', formerly named 'Lucifer Publishing'. Remember, Lucis Trust, is an avowed satanic organization that has promoted the idea of a New World Order/One World Religion, controlled by their Antichrist 'Maitreya'. Furthermore, their organization has called for the eradication of the United States Constitution, 90% of the world's population, freedom of speech, freedom to own a gun and defend ourselves, freedom to own land, implementation of 'Agenda 21', etc. It's Lucis Trust that has been instrumental in deciding matters related to the United Nations 'Economic and Social Council'.

From the time of its founding, in January 1, 1995, the World Trade Organization (WTO) accepted the standards of the Codex—and by the end of 2009, all 153 member countries of the WTO were required to implement the Codex "to harmonize the standards" for the global trade of foods. In the United States meanwhile, Congress passed the Dietary Supplements Health and Education Act (DSHEA) in 1994, which defined vitamins, minerals and herbs as foods, therefore not to be regulated by pharmaceutical standards. The Codex Alimentarius would reverse all that. It would treat those dietary supplements not as foods, but as toxins.

Dr. Rima Laibow is an expert on the subject of Codex Alimentarius. I highly recommend searching for her name on youtube.com, and you'll find a number of videos explaining in more detail how completely evil this final solution is for the global population.

In regards to how the United Nations plans to eradicate our God given right to the health benefits of Herbs and Vitamins, Dr. Laibow asks the question:

"How do you protect somebody from a poison? You use toxicology. You use a science called 'risk assessment.'"

Risk assessment, Dr. Laibow explains, works as follows:

"You take the toxin in question, feed it to lab animals and determine
the dose that kills 50% of them. That's called the LD 50. And you
extrapolate what the LD 50 for a human being might be. Then you go
down to the other end of the dosage range and you start feeding [little]
bits of it to test animals, and you come up with the largest possible
dose—the maximum permissible upper limit—that can be fed to an
animal before a discernible impact is shown. [...] Then you divide that
by 100. [...] And now you've got a safety margin, so you got 1/100 of
the largest dose that can be given with no discernible impact."

In other words, classified as toxins, vitamins, minerals and herbs
would only be allowed to be marketed in doses that have no discernible impact on anyone. Then why bother taking them? And that's not
all. Where our grocery and health food store shelves are now brimming
with supplements, only 18 of them would be on the Codex white list.
Everything not on the list, such as CoQ10, glucosamine, etc. would be
illegal—not as in "prescription-only" illegal, but as in "take it and you go
to jail" illegal.

But the mandatory requirements of the Codex will not only
concern vitamins and minerals, but all foods. Under Codex rules, nearly
all foods must be irradiated. And levels of radiation can be much higher
than previously permitted.

While irradiated, foods in America are currently treated with 1
– 7.5 kiloGray of radiation, the Codex would lift its already high limit of
10kiloGray—the equivalent of 330 million chest X-rays—"when necessary to achieve a legitimate technological purpose," whatever that may
be. Granted, the text says that the dose of radiation "should not compromise consumer safety or wholesomeness of the food." Note, however,
that it says "should," not "shall" (an important legal difference, since
"should" is not compulsory).

You buy rBST-free milk? Not much longer, because under the
Codex all dairy cows will have to be treated with Monsanto's recombinant bovine growth hormone. All animals used for human consumption
will have to be fed antibiotics. Organic standards will be
relaxed to include such measures. And did we mention that
under the Codex, genetically modified (GM) produce will

283

no longer have to be labeled?

Say good-bye to true organic food, and maybe even food that retains any resemblance of nutritional value. Moreover, in 2001, twelve hazardous, cancer-causing organic chemicals called POPs (Persistent Organic Pollutants) were unanimously banned by 176 countries, including the United States. Codex Alimentarius will bring back seven of these forbidden substances—such as hexachlorobenzene, dieldrin, and aldrin—to be freely used again. Permitted levels of various chemicals in foods will be upped as well.

Dr. Laibow has done the math. Using figures coming directly from the W.H.O and F.A.O, and according to those epidemiological projections, she believes that just the Vitamin and Mineral Guideline alone will result in about 3 billion deaths. "1 billion through simple starvation," she says. "But the next 2 billion, they will die from the preventable diseases of under-nutrition."

Dr. Laibow calls the new Codex standards "food regulations that are in fact the legalization of mandated toxicity and under-nutrition."

And for those of you who are thinking; 'hey, I'll just leave America and run to another Nation to escape this nutritional holocaust'. Think again, my friend. Once implemented, the Codex Alimentarius will set food safety standards, rules and regulations for over 97% of the world's population. Its curtains folks! Checkmate! This is why it's so incredibly important for the 240 million American Christians to band together and eradicate these demons before they exterminate us.

The merciless methods through which Satanic elites have chosen to murder our little innocent babies should come as no surprise to you. It should also come as no shock to anyone that simple picket lines, letters to state and federal officials, blogging and complaining to your mirror will achieve absolutely nothing; and will never extinguish our morally and financially ailing fireball of Nation. At this point, the only logical course of action for Americans is to completely start over. That means a 'Scorched Earth Policy' against all GMO corporations and their lab experiments which are illegally residing in our Nation's fields, as we speak.

284

My final thought on this subject is this. As Christian Americans, it's time that we set aside all of our differences, harness the power of our community, and begin freeing our brothers and sisters from their elite imposed mental and physical shackles. It's imperative that Christian Americans denounce moral and religious pluralism, assemble ourselves as one unbreakable chain, and with the power of our collective voices and resources demand that every last acre of land which has been contaminated with hybridized or genetically modified organisms is ripped up from our lands, and destroyed by those who illegally placed it there. This will be an extraordinary logistical undertaking and will result in a colossal financial burden to our Nation. We must demand once again that this burden be placed on the backs of those individuals and corporations who created these illegal toxic hybridized/GMO crops. And when all the dust settles, we replenish our soil with God's original creations e.g., Einkorn, Emmer, etc. And then demand American farmers to only grow organic, soy and hormone free meats, fruits and vegetables. And then finally, reward our hard working farmers and business owners by purchasing their organic, soy, and hormone free products.

CHAPTER
Body Balance Introduction 20

Whatever the prequel that's knocked your health into a chaotic state, you're there now. There's nothing we can do about our past, our only option is to pursue a happier and healthier present and future.

Nonetheless, it doesn't discount the frustration you feel having been subjected to years of ridicule by the Medical Industrial Complex, not to mention, the countless tests. And after all of this, all that you've been left with is a paranoid feeling that you're a hypochondriac. That's how every single doctor I met with during a frustrating period of my life made me feel. Well, I'm here to deliver some good news. Your health challenges, contrary to what the Medical Industrial Complex may be telling you, are not a figment of your imagination… Your challenge is something I refer to as 'Endocrine Toxicity Syndrome' (ETS).

Before we can address the many warning signs associated with ETS, we must understand the root cause of ETS. The vast majority of individuals living with this condition receive a number of 'red-flags' from their endocrine system. Initially, sufferers will dismiss these signs as nothing more than a stomach ache or 'heart-burn', completely oblivious to the fact, that these warning signs are in fact your body's way of telling you that something is terribly wrong within your body.

Unfortunately, for too many sufferers throughout America, their only health resource is a physician whose Medical Industrial Complex orthodoxy is limited to just two tests. They will propose a standard blood and/or urine test. Upon receiving your results, your physician will conclude one of two things. They'll either respond (A) 'You're fine' or (B) They'll suggest a list of chemical treatment options. The unfortunate reality is these chemical band-aids do absolutely nothing to address what's causing your body's 'red-flag' warnings.

What's causes gastrointestinal distress?

It will be remembered from previous chapters that I addressed the dangers related to hybridized American wheat and genetically modified Soy and Corn. These are the three chief villains, causing the epidemic of gastrointestinal and endocrine system related cancers. Simply put, Genetically Modified Organism's (GMO's) contain proteins, soil bacteria called Bt or Bacillus thuringiensis, which have been shown to be extremely toxic to the digestive system of every living creature on planet earth. All one has to do is educate themselves about the goal of GMO's and the pesticides they're bathed in. Take Monsanto BT Corn for instance.

Next time you visit your local grocery store, please take a minute to read the ingredients of the products you're purchasing. You will discover that 'Corn' is in the majority of products you're buying. What everyone must understand is that Monsanto Genetically Modified Corn contains something called Bacillus Thuringiensis or 'Bt' for short. Let's read what Bt does to the insects that try and eat Bt corn; then you decide, for yourself, if Monsanto Bt Corn could be one of the chief causes of the plague of gastrointestinal issues sweeping across the United States of America.

286

How Monsanto Bt Corn is killing Americans?

Monsanto's GM Bt corn is equipped with a gene, from soil bacteria. This bacteria is called Bt or Bacillus thuringiensis. This produces the Bt-toxin in the corn. When an insect ingests any part of Bt Corn, the toxic pesticide explodes the stomach of the insect and it dies.

Monsanto Bt corn was introduced into our food supply in the late 1990's, and since then we've seen a massive increase in gastrointestinal and endocrine system cancer.

Both the United States Government e.g., EPA, etc. and officials at Monsanto Corp. assured the American public that genetically engineered corn would only harm insects. They told us that the Bt-toxin produced inside the plant would be completely destroyed in the human digestive system. They assured the American consumer that Bt-toxin would not have any impact on the health of consumers.

Unfortunately, for millions of Americans suffering with gastrointestinal and Endocrine System Toxicity, Monsanto and the United States Government have been proven wrong. Not only is Bt corn producing resistant Super-insects, researchers also discovered that Bt is toxic to the human digestion system. Because of GMO toxins Americans are having their entire intestinal system ripped out, because it's riddled with ulcerative colitis, cancer, etc. Furthermore, America is facing a plague of diseases that include stomach cancer, colon cancer, pancreatic cancer, kidney cancer, hypothyroidism, hypoadrenia, etc.

In 2011, doctors at Sherbrooke University Hospital in Quebec Canada found high levels of Bt-toxin in blood samples taken from the following:

- 93 percent of pregnant women tested;
- 80 percent of umbilical blood in their babies; and
- 67 percent of non-pregnant women.

So much for the United States Government's and Monsanto's claims that Bt-toxins would be destroyed in the human digestive system!

287

The genetic abomination also poses countless health risks due to its high concentration of toxic proteins. For instance, non-GMO Corn is 20x richer in nutrition than GMO Corn. The following is a comparison between GMO Corn and non-GMO Corn:

- Non-GMO corn has 6130 ppm of calcium while GMO corn has 14 – non-GMO corn has 437 times more calcium.
- Non-GMO corn has 113 ppm of magnesium while GMO corn has 2 – non-GMO corn has about 56 times more magnesium.
- Non-GMO corn has 113 ppm of potassium while GMO corn has 7 – non-GMO corn has 16 times more potassium.
- Non-GMO corn has 14 ppm of manganese while GMO corn has 2 – non-GMO corn has 7 times more manganese.

As far as the energy content of non-GMO corn, it was shown to produce 3,400 times more energy per gram, per second compared to GMO corn. Overall, non-GMO corn is 20 times richer in nutrition, energy and protein compared to toxic GMO corn.

Regardless of how damning these findings are, the heavy-duty United States Government grade Teflon coated Monsanto Corporation will continue to make deceptive claims that their toxic genetically modified abominations are equivalent to or even higher quality than non-GMO crops. Any intelligent, rational human being, can clearly see that Monsanto is smoking too much of what their planting. There are quite frankly, too many studies to cite that all support my claims that GMO's will kill you if you eat them. Monsanto is a Corporation that is heavily protected by Satanic Theosophists, hell bent on murdering 90% of the global population. The desire to put them down should be in every cell of your body, not their GMO toxins.

The Bt Mind Connection

There are few substances that are allowed to permeate through the thin membrane of our intestinal tract. Those include: Carbohydrates, Proteins, Minerals, Fats, Cholesterol and Vitamins. The vast majority of substances in a healthy intestinal system never leave the secure walls of our intestinal system. This is why our creator placed a mucous barrier along with a substantial amount of our immune system, containing over ten trillion healthy bacteria.

What I would like readers to understand is that you cannot disconnect the link that binds our mind and intestinal system together. This connection is most profoundly realized when you're riding a roller coaster, or travelling at a high rate of speed over an elevation, on the freeway. And most people have experienced the uncomfortable feeling in our stomachs when we've broken up with someone or had someone break up with us. Or if you've ever been involved in a physical confrontation, people often describe this sensation as 'Butterflies in my stomach'. The scientific explanation is that our hypothalamus, which is the control center for many of our body's hormonal systems, produces hormone corticotrophin-releasing factor (CRF) in humans in response to most any type of stress, physical or psychological. The hypothalamus secretes CRF, which in turn binds to specific receptors on pituitary cells, which produce adrenocorticotropic hormone (ACTH). ACTH is then transported to its target and then the adrenal gland stimulates the production of adrenal hormones. The adrenal glands which are located on top of the kidneys then increase the secretion of cortisol. Then the release of cortisol initiates a series of metabolic effects aimed at alleviating the harmful effects of stress through negative feedback to both the hypothalamus and the anterior pituitary, which decreases the concentration of ATH and cortisol in the blood, once the state of stress subsides. But we'll just refer to it, as 'butterflies'.

Our brain/intestinal system warn us in less extravagant ways as well. Even though a person may be living a relatively healthy lifestyle, they may still be suffering with a painfully slow memory recall, bowel issues e.g., constipation, diarrhea, etc.

Over ninety percent of the output of our brains is dedicated to what is called the pontomedullary junction, also referred to as our brain stem. Vagus nerve stimulation originates here and links with our intestinal system. That is why we're so connected with what our stomachs are telling us.

A dysfunctional or deficient intestinal/mind relationship may result in a number of red-flag warning signs. This may include a substantial decrease in the amount of enzymes produced in our pancreas, an inefficient gall bladder, and an overall challenged digestive system. And because all of these organs are so intimately linked with the above mentioned organs, when they get sick, so does your brain.

It's critically important for people to understand that brain cells do not undergo what's referred to as 'apoptosis' a.k.a. programmed cell death. Furthermore, neurons do not die and regenerate like other cells in our bodies. When you kill off brain cells and neurons, you're not going to be a happy camper. That being said, it's critically important that you make every effort to avoid toxic substances such as: Genetically Modified Foods, Wheat, Gluten, Sugar, Fluoride, MSG, Aspartame, etc.

Human beings rely so heavily on an optimized brain and mind. With that being said, if you are ingesting any of the above mentioned substances, it's not a matter of if, but when, you're going to experience a catastrophic event. The most commonly misdiagnosed health condition in America is a damaged intestinal immune system. Symptoms derived from this condition are treated by the Medical Industrial Complex with steroids, antibiotics, antacids, and most troubling of all, with surgery. These broadsword band-aids do absolutely nothing, but mask the sufferers' condition or worse, exacerbate their condition.

I was recently introduced to a parent whose child was butchered by allopathic medicine. After diagnosing the child with colitis, the doctor strongly recommended removing a substantial portion of the child's intestine. Because the physician did not address the root cause of this particular child's condition, the frontal lobe of the child's brain sustained damage. I was both saddened and angered at how disturbingly incompetent, allopathic medicine was in this case. They completely failed this child and subjected the child to nothing more than butchery for profit. In my opinion, this is criminal. I've personally advised both human beings, as well as owners of animals whose loved ones were suffering with advanced colitis. The solution was nothing more than the elimination of toxic foods and products in their lives, and the introduction of herbal combinations. The final portion of my book contains a number of alternative suggestions to many of today's most common diseases.

Permeability characteristics of our small intestine increases exponentially when we bombard our endocrine system and digestive system with a diet of toxic food and stress. Intestinal permeability also referred to as 'Leaky Gut', can result in a significant decrease in your body's ability to circulate blood. This decrease in circulation can create inflammation throughout your intestinal system. This inflammation allows protein, such as the toxic proteins, produced in genetically modified foods, gluten, etc., to break through

290

what is commonly referred to as, your 'blood brain barrier' (BBB). This is why an elimination diet is crucial to repairing your intestinal system from systemic yeast, toxic bacteria, and parasites. The BBB is semi-permeable; that is, it allows some materials to cross, but prevents others from crossing. There are several areas of the brain where the BBB is weak. This allows substances to cross into the brain somewhat freely. These areas are known as "circumventricular organs". Through the circumventricular organs the brain is able to monitor the makeup of the blood. The circumventricular organs include the following:

- Pineal body: Secretes melatonin and neuroactive peptides. Associated with circadian rhythms.
- Neurohypophysis (posterior pituitary): Releases neurohormones like oxytocin and vasopressin into the blood.
- Area postrema: "Vomiting center": when a toxic substance enters the bloodstream it will get to the area postrema and may cause the animal to throw up. In this way, the animal protects itself by eliminating the toxic substance from its stomach before more harm can be done.
- Subfornical organ: Important for the regulation of body fluids.
- Vascular organ of the lamina terminalis: A chemosensory area that detects peptides and other molecules.
- Median eminence: Regulates anterior pituitary through release of neurohormones.

Once our BBB firewall has been breached by toxic substances, our brain now begins exhibiting the following red-flag warnings:

- Depression.
- Reduced communication with our intestinal tract, which compounds the problems associated with 'Leaky Gut'.

Toxic foods are the number one contributing factor to gastrointestinal disease and a toxic endocrine system. It's these conditions, which cause us to develop physical and/or mental disorders. The progressive loss of structure or function of neurons, including death of neurons, is responsible for neurodegenerative diseases including Parkinson's, Alzheimer's, and Huntington's. Both the elderly and children with autism have gastrointestinal disorders. Other symptoms include:

- Excessive mental and physical fatigue;
- Brain fog;
- Chronic intestinal challenges;
- Anxiety;
- Depression;
- ADHD;
- Cold Hands and Feet;
- Toe nail fungus;
- Reduced blood flow to extremities;
- Hashimoto's;
- Ulcerative Colitis; and
- Celiac.

Remember the poor little child whose parents were deceived by the Medical Industrial Complex? He sustained frontal lobe trauma following the removal of his small intestine. It's important to understand that the frontal cortex stimulates nerves that are responsible for stimulating emotion, HCL production, and a myriad of other digestive processes. In short, the front cortex commands all of our higher brain function. Now, if you're constantly bombarding your brain with toxic substances, we're going to experience perpetual depression, coupled with never ending digestive challenges.

Our Digestive Systems Nervous System

Our gastrointestinal system is a complex scaffolding of nerves. It's this densely populated tissue that's responsible for moving waste, etc. through our intestinal tract. In addition to movement, over eighty percent of our body's serotonin is created in our intestinal system. That's why, when you're constipated, you're less energetic, and unhappy.

Toxic Intestinal System – Toxic Brain Connection Facts:

- The human body, consisting of about 100 trillion cells, carries about ten times as many micro-organisms in the intestines. The metabolic activities performed by these bacteria resemble those of an organ, leading some to liken gut bacteria to a forgotten organ. It is estimated that these gut flora have around 100 times as many genes in aggregate as there are in the human genome.
  - Journal of Clinical Psychiatry 2001: 50-90% of IBS patients have a psychiatric disorder-depression, anxiety, social

withdrawal confirming the gut brain connection.

- 'IBS', a.k.a. doctors don't know what you have, is the second highest cause of seeing a General Practitioner in the United States after the common cold,
- The intestinal mucosa blood vessels are influenced by autonomic nervous system.
- Traumatic Brain Injury in mice results in 'leaky gut' within just six hours of their injury.

Biological Psychology 2009:

- Bacterial endotoxin increased gut pain - rats separated from mothers in early life had more of this toxin! There was massive increase in pain perception and this was permanent in the rats!! Although this could possibly be reversed in humans?

Journal of Neurotrauma 2009:

- Traumatic brain injury and intestinal dysfunction
Even small doses of pathogenic bacteria can cause brain problems, even in an environment where no intestinal symptoms exist. This proves that healthy intestinal bacteria strongly influence brain behavior and development.
- Anti-depression medication negatively impacts the intestinal tract and has massive side effects.
- Mast cells are present in most tissues characteristically surrounding blood vessels and nerves, and are especially prominent near the boundaries between the outside world and the internal milieu, such as the digestive tract, as well as the mouth.
- Interferon used for Hepatitis results in debilitating depression-65% taken on as depression patients- there are more side effects associated with Interferon than any other drug.

What all of the aforesaid demonstrate is that there is absolutely a correlation between a toxic intestinal system and a toxic brain. Moreover, all of the risk factors associated with toxic genetically modified foods and toxic products are all contributing to the hurricane of disease storming through America.

Endocrine System 101

The endocrine system is one of the more complex systems in our bodies. The vast majority of Americans will never find themselves asking the question: 'I wonder how my endocrine system is doing today?' That's because most of what our endocrine system does, is never seen or felt; and that's a good thing. Unfortunately, with the introduction of genetically modified toxins, Communist China's fluoride being mixed with our fresh water supply, mercury laced vaccines, dangerous, over-prescribes medications, and a host of other environmental risks, more and more people are beginning to experience problems as a result of a toxic endocrine system. Most of what your family doctor would see will cause him or her to refer you to an endocrinologist, who will most likely prescribe chemical solutions that don't actually rehabilitate the underlying problem. These chemicals only mask and ultimately compound the damaging effects of a toxic endocrine system.

The best way for me to describe the endocrine system is that it's the chemical brother of the nervous system. It's the job of our nervous system to transmit critical information, via electricity, whereas our endocrine system transmits critical life sustaining information via chemicals and biological compounds.

Our endocrine system manages the vast majority of biochemical pathways that occur in our bodies. The main tools used by our endocrine system are hormones. These hormones regulate how our bodies grow, how warm or cold we are, management of glucose, digestion, etc. The endocrine system can literally release a hormone that will affect the activity of cells throughout our entire body. The endocrine system is also unique in that it cooperates with glands and cells with organs that are related to other systems.

The significance of our endocrine system is realized throughout our one-hundred trillion plus living cells and it's the circulatory system that transports endocrine information. While our nervous system leverages neurons, our endocrine chemicals and hormones are circulated through blood vessels.

The vast majority of glands in our bodies secrete hormones into our blood. We have a pituitary gland, in the base of our skulls, which releases hormones. It's these hormones which control blood pressure and our excretory system.

Furthermore, we have a thyroid gland in our neck that controls bone growth rate and metabolism. And above our kidneys, we have a relatively small gland that releases adrenalin. Endocrine glands are throughout our entire bodies.

Creating a Toxic Environment

Our endocrine system is extremely delicate and because of that fact, it doesn't take a major event to create an unstable endocrine system. In today's world, there are physical, mental, and chemical traumas, all around us, which are capable of destabilizing the environment our endocrine system exists.

A rare and extreme condition, as a result of developing a toxic endocrine environment is what's known as 'Addison's Disease' or adrenal insufficiency. Addison's is named after Dr. Thomas Addison, the British physician, who first described the condition in 1849. Addison's, is a condition where the adrenal gland does not produce adequate levels of key steroid hormones. This can lead to chronic abdominal pain, extreme low blood pressure and even coma. What the Industrial Medical Complex won't tell you, is that your own immune system is causing this. How? By attacking glands throughout the endocrine system. When your immune system attacks your thyroid gland for instance, you may develop a condition called hypothyroidism. This is where your metabolism is substantially decreased, causing major weight gain, etc. Conversely, this same assault can result in an increase in metabolism or hyperthyroidism, causing among other conditions, substantial weight loss, insomnia, fatigue, hair loss, etc.

The vast majority of my readers who are physically exhausted on a daily basis, or suffer from hypothyroidism, hypoglycemia, depression or prone to mood swings, etc. may in fact, have a condition identified well over one hundred years ago, named non-Addison's hypoadrenia. Because it doesn't carry with it the extreme symptoms of full-blown Addison's, patients complaints are often ignored or worse discredited, which for the sufferer is a very lonely place to be. The sad truth is, if the Medical Industrial Complex would provide physicians with the basic tools and promote the very simply methods of identifying hypoadrenia, America would be a much happier and healthy place. What would all the elite owned pharmaceutical agents do with all of those unused pills?

So, why aren't doctors acknowledging critical data that has existed for over one hundred years? You've probably heard the saying: 'follow the money'. Well, this situation is no different. The bottom line is geneticists and pharmaceutical pushers have created an environment where one out of every three Americans will be touched by cancer. The Church of Babylon makes substantially more money creating and treating disease than they ever would by curing disease. Take for instance Harry M. Hoxey, a former coal miner who, in 1924, operated a number of cancer clinics using an herbal concoction handed down by his grandfather. Hoxey would be embroiled in a battle, between 1924 to 1960, with the newly formed American Medical Association (AMA). Hoxey would go on to win a slander suit against Babylonian Talmudist Dr. Morris Fishbein, head of the American Medical Association. The AMA went after Hoxey for two reasons. Number one, Hoxey had in fact cured thousands of people who had cancer. There was no doubt that Hoxey was curing cancer because there were so many cured patients who testified on his behalf. Second, Hoxey would not sell his formula to the American Medical Association and they bankrupted him in court. Again it's all about money, control, and reducing population size. If you're interested, there is a great video you can purchase titled: 'The Quack (?) Who Cured Cancer'.

"It's a pity [advantage] to get a man into a place in an
argument where he is defending a position instead
of considering the evidence."
– John D. Rockefeller

Endocrine Toxicity Syndrome

There are a number of risk factors which contribute to an inefficient endocrine system. Take for example, the rigors of modern life e.g., the passing of a loved one, our jobs, school; driving in a car, flying in an airplane, your wedding day, Godzilla smashing your city, the list goes on. There is one scenario however, where you would have had absolutely nothing to do with the destabilization of your endocrine system, and that's when you were inside your mother womb. It wasn't until I hit rock bottom, mentally and physically, that I learned my mother had suffered from a deficient endocrine system e.g., hypothyroidism, hypoadrenia, ovarian cancer, etc., which set the stage for me, later in life, to be more chemically susceptible to life's unpleasant surprises. All of these examples have the potential to generate

296

massive amounts of stress in our lives. These stresses however, become compounded exponentially when we throw, on top of it all, a poor diet and a reckless lifestyle. For example, in my case, I had literally broken the needle off of my physical and mental speedometer. I had lived a physically and emotionally taxing personal and business life, for too many years. Toss, into the bowl of my life, an abysmal diet, chop up and add a large quantity of harmful substances, and you've got yourself, one heck of a perfect storm salad.

What I would like for you, the reader, to consider is that your stress is relative, and it's in large part measured using your collective life experiences. From a physical perspective, we all respond differently to certain situations, e.g., 'fight or flight'. However it's the subconscious mind that manages our chemical responses to stress, and our only hope for effecting change, in our subconscious mind, is through the avoidance and expulsion of toxic chemicals in our bodies. Unfortunately, chemical changes and their damaging effects can go unnoticed for many years, and then all of a sudden, manifest themselves in many different ways. Sadly, we do not control how our endocrine system responds to certain stresses. For example, we can't yell at our adrenal glands: 'Hey, stop producing adrenaline'. Understand that the complex programming of our body's hormone management system can easily become corrupted to the point where we're only producing a finite supply of hormones. And just like the gas tank in your car, when you've run out of gas your car stops moving. This is exactly how our chemical system responds when we've depleted our body's natural supply of life sustaining hormones.

This is one of many hard lessons I've had to learn in life. My hope is that I'll be able to guide as many poor, unsuspecting souls away from that dark and destructive pathway. The idea of someone electing to be a guinea pig for the Rockefeller/Rothschild global cancer initiative, is just stupid. The troubling reality is there are millions of American men and women who are unknowingly swinging a chemical wrecking ball into their endocrine system, each and every day. Much like I did, these men and women are ingesting massive quantities of supplements by manufacturers who advertise them as being safe and beneficial to their overall health. What men and women must understand is that these supplements are literally battling their endocrine systems for supremacy. These unregulated, and in many cases, dangerous cocktails of herbs, aminos and vitamins are hijacking their bodies' normal, natural hormone production. I cringe, even to this

297

day, when I read an article, or see an advertisement that is promoting the idea of a 'natural' way to increase fill-in-the-blank hormone production. What these supplements are doing in reality is stressing the adrenals out, to the point of exhaustion, and the resulting effects for these poor men and women, later on in life, is going to be what I've gone through, and that is physical and mental anguish.

CHAPTER

21 Toxic Endrocrine System Profile

Just as stressful situations affect people in a different ways, our bodies externalize their chemical imbalances in many different ways as well. For example, in my case, my body went through a tectonic shift, both physically and mentally. Specific alterations to my body and mind, included:

Panic Attacks: For me the most terrifying experience was the first time I experienced a major panic attack. I was violently awakened, around 2 a.m., with this feeling that the blood had drained from all of my major organs and extremities e.g., hands, feet, etc. Upon rising from bed, blood began slowly circulating. Have you ever had your foot fall asleep? And then when the blood begins circulating again, you have that tickly, prickly sensation? That's how my entire body felt. I freaked out. I thought I was having a heart attack.

Dry Skin: Morning, noon, and night, I would have to rub lotion on my hands and feet. The webbing between my fingers would dry, crack, and bleed. In addition to dry hands, my feet and toe nails would become dry and brittle.

Zombie Mornings: In the mornings, I would literally have to peel my head off of the pillow, pry my eyelids open, and lift my legs over the edge of my bedside.

Starving in the Mornings: My symptoms, in the morning, became increasingly worse, as the days went on. At one point, I was forced to have ready a morning snack, etc. at my bedside, because if I didn't eat upon waking, I would be extremely lethargic, sick to my stomach, and dizzy. In short, I seriously felt as though I would die. I'm not exaggerating.

Wateraholic: I would have to drink a lot of water. My mouth would be continuously bone dry. First thing in the morning, I would drink at least 64 ounces of water, before I felt hydrated.

Tingling Hands and Feet: One of the many unnerving nuisances was a constant hot tingling in both my hands and feet. Sometimes this would keep me up the entire evening.

Communication Problems: The one symptom that I was most depressed about was my inability to communicate how I was feeling. And then when I did, I felt as though I was a bother to my loved ones. These feelings would pile up and eventually lead me to lash out at people unnecessarily, which compounded my depressed mood.

Brain Fog: Probably the most frustrating result of having a toxic endocrine system was that the 'file-guy' in my mind was constantly sleeping on the job. My mental recall was pitiful. There were instances in which I would order up some information at 10 a.m. from my file-guy, and he wouldn't deliver it until 9 p.m.
Weight Fluctuation: My body weight would expand and contract, regardless of what I ate.

Recuperation: Even though I was a mere shadow of my former physical self, I still enjoyed working out. What I found, however, is that my recovery time, following a relatively docile routine, would take 3 times to 4 times longer for my body to recuperate. I would feel sore and burned out for at least a week after working out.

When I meet with new clients, I go through my personal Top 10 list to see if any of my previous experiences resemble what their bodies are currently telling them. What I've found is that nearly everyone who I take on as a new client has experienced at least four or five of the ten symptoms listed. The question I would invite you to ask yourself is: How many of my symptoms do you identify with? If you are experiencing four or five of the above mentioned symptoms, there is a high probability that you're suffering from a toxic endocrine system.

The following is a checklist for individuals who may be suffering with a toxic endocrine system. I've created this resource for individuals who may not have access to the internet. It's a useful tool, for determining hormone deficiency, based on your body's current signs and symptoms

Preliminary Testing For a Toxic Endocrine System

There are tests that you can perform at home, that have existed for nearly ninety years. These tests will help you establish whether or not you are in fact suffering from a toxic endocrine system.

On January 2, 1924 Dr. Arroyo wrote the following Iris Contraction method. He writes:

"When exploring the pupil area reflex, I found that in the iris of those cases (adrenal insufficiency), although reacting readily to light, the contraction (of the iris) was flabby, lazy, in a word, asthenic. By making the patient look at the light we see that immediately after the initial miosis the pupil starts to dilate slowly as if it does not want to, seems to try to contract again but the dilation gains the upper hand and after a fight between miosis and mydriasis lasting for about 4-0 seconds. The pupil remains dilated in spite of the persistence of the exciting agent (the light). This sign is consistent and present in all cases of hypoadrenia in all of its clinical forms. In the normal individual, it does not appear as I have investigated. All patients presenting this sign, which I should like to call asthenocoria, have been benefited by suprarenal medication "
- Arroyo, CF. Med Jour.and Rac, Jan 2, 1924.CXIX.PG 25

In 1929, Harrower Laboratory, Inc. Henry R. Harrower in his Endocrine Diagnostic Charts, noted: "Hypoadrenia ordinarily spells hypotension".

One of the most common signs of a toxic endocrine system is low blood pressure. To perform this test, all you will need is a device to take your blood pressure. Next you will lie down, in a comfortable position, for ten to fifteen minutes. Once you've successfully recorded your blood pressure in a horizontal position, you will then safely stand. Now, while standing upright, record your blood pressure, once again. If your blood pressure drops upon standing, there is a strong possibility that you have hypoadrenia, one of the

300

markers of a toxic endocrine system.

SAFETY NOTE: A person who is suffering from a toxic endocrine system will oftentimes experience blood pressure changes upon standing. Understand that when your heart contracts, it pushes blood into the arteries causing an increase in blood pressure (systolic pressure). When your heart relaxes and refills with blood, the pressure in the arteries decreases (diastolic pressure). When you're lying down, 500 to 700 ml of blood is drawn into the legs, so there is less blood for the heart to pump. This results in a decrease in blood pressure. Special cells called baroreceptors (located close to the neck arteries) sense this decrease in blood pressure. They counteract by triggering the heart to beat faster and pump more blood in order to stabilize the blood pressure. Individuals with a toxic endocrine system will often experience dizziness, light headedness, blurred vision, and even loss of consciousness. With that being said, please be extremely careful, when performing this test.

Saliva Laboratory Testing

The Medical Industrial Complex is neither equipped, nor is it interested in pursuing methods which are less expensive and better qualified at accurately identifying the root cause of a particular health challenge. In 2014, we are beginning to see a trend, throughout the orthodox medical community, where a growing number of practitioners are referring to themselves as 'holistic healthcare providers'. Now, I've already addressed my issue with the Theosophical origins of the word 'holistic'. This slight alteration to their job description, at least shows, that the growing voices of dissent are beginning to resonate and financially impact the pocket books of those operating within the modern American medical community. Remember that the Medical Industrial Complex is no different than the giant elite controlled Corporations. They do not respond to threats, or grievances; they only respond to profit loss. And the most effective way of inflicting loss of market share is to extract you from the market. You do this, simply by seeking a more logical proactive and reactive method of healing that does not require the use of toxic narcotics, overprescribed antibiotics, unnecessary procedures, or going into bankruptcy.

Saliva testing is a method through which one is able to more accurately measure the deficit and/or surplus of hormones inside their body. This is by far the most accurate means of detection. Saliva testing detects hormone levels inside your cells, where actual hormone response occurs. Blood tests, in comparison, only account for the hormones flowing around our cells. Traditional blood laboratories are based on data collected from a community of individuals who were never screened for endocrine deficiencies. In other words, traditional orthodox methods are comparing apples to oranges, instead of analyzing a sufferer's lifestyle and health history.

The saliva collection process simply requires that you deposit small amounts of your saliva into four small vials, in the morning, noon, evening, and then right before you go to bed. It's that easy.

Please note: we suggest that you keep saliva samples inside your freezer until they are mailed back to the lab.

To contact a Silvanus premier Saliva laboratory please visit, SilvanusHealth.com. Unlike the Medical Industrial Complex, Silvanus' primary objective is to obtain the necessary data to make a functional diagnosis and get to the root cause of your health challenge. How you proceed, after an initial consultation, is completely up to you.

If you decided to work with a Silvanus authorized laboratory, you would simply choose from one of our health Packages. We recommend of course, that you first read this book in its entirety, as many of your questions may be answered. Upon completing this book, please visit SilvanusHealth.com and click on the 'COACHING PACKAGES' tab. There you will find a variety of packages to choose from.

Packages may include: A customized diet, supplement recommendations, and personalized fitness program, to achieve your individual health goals. Upon completion of your customized solution, a Silvanus Health Consultant will schedule a follow-up consultation to assess your progress. What's more, an authorized Silvanus Health Consultant will review your most recent labs and then determine your next phase of care. The Silvanus Team will work at your pace, and take the necessary steps to help you reach your personal health goals.

CHAPTER
Healing Yourself At Home **22**

The most distinguishing feature of naturopathy is that your body's response will in no way resemble that of someone else's. Just because two people may be suffering from a toxic gastrointestinal/endocrine system, their symptoms may be caused by a completely different set of chemical imbalances. Two people with the same health challenge may be experiencing similar symptoms; however, the actual chemical disparity between the two may be worlds apart.

Your particular solution may require a completely different herbal and/or whole food combination. A food or supplement that makes your intestinal system feel wonderful may aggravate someone else's. This is why the discovery process of naturopathy requires a great deal of patience and dedication on to your part. Remember, it took years of dedicated abuse to get your body into the toxic state that it's in; therefore it's going to take some time to heal years of damage. I have seen people recover in as little as a month, whereas it's taken others up to thirteen months.

Before we address anything related to hormone imbalance, etc., we must first address your toxic digestive system a.k.a. 'Leaky Gut'. It's paramount that you completely heal your gastrointestinal tract first, before introducing hormones into your body. If you do not address your diet first, there's not one herbal combination or replacement hormone on planet earth that will realign your toxic digestive system. In fact, if you were to stimulate your thyroid, adrenals, etc., with hormone therapy before repairing your distressed intestinal system, you would actually cause more harm than good.

Thankfully, the healing suggestions we are going to review next are fairly straight forward and relatively inexpensive. I have helped myself and many others using these methods, when allopathic medicine could not.

Elimination of Toxins

Cleansing your gastrointestinal system from all toxins will be vital to your success. This is what destroys the mucosal lining of your small intestine. To immediately stop any further destruction of your mucosal lining, you will need to immediately cease placing any of the following genetically modified toxins inside of your body: GM Corn, GM Soy, GM Sugar and Rockefeller Wheat. Completely eliminating any exposure to these killers is paramount to healing your distressed digestive system.

In order to achieve a clean intestinal system, you're going to first cleanse your refrigerator, cupboards, hidden desk drawer containing snickers bars, etc. At your earliest convenience, please go through your refrigerator, cupboards, and secret compartments, and box up anything that does not read 'Certified Organic', 'Gluten-Free', 'Wheat Free', 'Soy Free', GMO Free, etc.

IMPORTANT NOTE: Please don't throw your food into the trash. Given the condition of our Nation in 2014, there are millions of hungry Americans. And even though it's not 'Organic', it's food. Those Americans who have nothing, and are suffering, will be very happy to receive it. You can go online, to see where your nearest food shelter is located.

I'm predicting that once you've had an opportunity to audit your refrigerator and cupboards, you're going to be left with a kitchen that's pretty bare. When you go to purchase your new groceries, I would like for you to get into the habit of auditing the ingredients of each and every product that you want to buy. This includes any supplements that you buy. Before placing an item inside your cart, make sure that the outside of the box reads 'certified organic'. But that's just the beginning. Remember, that just because something reads 'organic' does not mean that it's ok to put into your stomach. Before placing this into your basket, make sure that its list of ingredients, does not contain any of the following digestive disrupters:

- Soy: (e.g., Soy Oil, Vegetable Oil, which is derived from Soy, Soy Lecithin, Edamame, Tofu, Citric Acid, etc.) If the outside of the container reads: 'May Contain Soy' or 'Made in facility that processes Soy', don't buy it. Please remember, that 'Citric Acid', is a common ingredient in most foods. Unfortunately most Citric Acid is derived from Soy. And if it's not organic, you

304

can guarantee, that it's derived from GMO Soy.

- All grains: wheat and/or gluten must be avoided indefinitely
- No sugar: I highly recommend that you eliminate all sugar from your diet, for at least thirty days. If you're buying already prepared foods, make sure that you read their ingredients. If it reads 'sugar', cane sugar, high fructose corn syrup, etc., don't eat it. After thirty days, you can begin to reintroduce small amounts of organic maple syrup and/or organic vanilla.
- Eggs. I highly recommend that you eliminate all eggs from your diet for at least thirty days. This way, you can gauge whether or not your intestinal tract registers eggs as disrupters.
- Nuts/Seeds/Legumes: Please avoid eating these foods for at least thirty days. Millions of intestinal tracts consider nuts and seeds disrupters. After thirty days, you can slowly reintroduce these foods back into your diet. If you experience headache, intestinal upset, etc., discontinue indefinitely.
- Do not drink: Tap water; bottled water; sodas; alcohol; caffeinated black tea, etc. If you're able to afford an under sink reverse osmosis system, I strongly recommend that you make the investment. An affordable solution can be found here: silvanusselect.com. Every region is different; in Northern California where I live, the impurities in the tap water are about 26ppm, bottled water is 68ppm, and a reverse osmosis system is 1ppm. Most people are unaware of the fact that there are chemicals/hormones, etc. inside you bottled water bottles that are seeping into your bottled water. Many of the people in China won't even drink from plastic bottles manufactured in China. And depending on where you live in America, your tap water may contain highly toxic, Chinese manufactured fluoride and chlorine, etc. Please do not drink anything else other than chamomile tea, peppermint tea and water. That's it. You should drink a cup of tea at the end of every meal.

Our goal in eliminating all of the above listed known toxins and suspected disrupters is to promote a harmonious environment inside of your gastrointestinal (GI) system. This is the only way you're going to restore your GI tract to its former glory.

Now, there are a number of GI tract healing diets on the market today. Some suggest eating foods that are associated with what your ancient ancestors ate, which is based on the religion evolution, others will promote a diet similar to the Macrobiotic Lifestyle that I was subjected to as a young person. All of these diets have their good and bad characteristics, and if you've looked into any of them and they are working, that's great. I would humbly suggest ignoring any suggestion to eat Soy, Wheat Corn or Sugar in any form whatsoever. The following meal plan is what has worked for me and countless other people. Please give it a try, for at least thirty days, and then evaluate how your body feels.

CHAPTER

23 Silvanus Body Balance Diet
30 Days to a Healthier, Happier You

The New Life Body Balance Diet™ borrows heavily from my culinary adventures during my youth, over thirty-five years ago. As much as I despised the transition from what I perceived as being a sugar rich utopia to one that seemed bland and downright torturous. The truth of the matter is, my health as a young person was bullet proof, and I was rarely, if ever, sick. In addition to the following healthful diet recommendations, I would also like to strongly advice that you discontinue using all of the following household items immediately. Healthier alternatives can be found at silvanusselect.com. All of the following products contain harmful toxins. They include:

- PFOA 'non-stick' coatings: Perflurooctanoic Acid (PFOA) is used during the creation process of Teflon, as well as a host of other non-stick products. For instance, it's found in candy bar packaging, microwave popcorn, fast food French fries, pizza boxes, bakery items, drinks, paper plates, and a host of "stain resistant" products. Those include well known brands, such as: Stainmaster, Scotchgard, Silver-Stone, Fluron, Supra, Excalibur, Greblon, Xylon, Duracote, Resistal, Autograph, and T-Fal. DuPont Corporation tells the American public that PFOA is only used during the creation of non-stick/stain resistant products, however PFOA toxins have been found in the bloodstream of 95% of American men, women, and children. Researchers have shown that PFOA toxins cause

306

cancer in the pancreas, liver, testicles, and mammary glands. It's also been shown to increase miscarriages, thyroid problems, weaker immune systems, and low organ weights.

- Fluoridated Products: Only use non-fluoride toothpaste; fluoride is also found in non-stick cookware, etc.
- Aluminum Products: Only use Aluminum free deodorant. And obviously don't cook with aluminum foil or eat out of aluminum containers of any kind. The aluminum in deodorant is absorbed into the body and causes, among other things, breast cancer, Alzheimer's, etc. The brand Tom's of Maine is sold in most stores, and they offer an aluminum-free option.
- Do Not Drink Tap Water or Bottled Water: Depending on where you live, toxins such as fluoride and chlorine are added to the water supply. And regardless of who the bottled water company is, their plastic bottles, leak estrogen mimickers, etc. into the water. A healthier alternative can be found here: silvanusselect.com
- Laundry Detergent: Only wash cloths in laundry detergent that is Bleach/Chlorine/Perfume free. They sell a product named 'ECOS' in most grocery stores that's good.
- Flame Retardant Baby Cloths and/or Toys: Eliminate all flame retardant baby toys. 80% of baby products tested contain toxic or untested chemical flame retardants.
- Baby wipes: Don't use wipes that are not 'organic' e.g., or contain perfumes, dyes, etc. or 'citric acid' - which is derived from genetically modified soybeans and highly toxic - especially given the fact that it's being applied to the rectum a short distance from the intestinal wall.

Before we review my detoxification suggestions, let's examine my lists of health disrupters and health advocates. The list of foods in my health advocate list comprises of all the ingredients you'll reference to make healthful and delicious meals throughout your 30-day New Life Body Balance diet™ and they include:

Health Disrupters

- Caffeine: Individuals who are suffering from a toxic GI and/or endocrine system must avoid all naturally and/or chemically derived stimulants, especially chocolate. No, this does not mean, you have to avoid your husband or wife. If you're using illegal drugs e.g., cocaine, speed, steroids, etc., use this opportunity as an excuse to get your life straight. It's important to understand that when you ingest stimulants, what little fuel is left in your adrenal tank, immediately evaporates, triggering a hypadrenia chain reaction.

Stimulants to avoid include:
- Chocolate, Coffee, Black Tea, Illegal Drugs, etc.

Foods That Contain Gluten
- Wheat: Beer, Flour, All Condiments, Brewer's Yeast, Bran, Couscous, Cookie Dough, Salad Dressing, Soy Sauce, Hot Dogs, Pasta, Malt Barley Flour, Malt Vinegar, Vegetable Protein, Seitan, Matzo, Meringue, Rye, Cold Cuts/Lunch Meat, Semolina, Spelt, Tabouli, Teriyaki Sauce, Udon. Note: Even avoid Einkorn Wheat for thirty days.

Foods Containing Corn
- Corn: High Fructose Corn Syrup, Boxed Cereal, Chips, Whiskey, Grits, Popcorn, Maize, Taco Shells, Corn Tortillas, Tamales, Vegetable Oil, Polenta, Corn Starch, Brown Sugar (brown color), Calcium Magnesium, Calcium Stearate, Bleached Flour, Ascorbic Acid, Artificial Flavorings, Artificial Sweeteners, Alcohol, Citric Acid, Ethanol, Glucosamine, Glycerin, Lecithin, Vitamin C, Vitamin E, Xanthan Gum, and Xylitol.

Foods Containing Soy
- Soy: Soy Milk, Soy Sauce, Tempeh, Tofu, Bean Curd, Edamame, Natto, Miso, Soybean Oil, Teriyaki Sauce, Chocolate, Bouillon Cubes, Asian Cuisine, Textured Vegetable Protein, Bean Sprouts, Boxed Cereal, Peanut Butter, Candy, Infant Formula, Mayonnaise, Vegetable Broth, Vegetarian meat substitute e.g., Veggie Burgers, Imitation Chicken Patties, and Imitation Bacon Bits, etc.

Vegetables:
Pickled Vegetables, Relish and Sauerkraut, All Mushrooms, Potatoes (Health Note: Yams will become your best friend, however I would avoid sweet potatoes), Tapioca, Cassava root, Yucca, Tomatoes, All Peppers and Products Which Contain Peppers. Note: Black/White Pepper is fine.

308

Seeds & Nuts:
Soy Nuts, Pumpkin Peanuts, Pine Nuts, Walnuts, Cashews, Brazil Nuts, Pistachios, Sunflower, Sesame, and Almonds.

Meat/Cold Cuts/Lunch Meat:
Beef, Veal, Calf Liver, Duck, Goose, Quail, Pheasant, Buffalo, Rabbit, Venison, Horse, All Processed Foods Containing Sodium Nitrite, Preservatives and Artificial flavors e.g., Hot Dogs, Lunch Meats, Bacon, Smoked Animal Protein, Deli Meat, and All Fatty Animal Protein.

Fish:
Avoid all Shell Fish e.g., crab, Clam, Shrimp, Lobster, etc. Avoid all bottom feeding fish e.g., Catfish, etc. Avoid Anchovy, Bass, Halibut, Sole, Octopus, Flounder, and Grouper.

Beans and Legumes:
Avoid all types of Beans.

Dairy & Eggs:
Avoid All Products Made With All Varieties of Milk and Eggs. (Health Note): It was the FDA which in 1994 allowed Monsanto's to begin exposing the American public to the toxic hormone Recombinant Bovine SomatoTropin (rbst). The FDA, in 2013, also proposed adding Aspartame; Aspartame, sold as NutraSweet or Equal, is an artificial sweetener, present in over 6,000 products. It is responsible for a host of health problems, including brain diseases, migraines and psychological ailments.)
Sugars:

Avoid All Sugars, Corn Sweeteners, Fruit Sweeteners, Xylitol, Splenda, Equal, Stevia, and Nutrasweet. (Health Note: Sugar may not be a fat; unfortunately our digestive process turns sugar into the exact same fats that make platelets sticky. Sugars interfere with insulin; the utilization of healthy fats e.g., avocados, olive oil, etc. sugar damages teeth, feeds bacteria, yeast, and fungus.

(WARNING: If you currently have cancer, sugar is the worst thing you can eat. Sugar increases serum triglycerides; interferes with vitamin C transport and immune function; increases adrenalin production, a powerful internal stressor, by up to four times,; cross-links proteins and speeds aging; and steals calcium, chromium, and other minerals from the body.)

Oils:

Hydrogenated or partially hydrogenated oils, found in the vast majority of processed foods, deep-fried foods, fast food, and junk food, Peanut Oil, Butter, Margarine, Mayonnaise, and Shortening.

The above listed foods are well known disrupters. However, there may be additional foods that you are personally sensitive to. For instance, Zucchini, Broccoli, Brussels Sprouts or Cauliflower may cause inflammation in some people. Unlike food allergies, whose symptoms reveal themselves quickly, food intolerance may take a longer time to manifest. Please be aware of potential food intolerance symptoms, if/when they do appear. If you feel tired, followed by headaches, etc., discontinue eating that particular food for at least thirty days. When symptoms subside, re-introduce the food to see if it was in fact that particular suspect. Unfortunately, repeated, long-term exposure to a suspected food may cause inflammation and further aggravate your toxic intestinal/endocrine system.

Health Advocates

Beverages: Drink a minimum of ten 8 oz glasses of water per day.

(Health Note: If you're able to afford an under sink reverse osmosis system, I strongly recommend, that you make the investment. The following link is to the best reverse osmosis system on the market: silvanusselect.com. Upon rising in the morning, drink a warm (Not Hot) glass of water with one teaspoon of organic lemon juice mixed in. After each meal, drink a cup of warm peppermint tea. Health Note: Don't drink spearmint tea, as this may cause inflammation). Right before bedtime, drink a hot cup of chamomile tea. It's rare, however, some people are allergic to chamomile and will experience an allergic reaction, similar to that of 'hay fever', etc.)

Probiotics: Your first glass of water in the morning should be accompanied with a probiotic capsule. The one I personally use, and the one that works best for my clients, may be purchased at www.silvanusselect.com. It's free from: GMO's, Yeast, Gluten, Wheat, Corn, Soy, Dairy, Artificial Colors, Preservatives and Flavorings. Be sure to keep your Probiotic refrigerated and always try to buy them directly from a store refrigerator.

Meat: Only eat organic, hormone-free, extra-lean white meat turkey, and chicken breast. Do Not eat red meat, for at least thirty days.

(Health Note: Ideally, buy all meat from a local organic grower, in your town/city/state. This way you're certain that the meat you're consuming is organic. Furthermore, you are contributing to what should be our ultimate goal and that's to strip power from global elite owned Mega-Corporations. Please visit silvanusselect.com to discover where to buy the best organic food in your area. Unearth family owned organic farms and farmer's markets selling vitamin rich organic produce. What's more you'll find growers of drug-free, grass-feed meat and related products. Please support, our aspiration of providing alternative health solutions to America's Christian majority, by shopping at silvanusselect.com for health related products that are unavailable in your hometown.)
Fish: Wild Salmon, Cod, Red Snapper, Carp, Trout, Pollack, Mackerel, and Sardine.

(Health Note: Most Farm Raised Fish are fed GMO Soy, etc.)

Digestive Enzymes: 20-30 minutes prior to eating a meal, please consider consuming a digestive enzyme supplement. This will help your body breakdown the protein and make the digestive process less aggravating to your intestinal tract. The product I personal use may be purchased at www.silvanusselect.com

Vegetables: Asparagus, Avocado, Basil, Bok Choy, Carrots, Celery, Cucumber, Kale, Onions, Artichoke Hearts, Dandelion Greens, Butternut Squash, and Yams.

Healthful Fats: Coconut oil and Avocado Oil for cooking. Extra Virgin Olive Oil should never be used for high-heat cooking. Only use Virgin Olive Oil as an additive on foods that have already been cooked. Else, you can sprinkle it on your vegetables, etc.

(Health Note: Some people may not tolerate Coconut Oil. If you experience constipation, etc., discontinue using as a cooking agent. Even though virgin coconut oil is an anti-bacterial, anti-fungal, and anti-viral agent, unfortunately, the fatty acids found in virgin coconut oil can boost your immune system. Therefore, if you're suffering from a toxic immune system, you may have to avoid Coconut Oil. You do not want to strengthen an already insatiable immune system. Again, everybody is different.)

Yogurt: If your body tolerates coconut, you should eat yogurt made with organic, sugar-free, soy-free coconut milk. Yogurt machines are relatively inexpensive and can be found on eBay for around $30. To make home-made yogurt, all you'll need is your yogurt machine, yogurt starter and time.

Spices and Herbs: Garlic, Ginger, Black Pepper, Turmeric, Basil, Oregano, Thyme, Peppermint, and Real Salt Brand Sea Salt.

Fruits: You should limit the amount of fruit that you consume for thirty days. The most healthful choices are Pears, Blueberries, Apples, Kiwis, and Strawberries.

The Healthy American Family Cookbook

The following are just a few of the recipes from my cookbook, titled: 'The Healthy Christian American Family Cookbook' that will be released soon at: silvanusselect.com. In it you'll find additional recipes related to detoxification.

For the first week, you will eat nothing but the following detoxi-fication soup for breakfast and lunch. For dinner, you pair turkey patty, chicken breast, or fish with one medium size yam and a vegetable. For every meal, you will need to add some sort of healthy fat to your dish, e.g., avocado slices, virgin olive oil, coconut oil, etc.

Silvanus Health Body Balance Detox Soup™ Recipe

Materials Needed:
- 6 qt soup pot
- Watermelon Baller
- Meat Ingredients:
- 1lb extra-lean organic white turkey meat or chicken breast
- 1 Tbsp organic Olive Oil
- 1 Tsp organic Paprika
- 1 Tsp organic Oregano
  - 1 Tsp organic Basil
  - 1 Tsp organic garlic powder

312

Soup Ingredients:

- 1/2 gallon purified water
- 1qty 32oz container of organic, gluten-free, free-range, sugar-free, soy-free chicken stock
- 1 Bunch of celery
- 8 Large Carrots
- 1 Bag of organic frozen green beans
- 10 Cloves of organic garlic
- 1 Tsp organic Paprika
- 1 Tsp organic Oregano
- 1 Tsp organic Basil
- 1 Tsp organic garlic powder

Instructions:
Pour purified water and organic chicken stock into 6 qt pot. Add all ingredients from the 'Soup Ingredients' list to the pot. Place your 1lb extra-lean ground turkey meat inside of a large mixing bowl. Add all of the ingredients from the 'Meat Ingredients' list to the meat and mix together really well. Using your watermelon baller, make the 1lb of turkey into small balls and place into pot. Bring water to boil, then reduce heat to medium/low and let cook for 1 hours.

Servings: 4-6
Preparation Time: Approximately 20 minutes
Cook Time: 1 hours

Baked Salmon w/Steamed Carrots Recipe

Materials Needed:
13 x 9in Clear Glass Baking Dish
Misto Gourmet Olive Sprayer – They cost $9.99 and are one of the greatest inventions. They allow you to place your own oils inside, simply give it a few pumps and voila, you have a healthy spray oil alternative to store bought PAM, etc. Make sure you store all oils in the refrigerator to avoid going rancid. (Health Note: Store bought organic spray oils, contain toxic Soy.)

Ingredients:
- 1 qty 2lb Salmon Fillet
- Misto Gourmet Olive Sprayer Filled w/Organic Avo-

313

cado Oil
- 2 Teaspoons Organic Paprika
- ¼ Teaspoon Real Salt™ Brand Sea Salt
- ½ Teaspoon Organic Pepper
- 2 Tablespoons Organic Oregano
- 2 Tablespoons Organic Basil
- ½ Teaspoon Organic Garlic Powder
- 6 qty Large Carrots

Instructions:
Spray bottom of dish with organic coconut oil. Note: If you become constipated, stop using coconut oil and use extra virgin olive oil. Pat salmon dry. Coat entire salmon well with avocado oil. Sprinkle all ingredients onto salmon. While salmon is cooking, place carrots into steamer and steam until fork tender.

Servings: 4-6
Preparation Time: Approximately 20 minutes
Cook Time: Bake at 425 degrees for 20 minutes or until salmon flakes easily with a fork.

Baked Sweet Potato Recipe

Materials Needed:
13 x 9in Clear Glass Baking Dish
Misto Gourmet Olive Sprayer – They cost $9.99 and are one of the greatest inventions. They allow you to place your own oils inside, simply give it a few pumps and voila, you have a healthy spray oil alternative to store bought PAM, etc. Make sure you store all oils in the refrigerator to avoid going rancid. (Health Note: Store bought organic spray oils, contain toxic Soy.)

Ingredients:
- 4-6 qty Large Organic Yams
- Misto Gourmet Olive Sprayer Filled w/Organic Coconut Oil. Note: If you become constipated, stop using coconut oil and use extra virgin olive oil.

Instructions:
Spray bottom of dish with Organic Coconut Oil. Wash yams thoroughly. Pat yams dry and pierce each yam two

or three times, with a knife. Be very careful not to cut yourself. Cut both ends off of each yam and place inside your baking dish. Cover each Yam with avocado spray and then place inside of your preheated oven. Yams are thoroughly cooked, when they are fork tender.

Servings: 4-6
Preparation Time: Approximately 10 minutes
Cook Time: Bake at 400 degrees for 1 hour and 15 minutes or until Yams are easily pierced with a fork. Split open and sprinkle organic cinnamon and organic vanilla into the Yam and then mix all together. Vanilla acts as a sugar replacement and the cinnamon neutralizes sugars.

CHAPTER

Silvanus Cellular Defying Formula   **24**

Once you've successfully completed the Silvanus Health Body Balance Diet™ and healed the chronic inflammation throughout your digestive system, you should have a feeling of calm and rejuvenation throughout your gastrointestinal system. Your digestive system should now be processing nutrients properly and you should begin to see some stabilization with regards to your weight gain/loss. I'd like to note that even though your immune system has been soothed and the inflammation in your intestinal tract has been healed and repopulated with billions of healthy, life sustaining bacteria, you still may be experiencing symptoms associated with a chemically imbalanced endocrine system. With that being said, let's move onto Silvanus' Body Balance Cellular Defying Formula.

Armed with knowledge about how your endocrine and gastrointestinal system functions, you're now equipped with the tools necessary to identify the myriad of toxins being promoted by the Church of Babylon controlled top 10 food companies. It's critical that when you see any of these toxic products on your store shelves, you do not pick them up, much less, place them inside of your grocery basket. What I invite you to do is imagine those toxic products with a giant 'skull & bones' poison decal pasted on the front of fill-in-the-blank box of cereal, can, bottle and/or jar. You must reprogram your subconscious mind to refuse these toxins as they are in large part responsible for inhibiting those health critical systems throughout your body from working efficiently and effectively. With that being said, you are now ready to move onto the formula through which you will balance your body's chemical and electrical system.

When an individual who has been suffering with one of the many symptoms of a toxic endocrine system, e.g. hypothyroidism, obesity, diabetes, hypoadrenia, unintentional weight loss, etc. achieve a balanced system, the way in which they define healthcare, moving forward changes completely. What you will find is that in order to continue down the path of wellness, you must adopt a proactive rather than reactive health awareness plan. It's within this new reality that you will accept the role of councilor, dietician, and physician. The overriding motivation that inspired me to write this book was that I grew tired of watching my fellow American citizens be slowing murdered. Moreover, my confidence on the Medical Industrial Complex was bankrupt. What I came to realize is that the Medical Industrial Complex would never be able to provide answers to my questions. The truth of the matter is they would never be equipped or willing to even understand, much less answer, my questions. What I learned, some twenty-years ago, is that no one is going to take better care of my health than me. This is the conclusion that I hope you have reached at this point in your life.

Balancing Your Way of Life

Hippocrates, a Greek physician who lived c.400 B.C. and is regarded as the father of modern medicine, first introduced the concept of disturbed physiology (organic processes or functions) as the basis for all illnesses, mental, or otherwise. Hippocrates did not describe disturbances of the nervous system as we do today, in terms of a chemical imbalance or a low level of neurotransmitters (neurotransmitters are the chemical messengers sent between brain cells). Instead, he used the notion of an imbalance of "humors." Humors were defined as bodily fluids, and were believed to be influenced by the environment, the weather, foods, and so on, producing various imbalances in a person's state of health.

The foundation of the healing philosophy that I'm going to share with you next is rooted in the idea that a life devoid of toxic substances, full of Jesus Christ and enzyme rich whole food and coupled with a healthy lifestyle and naturopathy based therapies is paramount in optimizing your hypothalamic-pituitary-adrenal axis.

The father of modern medicine, over 2,500 years ago, was convinced of the connection between healthy whole food and a healthy lifestyle. He promoted this philosophy, throughout his life, stating:
"Let food be thy medicine and medicine be thy food."
– Hippocrates

Leading up to my toxic endocrine/digestive system, I was arguably, one of the biggest offenders of the above principle. Today's fast paced world can be challenging, making it very easy to derail from what we know, deep down inside, to be nutritiously sound or conducive to a healthy lifestyle. Nonetheless, that fruitless and sterile existence is behind you now. Yes? This day forward, you are going to have a heightened sense of awareness from the time you wake up in the morning to the time you go to bed. You're going to be aware of all the background noise that's disrupted your health, right off a cliff and into a ravine. From this point forward, you are going to do everything in your power to avoid these external influences. Yes?

Avoiding Toxic Influences:

Stress is something everyone in modern society seems to understand. There are two basic kinds of stress: inner stress from previous traumas or wounds that affect one's present life, and outer stress, or the environmental issues that complicate life on a daily basis, such as work or family challenges. The interplay of these two forms of stress affects brain chemistry just as it can affect physical health. Numerous studies have shown that when people are chronically stressed in life, they are vulnerable to depression, anxiety, and other disorders. Interestingly, 70% of the adults in one recent war situation were found to have depression, which is a normal human response to relentless stress. Researchers presently think that the mechanism that triggers this depression is the depletion of certain neurotransmitters, particularly serotonin and norepinephrine, which may lead to other biochemical imbalances. For instance, most people diagnosed with schizophrenia have their first psychotic episode during such stressful situations as leaving home for college or military service.

317

In order to successfully purge your life of any and all toxic energy, it will be necessary for you to honestly and meticulously audit everyone and everything that influences your personal space. When I emerged from this informative exercise, I quickly determined that I would need to limit and/or completely eliminate exposure, not only to toxic substances, but a number of toxic individuals, people that I had known for a number of years. We're all too familiar with these types of personalities. They can be most politely described as being disruptive or dramatic, and if you're someone who is trying to heal themselves of a toxic endocrine system distancing yourself from these types of personalities is a critical first step. And if you happen to be this type of personality, it's equally important to change the way in which you both internalize information and emotions and how that processed information and energy is then externalized. In other words, if what you're about to think or speak could be considered toxic in nature to either yourself or those around you. Stop!

Now, there are obviously going to be instances in all of our lives where we're forced into situations where toxic personalities are unavoidable. Just a few examples might include your workplace, a family gathering, the gym, an airplane, sporting event, an elevator, etc. In the case of forced cohabitation with a toxic co-worker, boss, family member, or some random member of society it's vital that you do everything in your power to avoid conflict. In my practice, I commonly refer to these types of individuals as 'Energy Vampires' because they literally suck the energy right from your body. Avoiding energy vampires is paramount, prior, during, and following the healing process of your endocrine system. When I'm forced into a toxic situation or around toxic people, I just quietly think to myself:

"Peace I leave with you, my peace I give unto you: not as the world giveth, give I unto you. Let not your heart be troubled, neither let it be afraid." - John 14:27

Recharging Your Batteries:

Second only to avoiding toxic substances and people is ensuring that you're properly recharging your mind, body, and soul. To achieve this, you must make every effort to be in bed by 10 p.m. and get no less than eight to ten hours of uninterrupted sleep, each and every night. As someone who has personally suffered with hypoadrenia, I will tell you that being forced awake, at 2:00 a.m., on almost a nightly basis, played havoc with both my digestion and mind. This exhaustive experience was compounded when I awoke with a ravenous appetite. To avoid this from happening to you, I'm going to make some suggestions that helped me through this challenging period of my life and continues to help those individuals I advice.

The Sleep Challenge:

If you find yourself waking up in the mornings, feeling like a starving zombie, this is reminiscent of a body whose cortisol levels are low. If this describes your physical and/or mental condition in the mornings, I highly recommend submitting a saliva sample to one of our Authorized Silvanus Health Labs. Please visit the website silvanushealth. com and click on the 'COMPANY' link at the top of the page. Once on the 'COMPANY' Page, you will see a 'lab test' link on the left side of the page. Once on our lab partner site, you will be able to order a test kit. Please consider the following tests:
Saliva Hormone Testing:

- HORMONES
- Estrone (E1)
- Estradiol (E2)
- Estriol (E3)
- EQ (E3/(E1+E2)
- Progesterone (Pg)
- Ratio of Pg/E2
- Testosterone (If you're male)
- Estrogen (If you're female)
- ADRENALS
- DHEA
- Cortisol Morning
- Cortisol Noon
- Cortisol Evening
- Cortisol Night

One of the most disturbing symptoms of hypoadrenia are the panic attacks one may experience in the middle of the night, or shortly after falling asleep. These attacks can range anywhere from a mild disruption to a severe episode, mimicking that of a heart attack or stroke. Additional symptoms may include

319

increase heart rate, numbness in your extremities, confusion, dry mouth, etc. When this happens, you may want to consider reassuring yourself that what you're experiencing may not be life threatening. Next, focus on slowing your breathing and heart rate. If you believe you're in danger or it's an emergency, call 911 immediately or go to the Emergency Room.

My first experience with hypoadrenia induced panic attacks was quite unnerving, to say the least, so much so that it prompted me to dial 911. I eventually discovered the root cause of these attacks and began adjusting my diet and lifestyle accordingly. If you are currently experiencing panic attacks similar to ones described above, please consider consuming a lean, protein rich snack, accompanied by some sort of healthy fat and uncooked vegetables prior to turning in for the evening. This will ensure that your blood sugar levels stay within a healthy range throughout the evening. Additional measures you can take to avoid evening panic attacks include:

• Meditation: The Holy Bible instructs Christians to 'meditate' on God's word 'day and night'. Christ centric prayer prior to bedtime is a great stress reliever. However, Christians must not allow themselves to be deceived into believing that Christ centric 'meditation' is in any way similar to that of 'Transcendental Meditation' ['TM'] this is a 'New-Age' concept.

The Holy Bible teaches that God possesses the characteristics of a living individual e.g., emotions, intelligence, power to make choices, etc. The Christian God is the Creator of all things. Contrary to the religions of TM and Hinduism, Man cannot become God. This is the oldest lie ever told to Man. "...and ye shall be as gods" - Satan, Genesis 3:5. Performing any mental or physical techniques, religious or health protocols which invoke the idea that you are 'God' is blasphemous. It will be remembered from previous chapters that 'The David Lynch Foundation' is promoting the religion of TM inside of the American school system. Christian parents must not allow their children to be taught the TM religion. "The Third Circuit recently held in Malnak v. Maharishi Mahesh Yogi that a public school course in the 'Science of Creative Intelligence - Transcendental Meditation' was 'religious in nature'..." - Harvard Journal of Law and Public Policy. The appellate court agreed and added that "the puja, or initiation, ceremony constitutes a prayer through 'invocation of a deity or divine Being.' "The court noted that the Maharishi is a 'Hindu monk,'" ... and that he first offered Transcendental Meditation [TM] under the auspices of the 'Spiritual Regeneration Movement Foundation' ... It observed that the organization was incorporated as a 'religious' corporation, ... and that the 'field of creative intelligence' closely resembles the 'Hindu concept of the Supreme Being." The courts have ruled that TM is religious and is Hinduism. This should exclude TM from being practiced inside of schools. After all hasn't it been under the guise of separating the Church and State that Christianity has been eliminated from U.S. schools? Not surprising, we see efforts made by the Church of Babylon to omit sanctions for TM, Hinduism and Islam. For instance, there have been great efforts made to build entire prayer rooms for Muslim students in schools all over the U.S. This at a time in history when innocent Christian children are being kidnapped, beheaded and crucified throughout Asia and Africa.

- Stop watching television or P.C. use at 6 p.m.: If you absolutely must be on your computer late, be sure to turn the brightness of your monitor down to its lowest setting.

- Exercise: Low impact exercise for at least thirty minutes every day is helpful.

- No Stimulants: Avoid any substances, throughout the day, which contain stimulants.

Those suffering with hypoadrenia are usually deficient in a number of vitamins and minerals. Introducing a high quality liquid multi-vitamin/mineral, Licorice Root, Lemon Balm, Magnesium Citrate, Calcium Citrate and/or Valerian Root may help to promote a restful night sleep. Please visit silvanusselect.com for these products.

Proper Care & Feeding of Your Adrenals:

The chemical romance between your endocrine system and the substances that you eat is about as volatile as a Hollywood marriage. Those of us who are suffering with an imbalance in our endocrine system, e.g., hypothalamic-pituitary-adrenal axis, are already operating on a quarter tank – chemically speaking. Throw a high-stress situation at us, and couple it with a missed meal or two, and you've immediately reduced us to zombie status. This brings me to one of the most important habits a sufferer must develop, 321 and that's a subconscious reflex to maintain a healthy and steady flow of nutrients throughout the day. The only logical way one can achieve this is through a routine of three to four high quality meals throughout the day. I learned very quickly that this was paramount to rehabilitating a chemically parched system. Keep in mind, those 'mood swings' and/or 'energy drops' you're experiencing throughout the day are your body's 'red-flags'. Sufferers of a depleted endocrine system are prone to hypoglycemia; because of this fact, you must be vigilant about maintaining healthy blood sugar levels throughout the day.

We discussed extensively the importance of a proper diet in previous chapters and how this was vital not only to healing process, but also to the maintenance of your gastrointestinal tract. The eating regimen for a depleted endocrine system is a continuance of my gastrointestinal diet found in chapter 25. I have provided in the next chapter a sample routine to follow on a daily basis. In order to ensure that your hypothalamic-pituitary-adrenal axis is healthy and performance optimized, your emphasis moving forward must be on maintaining a healthy balance throughout your gastrointestinal system. If you abuse or neglect this part of your body's support system, please understand that your chemical and electrical 'house of cards' will come crashing down.

Silvanus Hormone Support Formula **25**

DISCLAIMER: Because a hormone imbalance can turn severe, you should always be monitored by your doctor. The following information and opinions are not a substitute for professional medical prevention, diagnosis, or treatment. Please consult with your physician, pharmacist, or health care provider before taking any home remedies or supplements or following any suggestions in this book. Only your health care provider, personal physician, or pharmacist can provide you with advice on what is safe and effective for your unique needs or diagnose your particular medical history.

The decision of where to begin can be somewhat of a daunting proposition. For this reason, I have provided the following routine to get you started in your new important position of counselor, dietician, and physician. Once you become familiar with all of your choices and how your body responds to those choices, you'll be better equipped to customize your own personal routine.

- 8:00am: Upon waking, you will head down to the kitchen and drink a 16 oz glass of water with a ½ teaspoon of Organic Lemon Juice. Accompanying your morning water intake should be your Organic Probiotic. NOTE: It's important to drink all liquids from glass, not plastic.
- Morning Supplement Suggestion: 15-30 drops organic liquid Licorice Root, 15-30 drops organic liquid Milk Thistle Seed, 15-30 drops organic liquid Olive Leaf. Note: These supplements are available at: silvanusselect.com
- 8:30 a.m. – (Meal #1): Using a stainless steel juicing machine, juice the following ingredients.

(PLEASE NOTE: Wash all vegetables in purified water and trim their tops and bottoms off. Core your apple. Makes approximately 8oz)

2qty whole organic carrots
1qty organic beet
2qty stalks of organic celery
2qty sprigs of organic parsley

1qty clove of organic garlic
1qty organic apple
2qty organic parsnips

- 9:00 a.m. – 30 minute low impact exercise: This may include taking a relaxing walk around the neighborhood, operating an elliptical machine slowly, soft martial art techniques, etc. As soon as your system has become stabilized, it will then be appropriate to incorporate some light weight lifting, etc.
- 9:30 a.m. – (Meal #2): Using the Health Advocates Food List provided in Chapter 25, create a meal which includes Organic Protein, Organic Vegetable and healthy Organic Fat.

Beverages: should include a cup of Organic Peppermint Tea.

Supplements: Take your Organic multi-vitamin and Organic Ashwagandha.

- 10:30 a.m. – Relaxation & Snack Time: Borrowing ideas from the Health Advocates Food List in Chapter 25 eat a very light snack which includes Organic Protein, Organic Vegetable, and Organic Healthy Fat. If possible, close your eyes for 15 minutes and meditate or just sit quietly, doing your best to block out all of life's background noise.
- 11:00 a.m. – (Meal #3): Using the Health Advocates Food List in Chapter 25 create a lunch that consists of Organic Protein, Organic Sweet Potato, and Organic Vegetable.

Beverages: should include a cup of Organic Peppermint Tea.

- 2:30 p.m. - Relaxation & Snack Time: Borrowing ideas from the Health Advocates Food List in Chapter 25 eat a very light snack which includes Organic Protein, Organic Vegetable, and Organic Healthy Fat. If possible, close your eyes for fifteen minutes and meditate or just sit quietly, doing your best to block out all of life's background noise.
- 6:30 p.m. – (Meal #4): Using the Health Advocates Food List in Chapter 25, create a lunch that consists of Organic Protein, Organic Sweet Potato, and Organic Vegetable.

Beverages: should include a cup of Organic Peppermint Tea.
Supplements: Consider taking 15-30 drops organic liquid Lemon Balm

- 8:30 p.m. - Relaxation & Snack Time: Borrowing ideas from the Health Advocates Food List in Chapter 25 eat a very light snack which includes Organic Protein, Organic Vegetable, and Organic Healthy Fat. If possible, close your eyes for fifteen minutes and meditate or just sit quietly, doing your best to block out all of life's background noise.
- 9:00pm – Go to sleep.

Supplementation:

I have intentionally saved the discussion of supplementation for last. I know that many alternative health practitioners present hormone replacement as their first line of defense. I personally do not subscribe to this methodology and here's the reason why. If you're suffering with a chemical imbalance caused by GMO toxins, it's because your hypothalamic-pituitary-adrenal axis is being assaulted by an out of control immune system, commonly referred to as 'autoimmune disease'.

By stimulating your thyroid, adrenals, etc., through hormone replacement, you are in essence painting a giant bulls-eye on those said glands and motivating your immune system to increase its lethality with which it's attacking those glands. The only way to stave off these attacks is to eliminate the power source of your enraged immune system; this power source being an inflamed, Toxic GMO protein leaking intestinal system. Introducing supplementation prior to achieving balance throughout your GI tract is like poking a stick at a beehive. It's just a matter of time before you get stung.

Individually, autoimmune diseases are not very common, with the exception of thyroid disease, diabetes, and systemic lupus erythematosus (SLE). Taken as a whole, they represent the fourth-largest cause of disability among women in the United States. If we also consider other conditions, such as environmental allergies and Chrohn's Disease, an even larger number of people are affected, and included in this ever increasing number are men.

An example of this is a friend of mine whose mother had suffered from and ultimately succumbed to complications associated with Chrohn's. When my friend became symptomatic, he was immediately absorbed, both psychologically and financially, into the Medical Industrial Complex of toxic medication and butchery. As the severity of his condition grew, so did his desperation and ironically enough, his complacency and unwillingness to make simple changes to his lifestyle. Instead of prescribing a solution, the complex of medication and surgery, of course, recommended my friend undergo gastric bypass surgery. Against my strong recommendations for this particular treatment protocol, my friend chose to be butchered.

It will be remembered from previous chapters where I shared a disturbing story about a small child who was recently butchered by the Medical Industrial Complex and why this did nothing but compound his already complex condition. The resulting effects of my friend's surgery were no better. As a matter of fact, the gastric bypass 'solution' did nothing, but magnify his Chrohn's disease. Flash forward, one year later, and his condition has developed into ulcerative colitis throughout much of his small intestine, and instead of suggesting a non-evasive, naturopathic method of treatment, the Medical Industrial Complex presented more butchery. Again, my friend chose to be butchered, rather than the substantially less complicated correction to his lifestyle. I have known a couple of people who chose to be butchered to eliminate large quantities of Rockefeller Hybridized/GMO toxic related fat and the resulting effects have all been catastrophic. The end result for my friend was no different. Those poor souls who have been victimized by the Medical Industrial Complex, and have been 'consulted' into losing one of the most important parts of their bodies are a source of great sorrow for me. If I had to choose which condition as a result of my friend's butchery affected him the most, it would have to be his alcoholism. Because of his gastric bypass, his body was unable to process alcohol properly; therefore, it was essentially dumped straight into his blood stream. The result was that he would become drop down drunk after just a few sips of alcohol. Suffice it to say, someone in his condition should not be drinking alcohol in the first place, nonetheless he did. My friends mind became so toxic that I ended up having to distance myself from him. I remember one of our last conversations over the phone, where he asked the following question:

"Will you please help put a hit out on me? I can no longer live with this [expletive deleted]"

I of course renounced this idea and eventually convinced him that this was in no way a logical solution. I have to tell you, prior to my friend's butchery sessions, he was one of the brightest characters I've come across. He was a brilliant writer and a talented diplomat.

I share the above personal story to illustrate just how devastating a toxic lifestyle and diet can be, not only to the individual sufferer, but to those around them. I often find myself sitting down, calculating the loss of human capital that we as a Nation are losing on a daily basis. Many are citizens who at their best were once considered extraordinary. It's through toxic substances that these once exceptional individuals are being reduced to ulcerate ridden, cancerous piles of meat.

I wish that stories like my friend were uncommon. Unfortunately for a growing population of Americans, diseases that fit within the spectrum of gastrointestinal toxicity have wormed their way into the lives of millions of people across our Nation. My hope is that the Christian American majority discover my elimination diet and lifestyle change recommendations featured in previous chapters, along with the following suggestions to help diffuse the ticking time-bomb, lurking inside of their gastro-intestinal tract.

INTESTINAL DISTRESS REMEDIES:

***DISCLAIMER: Because intestinal distresses, e.g., ulcerative colitis, etc., can turn severe, you should always be monitored by your doctor. The following information and opinions are not a substitute for professional medical prevention, diagnosis, or treatment. Please consult with your physician, pharmacist, or health care provider before taking any home remedies or supplements or following any suggestions in this book. Only your health care provider, personal physician, or pharmacist can provide you with advice on what is safe and effective for your unique needs or diagnose your particular medical history.

***WARNING: There is a growing population of websites promoting 'Candida Cell Wall Suppressor' supplements. It's critical that my readers understand that the vast majority of these sites are in fact selling nothing more than a Chinese pesticide-grade Lufenuron containing heavy metals, fluoride and organic solvents. Heavy metals may cause neurological damage, fluoride causes a long list of health issues and the organic solvents in 'Made in China' Lufenuron can cause cancer. Pet owners will be interested to learn that Lufenuron is an active ingredient in animal flea and heartworm medication. These products are known to kill hundreds of pets each year and injure tens of thousands.

Destroy Candida Overgrowth with Liquid Oxygen – Contrary to what the Medical Industrial Complex will have you believe, the human body has never been, nor will it ever be, deficient in pharmaceutical drugs. What are deficient are oxygen levels throughout our bodies. It's hard to believe, but the United States Geological Society tells us that earth's atmosphere once contained over 35% oxygen. Compare that with current levels, which measure around 21%, and if you live in a big city, your levels are even lower. This should be of great concern for anyone aspiring to be the very best version of themselves physically; after all, the very core of our being is based on our ability to provide a nutrient and oxygen rich ecosystem for our cells. If more people accepted the universal reality that we live and die on a cellular level, disease would not have such a strong hold on our Nations populace. Nevertheless, it must be your supreme goal to furnish each of your 100 trillion cells with premium nutrients, while eliminating toxins. Following my elimination diet, you still may be hosting yeast infections, candida overgrowth, and even systemic candidiasis. All of these are common in our environment. Because yeast, candida, etc., produce symptoms similar to other conditions, it is vital that you complete our elimination diet to ferret out obvious symptomatic causes first. If after my elimination diet, you still maintain a majority of the symptoms that we've discussed through previous chapters, and your doctor is clueless as to what may be wrong, you may want to consider the products found here: silvanusselect.com as well as the following protocol.

STEP #1:
Take 1 teaspoon of liquid oxygen, three times daily, for three weeks. Take on an empty stomach, under the tongue, and hold for five minutes.

STEP #2:
Re-implant healthy bacteria. Take a multi-source acidophilus, ten capsules daily for ten days.

328

(NOTE: Begin multi-source acidophilus the first day after the last day of liquid oxygen.)

Braggs Apple Cider Vinegar - If you find that you are unable to tolerate the oxygen therapy you should consider the following solution:

STEP #1:
Mix two tsp of Braggs Apple Cider Vinegar in an 8oz glass of filtered water. Drink at 8am, 12 noon and 5pm.

STEP #2:
Re-implant healthy bacteria. Take a multi-source acidophilus, ten capsules daily for ten days.

(NOTE: Begin multi-source acidophilus the first day after the last day of liquid)

"And the dove came in to him in the evening, and lo, in her mouth was an olive leaf plucked off. So Noah knew that the waters were abated from off the earth." – Genesis 8:11

- Organic Olive Leaf: Within the pages of The Holy Bible, God describes a tree with medicinal properties: "and its fruit shall be for food, and its leaf for medicine." Was God describing the olive tree? And in Revelations 22:14, we read about the "Tree of Life". Cultures throughout history have highly regarded the olive tree as a source of power. Ancient Egyptians utilized its oils for mummification, a complicated process that modern day science cannot replicate. However, we've learned that the vast majority of cultures throughout world history have used Olive leaves, more often for the benefit of improving health. The very first account of Olive Leaf's ability to cure disease was made nearly 150 years ago. In 1854, Daniel Hanbury provided the following therapy recommendation inside Pharmaceutical Journal, which he discovered in 1843 and used it with great success ever since:

"Boil a handful of leaves in a quart of water, down to half its original volume. Then administer the liquid in the amount of a full wine glass every 3 or 4 hours until the fever is cured." 329

In 1962 an Italian scientist concluded that the bitter substance found in the Olive Leaf, called 'Oleuropein', actually lowered blood pressure in animals. Several other European scientists discovered this substance increased blood flow and corrected arrhythmias. Later a Dutch researcher would discover an ingredient in oleuropeinIn which he named 'elenolic acid'. In the early 1960's scientists at a leading American pharmaceutical corporation named UpJohn determined that elenolic acid inhibited the growth of viruses. According to their research, elenolic acid killed every virus they introduced it to, including the common cold virus, influenza, leukemia, and herpes. Moreover, it was effective in killing the following parasites and bacteria: E. coli, salmonella, and malaria. Furthermore, researchers concluded that even at high doses, elenolic acid was safe and non-toxic.

- Organic Probiotics: Your first glass of water, in the morning, should be accompanied by a hi-quality refrigerated Organic Probiotic Capsule. The one I personally recommend is a product, by the name of 'ImmunProbio'. It's free from GMO's, Yeast, Gluten, Wheat, Corn, Soy, Dairy, Artificial Colors, Preservatives, and Flavorings. Be sure to only buy probiotics which are kept in a refrigerator at your Whole Foods, Health Food Store, etc.

- Organic Liquid Multi Vitamin and Mineral Supplement: As obvious as this might be to some people, the vast majority of Americans are completely unaware of the fact that they are not supplying their bodies anywhere near the necessary amount of vitamins and/or minerals needed to function, let alone repair itself. Years of exposure to toxic Hybridized and GMO foods has literally put our bodies into a state of malnutrition. What should cause everyone reading this to turn off their television and focus 110% of their efforts, eliminating The Church of Babylon from American soil, are the nutritional guidelines 'suggested' by Church of Babylon members who have created what is known as the 'Codex Alimentarius' (CA). Using figures coming directly from the 'CA', experts project that just the Vitamin and Mineral Guideline alone, will result in about three billion deaths. One billion through simple starvation and the next two billion will die from preventable diseases caused by malnutrition. With that being said, you should consider taking an Organic Liquid Multi-Vitamin and Mineral Supplement. I personally have found the liquid vitamin/mineral supplement found here: silvanusselect.com to be the best.

- Organic Slippery Elm Powder: This is by far one of the single best solutions for repairing a distressed GI tract suffering from Ulcerative Colitis, IBS, IBD, and Crohn's Disease. Using Organic Slippery Elm Powder is like putting a thin layer of Aloe Vera over the top of a burn etc. Organic Slippery Elm protects the thin lining of your intestinal system and allows it to heal itself. In addition to being incredibly effective, it's extremely inexpensive. I'd like to make mention of the following when buying and using Organic Slippery Elm:

1. Make sure that is in fact Organic; and
2. Buy it in powder form, not in capsules. The capsules are not going to provide you with a large enough dosage to coat your entire intestinal wall.

Dosage Recommendations:
3 times per day – mix 1 teaspoon in 2 oz of filtered water.

Preparation:
Be sure to dissolve the powder thoroughly. This may require that you smash all of the clumps against the side of the glass. You'll know that you've reached the proper consistency when the Organic Slippery Elm has turned into almost a gel like substance. When it's reached this state, be sure to drink it right away.

***Slippery elm may interfere with the way that other medications or herbal remedies are absorbed by your body. To avoid this, take slippery elm several hours before or after taking other medications.

- Organic Aloe Vera Gel: Second only to slippery elm, for its healing qualities. I have personally used Aloe Vera for years to remedy ulcers in both the stomach and intestinal tract of clients. Aloe Vera gel has been shown in studies to have an anti-inflammatory effect. A double-blind, randomized trial examined the effectiveness and safety of aloe vera gel for the treatment of mild-to-moderate active ulcerative colitis. Researchers gave 30 patients 100 ml of oral aloe vera gel and fourteen patients 100 ml of a placebo twice daily for four weeks. Clinical remission, improvement and response occurred in nine (30 percent), eleven (37 percent) and fourteen (47 percent), respectively, of aloe vera patients compared with one (7 percent), one (7 percent) and two (14 percent), respectively, of patients taking the placebo.

331

When buying Aloe Vera gel, look for "whole" organic Aloe Vera gel, and not products featuring juice from concentrate. Most health food stores carry Organic Aloe Vera gel.

Dosage Recommendations:
2 oz – 8 times per day for at least three weeks (Note: continue taking the aloe vera gel for the full three weeks, even after your intestine has been healed.)

Preparation:
I recommend adding 1 teaspoon of high quality organic liquid chlorophyll every time you take your aloe vera gel.

- Organic Boswellia: Boswellia is an herb that comes from a tree native to India. Similar to Slippery Elm, the active ingredient is derived from tree bark. Boswellia is a wonderful solution to calming down intestinal inflammation. I have used this solution with success, to treat people suffering with ulcerative colitis, rheumatoid arthritis, and other inflammatory conditions. Unlike toxic medications, Boswellia does not cause GI upset. A 1997 study of people with ulcerative colitis found that 82 percent of those who took a Boswellia extract - 350 milligrams, 3 times per day - experienced complete remission.

Dosage Recommendations:
350 mg – 3 times per day, for six weeks.

***Very rare side effects of Boswellia include diarrhea, nausea, and skin rash. You should not take Boswellia for more than 8-12 weeks, unless you do so under the supervision of a qualified health practitioner.

- Organic Fiber: As the inflammation in your intestinal system is diminished, I strongly recommend that you increase your fiber intake. As you begin to repair your toxic endocrine system, those toxins will be processed by your liver and ultimately routed to your intestinal system. Once introduced into your intestinal tract, it's vital to eliminate that waste from your body. A great source of fiber is Nutiva Organic Hemp Protein 'Hi-Fiber' Protein Powder. If you're intestinal system is fully repaired, and your body is chemically balanced, you should consider drinking the follow shake in the mornings.

332

6 qty teaspoons – Nutiva Organic Hemp
½ cup of Organic Pure Pineapple Juice
½ cup of purified water
1 teaspoon of Organic Cinnamon
1 teaspoon of Organic Alcohol Free Vanilla Extract
½ cup of Organic Frozen Blueberries
½ cup of Organic Frozen Strawberries
Blend the above ingredients, for 2-3 minutes and drink.

- Organic Milk Thistle: During the cleansing process of toxins from your body, your liver, which is an amazingly resilient organ, is under a great deal of stress. Milk Thistle is remarkable because of its ability to both protect and regenerate the liver in most liver diseases. Examples of the types of diseases Milk Thistle helps to cure include Cirrhosis, Jaundice, Hepatitis, and Cholangitis (inflammation of bile ducts resulting in decreased bile flow). Milk Thistle, is by far, one of the single best solutions for individuals seeking a proactive/ preventative medicine as Milk Thistle protects each and every cell of the liver from incoming toxic and simultaneously encourages the liver to cleanse itself of damaging substances such as alcohol, drugs, medications, mercury and heavy metals, pesticides, anesthesia. Milk Thistle has even been known to cleanse and protect the liver from even the most poisonous of mushrooms, the Amanita or Death-cap mushroom. Furthermore, Milk Thistle is one of the most effective solutions for people who are under significant stress, drink excessively, have a controlled substance problem, take prescription toxins, and are exposed to pesticides or environmental toxins and pollution. Virtually everyone seeking optimal health can benefit from Milk Thistle. One of the special qualities of Milk Thistle is that it cleanses and detoxifies an overburdened and stagnant liver while also being able to strengthen and tonify a weak liver, thus delivering potent medicine to clogged, excess conditions as well as to weakened, deficient conditions. One of the tasks of the liver is to cleanse the blood. If the liver energy is stagnant it will be unable to effectively cleanse the blood. This can result in skin problems ranging from acne to psoriasis, eczema, and dermatitis. Milk Thistle is a powerful herb for supporting the liver to purify the blood and is one of the best herbs for the skin disorders mentioned above. It is also effective for treating congestion of the kidneys, spleen, and pelvic region.

333

Milk Thistle & Your Bowels: Milk Thistle is a gentle and mild laxative due to its ability to increase bile secretion and flow in the intestinal tract. This herb can have actions ranging from lubrication and softening of the stools to a mild laxative effect, to actually balancing individuals that alternate between diarrhea and constipation. (In patients with stools that alternate between constipation and diarrhea, Oriental Medicine would most likely suspect liver involvement.) This formula has been seen to improve bowel regularity and stool consistency in individuals with this type of alternating presentation. This is due to the astringent nature of the Dandelion Root combined with the softening and moistening nature of the Milk Thistle).

Milk Thistle & Inflammation: Milk Thistle is also a Demulcent, meaning that it soothes and moistens the mucus membranes, kidney and bladder irritations, and inflammations in general. Being a demulcent, it also greatly softens and moistens the skin. Patients with skin problems ranging from acne to severe eczema have reported a clearing of skin impurities, healing of redness and inflammation, a dramatic softening and moistening of dry, cracking skin, and a noticeable glow and radiance to the skin quality.

Milk Thistle & Liver Disease: Milk Thistle has been found in recent years to be a major player in the treatment of Liver Disease. Because it helps lower enzyme levels and facilitates the liver in its process of detoxifying the body. Among all known herbal remedies, Milk Thistle finds its place as the leader in herbs to treat liver disease. Physicians have prescribed Milk Thistle for Hepatitis to keep down inflammation, Cirrhosis to soften the liver, Liver Cancer to aid in detoxification, and many dysfunctions of the Gall Bladder System. It also helps protect the liver for those individuals that are taking prescription medications known to elevate liver enzymes.

Milk Thistle & Gall Bladder Disease: Because Milk Thistle is both a demulcent and it stimulates bile flow, it is a natural for treating a wide array of Gall Bladder diseases and symptoms. Milk Thistle can calm down an inflamed Gall Bladder while at the same time clearing out any stagnation that might be present. When using Milk Thistle to combat Gall Bladder symptoms, it is important to verify that there are no Gall Stones present which would be too large for the Gall Bladder to pass. The only way that this can be known is to visit your local physician and get a clearance from them to proceed.

The regenerative effects of milk thistle on the liver have inspired the curiosity of researchers searching for a substance that would provide similar benefits for the kidneys. After all, both organs provide filtration of toxin and both are susceptible to their damaging effects. According to "PDR fro Herbal Medicines", clinical studies showed Milk Thistle prevented toxicity-related damage to the kidney cells. This makes Milk Thistle a logical candidate for countering the side effects associates with toxic prescription drugs. Moreover, Milk Thistle has been shown to re-generate kidney cells and may even provide protection against kidney cancer. It accomplishes this by protecting kidney cells from oxidative stress and inflammation by eliminating free radicals.

***WARNING: Milk Thistle has been shown to be safe, it has also been proven to cause thinning of the blood. Consult your doctor.

- Organic Bromelain: Bromelain is an enzyme that is extracted from the stem and juice of pineapple. It was first discovered in the late 1800s, but was not used as a dietary supplement until the 1950s. Bromelain is an anti-inflammatory and has been used as a digestive aid and a blood thinner, as well as to treat sports injuries, sinusitis, arthritis, and swelling. Bromelain is also being studied for use as a supplement for inflammatory bowel disease (IBD), especially ulcerative colitis. Bromelain digests proteins, which is why it is also used as a meat tenderizer. As a supplement, it is available as capsules or tablets. As a digestive aid, the recommended dosage is generally 500 mg three times per day. It can be taken with food, but is more effective in reducing inflammation when taken on an empty stomach. Bromelain is approved in Germany for use after surgery, where dosages range from 80 to 320 mg per day. The optimal dosage for other uses, such as arthritis, is not known. Bromelain is normally taken for eight to ten days.

Bromelain is an anti-inflammatory, but there is not much research to support its use in either Crohn's disease or ulcerative colitis. There is a case report of two patients with ulcerative colitis who responded well to treatment with Bromelain. Bromelain has not been studied on humans with IBD, but there is one study that was done on the biopsy tissue taken from the intestine of people with Crohn's disease and ulcerative colitis. The tissue did appear to respond positively to the Bromelain, and

335

showed fewer IBD markers than the tissue that was not treated with Bromelain.

Eating large amounts of the fruit of the pineapple will not give the same effect as taking a Bromelain supplement. Bromelain is primarily found in the stem of the pineapple, which is not normally eaten.

Interactions with Other Drugs and Supplements:

Bromelain may increase the effectiveness of some antibiotics, including amoxicillin. It may have a similar effect on tetracycline, but the current research on this is conflicting.

Bromelain also has an effect on the blood, and may affect the ability of the blood to clot. Therefore, it should not be taken along with any drugs or supplements that also thin the blood or that increase the risk of bleeding, including:

- Coumadin (warfarin)
- Garlic
- Ginkgo biloba
- Heparin

***DISCLAIMER: Because hormonal distresses e.g., hypoadrenia, hypothyroidism, etc., can turn severe, you should always be monitored by your doctor. The following information and opinions are not a substitute for professional medical prevention, diagnosis, or treatment. Please consult with your physician, pharmacist, or health care provider before taking any home remedies or supplements or following any suggestions in this book. Only your healthcare provider, personal physician, or pharmacist can provide you with advice on what is safe and effective for your unique needs or diagnose your particular medical history.

HORMONE DISTRESS REMEDIES:

Organic Liquid Multi Vitamin/Mineral Supplement: As obvious as this might be to some people, the vast majority of Americans are completely unaware of the fact that they are not supplying their bodies anywhere near the necessary amount of vitamins and/or minerals needed to function, let alone repair itself. Years of exposure to toxic Hybridized and GMO foods has literally put our bodies into a state of malnutrition. What should cause everyone reading this to turn off their televisions and focus 110% of their spare time to evicting the United Nations from American soil are the nutritional guidelines 'suggested' by the Satanic Theosophist controlled United Nations. It's this organization who has created the 'Codex Alimentarius' (C.A.) In early chapters of this book I have addressed in detail the Codex Alimentarius and how just by using figures from C.A. it is projected that just following the Vitamin and Mineral Guideline alone in the United Nations' created C.A. will result in about 3 billion deaths. One billion is projected to die through simple starvation, and the other two billion are projected to die from preventable diseases caused by malnutrition. With that being said, you should consider taking a high quality Organic Liquid Multi-Vitamin/Mineral supplement. I personally have found the following liquid vitamin/mineral supplement to be the best: silvanusselect.com

"If a substitute for cod-liver oil is given, it ought to be at least as powerful as this oil in its content of both vitamins A and D."
- Edward Mellanby circa 1920

Barlean's Cod Liver Oil: Hippocrates first recorded the medicinal use of fish oils, subsequently this ancient wisdom has been passed down to modern day generations. As relentless as the Medical Industrial Complex has been towards the superior effects of whole foods, herbs, etc., Cod Liver Oil still stands as one of the most dynamic healing solutions on Planet Earth. Cod Liver Oil is a combination of highly beneficial nutrients, a blend which has been scientifically prove to cure a number of diseases. These nutrients include:

- Vitamin D – 1 teaspoon provides approximately 2000IU's.
- Vitamin A – 1 teaspoon provides 10,000IU's of immune health, healthy vision, testosterone development, and prostate health.
- EPA and DHA – Cod liver oil provides your body with omega-3 fatty acids EPA/DHA, nutrients which are critical to a healthy brain and nervous system.

Cod Liver Oil has also been used to prevent and treat the following conditions:

1. Heart Disease;
2. Diabetes and Insulin Resistance;
3. Cancer and Other Diseases;

337

4. Various Children's Health Conditions; and
5. Healthy Skin and Hair.

- Organic Licorice Root: Licorice root is one of the most important herbs that I use in my practice. Organic Licorice Root is incredible at balancing cortisol levels, which is paramount in resolving challenges associated with a toxic endocrine system. I was personally made aware of this versatile herb over 22 years ago, when my mother who used the herb to treat hypoadrenia, introduced it to me. I cannot overstate the importance of Organic Licorice Root, as it was quite literally, the herb that pulled my chemically challenged system back to center.

Not surprising, considering Organic Licorice Root is the single most widely used herb throughout Chinese Medicine. An astonishing number of Chinese herbal formulas, over 5,000, to be exact, use licorice to sweeten teas and to "harmonize" contrasting herbs. Its first documented use dates back to the time of the great Chinese herbal master Zhang Zhong Zhing, circa 190 AD; and was certainly used for many centuries prior to that time. Organic Licorice Root was even used in ancient Egypt as a drink flavoring called 'Mai-sus'. King Tutankhamun (Circa 1324 BC) must have had a taste for Licorice Root, given the fact that large quantities of this stuff were discovered in his tomb. Even one of history's greatest conquerors, Alexander the Great, relied heavily on Licorice Root as a stamina enhancer for his soldiers. In addition, his men used a licorice laden drink to quench their thirst following a long day of fighting. The root was first brought to the England in 1090 AD by Crusaders returning from their Middle East campaigns, and was later grown in the 14th century by Spanish monks who settled at Pontefract Priory and other parts of northern England where the root was even nicknamed 'Spanish'. Its main purpose then was as a medicine used to ease coughs and stomach complaints. By 1614 AD, licorice extract was being formed into small lozenges. But it was not until 1750 that a local apothecary, George Dunhill, decided to add sugar to the recipe and licorice became a sweet known as the Pomfret or Pontefract Cake. Nearly 100 years ago, in 1914, the Chicago Licorice Company began to sell Black Vines, the first in a very long line of licorice based candies.

***WARNING: Don't use Organic Licorice Root if you have high blood pressure, and don't use Organic Licorice Root if you have not yet completed your 30-day Silvanus Health New Life Body Balance Diet.™ If you are still eating an unhealthy diet filled with red meat and white potatoes, it's ill advised. Your body will only benefit from Organic Licorice Root if you are consuming organic vegetables, fruit and lean animal protein e.g., white meat turkey and/or chicken. In addition, if you use steroids and/or asthma inhalers, please be aware that Organic Licorice Root will increase both the effectiveness of the drug and the severity of its side effects. Its long term use is not recommended, and it is not recommended for use by pregnant women. It may cause stomach upset if taken in large quantities.

- Organic Ashwagandha: Ashwagandha is similar to ginseng but far less expensive. Ashwagandha is commonly referred to as "Indian Ginseng". Ashwagandha is a superior herb for the rejuvenation of muscles, bone marrow, and male/female fertility. This herb is superior for stress, weakness, tissue deficiency, the elderly, overwork, lack of sleep, nervous exhaustion, sexual debility, problems of old age, loss of memory, loss of muscular energy, insomnia, weak eyes, cough, infertility, and glandular swelling. It inhibits aging and catalyzes the anabolic processes of the body, nurtures, and clarifies the mind promoting dreamless sleep. Ashwagandha helps the body adapt to stress, but it also rebuilds the nervous system without stimulating it, a wonderful sleep tonic. In the morning it helps build the immune system and muscular-skeletal systems, both of which are negatively impacted by stress and helps those under stress.

Researchers at the University of Texas Health Science Center have studied Ashwagandha, and what they found that extracts of the shrub had activity that was similar to GABA, which could explain why the plant is effective in reducing anxiety. Scholars from the University of Leipzig, Germany, looked at the effects of Ashwagandha on the brain. The research showed Ashwagandha led to more acetylcholine receptor activity. The scholars concluded that the increase of activity in that particular neurotransmitter could account for the increase in cognitive ability and memory attributed to Ashwagandha. Scholars at Banaras Hindu University, Varanasi, India, conducted research which proves many of the elements of Ashwagandha are antioxidants. The researchers found that Ashwagandha led to larger amounts of three different natural antioxidants: superoxide dis-

339

mutase, catalase, and glutathione peroxidase. The antioxidant effect of active principles of Ashwagandha may explain the anti-stress, cognition-facilitating, and anti-aging effects produced in clinical situations.

- Iodine: Iodine is an essential element for a vibrant and radiant body. It is a key player in the integrity of our DNA; it boosts the immune system, keeps our metabolism in balance, and even aids cardiovascular health. Estimates show that more than half of the United States' population may be deficient in iodine. Studies show lower incidences of breast cancer and fibrocystic disease in women who had higher iodine levels. If we look at the amount of iodine typically consumed by the modern American (240 micrograms (μg) of iodine a day) with amounts in Japan (12,000 μg), a country typically associated with lower rates of breast cancer, we may be witnessing a startling lack.

  Furthermore, iodine plays an important role in the function of the thyroid gland, particularly in the creation of the hormones T3 and T4, which are important for the body's ability to regulate its own metabolism. More than thyroid help, iodine is also critical for many other basic physical functions, including the body's detoxification process from the negative effects of environmental and radiation pollution. Lack of iodine can also lead to emotional disorders, malfunctioning glandular systems, and weight gain associated with hormonal imbalance. Iodine deficiency may be linked to breast, ovarian, uterus, and prostrate cancers and cysts. I personally have found the following supplement to be the best source of iodine: silvanusselect.com

- Organic Ginger Root: Ginger Root is commonly used for people who are suffering from upset stomach, due to motion sickness, gastrointestinal challenges, etc. Moreover, the ability of Ginger Root to stabilize cortisol levels, and heart related issues, is well documented. Furthermore, Ginger Root is extremely effective at inspiring the use of body fat storage, increasing energy levels, amplifying your metabolic rate, and promoting good digestion. I recommend buying Organic Raw Ginger Root, peeling the outer skin, grating a teaspoon inside a hot cup of water and letting it steep for 5-10 minutes, before drinking it. This, coupled with a bag of Organic Peppermint Tea, will balance even the most upset stomach.

340

- Organic Lemon Balm: Lemon Balm has been one of the most effective herbal remedies that I've used for the regulation of thyroid hormonal production. This ability along with its herbs anti-viral characteristics make Lemon Balm my number one herbal solution for stabilizing hormone levels throughout the endocrine system. Lemon Balm is also extremely effective at reducing anxiety, stress, and sleeping disorders. Research has shown that Lemon Balm is also effective at improving an individual's ability to concentrate.

Other studies have shown Lemon Balm's effectiveness at treating viral afflictions, including herpes, cold sores, and shingles.

***Caution: Do not use Lemon Balm while driving a car or machine that could cause harm to yourself or others. Lemon Balm is a sedative and may induce sleep.

CHAPTER

An Address To Christians On 26 The Elimination Of The "Synagogue Of Satan"

"Who will rise up for me against the evildoers? or who will stand up for me against the workers of iniquity?" - Psalm 94:16

Lord Jesus Christ prophesized that his followers would be infiltrated by demons which would ultimately deceive many into believing that they were teachers and warriors of Lord Jesus Christ, when in reality, they were scouts and soldiers for the synagogue of Satan. Based on the aforementioned knowledge, I strongly believe that the Church of Babylon and its Satanic proxies e.g., Freemasonry, etc. are in fact a modern day interpretation of what Christians have fought against for thousands of years. It's this fashionable proxy of satanic heretics which Lord Jesus Christ calls out and names as the synagogue of Satan.

"I know thy works, and tribulation, and poverty, (but thou art rich) and I know the blasphemy of them which say they are Jews, and are not, but are the synagogue of Satan." - Revelation 2:9

341

Every Saturday and Sunday, Christians ascend onto their local houses of worship. Numbering in the tens of millions, American Christians sit and listen to Christ's repeated warnings regarding demonic influence, and yet there are a staggering number of Christ's followers who believe these warnings are simply things of legend.

Defeating the 'synagogue of Satan' requires a clear understanding of the type of evil Christian America is up against, and the method by which to evict it from our Nation. I expand on the, "synagogue of Satan," subject thoughout my book, "On The Jews and Their Lies: 9/11" at, GoyToy.net.

"Behold, I will make them of the synagogue of Satan, which say they are Jews, and are not, but do lie; behold, I will make them to come and worship before thy feet, and to know that I have loved thee."
-Revelation 3:9

With that pursuit in mind, it's to our tactical advantage to both study and understand its strengths and its weaknesses. Contrary to what cowardly men may tell you, nothing and no one is without weakness. Ironically, this has been the seminal feature of every campaign that's been waged against Christian Americans throughout our history. We are perceived by Satan and his followers as weak, when in truth, it's he who is powerless against the one true God. We must condition our subconscious with the above declaration and upon every activity we endeavor.

Let's discuss the primary disability of Luciferians. Regardless of their station in life, its members work tirelessly to conceal their true nature, when in actuality their desire is to be known. The consequence of this is that they eventually reveal their true nature to us, through words, actions, etc. Just as the plant cannot grow without the protection of its soil, Luciferians cannot grow without their safeguard of concealment. Stripping them of this defense is paramount in defeating them.

"For every one that doeth evil hateth the light, neither cometh to the light, lest his deeds should be reproved." - John 3:20

For more than 160 years, American Christians have failed to eliminate the "synagogue of Satan" from our Nation, because of our fervent willingness to accuse and prosecute Luciferian designed scapegoats, rather than the designers themselves.

Moreover, through Skinnerian/Wundt/Jungian Human Exploitation Psychology, the vast majority of Christian Americans, just over the past sixty-years, have been reduced to nothing more than a silent majority of geldings, with little disposition to reprimand those in governmental, corporate, and clergy leadership positions whose words and actions are clearly worthy of rebuke. Even more detrimental to the Christian faith has been our inability to resist the reprisal of the enemy. Those who hate Lord Jesus Christ have always been among us. It's only been within the past sixty years though that they've sensed significant weakness throughout our ranks. It's been throughout this period where we have witnessed "the Synagogue of Satan's" most bold advances against Christian America. Christians must recognize the fact that these attacks will only grow in frequency and furry. Therefore, it's incumbent upon each one of us to regain an appetite for the surgical work that is now before us, for this work that is absolutely necessary in order to disrupt and destroy Christian America's one true enemy.

> "The most unhappy man in the world is he that is not patient in
> adversities; for men are not killed with the adversities they
> have, but with ye impatience which they suffer."
> – Sir Charles Bailly, Secretary of the Queen of Scots

As an aside, Mary Queen of Scotland was known for her regal, beauty, and allegiance to the Papacy. Her life was cut short by a cruel cousin obliged to the Serpent Death Cult. Before Mary was beheaded, her qualities were rooted in her son, King James VI and I, one of the greatest champions of Jesus Christ and benefactor of The King James Bible. To discover Queen Mary and King James ancient struggle with the Serpent Death Cult, please read my book, 'Queen Mary & The Serpent Cult' release date: March 1, 2017.

The only way in which Christian Americans will seize victory over Luciferianism: (i) Wisdom. (ii) Choice. (iii) Patience, and (iv) the sensibility of a diplomat. Fly-paper, public protests, radio/internet rants and the murder of innocent people, do nothing more than embolden the "synagogue of Satan" and their ever increasing surplus of resources, lying in wait. Christians must begin fostering an imperative sense of duty throughout our community of 240 million brothers and sisters prior, during, and following our non-violent movement, and that our collective faith always remain in Lord Jesus Christ.   343

Whether their intentions originate from a place of naiveté or willfulness, the fact is, there is a growing population of esoteric Christian ministers who are deceiving a large swath of the Christian American majority through disinformation campaigns. It's these types of campaigns that are responsible for misleading Christians into believing such lies as Spanish Jesuit Francisco Ribera's Big-Lie regarding Daniel's 70 Week Prophecy, Cyrus Scofield's Pre-Tribulation Rapture and turning ones cheek to Satan, and his chief propaganda minister Azazel, as a means to defeat the Church of Babylon's demonic onslaught.

"Now I beseech you, brethren, mark them which cause divisions and offences contrary to the doctrine which ye have learned; and avoid them. For they that are such serve not our Lord Jesus Christ, but their own belly; and by good words and fair speeches deceive the hearts of the simple." - Romans 16:17

Now read Christ's method of identifying and defeating Church of Babylon leadership:

"For we wrestle not against flesh and blood, but against principalities, against powers, against the rulers of the darkness of this world, against spiritual wickedness in high places." - Ephesians 6:12

Jesus Christ clearly differentiates between the flesh and blood of mankind and the 'spiritual wickedness in high places'. In wrestling against flesh and blood, we are commanded to use one solution only and that's 'forgiveness'. In terms of destroying evil, Christ clearly states the method by which Christians are to eliminate Satan and 'the rulers of the darkness of this world'. Here's a hint. It doesn't involve weakness or diplomacy and it certainly does not include 'turning one's cheek':

"Think not that I am come to send peace on earth: I came not to send peace, but a sword." - Matthew 10:34

It's imperative that Christian Americans abandon the spiritually toxic, Church of Babylon created ideology of 'political correctness' which can be traced back to Karl Heinrich Marx and Friedrich Engels. It's this ideology which has allowed our children's minds to be poisoned with the religion of 'evolutionism', as well as the alternative lifestyle of homosexuality.

If you are unfamiliar with Marx and Engle's, Religion of Communism, please listen. Carl Marx's is the offspring of Satanic Talmudists. Marx maternal grandfather was a Dutch rabbi, while his paternal line contained rabbis since 1723. Friedreich Engels was also the offspring of Babylonian Talmudists. Both Marx and Engels created, "The Communist Manifesto," which was issued on 1848 in London. The Babylonian Talmud is the source from which Marx and Engels communist philosophy originated. This led directly to the rise of Communism, Socialism and Nazism and has paved the way for the Babylonian Talmudist, "New World Order" and "One World Religion."

Engels was not only a Prussian-German philosopher and revolutionary socialist, like Adolf Hitler, Engels was a student and admirer of Helena Blavatsky's Satanic Theosophical ideology of ushering in a New World Order. Throughout my many years of studying communist societies, not to mention being married to a woman who grew up and escaped Communist Romania (which lasted in Romania until 1989), I have come to the conclusion that the communist weapon of propaganda was never implemented with the intention of influencing or encouraging its people. Rather, communist propaganda has always been used as a means to disgrace and debase its populace. And as we've seen throughout history, the more outrageous the claims, the more likely the population is to accept it.

"Why may not the Bible, and especially the New Testament... be read and taught as a divine revelation in the [school] its general precepts expounded... and its glorious principles of morality inculcated?... Where can the purest principles of morality be learned so clearly or so perfectly as from the New Testament?"
– U.S. Supreme Court, Vidal v. Girard (1844)

The omission of America's exceptional Christian heritage from U.S. textbooks has been made possible through the systematic dismantling of our once superior Christian American educational system. This system owes its past success to the Christian based McGuffey educational system created by Scottish American William H. McGuffey. These were a series of graded prim-

345

ers that were widely used as textbooks in American schools from the mid-19th century to the mid-20th century, and are still used today in some private schools and in home schooling. It is estimated that at least 120 million copies of McGuffey's Readers were sold between 1836 and 1960, placing its sales in a category with the Bible and Webster's Dictionary. Since 1961 they have continued to sell at a rate of some 30,000 copies a year. No other textbook bearing a single person's name has come close to that mark.

The world renowned inventor Henry Ford cited McGuffey's Readers as one of his most important childhood influences. He was an avid fan of McGuffey's Readers first editions, and claimed as an adult to be able to quote from McGuffey's by memory at great length. Ford republished all six Readers from the 1857 edition, and distributed complete sets of them, at his own expense, to schools across the United States. In 1934, Ford had the log cabin where McGuffey was born moved to Greenfield Village, Ford's museum of Americana at Dearborn, Michigan.

To understand why the McGuffey educational system was eliminated from the vast majority of private and public schools by the, "synagogue of Satan," throughout America, and why it's paramount that the Christian American majority return to this educational system, all one must do is read the following quote:

"The Christian religion, is the religion of our country. From it are derived our prevalent notions of the character of God, the great moral governor of the universe. On its doctrines are founded the peculiarities of our free institutions." – William McGuffey

McGuffey was known for his philanthropy and generosity among the poor and newly emancipated African Americans. William McGuffey died in 1873.

Americans are beginning to see the corrosive nature of 'political correctness' throughout America. Evidence of this fact can be seen in America's response to the recent April, 2013 bombing in Boston, MA. More people are awake and understand that this event had all of the hallmarks of a 'false-flag', now those who have trusted and been asleep for far too long are demanding answers. This uprising is a result of the Marxist political correct police forcing people to remain silent for so many years. Americans are fed up with being fed Nazi like 'Big Lie' propaganda. When Hitler dictated his 1925 book Mein Kampf, he advocated using a lie so "colossal" that no one would believe that someone "could have the impudence to distort the truth so infamously."

Americans are dizzy from being forced fed lies. Moreover, they're mentally and physically short circuited because of this expectation that they must wholeheartedly believe in those lies. Only slightly more aggravating is how propagandists expect the American population to not only believe in these lies, but parrot those lies to others. This is a control method that has been used by tyrants for generations to strip their populace of any semblance of decency.

American Christians are either affirming or rejecting the, "synagogue of Satan," with every purchase they make, movie they watch, CD or music they download, food they buy, water they drink, schools they choose to educate their children in, cities they live in, churches they worship in, etc. When Christian Americans audit their lifestyles and find that they're affirming the interplay between the money they spend and the, "synagogue of Satan," they must come to the conclusion that they have in fact been deceived into following Satan. When the Christian American majority stops developing their spiritual muscle to resist Satan, the spiritual strength of every American Christian is eroded and lost.

Christians must not allow Satan to turn our Nation into a society of emasculated liars who are easily controlled. If one studies the Marxist origins of 'Political Correctness', they will learn that it has always had this effect on a Nation and its citizenry's spiritual liberty. Lord Jesus Christ does not say 'Seek Ye Political Correctness and the Political Correctness will make you free'... He told us to seek the 'Truth' and unadulterated truth is what I've provided throughout preceding pages.

The Holy Bible speaks about spiritual liberty [Isaiah 61:1], but Luciferian carnal hearts feel no other grievances than those that molest the body and distress their worldly affairs. Talk to them of their liberty and property, tell them of waste committed upon their oceans or lands, or damage done to the value of their homes, and they understand you very well; but speak about the origins of bondage and sin, captivity to Satan, and liberty by Christ, tell of wrong done to their precious souls, and the hazard of their eternal wel-   347 fare, and they look at you as does a deer caught in the headlights of a car. Jesus plainly reminds us that the man who practiced any sin was, in fact, a slave to that sin, which is the case with many Christian Americans today. Lord Jesus Christ offers us true Liberty, and those whom Christ makes free are truly Liberated. But often we see persons disputing about Independence of every kind, while they deny the existence of God and remain slaves to Luciferian sinful lust.

"The fool hath said in his heart, There is no God. They are corrupt, they have done abominable works, there is none that doeth good."
- Psalm 14:1

Relative to a single Christian, the vast empire of U.S. elites throughout our Nation's history e.g., The Rockefellers, Morgan's, Vanderbilt's, Gould's, Astor's, Havemeyer's, MacKay's, Huntington's, Armour's, Carnegies, Sloane's, Whitney's, etc. who at one time collectively possessed more than twenty-five percent of all the circulated wealth of the United States have always been an imposing force. Their minions have always occupied positions of influence in virtually every government, corporation, and non-profit organization around the world. For centuries, they have worked fervently to construct a complex network of loyal proxies, willing and capable of executing the most nefarious of orders and because of these despots, Luciferians have nearly reached the pinnacle of control over the United States of America. There has however been one massive barrier obstructing their goal of constructing a One World Government. That barrier is Lord Jesus Christ and his Christian American majority.

On Jan. 10, 1963, Congressman Albert S. Herlong Jr. of Florida read a list of 45 Communist goals into the Congressional Record. The list was derived from researcher Cleon Skousen's book "The Naked Communist." Step #27 reads,

"Infiltrate the churches and replace revealed religion with "social" religion. Discredit the Bible and emphasize the need for intellectual maturity, which does not need a "religious crutch."

To understand how wicked the Talmud is please read, 'On The Jews and Their Lies: 9/11' at, GoyToy.net.

348

Nothing but the Christian faith remains undefeated by Satan, and yet so grand are the resources of Luciferianism that even the greatest among us have abandoned the daunting task of supplanting the, 'synagogue of Satan' from our lands. Other Nations have tried to segregate it, but while segregation was pursued from one side, their minions infiltrated from the other. For centuries, Nations and their most prominent citizenry have plotted against 'synagogue of Satan' leadership, enlisting the persuasion of violence, only to be confronted with defeat.

The question that we must ask ourselves is "Why has the Christian majority been so unsuccessful, over the past 160 years, at displacing the, 'synagogue of Satan' from The United States?" The answer may not be as complicated as you may think. It's because the above said techniques are precisely the methods in which 'synagogue of Satan' members hope to provoke. It's because synagogue of Satan members already know the futility of such a fool's errand. Unfortunately Christians end up figuring this out after the fact. And before the dust settles, 'synagogue of Satan' members know how the failed Christian campaign will positively impact 'synagogue of Satan' propaganda.

The most important contribution each and every Christian can make towards the goal of supplanting Luciferianism is to read and understand The Holy Bible. Only then will the solution of eliminating the, 'synagogue of Satan' be revealed. History shows only those who are unconditionally dedicated to Christ's message will answer this call, even after reading the mountain of data that's been provided establishing the fact that our Nation has been infiltrated by the very demons they have convinced themselves don't exist. Even with all of the evidence that's been presented in this book, this call to action will not be embraced by the majority, which thankfully, isn't necessary. In truth, this Christian Revolution may resemble the American revolution of 1776, where only three percent of Americans fought and won against a much stronger adversary. Similarly, the Christian American Revolution may only garner support of approximately seven million Christians, an imposing threat to any standing army, to only a few thousand Luciferians nightmarish.

It is time for the timid and soft literary men in pulpits, the false preachers of 'peace', the shouters for 'fairness' and all who are afraid of the truth in its surgical forms. It's these men and women who have no place in the healing of this Nation; they are wedded to their softness. Nothing should be a greater source of shame to a Christian than the deafening silence that has fallen over the millions of children who have been aborted, molested, or sold as sex slaves and the lecherous, 'synagogue of Satan' that has sowed, cultivated, and peddled this filth.

What shall Christian America do? This is the question. How shall we draw back from this system which surrounds us and infects so much of our lives? For the past sixty-five years, Luciferians have skillfully maintained a tame and compliant Christian American majority. By strictly limiting the choices through which an acceptable public opinion is formed, their control system has allowed for seemingly lively debate within a heavily monitored and controlled environment of falsehoods. To destroy this system Christians must: IDENTIFY IT, OBSERVE IT, AND TURN THEIR BACKS ON IT! More powerful than guns, bullets, and bombs, is the active opposition to every Luciferian organization and/or individual throughout our Christian Nation. A well informed, knowledgeable Christian majority is something even the 'synagogue of Satan' cannot endure.

"The Lord trieth the righteous: but the wicked and him that loveth violence his soul hateth." - Psalm 11:5

The most powerful action our Christian majority can take is to completely reestablish Christian Morals throughout our communities, which the, 'synagogue of Satan' has broken down over the past sixty-five years. Just this one accomplishment would topple their entire control system. Quietly and Peacefully reestablishing our Christian principles, while we migrate the economic powerhouse of 240 million American Christians over to U.S. based Christian owned and controlled businesses, communities, States, schools, organic agriculture, music, and television corporations, etc., will sustain the Christian majority for thousands of years. The aforesaid direct action is one that has been discussed but never tried, and one which Luciferians cannot defend against.

Before a Christian American patrons any business or buys a particular product, he or she must research and verify the origins and intentions of that company or product. If it's a product that was manufactured by one of the top 10 global elite controlled promoters of genetically modified products, do not support their business. Imagine what would happen to McDonald's if a quarter of a billion Americans stopped supporting their American

350

operations. It will be remembered from previous chapters where I suggested identifying capable executives from every industry, then motivating these men and women to spin-off businesses whose foundation is built upon Christian morals and focused on the health and wellbeing of not only Christian citizenry, but the whole of America.

It is time for the Christian Majority to once again embrace the superior concept of high quality American manufactured goods and services. We must completely divorce ourselves from the economically toxic concept of 'outsourcing', or a 'North American Union'. These measures are paramount in order for the United States of America to regain control over its financial destiny. Christian Americans must understand that off shoring is nothing more than a few select Luciferian CEOs complying with, and executing their anti-Christian doctrine, to achieve a 'One World Economy'. In no way can Christian Americans look at off shoring any other way but an abysmal failure. There is a number of industry experts who cite a number of reasons for the failure of the, 'synagogue of Satan' based off shoring model. These include a company's inability to execute its business strategy, lack of intellectual property (IP) protection, IP theft, inconsistent and/or complete lack of business ethics, indigenous company's inability to measure up to traditional standards of performance, indigenous company's subpar logistical and/or communications infrastructure, massive hidden costs e.g., government 'kick-backs' and 'greasing palms', onerous contractual models, etc.

I have personally assisted with the creation of a number of manufacturing facilities throughout Asia and have worked with the designer of the completely automated $100 million Webvan facility located in Northern California. I can tell you with absolute confidence and authority that the above-mentioned off shoring challenges are just a short list of the many capital vampires awaiting every naïve entrepreneur overseas. In this day and age, setting up a manufacturing facility in America e.g., AutoCad inventor designers, product mold development, automated assembly line design, logistics, etc., are all painfully simple. Christian America, close your eyes and imagine a few thousand manufacturing facilities incubating within a Christian, business, tax and patriot friendly State such as Tennessee, Montana, Texas, etc. and you've got a recipe for secession from the 'synagogue of Satan.

Another requirement for healing our Nation's economic and spiritual fractures is the examination of modern day 'liberalism', the source of its ideology, its effects on the American population and its historical tendencies towards the American Christian. American Christians for example, irrespective of skin color or financial station in life, must be completely honest with themselves and come to terms with the fact that the, 'synagogue of Satan' manufactured deception such as 'The Sexual Revolution', Abortion, Pornography, Infidelity, Arrogance, Lying, Freemasonry, Theosophy, The Occult, Satanism, Drugs, Alcohol, Violence, etc. have poisoned them morally, socially and economically. These biblical abominations have twisted the American men's and women's mental wellness and turned our society into a sewer.

"There are six things that the Lord hates, seven that are an abomination to him: haughty eyes, a lying tongue, and hands that shed innocent blood, a heart that devises wicked plans, feet that make haste to run to evil, a false witness who breathes out lies, and one who sows discord among brothers." - Proverbs 6:16-19

The only way in which our Christian Nation can defend itself from Luciferian engineered psychological waste is to completely eliminate the immigration of 'synagogue of Satan' ideas into our communities. Christian Americans must be vigilant when choosing the types of businesses, movies, music, and writers we support. If we know that a particular television, movie, book, band, or radio host is spewing anti-Christian propaganda, why then would you support that? After all, it's through these media, Luciferians mix in their toxic anti-Christian propaganda. It will be remembered that the, "National Academy of Television Arts & Sciences" (NATAS) is SATAN in reverse.

In today's world, there is an ever increasing number of Christians who are practicing a Luciferian version of Christianity that is woefully inaccurate and blatantly contrary to what Christians know deep down inside to be the truth and the life of Lord Jesus Christ.

Inexperienced in basic biblical edicts, Christians have unwittingly become proselytizers for the, 'synagogue of Satan'. Through vanity and "doctrines the commandments of men" [Matthew 15:9], Christians have been tricked into believing salvation is obtained through the worship of Israel and its inhabits, ignoring God's divine proscription which states,

352

"...the LORD had said unto Abram [Abraham], I will bless THEE, and make THY name great. I will bless them that bless THEE, and curse him that curseth THEE: and in THEE shall all families of the earth be blessed." – Genesis 12:1-3

The Holy Bible clearly states in Genesis 12:1-3 that God's blessing is bestowed upon Abraham. The beneficiary of God's promises is further clarified in Galatians 3:16 which states:

"Now to Abraham [Abram] and HIS seed were the promises made. He saith not, And to seeds, as of many; but as of one, And to THY seed, WHICH IS CHRIST."

What the abovementioned scripture is communicating to believers is that Abraham's seed [singular] has been granted God's promises and the only way we are to receive God's promises is when we 'believeth' on Lord Jesus Christ [John 3:16; John 14:6; John 6:47; John 5:24; John 3:36; Acts 16:31; John 8:24; Romans 10:9; Ephesians 2:10; Romans 8:28; 2 Peter 3:9; 1 John 1:7]. Contrary to modernist false prophets who promote One World Religion Cults such as 'Chrislam' [Christianity/Islam] and 'Judeo-Christianity', salvation is neither gained through faith in Baal, Moloch, Remphan, nor is it found in the ruse of Israel, Judaism, Islam, Buddhism, Hinduism, etc. All of these said cults have one thing in common, infidelity towards God. To substantiate my assertion read what The Holy Bible teaches about those who deny Jesus Christ:

"Who is a liar but he that denieth that Jesus is the Christ? He is antichrist, that denieth the Father and the Son." – 1 John 2:22

If Christians were to adhere to the very basic above mentioned principles, what they would quickly realize is that all of the monies that were once being funneled through Luciferian controlled governments and organizations to fund the very lifestyles, the very murderous war mongering, the very anti-Christian propaganda to which Christian Americans are vehemently opposed, would disappear overnight. And if properly choreographed, a modern day Christian American economic tsunami would ensue. All that's required to initiate this reemergence of greatness is the awakening of the Christian American Giant.

Alternatively, if Christian America chooses to ignore the warnings issued throughout this book and continues to support corrupt 'Big Lie' economic strategies, all the while deluding themselves into believing that the Luciferian controlled United States government actually have a plan in place, that will realign the myriad of fundamental problems facing our Nation… Its curtains for America. The spiritual, moral, and economic path in which our Nation has been travelling is unsustainable. The intellectual oligarchs [Rockefeller, Rothschild, George Soros, Rupert Murdoch, Ted Turner, etc.) governing the ship of America will not deviate from their current trajectory until they've obliterated us from the annals of time. If Christian America does not wake up soon, the destruction of Christianity and life as we know it in America is at hand. The financial collapse of America will be unlike anything anyone could have ever imagined.

Christian Americans have been dissuaded from the place of true Christian leadership, and we must change this course. They have chosen leaders based on material gain, narrative, and fleeting attributes. The 'meat-suits' throughout much of Washington D.C. and Corporate America are nothing but a den of vipers, false leaders, whose blood lust, chaos, and foreign agendas have deceived our altruistic and generous Christian majority for generations by telling them what their itching ears want to hear. The truth is not kind. Christian Americans must reinvigorate the shortage of dissent throughout our majority and challenge all anti-Christian laws and orders which disparage the divine legacy that's alive in each and every one of us.

"Commit thy way unto the Lord; trust also in him; and he shall bring it to pass" - Psalm 37:5

It is incumbent upon every American Christian to keep alive Lord Jesus Christ's message throughout our schools, churches, legislatures, jury rooms and the Government, for these are the most powerful tools of resistance against evil. The Church of Babylon will only succeed if the American Christian majority allows it to bloom into something that it ought not to. If Christian Americans resort back to the landmarks that made us the greatest Nation on earth, the, 'synagogue of Satan' will fail.

354

The American Christian majority must begin to aggressively re-Christianize our Nation. In addition to actually bringing our children through the birth canal and not an abortionist's suction device, we need to proactively introduce Christian American exceptionalism to all new immigrants coming into our Nation.

"Before I formed thee in the belly I knew thee; and before thou camest forth out of the womb I sanctified thee, and I ordained thee a prophet unto the nations." - Jeremiah 1:5

That being said, our Christian brothers and sisters from Mexico should be welcomed not by the 'synagogue of Satan' – which is what is currently happening – but by the hand and face of an exceptional Christian American. I do not support the idea of illegal entry into any Nation and fixing our Southern Border is a priority. Unfortunately, the Luciferian agenda to destroy all borders e.g., the North American Union has created a situation that Christian Americans must now embrace in a Christian manner. By absorbing these new Christian brothers and sisters into our American Christian family, we are strengthening our spiritual influence throughout America, opposed to weakening it. Again, one of the most powerful tools that we can use to defeat Luciferianism is 'Truth', and the truth of the matter is, seven to nine million Mexican immigrants are not going to 'self-deport', nor is the pro-North American Union, Luciferian controlled United States Government going to force them out. As difficult as this strategy might seem to many Americans, Christian Americans must compare the advantages of having seven to nine million new Christian brothers and sisters with that of seven to nine million new Luciferians. Having read the history and objectives of the, 'synagogue of Satan', which would you prefer?

It's important to understand that Luciferian controlled global elites are neither brilliant nor does their wealth provide them absolute safety and security. They have captured our castle from within through duplicity and deception. Luciferians are master deceivers not master negotiators, nor are they diplomatists. As Christian Americans regain control of America, and we will, Americans must work towards the goal of returning our economy back to a Christian centric economy and eliminating all unconstitutional, corporate and/or government money making schemes. For example, why would any American Christian place their money inside of CHASE Bank? After all, it's owned by David Rockefeller, a man who has bragged

355

openly about his family's involvement in a plan to overthrow the American Constitution, and usher in the Satanic 'New World Order'.

Throughout our American Christian Revolution we must always be committed to Biblical Truth and Forgiveness. We must never be prejudicial, abusive, hateful, scornful, or in any way ridicule our flesh and blood brothers and sisters. Christian Americans must always remember this... The, 'synagogue of Satan,' does not fear lies, nor will they hesitate in miring the Christian majority in lies and deceit if it pleases their master [Satan]. Luciferians, over the past 160 years, have demonstrated, through quotes and behavior that they are deathly afraid of Christianity's spiritual wealth. This is why they tirelessly labor at destroying anyone who believes in or promotes the morally superior principles of Lord Jesus Christ.

Luciferians know they cannot defend their actions and deeds against Jesus Christ's spiritual truths and a well educated Christian American majority. This is why Spiritual truth alone, not force, violence, or lies must be our prevailing wisdom and power throughout America's coming spiritual struggle. Spiritual truth is the genesis of Christianity, and it's through Lord Jesus Christ's guiding light that our collective enemy [Satan] will be exposed and destroyed. It's through the lens of truth through which the Christian majority of America should measure all men and women. If a person's words or actions do not match those in the Holy Scriptures, then Christians must not follow that person. Working together to produce an ever greater abundance of material and Christian values for all has always been the secret to the prosperity of the Christian American majority and the state in which Christians must return their Nation.

"If my people, which are called by my name, shall humble themselves, and pray, and seek my face, and turn from their wicked ways; then will I hear from heaven, and will forgive their sin, and will heal their land." - 2 Chronicles 7:14

356

Dear Reader,

Thank you for investing your valuable time into reading my book. I created this book, to warn the American people of the very real threat facing our Nation. My aim is to strengthen the United States by exposing the seditious, covert campaign which seeks to slow-kill and destroy our Nation from within. I hope that in some measure I've achieved this goal.

If what you've read has inspired you in any way, please recommend its content to those you care about in person and on social media. I would also very much appreciate it if you would leave me a positive review at ThinkAmerika.com. Thank you!

If you are a non-Christian and the information inside of this book has opened your eyes, to the deceptions of Satan and inspired you to know the real message and meaning of Lord Jesus Christ, please pray with me now.

"Father, I know that I have broken your laws and my sins have separated me from you. I am truly sorry. I want to turn away from my past sinful life toward you. Please forgive me, and help me avoid sinning again. I believe that your son, Jesus Christ died for my sins, was resurrected from the dead, is alive, and hears my prayer. I invite Jesus Christ, to become the Lord of my life, to rule and reign in my heart from this day forward. Please send your Holy Ghost to help me obey You, and to do Your will for the rest of my life. In Jesus' name I pray, Amen."

"Neither is there salvation in any other: for there is none other name under heaven given among men, whereby we must be saved." – Acts 4:12

Follow me on Twitter:
@SilvanusBooks

Connect with me on LinkedIn:
Linkedin.com/In/SilvanusPublishing

Subscribe to my Blog:
SilvanusPublishing.com/blog

INDEX

A

B

C

D

E

F

G

K

L

M

Q

R

T

U

V

W

Y

Z

Inside Satanism +
the Satanic church
Documentary film

Killing Ireland, com

Deception book by Boze

answering muslims . com

Zeitgeist challenge . com

Hollywood Unmasked . com

Obama's real father . com

russian heads . com

goy toy .net

From Torah to Kabbalah

about the sky

Book - Lincoln + the Jews

freedom to fascism .. com

BOOK - The World's Last Dictator
         Dwight L Kinman
Creation seminar — ww 2 peter 3 . com

Made in the USA
Middletown, DE
06 September 2018